THE NEW

L

LEXINGTON
PRESS

CORPORATE GLOBAL CITIZENSHIP

CORPORATE GLOBAL CITIZENSHIP

Doing Business in the Public Eye

Noel M. Tichy

Andrew R. McGill

Lynda St. Clair

•

Editors

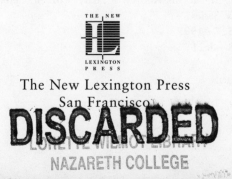

The New Lexington Press
San Francisco

Substantial discounts on bulk quantities of The New Lexington Press books are available to corporations, professional associations, and other organizations. For details and discount information, contact the special sales department at (415) 433-1740; Fax (800) 605–2665.

For sales outside the United States, please contact your local Simon & Schuster International office.

The New Lexington Press Web address: http://www.newlex.com

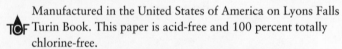 Manufactured in the United States of America on Lyons Falls Turin Book. This paper is acid-free and 100 percent totally chlorine-free.

Library of Congress Cataloging-in-Publication Data
Corporate global citizenship : doing business in the public eye /
  Noel M. Tichy, Andrew R. McGill, Lynda St. Clair. — 1st ed.
      p. cm. — (New Lexington Press management and organization
  sciences series)
    ISBN 0–7879–1095–3 (cloth : acid-free paper)
    1. Social responsibility of business—Case studies. I. Tichy,
Noel M.   II. McGill, Andrew R., date.   III. St. Clair, Lynda,
date.   IV. Series.
HD60.I527   1997
658.4'08—dc21   97–21181

FIRST EDITION

HB Printing 10 9 8 7 6 5 4 3 2 1

The New Lexington Press Management and
Organization Sciences Series

This book is dedicated to the late Father William Cunningham, cofounder of Focus: HOPE. His commitment to taking "intelligent and practical action to overcome racism, poverty, and injustice and to build a metropolitan community where all people may live in freedom, harmony, trust and affection" has led to the creation of a model organization that reflects the three pillars of ethics, social benefit, and economic profitability that undergird all effective corporate global citizenship efforts. It is through his creation of Focus: HOPE against all odds that Father Cunningham's contribution will truly be everlasting and provide a constant beacon for hard work and brotherhood among all peoples. As a small step toward that end, all proceeds from the sale of this book will be donated by the editors, authors, and publisher to fund scholarships and fellowships for the continued betterment of citizens of the Focus: HOPE community in the memory of Father Cunningham.

CONTENTS

PREFACE

EVERY YEAR, BEFORE sending thirty senior executives from Fortune 100 global corporations to study business issues in China, India, Russia, or Brazil for two intensive weeks, they are each asked to write and present their answer to the following dilemma:

> There are 5.7 billion people in the world.
>
> The gross domestic product (GDP) of the U.S. is $7.4 trillion, the GDP of the European Community is $7.5 trillion, and the GDP of Japan is $4.7 trillion. The combined population of those areas is 710 million people.
>
> The GDP of India is less than $400 billion and China's GDP is $600 billion. The combined population of those countries is 2.2 billion.

Given the fact that the corporations you represent are thirty of the world's largest, with awesome economic power—General Electric, Shell, Sony, NEC, and General Motors alone have combined annual sales that exceed the combined GDPs of China and India, for instance—what role should your company be playing as a citizen of not just your homeland but also of the world?

In the twenty-first century and beyond, with business now the most global of all institutions, you are unlike politicians who win all of their votes from a local power base. You collect your votes from the world—from customers. And increasingly you must be able to answer for them and all constituents:

> What is your definition of global citizenship—for your company?
>
> What is your personal role—indeed, obligation—as an executive and influential human being in global citizenship in the world, given your power?

Having worked with thousands of executives on these challenging dilemmas, we are fully aware of the inadequate responses most people initially come up with. We are also encouraged by what can happen after engaging people from all levels of corporations—from chief executive officers to entry-level managers—with the intellectual and emotional challenges around these issues. After direct involvement, people come alive with ideas and commitments that give us real optimism for the role that business can and should play in the twenty-first century in dealing with the world's most pressing problems.

Precisely with this idea in mind, retired General Colin Powell and all the living U.S. presidents summoned corporate and community leaders to a Philadelphia conference this spring to promote volunteerism. Corporate leaders and philanthropists, from Bill Gates of Mircosoft to Larry Bossidy of Allied-Signal, are giving their money and, more importantly, their time to make a mark.

Global citizenship is a growing challenge for business leaders as the twenty-first century approaches. On this, we have a clear point of view: The wealth-producing institutions of the world—business—must have a clearly articulated agenda regarding environmental and human capital issues. Because of that, MBA students at the University of Michigan Business School spend their first two days at the school, during orientation, participating directly in community service activities in the inner city of Detroit or similar locales. Executives in the Michigan Global Leadership Program spend 20 percent of their time on these issues over five weeks as they study and travel to China, Russia, India, or Brazil. Every corporate client we work with in CEO-driven transformations—Shell, Ford, and Ameritech, among them—involves thousands of executives in community activities as part of their leadership development process. A few examples of their impact:

- A research executive from Otsuka, the Japanese pharmaceutical manufacturer, had just led his research team's development of an anti-AIDS drug. However, it wasn't until he visited a Washington, D.C., clinic during the Global Leadership Program that the executive actually met people suffering from AIDS and began to understand the human side of the disease. He left even more committed to his research and to finding an AIDS cure.

- Workers from Ameritech donating thousands of hours to do volunteer work at Focus: HOPE in Detroit, distributing food to shut-ins, helping children in the day-care center while their (mostly single) parents develop job skills, and urging their corporation to donate millions of dollars in computers to help in Focus: HOPE's educational efforts.

- University of Michigan MBA students launching hundreds of community service projects, including a Habitat for Humanity project for which they raised money and did the physical work as well.

- Royal Dutch/Shell donating money and volunteer time in inner-city London to Community Links and other community development groups.

We personally wrestle with these citizenship issues in our own roles as academics and consultants to the wealth-producing institutions of the world. There are no clear answers for us, other than our commitment that we must stay engaged and that we must—as leaders, advisers, and coaches to business leaders—continually underscore the importance of citizenship issues.

In pursuing those interests in this book, our objectives were threefold. First, we wanted to explore the variety of ways in which organizations engage in corporate global citizenship and the impact of those activities on organization members. Second, we wanted to learn in greater depth how corporations understand their role in the global community and how they articulate their participation in corporate citizenship activities. Finally, we wanted to create a book that could be used by organizational researchers and teachers, as well as by practitioners in community service organizations and by individuals interested in advocating increased corporate attention to issues of global citizenship.

Our first objective was met with the benefit of a grant from the Commonwealth Fund. We began a research program to review different types of corporate involvement in community problems. Those data, which are included in the Appendix of this book, help to describe the breadth of corporate global citizenship programs that are being conducted at a dozen of today's leading corporations.

After gaining some insight into the breadth of citizenship programs, we turned our attention to focusing on several corporate programs in more depth. We contacted organizational scholars interested in corporate citizenship issues who worked with us in developing a series of case studies on corporate global citizenship. The majority of those cases were based on different organizations as a way of expanding the breadth of our coverage. To help represent issues that are likely to face organizations as they become more and more global, we also included cases that focus on specific countries rather than specific companies.

To provide a framework for thinking about issues of corporate global citizenship, the chapters in Part One discuss some of the complex aspects of these issues from a variety of perspectives. Our hope is that the resulting book will contribute to the literature in organizational corporate citizenship and benefit a variety of audiences.

INTENDED AUDIENCES

Teachers

The readings and cases in this book can be used to form the core of a stand-alone course on corporate global citizenship. They can also be used to supplement other, related courses. For example, an accounting course might use the Merck case described in Chapter Seven to discuss ways in which the costs associated with the *Mectizan* program could have been captured to provide information on the overall cost of the program. The J.P. Morgan case discussed in Chapter Six could be used to supplement a marketing course by having students debate the benefits of expanding the exposure of J.P. Morgan's global citizenship activities and developing a marketing strategy that increases public awareness, while at the same time meeting the company's desire for a low-key approach.

Researchers

The readings in Part One offer provocative questions that we hope will stimulate additional research in the area of corporate global citizenship. For example, more work is clearly needed on the implications of government policies for corporate citizenship. Debates in the political arena over who will pick up the slack as government programs are cut make far-reaching assumptions about what and how much corporations can and will do to contribute to revitalization—making employees feel as though they are part of a broader community and making the community feel as though the organization is working for them, rather than against them.

SCOPE OF THE CASES

Because we wanted to highlight the global nature of corporate citizenship, all the cases included center on very large, internationally known organizations. Many other large organizations could have been included; several of these are represented in the Appendix. Likewise, many smaller organizations have been leaders in corporate citizenship for many years. Some of these are detailed in *Companies with a Conscience,* by Scott and Rothman. Their 1994 book includes detailed descriptions of 12 smaller-scale organizations that rank high on corporate citizenship. They also include shorter descriptions of other companies that have social responsibility as a central tenet of their organizations.

OVERVIEW OF THE BOOK

Part One introduces the concept of corporate global citizenship and places it within the broader context of corporate social responsibility. The Introduction sets the stage by discussing the importance of corporate global citizenship in today's society. It uses data from *Fortune* magazine's annual surveys of corporate social responsibility to provide a descriptive analysis of what has been taking place in the realm of corporate global citizenship. Then in Chapter One, Charles J. Fombrun addresses the question of whether or not corporate intervention in social policies is an appropriate use of the corporation's resources. In Chapter Two, based on a series of conversations with Amitai Etzioni, Laurie Richardson discusses the implications of good corporate citizenship for our communities. She argues that an overemphasis on individual rights has led to the neglect of the importance of individual responsibility to the whole. In Chapter Three, Mary Tschirhart outlines the impact of governmental policies and activities on corporate participation in citizenship activities, especially those conducted through links with nonprofit organizations. In the final chapter in Part One—a chapter by Charles Kadushin and Lynda St. Clair—the authors consider how corporate global citizenship activities can become institutionalized.

After providing this introduction to some of the central issues of corporate global citizenship, Part Two moves to some specific examples, including: American Express (Chapter Five by Michael Brimm), J.P. Morgan (Chapter Six by Charles J. Fombrun), Merck (Chapter Seven by Jane E. Dutton and Michael G. Pratt), General Electric and Ameritech (Chapters Eight and Nine by Jeanette L. Jackson), Sara Lee (Chapter Ten by Ann E. Tenbrunsel, Zoe I. Barsness, and Paul M. Hirsch), Procter & Gamble (Chapter Eleven by Paul Shrivastava), and Compaq Computer Corporation (Chapter Twelve by the employees of Compaq Computer and Lynda St. Clair). The eight cases in this section can be used in courses designed around corporate global citizenship in general, or specific types of corporate activities. The data presented in these case studies generally reflect the situation in the first half of the 1990s. This allows student projects to be designed around evaluating how these companies have done in subsequent years with their corporate global citizenship activities. The large size of these organizations helps to ensure that adequate research materials can be obtained by students pursuing that type of project.

Part Three points toward the future and how one might develop an agenda for corporate global citizenship. The next four chapters look at corporate global citizenship activities from the perspective of different countries or regions, rather than different companies. In Chapter Thirteen, Stuart Hart argues that preserving the environment of the world requires companies to establish sustainable development as their central goal. Chapter Fourteen by Erik C. Olson discusses issues facing organizations interested in practicing corporate global citizenship in China. Benjamin E. Goldsmith discusses general citizenship issues in Russia, Ukraine, and Kazakhstan in Chapter Fifteen and provides examples of successful and not-so-successful citizenship efforts in India in Chapter Sixteen. Chapter Seventeen, by Lynda St. Clair, brings us back to the United States with a discussion of Focus: HOPE, a not-for-profit organization that provides an inspiring model of how organizations can build integrated systems that serve society, while resting firmly on the three pillars of ethics, social benefit, and economic profitability that serve as a foundation for effective corporate global citizenship efforts. Finally, in Chapter Eighteen we set forth our personal agenda for the future of corporate global citizenship, using the frameworks provided in the first part of the book as a guide. We reflect on the many sides to the issue of corporate global citizenship and discuss the pros and cons; we also discuss the paradoxes of corporate global citizenship. We conclude the book with our own normative opinion that corporations should and must make a contribution back to the global community that serves as their suppliers, their employees, and their customers as a ticket to admission to the 21st century.

This book represents a milestone in our own personal journeys.

For Noel, it is a reflection of his attempt to integrate a social activist's agenda from the 1960s and 1970s, when he spent a great deal of time in community development and health care, leading to his first book, *Organization Design for Primary Health Care: The Dr. Martin Luther King Jr. Health Care Center.* The book chronicles one of the big successes of the War on Poverty, a community-based health care delivery system in the worst section of the South Bronx in New York that provided health care to 49,000 residents as well as jobs to over 500 previously unemployed African American and Puerto Rican residents. This led Noel to try to replicate the Martin Luther King Center in the hills of Appalachia, where he worked full-time for a year establishing the

Hazard (Kentucky) Family Health Services, which was dedicated to reducing infant mortality in one of the worst areas of the United States. It was from those roots to the mid-1980s before Noel was able to make the linkage between such community service efforts and big business and leadership for the twenty-first century. Since that time he has been on a mission, proactively making it part of his life's work as an academic, teacher, and consultant.

For Andy, this represents the culmination of three decades of observing the underside of society and working to improve things. From the streets of Detroit in 1967, where as a journalist he witnessed the Detroit Riot, the most devastating and divisive race riot in modern U.S. history, Andy reported on the economic frustration that lay beneath the rubble and saw the optimism with which Focus:HOPE and numerous other organizations rallied forces to improve conditions. In the 1970s, as a seminarian he helped young African American children learn basic academic skills and see the value of staying in school in the inner city of Chicago. He later used his network analysis skills as an academic to research social network connections in metropolitan Detroit and Camden, New Jersey, to help spark the revitalization of the areas, leading to two Pulitzer Prize nominations. Andy began to see the sparks of optimism that could result when caring people—individually and in corporations—came together to make a difference, especially when they had enough money. Against that backdrop, this book represents for Andy a collection of best practices from around the world and the incredible potential for their replication.

For Lynda, this book provided an opportunity to advance her understanding of the relationship between the individual and the organization and to think about what that means. Although the most obvious impact of corporate global citizenship programs is on their intended beneficiaries, such efforts also affect the members of the corporate organizations. In some cases, the impact is through creating a corporate identity that is consistent with the values and beliefs of organization members, further reinforcing the bond between the individual and the organization. In other cases, where there are profound disagreements about how best to serve the needs of the community, some types of corporate citizenship activities may actually fray the bond between some individual members and the organization. Finally, in still other cases, the impact may be much deeper—by taking part in citizenship activities, employees who previously had been insulated from the needs of the community around them may develop new personal beliefs and values as a result of their relationship to the organization. It is clear that as corporations move ahead with global citizenship efforts, they need to think about such potential outcomes.

From such disparate experiential beginnings, we came together to methodically assemble what we had learned or knew to be the best corporate global citizenship practices in the world.

July 1997

NOEL M. TICHY
Ann Arbor, Michigan

ANDREW R. MCGILL
Ann Arbor, Michigan

LYNDA ST. CLAIR
Smithfield, Rhode Island

THE EDITORS

Noel M. Tichy is professor of organizational behavior and human resource management at the University of Michigan Business School. He holds a Ph.D. from Columbia University. Professor Tichy is the director of the Global Leadership Program at the University of Michigan. He is the author of several books, including *Managing Strategic Change: Technical, Political, and Cultural Dynamics; Strategic Human Resource Management* (coeditor), *The Transformational Leader* (with Mary Anne Devanna), *Control Your Destiny or Someone Else Will: How Jack Welch Is Building the World's Most Competitive Enterprise* (with Stratford Sherman), *Globalizing Management: Creating and Leading a Competitive Organization* (coeditor), and *The Leadership Engine: Winning Companies Build Leadership at Every Level.* Formerly, Dr. Tichy was manager of management education for General Electric, where he directed its worldwide development efforts at Crotonville between 1985 and 1987. He consults widely in both the business and public sectors. He is a senior partner in Action Learning Associates, where his clients have included Ameritech, AT&T, HarperCollins Publishers, Mercedes-Benz, BellSouth, CIBA-GEIGY, Chase Manhattan Bank, Citibank, Exxon, General Electric, General Motors, Honeywell, Hitachi, Imperial Chemical Inc., IBM, NEC, Northern Telecom, Nomura Securities, and 3M.

Andrew R. McGill is director of the Michigan Global Business Partnership and associate professor of organizational behavior and human resource management and associate research scientist (visiting) at the University of Michigan Business School, where he teaches "Developing the Customer-Driven Organization" and "Human Resources as a Competitive Advantage." He received his Ph.D. in business administration at the University of Michigan in organizational behavior and human resource management. His research interests focus on the cognitive aspects of managerial change, with an emphasis on turbulent environments in which organizations are attempting to become more customer-driven. Much of his research and consulting are concentrated on the banking, consumer goods, health-care, insurance, telecommunications, and automotive industries, with clients including Ameritech, Blue Cross and Blue Shield, Ford, Harley-Davidson, General Motors, Mercedes-Benz, Nissan, Royal Bank of Canada, Toshiba, and the Saudi Arabian Monetary Authority.

Lynda St. Clair is associate professor of management at Bryant College in Rhode Island. She earned her Ph.D. from the University of Michigan in organizational behavior and human resource management. Her research interests center on the relationship between the individual and the organization. She has written about individuals' attachment to their employing organizations, the implications of the changing psychological contract, and the impact of family responsibilities and career identity salience on performance outcomes of professionals (with Sharon A. Lobel). She has also coauthored papers on the concept of group entities (with Lloyd E. Sandelands), coping with incompatible expectations (with Anne S. Tsui, Susan J. Ashford, and Katherine Xin), and psychological intimacy at work (with Sharon A. Lobel, Robert E. Quinn, and Andrea Warfield). Her work has been published in the *Academy of Management Journal,* the *Journal for the Theory of Social Behaviour,* and *Organizational Dynamics.*

THE CONTRIBUTORS

Zoe I. Barsness is assistant professor of management at Texas A&M University. She received her A.B. in comparative history from Harvard University in 1987, an M.S. in organization behavior in 1993, and a Ph.D. in organization behavior in 1996 from the J.L. Kellogg Graduate School of Management at Northwestern University.

Michael Brimm is professor of organizational behavior at INSEAD (European Institute of Business Administration in Fontainebleau, France), where he is also a founding faculty member of the Corporate Renewal Initiative (CORE). He received his bachelor's degree in 1964 from Cornell University, his master's degree in 1969 from Northeastern University, and his Ph.D. in 1975 from the Harvard Graduate School of Business. His research interests include the change process in large multinational organizations and the role of leadership in achieving organizational excellence. He is currently studying outstanding French restaurants.

Jane E. Dutton is the William Russell Kelly Professor of Business Administration at the University of Michigan Business School, where she is also the area chair of the Department of Organization Behavior and Human Resource Management. She received her bachelor's degree (1974) from Colby College, her master's degree (1981), and her Ph.D. (1983) in organization behavior from Northwestern University. Her research interests include strategic agenda building and invisible relational work in organizations.

Amitai Etzioni is an eminent sociologist and social philosopher and university professor at George Washington University. He received his B.A. (1954) from Hebrew University in Jerusalem, his M.A. (1956) and Ph.D. (1958) in sociology from the University of California at Berkeley. He is director of the Center for Communitarian Policy Studies, which he founded in 1995. He has written many pathbreaking books and articles on individual participation in communitarian activities, prominent among them, *The New Golden Rule* and *The Spirit of Community*.

Charles J. Fombrun is professor of management at the Stern School of Business of New York University. He earned a B.S. in physics from Queen's University (Canada) and completed his Ph.D. at Columbia University in 1980. He is the cofounder and editor-in-chief of the *Corporate Reputation Review,* a new quarterly journal published beginning in June 1997. His research interests include reputation management and organizational change.

Benjamin E. Goldsmith is a Ph.D. candidate (1999) in the department of political science at the University of Michigan. He received his bachelor's degree (1991) in Russian studies from Columbia University and his master's degree (1995) in Russian area studies from Georgetown University. His research interests include comparative foreign policy and international relations.

Stuart Hart is professor of corporate strategy at the University of Michigan Business School, where he is also director of the Corporate Environmental Management Program. He received his bachelor's degree in 1974 from the University of Rochester, his master's degree in 1976 from Yale University, and his Ph.D. in 1983 from the University of Michigan. His research interests include strategy and the environment.

Paul M. Hirsch is the James L. Allen distinguished professor of strategy and organization behavior at Northwestern University, where he is also a faculty fellow at the Institute for Policy Research. He received his bachelor's degree in 1966 from the City College of New York, his master's degree in 1968 from the University of Michigan, and his Ph.D. in sociology from the University of Michigan. His research interests include the framing of social issues (from downsizing to rightsizing, for example) and business, work, and family.

Jeannette L. Jackson is president of Grosvenor Associates, Inc., in Ann Arbor, Michigan. She received her bachelor's degree (1985) from Smith College and her master's degree (1991) in business administration from the University of Michigan. Her research interests include citizenship, leadership, and organizational change.

Charles Kadushin is professor of sociology and psychology, Graduate Center, CUNY, and is a coordinator of its advanced social research concentration. He received his Ph.D. in sociology from Columbia University (1960) and his A.B. from Columbia College (1953). His special expertise lies in bringing the methods and findings of modern social science research together with the methods and techniques of action learning and organization development.

Erik C. Olson received his interdisciplinary bachelor's degree (1981) in the political and economic dimensions of international relations from California Lutheran University; he expects his master's degree (1997) in agricultural economics from Michigan State University and his Ph.D. (2000) in political science from the University of Michigan. His research interests include formal and empirical approaches to the political economy of development in developing countries, particularly China.

Michael G. Pratt is assistant professor of business administration at the University of Illinois at Urbana-Champaign. He received his B.A. in psychology from the University of Dayton and his M.A. and Ph.D. in organizational psychology from the University of Michigan. His interests include organizational culture and identity, socialization, organizational attachment, organizational sensemaking, and emotions in organizations.

Laurie Richardson is a Washington, D.C.-based community development management and training consultant to public, private, and nonprofit organizations. She has a bachelor's degree in international affairs from the Georgetown University School of Foreign Service (1979), a certificate in cross-cultural training from the Society for Intercultural Education, Training, and Research (1981), and a master's degree in public and private management from Yale University (1991).

Paul Shrivastava is the Howard I. Scott professor of management at Bucknell University. He received his bachelor's degree in mechanical engineering from Bhopal University, India, his master's degree in management from the Indian Institute of Management, Calcutta, and his Ph.D. in business from the University of Pittsburgh. His interests include environmental management and strategic management.

Ann E. Tenbrunsel is assistant professor of management at the University of Notre Dame. She received a B.S. in industrial and operations engineering (1986) from the University of Michigan. She received a master's degree in management in 1990 and a Ph.D. in organizational behavior in 1995 from the J.L. Kellogg Graduate School of Management at Northwestern University.

Mary Tschirhart is assistant professor at the School of Public and Environmental Affairs, Indiana University, and a member of the Philanthropic Studies faculty of the Center on Philanthropy. She received her Ph.D. in organizational behavior and theory from the University of Michigan's Graduate School of Business Administration. She earned a B.A. in philosophy from Michigan State University and an M.B.A. from the State University of New York. Her work is on the relationships of organizations to their stakeholders, with a particular emphasis on how nonprofit organizations attempt to influence individuals' attitudes and behaviors.

CORPORATE GLOBAL CITIZENSHIP

INTRODUCTION: CORPORATE GLOBAL CITIZENSHIP—WHY NOW?

Noel M. Tichy, Andrew R. McGill, and Lynda St. Clair

Globalizing markets, instantaneous communications, travel at the speed of sound, political realignments, changing demographics, technological transformations in both products and production, corporate alliances, flattening organizations—all these and more are changing the structure of the corporation. The once very rigid and unbreachable boundaries of business are fading in the face of change (Harvard Business Review, *May-June 1991, p. 151*).

AS SOCIETY PAYS THE PRICE of enormous upheavals resulting from the rapid changes and increased competition in the business community just described, more attention has been focused on the role that business can—indeed must—play in serving the needs of society. As federal government deficits have skyrocketed in the United States and Western Europe, and budget balancing has become tricky even in the emerging economies of Asia, many eyes are turning toward corporations to help make up losses in funding for a variety of social programs. Many business executives seem to agree. For example, the *Harvard Business Review* article cited earlier goes on to report that three out of four U.S. executives approve of a very active role for their companies in improving the quality of education; fewer than 20 percent think their companies should limit their social contributions to financial support. American executives also rate unsafe cities, substance abuse, and environmental problems as requiring more active corporate involvement in the years ahead.

In this book, we consider specific instances of how and why corporations have been responding to this pressure. Although familiar arguments about ethical and economic motivations for engaging in citizenship activities are included, our intention is not primarily to argue for one rationale

1

over another. Rather, it is to help explain the movement by corporations toward corporate citizenship activities from the companies' perspectives, as well as from broader theoretical perspectives that introduce sociological, psychological, and economic concepts to help make sense of these actions.

USHERING IN A NEW ERA

The level of corporate interest in pressing social problems in their communities is moving beyond traditional corporate philanthropy. It is taking the form of large-scale, strategic projects that mobilize companies' own people power as well as their resources. Companies are beginning to take a direct, hands-on approach to correcting social problems. Landmark projects by such companies as Merck, Ameritech, GE, Sara Lee, Levi Strauss, Procter & Gamble, and J.P. Morgan, to name a handful of prime examples, are being scrutinized by corporate managers and university researchers and heralded as the beginning of a new era of enlightened capitalism.

This book provides an examination of the potential of this relatively recent phenomenon to add substantially to our problem-solving capacity within organizations, extending to society as a whole. Our bias, which we state freely, is clearly toward increased citizenship activity by corporations, especially those with global business activities or aspirations, because these organizations bear the burden of contributing to the social well-being of those communities where they do business the world over, not just in their traditional home bases. It is our primary intention in this book to accurately reflect what organizations are doing in the area of corporate global citizenship, how they explain and justify those activities, and what impact those activities have on the broader social and business context. Thus, we hope that the cases in this book can inform our readers about how corporations can use their enormous capacities and resources effectively toward shared pursuits, and that the articles present a useful backdrop for creating a framework to better understand corporate global citizenship.

CORPORATE GLOBAL CITIZENSHIP

We see corporate global citizenship as one of the many different types of activities that make up the broader concept of corporate social responsibility. In particular, we are interested in organizational activities and programs that go beyond the traditional definition of profit making, and even beyond corporate donations to good causes. *Corporate global citizenship aims to enhance the quality of community life through active, participative, organized involvement.*

Our inclusion of the word *global* is not accidental. First, many organizations are moving into the global arena, with operating units in multiple countries. Thus, considering only citizenship activities in the United States for an American firm, for instance, would greatly restrict the focus on this critical issue. In addition, if corporate citizenship and social responsibility are only viewed within the narrow context of a single community, decisions that might benefit one community could be detrimental to the broader global community. We will return to this idea in the last section of this book in our chapter, "An Agenda for Corporate Global Citizenship."

Unlike the broader concept of corporate social responsibility, we have not sought to include those activities such as obeying the law, which are considered to be a priori, that is, basic and fundamental. Rather, our focus is on major projects that corporations have undertaken to provide support for the communities in which they operate. Although these activities are not directly aimed at profit making, we believe that effective corporate global citizenship does have positive bottom-line consequences. Corporate global citizenship is good for both individuals and companies. It makes people feel good about themselves, their company, and their world. By personally engaging in citizenship activities, by tackling and overcoming difficult challenges, employees acquire the ability to work more effectively in diverse organizations, classes, and cultures.

Not only does the corporation directly benefit from the increased understanding and energy of its workers, but its image to governments, stockholders, and consumers is likely to be greatly enhanced. Good corporate citizenship provides numerous benefits that are standard rationales for involvement: improved community and public relations, visibility, and reputation; better marketing; and an increased ability to attract high-quality people.

POWER, ACCOUNTABILITY, AND CITIZENSHIP

Modern corporations can mobilize human and capital resources to an extent unimaginable before this century. In many instances, individual corporations have more wealth at their command than the governments of some countries in which they do business. Because they operate in a multinational, global environment, corporations are accountable not to national governments but to their shareholders for most of their actions.

Regulatory constraints notwithstanding, corporations face relatively few externally imposed limits on their activities. This combination of great wealth and broad discretion makes modern corporations enormously powerful. And even seemingly trivial decisions by corporations can affect—for good or ill—individual well-being on a global scale.

Because corporations exercise such great power, many people maintain that corporations should operate under some form of self-accountability. This kind of self-accountability is usually referred to as "corporate social responsibility" or "corporate global citizenship." These terms are rarely stated precisely. Good (and bad) corporate citizenship seems easy to identify but hard to define.

Here, nonetheless, we will attempt such a definition and a rationale for it.

As we approach the end of the 20th century, nations the world over and corporations doing business in them are struggling with a web of issues relating to population, the environment, social justice, poverty, health, and education. The issues affect the well-being of nations, the productivity and effectiveness of corporations doing business in them, and the quality of life of the world's population. Traditionally, corporations have exempted themselves from social and environmental problems, focusing instead on performance and shareholder return. However, as it becomes apparent that the complex issues of today demand more than government intervention can accomplish or should attempt, businesses are rethinking their role as global citizens. Motivated by concern and enlightened self-interest, corporations are enlarging their definition of appropriate involvement and beginning to address environmental and human capital challenges.

Global citizenship is not the old style of good citizenship—simply doing good deeds or offsetting the damage a corporation might do to the local ecology with compensating measures. Nor does it simply mean inculcating employees with a sense of civic obligation to their local communities. While these are important aspects of corporate responsibility, they are not how we define global citizenship. *Global citizenship entails an understanding and awareness of future trends that will affect both the climate for doing business and the quality of life of the world's population. As we move into the 21st century, global businesses will find themselves increasingly intertwined with global political, social, and environmental issues that will force them to redefine their role as a potent force for world integration. This force, coupled with the pressure being exerted by a burgeoning world population, is determining the need for global citizenship.*

World population growth is the single most pervasive factor affecting the world today. Demographic projections by the World Bank estimate a doubling of today's population by the middle of the next century, with the highest growth rates occurring in the world's poorest countries. Accompanying this massive population growth is a rapid increase in urbanization. U.N. projections suggest that 60 percent of the world's population will be urbanized by early next century, compared to only 25 percent in 1950. When the population growth since 1950 is factored in, this translates to very large numbers indeed. And since resources are scarce, population has a dramatic impact on every other social and environmental issue, with effects that ignore geopolitical boundaries. A rapidly growing population can strain a country's ability to produce enough food and provide sufficient housing, education, and health care. Often overlooked, the size of the human population is the most pressing environmental problem. People drain the earth's renewable resources, release toxic chemicals into the environment, consume fossil fuels (which add greenhouse gases to the atmosphere), and cause the extinction of other species. Overpopulation directly determines or greatly contributes to virtually every environmental and social problem facing the nations of the world today.

A corporate global citizenship response to such challenges, then, encompasses the five cornerstones shown in the accompanying chart (see Figure 1): *understanding, values, commitment, actions,* and *cooperation.*

Figure 1. The Corporate Global Citizenship Approach.

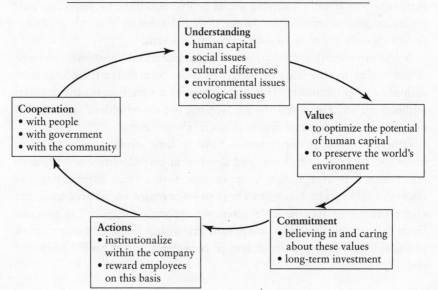

The elements of the approach are as follows:

Understanding—Corporate global citizenship starts with understanding social issues, cultural differences, environmental problems, and ecological issues.

Values—It means having values that optimize the potential of human capital and preserve the world's environment.

Commitment—It takes commitment, caring about the values, and making long-term investments.

Actions—It encourages action that institutionalizes the values and commitments within the company and rewards employees on that basis.

Cooperation—It is above all a cooperative approach between people, community, and government.

JUSTIFYING CORPORATE GLOBAL CITIZENSHIP

A variety of perspectives exist regarding what a corporation must do in order to be labeled a good corporate citizen. The most conservative view of corporate social responsibility is associated with the economist Milton Friedman, who argues that corporations have no social obligations beyond their fiduciary duty to shareholders. Pursuit of goals besides profit is harmful to the extent that it conflicts with this duty. In this view, the market is best suited to solving social problems, either by providing corporations with incentives to change their behavior or through organizations explicitly designed to address social concerns.

A less conservative view argues that corporations must assume some responsibility for the state of society in order to preserve their long-term viability and profitability. This can be seen as a variation on the position outlined earlier. The definition of "serving the shareholders' interests" is extended to include some degree of social involvement.

Others argue that corporations have at least some responsibility to make society better off, long- and short-term profitability notwithstanding. Often it is argued that corporations have unique capabilities and resources that can be brought to bear to solve major social problems that might otherwise receive little attention through the political process. From this perspective, good corporate citizenship involves some amount of social involvement, independent of considerations of profitability and viability.

Finally, some argue that corporations should not engage in social activism at all, not because they have no responsibility to do so but because they can offer no more than token assistance. These individuals argue that the solutions to social problems fall outside the competence of most managers and that managers will be inherently conservative, offering piecemeal, incremental solutions when major social reform is required. In this view, corporate social activism may simply delay the implementation of necessary solutions, thereby worsening whatever problem is under consideration.

In practice, a combination of purely altruistic and purely pragmatic motivations impels corporations to be good citizens. One concern rarely appears in isolation from all others. Reasons often cited for being a good corporate citizen include a genuine commitment to change on the part of managers, concerns of enlightened self-interest involving long-term profitability and sustained economic growth, and a simple desire to cash in on consumers' political sentiments. All three of these reasons seem to lie behind the recent growth in the number of environmentally friendly products available to consumers, the so-called green movement.

THE PROBLEMS OF MORE PEOPLE

Population growth is the primary driver of the world's human capital and environmental problems. These are problems brought on by a burgeoning world population, and they respect no boundaries; they challenge local communities and the world with equal persistence. The convergence of these issues and business's unique global position defines the need for global citizenship. While the broad global issues can be categorized into main headings, their magnitude and specific local needs can vary dramatically from country to country. The successful global company orients its citizenship approach to meet the requirements of the local conditions. Figure 2 suggests how these problems converge.

With such a growing population comes the confluence of human capital and environmental issues.

THE PRESSURES OF POPULATION GROWTH

Most of today's high-level corporate executives grew up in the 1940s and 1950s. During their lifetime the world's population has more than doubled. Rapidly growing populations can strain a country's ability to

Figure 2.   The Corporate Global Citizenship Challenge.

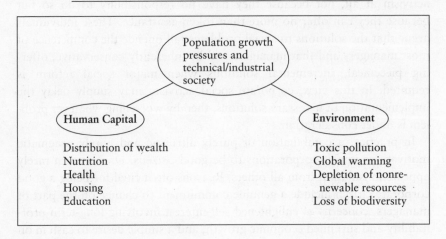

produce enough food and provide sufficient housing, education, and health care. If current trends continue, millions of people will eventually starve to death as agricultural capacity fails to keep up with population growth.

The facts of the population problem are simple. There are currently 5.7 billion people in the world, and the population is growing at about 1.8 percent a year. This translates to 95 million more births than deaths each year. This is equivalent to the population of Austria, Belgium, France, Luxembourg, the Netherlands, and Switzerland combined being reproduced each year.

Population has traditionally been viewed as a problem for only a few countries, either extremely populous ones such as China and India or poor ones such as Somalia. Increasingly, however, more and more countries will face human and environmental challenges as their population rises. Additionally, globalization of economic, agricultural, and energy systems and the integrity of the earth's physical system have made population a worldwide concern.

It is often politically expedient to focus on the *effects* of overpopulation instead of identifying it as the *cause* of many social problems (especially in countries that are sensitive to population control). For this reason, as the world's population rises it may be increasingly hard to get the nations of the world to address the issue of overpopulation for its own sake.

HUMAN CAPITAL ISSUES

Distribution of Wealth

The gaps between the world's rich and poor are staggering. Consider that the three wealthiest economies in the world—the United States, the European Union, and Japan—generate a combined annual gross domestic product of almost $20 trillion for the 710 million people who live there, or almost $28,600 per capita. Compare that with the developing countries of China and India, the world's most populous, where the combined gross domestic products equal $980 billion for the 2.2 billion people living there, or less than $450 per person. That represents one segment of the global population producing wealth 65 times more than another—a dramatic and scary disequilibrium.

Even when the controversial but far more generous purchasing power parity numbers are considered, China and India would have a combined economy of only about $4 trillion—one-fifth that of the First World triad—for three times the population.

To be sure, if this gap is to be acted upon and narrowed by the citizens of the world, it will come at the hands of the giant Western corporations that are beginning to face their corporate citizenship responsibilities as they increasingly do business in China, India, and the emerging world.

Among the questions they need to examine are those developed in the Global Leadership Program:

- What are the local standards of rich and poor?
- Are there major observable differences between rich and poor?
- What is the relative number of rich and poor people?
- How important is the middle class?
- Within a company, what is the range of wages?
- What are the differences in standard of living between people earning the highest and lowest wages in a single enterprise?
- Is there much mixing between people of different incomes?
- How do members of one socioeconomic group view members of other groups?
- Are differences in the distribution of wealth more noticeable within or between regions of the country?
- Is money the primary means for obtaining goods and services, or are they allocated by other means such as rationing?

Nutrition

Obtaining a proper diet is one of the most basic human needs, yet hunger is a fact of life for millions of people around the world. Hunger contributes to a variety of health problems and is a factor in millions of deaths each year. In many areas there are simply too many people to be fed on the resources available. An assessment of the nutritional status of a region should include a determination of the following:

- What is the local definition of a minimum-standard diet?
- What percentage of the population is able to obtain that standard?
- Do levels of nutrition contribute to health problems for many people?
- Is nutrition considered a national priority?
- Are a wide variety of foods readily available?
- Does the country have significant surplus food in storage to buffer against future poor harvests?
- Does the country have the resources to feed its population, or does it depend on imports of food?
- How reliable is the source of imports?
- If food shortages exist, what is their underlying cause? (Too many people? poor farming techniques? inadequate distribution systems?)

Public Health

The level of health and availability of medical care will vary tremendously within countries. Many cities have modern hospitals, whereas rural areas have almost no health care. A wide variety of information goes into an assessment of the health status of a region.

Some factors to consider include:

- Are the major sources of mortality infectious diseases or chronic conditions of aging such as heart disease and cancer?
- Do mothers receive adequate prenatal care?
- Are babies born healthy?
- Does nutrition play a major role in a significant portion of health problems?

- Does sanitation play a major role in a significant portion of health problems?
- What percentage of people have reliable access to clean drinking water and adequate sewage facilities?
- Are people aware of the cause of the most prevalent ailments?
- Is the focus of the health care system treatment or prevention?
- Is the focus appropriate to the needs of the community?
- Are there significant regional differences in the health status of the population?

Housing

The availability and standards of housing differ greatly within and between countries. A general assessment should consider the following topics:

- What percentage of the population has housing?
- What is the local definition of minimum-standard housing?
- What percentage of the population lives in housing that meets that standard?
- How do living conditions contribute to public health problems?
- Is housing considered a national, regional, or local priority?
- Does the government have a housing policy? If so, what is it?
- Are companies expected to provide or help workers obtain housing?
- What percentage of annual income do most people pay for housing?
- Are most workers able to live close to employment?
- Is transportation to and from work a logistical or financial problem for many people?
- Does the availability of housing vary greatly within the country?

Education

Education levels may vary greatly within and between countries. A general assessment of the quality of education in a country should include the following:

- What is the average level of education?
- What percentage of children attend school regularly?
- Is education overseen by the national or local government?
- What are the strengths and weaknesses of the system?
- Are people adequately educated for the jobs they hold?
- Is the education system meeting the country's needs? Is the labor force adequately and appropriately trained?
- Do people make full use of the education they have?
- Are there differences in levels of education between men and women? between young and old?
- Do many people study overseas? Do those who study overseas return?
- Is teaching a respected profession in the community?
- Are teachers well paid relative to other workers?

ENVIRONMENTAL ISSUES

Capital Depletion

The safest route to long-term financial security, in theory, is to invest your capital and live only off the income it generates. Routinely depleting capital for day-to-day expenses is usually regarded as unwise. Unfortunately, this principle, generally accepted and occasionally followed in matters of finance, is barely recognized in the use of natural resources. In a very real sense, most of modern society is based on the depletion of capital. We do not live on income.

Careless exploitation of any nonrenewable resource is worrisome. But three types of capital depletion are especially significant. The first is familiar to most people; the others generally are not.

Nonrenewable energy sources. These are fossil fuels in affluent nations, fuelwood in less-developed countries. Despite low prices in the 1980s and 1990s, most people and governments are aware of the world's dwindling resources of oil and natural gas. Coal and other less accessible sources of petroleum are somewhat more abundant, but even the most optimistic estimates suggest at most a 100–200-year supply of fossil fuels. This shortage is cause for concern but is the one that is most likely to be counterbalanced by the market-driven development of new technologies. As petroleum prices rise, it will become more profitable to invest in alternative sources of energy, many of them already identified and waiting to pump into action at the right price.

The situation in poor nations is more difficult to project. In many areas of the world the primary source of energy remains firewood. Theoretically, fuelwood is a renewable resource, but demand, which is rapidly rising, already far outstrips supply in most places. In many regions, large areas have been deforested by people gathering fuel. Because the need for fuel will not abate, these areas will most likely not regenerate for generations, if at all. The energy future of such regions is uncertain. How people who cannot now afford oil will be able to purchase more expensive alternate technologies is unknown.

Groundwater. Most of modern agriculture depends on stored groundwater, which has accumulated over thousands of years. This groundwater is being "mined" at alarming rates. The problem is perhaps most acute in North America and India. All agriculture in the southwestern portion of the United States depends on the enormous Ogallala aquifer, which is being pumped out at about 2 meters per year. It is naturally replenished by less than 2 centimeters per year. Similar problems exist in India, where tube wells have lowered the water table by as much as 20 meters in some important areas.

Topsoil. Equally important to agriculture as water is fertile soil. The amount of arable land worldwide actually declines each year for two important reasons—erosion and contamination. Poor land management practices like overgrazing on rangelands, overcultivation of few crops, and deforestation all result in a decline in soil productivity—degradation—and its actual physical loss—erosion. For example, in China over 1.5 billion tons of fertile soil wash down the Huang He (Yellow) and Chang Jiang (Yangtze) rivers annually. Poor irrigation practices in both humid and arid regions can contaminate agricultural land. In moist areas such as the Indian state of Madhya Pradesh, irrigation has raised water tables into the root zone, which damages crops. In dry areas like China's North Plain, extensive irrigation is accompanied by evaporation, which leaves behind salts and other dissolved chemicals toxic to crops. Build-up of these chemicals can effectively ruin once-productive agricultural lands.

Global Warming and Climate Change

Given much attention in the recent press, global warming has become the subject of tremendous controversy. Here, stated as simply as possible, are the facts:

- In the past 200 years, since the beginning of the industrial revolution, the amount of certain gasses in the atmosphere has increased dramatically.
- The dramatic increase in CO_2, water vapor, methane, chloroflorocarbons (CFCs), nitrous oxide, and various other trace greenhouse gasses is directly correlated with human activities.
- These gasses play an important role in the greenhouse effect. Despite public confusion, the greenhouse effect is not controversial. It is a fact accepted in the scientific community. Various atmospheric gasses trap solar energy and reradiate it toward the surface of the earth. Without the greenhouse effect, the earth would be too cold to sustain life.

What is controversial is to what extent—and how rapidly—increasing the amount of greenhouse gasses in the atmosphere will result in trapping more energy and what the consequences will be. The debate centers on whether the earth's temperature will increase by 1°, 4°, or 8°C; whether it will happen in 50, 100, or 200 years, whether it will be drier in Iowa or wetter in India, and whether these changes are good or bad, and for whom. The arguments take many forms and most have no clear cut answers. What is certain, however, and really the root of most scientists' concern, is that we are causing changes of uncertain consequence at a much greater rate than at any time in the earth's recorded history.

Toxic Pollution

The dangers of toxic pollution have been recognized for many years. Major strides have been made in many developed countries in cutting the level of many types of pollutants. In most poorer countries, nevertheless, serious problems persist. The major factors responsible for the differences between developed and developing countries are more efficient and cleaner industries, more stringent governmental oversight, and a better-informed, more outspoken population. Numerous types of toxic pollution are eminent.

Air Pollution

Air quality has improved markedly in many developed countries. Smoke and sulphur pollution have been cut dramatically, but auto emissions remain a problem in many urban areas. In poorer countries, toxic industrial emissions occur at higher levels, and smoke from charcoal fires remains a serious problem. The air in cities such as Sao Paulo, Bombay, and Beijing is among the most unhealthy in the world. An important difference between rich and poor countries is in restrictions on smokestack and automobile emissions. For instance, most developed countries mandate catalytic converters on automobiles, which are required to burn unleaded fuel. Such requirements are rare outside of Japan, Europe, and North America. Acid rain is a difficult problem in North America and Europe that results from coal-fired industries.

Water Pollution

Water contamination comes from two sources: human and animal wastes and industrial discharges. Well over half of all citizens in developing countries do not have access to plentiful clean water, and three out of four have no acceptable form of sanitation. India has serious shortages of clean drinking water for large segments of its population. Fouled water is implicated in a host of diseases from trachoma blindness to typhoid and yellow fever, but most severe are diarrheal diseases that kill or debilitate millions of people each year. In addition to causing deaths, water-borne diseases leave people seriously disabled. In India, water-borne diseases claim 73 million work days each year; the cost of medical treatment and lost production amounts to almost $1 billion.

Hazardous Chemicals

The horrendous accident at Bhopal, India, which killed 3,000 people in the mid–1980s, is perhaps the most memorable example of the problem of toxic pollution in developing countries. Industry and agriculture contribute thousands of tons of toxins to the environment each year. The roots of pollution are very different in poorer countries such as India and in command-economy countries like China and the former USSR. In India, toxic pollution accumulates mostly because there is no regulation of small industries and agriculture. In most communist countries, ideology called for industrialization at the expense of the environment. Only in the last decade have serious environmental efforts begun in these nations.

Nuclear Power

The nuclear accident at Chornobyl in 1986 highlighted the dangers of nuclear power to the world environmental community, but atomic energy remains an important component of many nations' development plans. Incredibly, the two remaining reactors at Chornobyl, identical to the one that malfunctioned, continue to be used by the Ukranians. India, China, and Russia all have independent nuclear energy programs. Nuclear power continues to present a difficult choice for all nations, which must weigh the need for electricity against the horrifying prospect of a reactor accident and the still unsolved problem of nuclear waste disposal.

Biodiversity

Human effects on the world's ecosystems have precipitated what has been labeled an extinction epidemic among other plants, animals, and microorganisms. Thousands of species a year disappear, most without much public notice or comment. Controversies such as that surrounding the spotted owl in the United States are very much the exception. There are three classical types of argument for why we should be concerned about the loss of biodiversity:

Aesthetic and ethical arguments. These contend that nature and the planet intrinsically deserve respect, and it is morally wrong to exterminate other forms of life. This argument is gaining favor in certain segments of western society.

Direct economic and natural resource arguments. Human civilization depends heavily on other species for food, transportation, medicines, and industrial materials. By eliminating diversity we are limiting our potential to grow new crops, develop new pharmaceuticals, and exploit certain resources. This type of argument is frequently used by people concerned about the destruction of tropical rainforests.

The earth as integrated system argument. This argument works best by analogy. A modern jetliner is redundantly designed for safety. If you remove one of the rivets attaching the wing to the fuselage, the airplane will almost certainly still fly. It will probably fly if you remove five, ten, or even a hundred of the many thousands of rivets holding the wing in place. But at one point, you will remove one rivet too many, and the wing will fall off. To complete the analogy, imagine earth as the airplane and different species as individual rivets. It is hard to argue in the specific that losing the snail darter, spotted owl, Furbish's lousewort, or any other single species will have significant consequences. Removing species from the earth's ecosystem may have profound results, nevertheless. Most serious are losses of species that play a role in maintaining fundamental life-sustaining processes like regulation of the hydrologic cycle and control of the proportion of gasses in the atmosphere.

CORPORATIONS: IN THE PUBLIC EYE

Corporations are beginning to recognize that the effects of this social and environmental discord land squarely on business's doorstep. If businesses do not assist in the improvement of human and environmental conditions, needed changes will not occur, and ultimately corporations will suffer the direct consequences of a damaged society and global infrastructure. Although good public relations are not the only motivation, it should come as no surprise that the surge of interest and activity in corporate global citizenship has been reflected in media reports of corporate performance in the citizenship arena. Beginning in 1983, *Fortune* magazine has conducted annual surveys to assess the reputation of corporations. One of the eight components included in that survey is "community and environmental responsibility" (referred to here as corporate global citizenship). By tracking and publicizing corporate reputations, including a measure of social responsibility, *Fortune* has identified this type of activity as "defining" the best corporations. The mere fact that this information is being gathered is likely to change people's behavior because it makes salient corporate citizenship available in a way that it was previously not.

The *Fortune* data indicate that Johnson & Johnson stands head and shoulders above the rest when it comes to community and environmental responsibility. J&J was ranked in the top three 12 times from 1983 through 1996. In five of those years, they were ranked No. 1. Merck rates second place with six top-three finishes in the same fourteen years and two No. 1 rankings in the six. Eastman Kodak and 3M both had five top-three finishes, but Eastman Kodak ranked first three times, and 3M ranked first only once. Other multiple-year winners include IBM and Rubbermaid, with four top-three finishes, DuPont with three, and Coca-Cola with two. Procter & Gamble made the list once in 1988 but hasn't been back since. Two other companies also have one top-three finish each (Corning in 1994 and Levi Strauss Associates in 1996). (See Table 1.)

Fortune's ratings are based on a survey of executives, outside directors, and financial analysts. Respondents rated only companies that were in their same industry or the industry that they followed in the case of financial analysts. In the first year of the survey, Fortune included 200 of the largest U.S. corporations and surveyed nearly 6,000 individuals. By 1996 the survey had grown to 417 companies and 11,000 raters. Because some industry groups have been added along the way, not every company was included in all of the years of the survey. For example, Coca-Cola first came into the survey in 1984.

Table 1. Top Three Community/Environmental Responsibility Scores from *Fortune* Magazine's Annual Survey of Corporate Reputation from 1983 Through 1996.

Company	1983	1984	1985	1986	1987	1988	1989	1990	1991	1992	1993	1994	1995	1996	Times in top 3
Eastman Kodak	8.32	8.26	8.35	8.43		8.11									5
IBM	7.85	7.95	7.96		7.92										4
Johnson & Johnson	7.76	**8.44**	8.09	7.88	**8.51**	8.39	8.31	8.23	8.22	8.29		7.89		8.06	12
3M			7.96	7.92							**8.09**		7.63	7.99	5
Coca-Cola (1st incl'd 1984)				7.88									7.77		2
Merck					7.68		8.1	8.19	**8.27**	**8.32**	7.92				6
DuPont							8.16	7.99	8.15						3
Procter & Gamble						8.1									1
Rubbermaid										8.19	8.05	**8.03**	**8.22**		4
Corning												7.9			1
Levi Strauss Associates														8.13	1

Note: Highest rankings are shown in bold; second-highest rankings are shown in italics and underlined.

Community and environmental responsibility is only one of the eight attributes that *Fortune* uses to evaluate corporate reputations. The others are: quality of management; quality of products or services; ability to attract, develop, and keep talented people; value as a long-term investment; use of corporate assets; financial soundness; and innovativeness. In 1996 the magazine noted that community and environmental responsibility was rated as the *least* important of these attributes. Thus it is no surprise to find that making it into the top three on the community and environmental criteria did not necessarily catapult a company into the top ten overall in terms of corporate reputation. For example, in six of the twelve years that J&J was ranked in the top three in community and environmental responsibility, they were not ranked in the top ten overall. (See Table 2.)

These companies that *Fortune* has recognized are not only in the public eye because of their corporate global citizenship activities, but they have also caused people to stand up and take notice because of their ability to generate substantial returns for their shareholders. As shown in Table 3, all of the companies on which data were available outperformed their relevant industry in terms of return on equity (ROE) from 1983 through 1996 (ROE data were not available for Levi Strauss). For example, over those 14 years, Coca-Cola generated a whooping 3,345.05 percent return on equity. In contrast, the beverage industry returned only 748.90 percent, about equal to the ROE for the Standard & Poor's 500 (742.60 percent). (See Table 3.)

The companies described in the detailed cases later in this book are no slouches when it comes to stock market performance, either. For example, American Express returned 525.05 percent, compared to the S&P's Financial-Miscellaneous category's return of 344.05 percent. J.P. Morgan's return of 939.65 percent handily beat the S&P Money Center Bank category (300.15 percent). Even more impressive was General Electric's return of 1,173.33 percent, which stood in stark contrast to the S&P Electrical Equipment group's modest return of 237.90 percent. Sara Lee also had outstanding results, returning 1,898.25 percent to beat the S&P Food group's 249.97 percent return. Two companies' results are available for slightly shorter time horizons but are no less impressive. From November 10, 1983, through December 31, 1996, Ameritech returned 1,094.48 percent compared to the S&P Telephone group's 104.74 percent return. Finally, Compaq Computer Corporation had more than enough time from February 29, 1984, through December 31, 1996, to outperform the S&P Computer Systems group's return of 23.16

Table 2. Overall Ranking from *Fortune* Magazine's Annual Survey of Corporate Reputation for Those Companies with the Top Three Scores in Community/Environmental Responsibility for Companies That Were in the Top Ten Overall from 1983 Through 1996.

Companies with top three community and environmental responsibility scores	1983	1984	1985	1986	1987	1988	1989	1990	1991	1992	1993	1994	1995	1996
Eastman Kodak	4		9											
IBM			1	1	7	4			8	6	4			
Johnson & Johnson		5		2	8	6	6		7	8				
3M	3		4	4			4		6	7	5	5	8	4
Coca-Cola (1st incl'd 1984)		9		4	5	1			1	1	1	3	3	1
Merck	5	4	10	5					3				3	6
DuPont								10						
Procter & Gamble				8	8	4			3	9	6	6	7	2
Rubbermaid				7	7	5	1		2	2	2	2	1	3
Levi Strauss Associates														

percent. During that time Compaq provided their shareholders with an awe-inspiring 5,073.91 percent total return on equity.

Hence, there is powerful evidence that those firms active in corporate global citizenship financially outperform their competitors. The following chapters offer several arguments for why that linkage should be seen as more than coincidental.

CONCLUSION

Companies today are truly in the "public eye." They are being watched not only by a society that has grown to expect corporations to give something back to the communities that support them, but also by shareholders who expect lucrative returns on their equity investments. Balancing these two responsibilities may at first appear to be impossible, but as the elite organizations profiled in this book attest, it can and must be done.

We are grateful to the Commonwealth Fund for its generous funding of some of the cases in our book (Grant Nos. 90–67 and 92–41). These cases—

Table 3. Total Return on Equity from 12/31/82 Through 12/31/96
for Companies That Ranked in the Top Three Community/
Environmental Responsibility Scores from *Fortune* Magazine's Annual
Survey of Corporate Reputation from 1983 Through 1996.

Company	Total return on equity—12/31/82 through 12/31/96	Standard & Poor's industry measure of return on equity[1]	Industry category description
Eastman Kodak	354.85%	91.69%	photography/ image industry
IBM	149.40%	23.16%	computer systems
Johnson & Johnson	993.12%	263.91%	health care division
3M	648.05%	182.47%	miscellaneous
Coca-Cola	3345.05%	748.90%	beverages
Merck	2314.56%	340.02%	drugs
DuPont	1276.52%	179.70%	chemicals
Procter & Gamble	1012.88%	343.85%	household products
Rubbermaid	646.36%	251.76%	housewares
Corning	690.91%	182.47%	miscellaneous

[1]*The total return for the S&P 500 for this period was 742.60 percent.*

and the many leaders their authors had occasion to meet in reporting them—provide some of the best examples in the world of blending know-how and societal improvement. We also appreciate the valuable contributions from all of our colleagues at the University of Michigan Global Leadership Program and our years of traveling the world together in search of citizenship lessons, especially Michael Brimm, Hirotaka Takeuchi, Paul Kreisberg, Kenneth Lieberthal, Erik Olson, Benjamin Goldsmith, Robert Marcus, Jeannette Jackson, and Martin McDermott. Our longtime colleagues Charles Kadushin and Charles Fombrun have provided ongoing support over the many years of this project. And the numerous administrative coordinators of the effort, notably Laurie Richardson and Marjorie Heinzman, helped in keeping us focused on the project—its importance and completion.

We hope that our readers will leave this book feeling encouraged by the good works that are reported here. We also hope that the warm glow they are left with will burst into a flame of inspiration, leading them to encourage their own organizations to become better citizens in the countries and regions in which they do business. The time has come for corporations to accept their responsibility to global society and to place their corporate global citizenship agendas on center stage for all to see.

PART ONE

THE THEORY OF CORPORATE GLOBAL CITIZENSHIP

A SUCCESSFUL LEADER must have a clear point of view on corporate global citizenship and be able to articulate it. On this we take a firm stance. Furthermore, it is not enough for leaders merely to hold this perspective—they must be able to teach it, so that they can help other leaders shape their own teachable points of view.

There is a clear link between great leadership and great teaching. Examples ranging from chief executive officers—Jack Welch at General Electric, Andy Grove at Intel, Larry Bossidy at Allied-Signal—to the late Father William Cunningham, the cofounder of Focus: HOPE, demonstrate this amply. These and other successful leaders are able to articulate and teach various dimensions of leadership:

- *Ideas* They have clear ideas of what it takes to win in the marketplace and on how the organization should operate.
- *Values* They articulate the values that support their business ideas, and they are well understood throughout the organization.
- *Emotional Energy* They are not only highly energetic people but they know how to energize others around the organization's ideas and values.
- *Edge* They can make tough decisions, and they encourage and reward others who do the same.

In addition, winning leaders must have a teachable point of view on global citizenship. The first part of this book provides both experienced and emerging leaders with a chance to gauge their own thinking against the ideas and values of our authors. The challenge for all readers is to have their own point of view that, over time, they can teach to anyone. This requires having intellectual ideas about how the organization will deal with environmental and human capital issues, health and nutrition, and economic haves and have-nots and understanding how those ideas relate to products, services, distribution channels, new plants, customer segments, and other such elements that lead to making money in the marketplace.

There must be a teachable point of view regarding the value system that supports global citizenship and ties to other organizational values. There must also be ways of generating positive emotional energy among the employees of the organization for global citizenship. Finally, there must be an ability to make tough yes-no decisions regarding environmental and human capital issues.

When reading the chapters in this part, readers should work toward a teachable point of view. Can you, our reader, list three to five bullet points for each of the four categories mentioned earlier that would help you present your teachable point of view? Such a list will help you wrestle with the problems facing society that were outlined in the Introduction—problems that are enormous in both scale and scope. No single effort or prescription can begin to solve them all. Efforts to address specific aspects of the problems, however, can be highly efficacious.

In Part One we focus on the theoretical issues that are central to the effective implementation of corporate global citizenship programs with sufficient power to successfully address problems of such magnitude. In particular, we consider how organizations can justify their participation in corporate global citizenship activities and how they can be more effective in those efforts by working alongside other organizations.

Justification for corporate citizenship: The first two chapters focus on different rationales that can be used to justify a corporation's participation in global citizenship activities. In his analysis, Fombrun identifies three basic justifications for corporate global citizenship: it is the "right thing to do" based on ethical grounds; it is the "responsible thing to do" as a member of a social community; and it is the "profitable thing to do" based upon economic analysis. Richardson captures Etzioni honing in on the concept of responsibility and reflecting on the need to balance the "spirit of self-interest" with a "commitment to the community." They suggest that such a balance can be achieved by nurturing a nascent social movement that is directed toward "enhancing social responsibilities, public and private morality, and the public interest."

Juxtapositions in corporate citizenship: The authors of the last two chapters begin with the premise that global citizenship is an appropriate corporate objective. With that as an underlying assumption, they turn their attention to how those activities can be accomplished efficiently and effectively (Chapter Three) and how they can be made ubiquitous (Chapter Four). The accomplishment of both of these goals depends on the appropriate juxtapositions of proactive organizations. As Tschirhart explains, corporations working on their own will find it difficult to be as effective as corporations working along side nonprofit and governmental agencies. Kadushin and St. Clair argue that corporate global citizenship can become ubiquitous through the process of institutionalization. As companies discover through their corporate networks that other organizations are proactive participants in citizenship activities, these types of programs will become even more diffuse, further fueling the drive to become exemplary corporate citizens.

The ideas and frameworks in these first four chapters set the stage for the cases and examples in the remainder of the book. Each case, for example, can be evaluated in terms of the justifications for participation in the particular citizenship activities in which they have chosen to take part. They can also be evaluated in terms of the number and kinds of organizations with which they have juxtaposed themselves to accomplish their objectives.

I

THREE PILLARS OF CORPORATE CITIZENSHIP

Ethics, Social Benefit, Profitability

Charles J. Fombrun

*A people among whom individuals lost the power of achieving
great things single-handed, without acquiring the means of
producing them by united exertions, would soon lapse
into barbarism.*
—Alexis de Tocqueville, *Democracy in America*

Democracy reads well, but it doesn't act well.
—George Bernard Shaw, *Misalliance*

IS THE BUSINESS OF BUSINESS simply to generate profits, or is it to fulfill other societal objectives? Should managers make decisions based solely on the bottom line, or should their decisions recognize broader social obligations? Are corporations owned merely by their shareholders, or are they a form of social architecture designed to serve and preserve the interests of a diverse polity?

THE CRUSADE

Increasingly these questions are being asked, not only by ivory-tower intellectuals but more significantly by critics, activists, reporters, entrepreneurs, and managers themselves. Collectively they ponder whether, in granting corporations the right to exist, we also should not expect them to fulfill diverse social obligations. If individuals and corporations have nearly equivalent legal and political standing, should we not demand of them equivalent *moral* standing? In which case, just as a democratic society bestows both rights and responsibilities upon its individual citizens, should it not also ascribe to its corporations not only the rights of citizenship but a corresponding set of duties to perform?

By *corporate global citizenship,* we—the author and the editors—mean the responsibilities that attach to a corporation by virtue of its membership in society. We use the term *citizenship* to crystallize a corporate mindset that is slowly taking root in companies large and small throughout the world, but especially in America. As corporations have moved to center stage in the economic sphere, whether as employers, producers, or service providers, we have conceded to them many of the rights of individuals but with few, if any, corresponding societal responsibilities. There is movement afoot to alter that prevailing *zeitgeist,* to recognize that companies are not only engines of economic growth but also pivotal agents of social and political integration. In their thoughtful and timely book, *The Good Society,* Robert Bellah and his coauthors (1991) argue that:

> We need to understand how much of our lives is lived in and through institutions, and how better institutions are essential if we are to lead better lives. In surveying our present institutions we need to discern what is healthy in them and what needs to be altered, particularly where we have begun to destroy the nonrenewable natural and nearly nonrenewable human resources upon which all our institutions depend [p. 5].

Traditional exhortations that companies should behave responsibly have largely failed, we contend, because they have relied principally on ethical reasoning to defend corporate citizenship without sufficiently accenting the desirable *social and economic consequences of citizenship.* Against the moral concept of *responsibility* and the political concept of *citizenship,* we therefore juxtapose two others: the social concept of *integration* and the economic concept of *reputation. Corporate citizenship, in our view, is justified by a fusion of moral and teleological reasoning that champions ethical behavior, social integration, and long-run profitability.*

Like Bellah and his colleagues, we believe that a philosophy of extreme individualism teaches us:

There is no such thing as the common good but only the sum of individual goods. But in our complex, interdependent world, the sum of individual goods, organized only under the tyranny of the market, often produces a common bad that eventually erodes our personal satisfactions as well.

A commitment to corporate citizenship defines not only a moral basis for management practice but also a dedication to creating stronger ties between people and the larger communities to which they belong. Companies pledged to a mindset that identifies citizenship as a core value recognize the importance of enabling closer integration between work and leisure, between individual and organization, between individual and community, between organization and community. The trend toward company-supported volunteerism, community networking, environmentalism, employee participation, and workplace equity are practical means that path-breaking companies are taking to reduce employee alienation, to achieve social integration, to improve company reputations, and so to sustain their long-term viability.

In fact, our rationale for corporate citizenship is built on three core arguments—three pillars, as it were, of good practice. First is the belief that *corporate citizenship is ethical*. Undersocialized individuals often pursue their self-interest at the expense of others. Corporate citizenship encourages development of a cultural context that channels managerial acts and decisions in morally defensible directions.

Second is the belief that *corporate citizenship is socially beneficial*. Where individualism prevails, community suffers. A society committed to the pursuit of self-interest finds it difficult to build and maintain a degree of unity, of common purpose, of shared values. To call for greater corporate citizenship is to encourage social integration and so to strengthen our experience of community.

Third is the belief that *corporate citizenship is profitable*. Bottom-line thinking provokes a short-term outlook to investments. Corporate citizenship focuses attention on the reputational consequences that come from fulfilling the expectations of a diverse group of corporate stakeholders, and so encourages a long-term view of economic returns.

WHY CORPORATE CITIZENSHIP?

Various trends reinforce the notion that corporate citizenship is an idea whose time has come. For one, the laissez-faire decade of the 1980s demonstrated how recklessly corporations and managers could behave when left to their own devices. Although mergers and leveraged buyouts were widely defended in the go-go years as strategies to enhance corporate efficiency, most proved to be motivated more by exploitative managers and raiders eager to capitalize on market failures, with little concern for the people left behind, for the communities that were frequently devastated, or for the companies that were themselves subsequently bankrupted by debt. Ultimately, we pay a high price for endorsing a short-run view of corporate self-interest and for disregard for the social implications of those corporate decisions.

Public activists have also become increasingly vocal about the reprehensible role that companies play in damaging our natural environment, with catastrophic potential for the global community. By aggressively boycotting products and generating media hype through attention-getting events, interest groups point to the deficiencies of an economic system that champions the self-interested actions of its members at the expense of society's well-being and the survival of future generations. In 1992, Al Gore wrote of our disintegrating ecology. His best-selling book was doubtless instrumental in his becoming vice president of the United States, and his election served notice of a sea change in social attitudes.

Environmentalists like Gore ask that companies incorporate so-called "externalities" into their strategic decisions, that they internalize the clean-up costs of industrial waste and of air, water, and land pollution. Beyond asking that companies pay economic penalties, however, one also hears in their demands a clear expectation that companies demonstrate responsible citizenship in the societies in which they operate. Much as populations of a prey can be wiped out by overconsuming predators, so is the human species threatened, they point out, by irresponsible companies who overconsume our natural and human resources. For them, citizenship means favoring *sustainable business* activities that take out of society and the environment no more than they put back.

Heightened global interdependence has also prompted some convergence around shared values. The dismantling of the Soviet empire not only shifted the axis of global dialogue away from the polarized East-West and North-South descriptions of the postwar era, but increased the potential for global cultural integration. Since 1990, an invigorated United Nations has found itself returned to the center stage of international efforts to champion human rights. The UN's post–World War II "Declaration of Human Rights" reflects some of these shared values. By specifying work standards that include nondiscrimination, equal pay for equal work, and a clean environment, the charter conveys jointly held values that define a company's responsibilities to the global community—values that also constitute a benchmark for corporate citizenship.

A more exciting development of recent years, perhaps, is the formation of numerous private groups and organizations that explicitly advocate practices consistent with a concept of corporate citizenship. The Franklin Research and Development Corporation, for instance, was among the first advisory firms to specialize in socially responsible investing. Founded in 1982, the employee-owned company has since spawned two other organizations: (1) the Social Investment Forum, a professional association working to build support for social investing and (2) the Coalition for Environmentally Responsible Economies (CERES), sponsors of the CERES Principles—a corporate code of environmental conduct. Another investment advisory firm of this sort is Kinder, Lydenberg, Domini & Co. In 1992, the firm's senior staff published the *Social Investment Almanac* (Henry Holt Co.), a guide to social investment practices.

The Council on Economic Priorities is an independent research organization that regularly assesses and publicizes the social performance of corporations. Its purpose is to heighten public awareness and thereby to channel corporate decision making in socially desirable directions. Its annual Corporate Conscience Awards are presented for exemplary environmental performance, employee responsiveness, charitable contributions, and community outreach. Recent winners have included such companies as Herman Miller, Prudential, Kellogg, Avon, H.B. Fuller, and Pitney Bowes. According to *The Washington Post* (Skrzycki, 1990, p. C1), "The awards ceremony is the business equivalent of an Oscar"—a suggestive parallel since, as movie buffs know, an Oscar virtually guarantees the economic success of a film—an impact that the Conscience Awards would surely like to have on the corporate world.

Most recently, leading representatives of American business, academia, labor, and the media founded the Business Enterprise Trust in 1989, a national organization seeking to shine a spotlight on acts of courage, integrity, and social vision in business. The Trust gives five annual awards to individuals and companies that recognize exemplary acts of business responsibility. Prudential was among the 1992 recipients and was lauded for designing innovative policies for providing terminally ill patients early access to their insurance savings.

By granting high-profile awards and publicizing relative ratings of comparable firms, pressure groups, advisory firms, and investment funds call attention to the merits of activities and programs that better integrate employees and companies into their communities, increase their social responsiveness, and so enhance their reputations. These rankings not only strengthen better-regarded companies' public profiles but also make their products more attractive to consumers, their jobs more attractive to prospective employees, and their stock more attractive to investors.

THE GOOD CITIZEN

Corporate global citizenship can be assessed from different perspectives. We propose a three-part view of citizenship as: (1) a reflection of shared moral and ethical principles; (2) a vehicle for integrating individuals into the communities in which they work; and (3) a form of enlightened self-interest that balances all stakeholders' claims and enhances a company's long-term value. The model that we propose fuses these moral, social, and economic viewpoints. We argue that companies whose actions and decisions demonstrate citizenship work actively to enhance employee morale and loyalty, to create consumer credibility, to develop community trust, and to secure investor confidence. In doing so, they build valuable *reputational capital* that becomes a source of competitive advantage for better-regarded companies; eventually it translates into higher long-term profits.

Taken together, this concept of corporate global citizenship therefore rests on the three supporting pillars of social responsibility, community integration, and reputation building. Shared values are maintained by programs that stress the integration of the individual into the community. Over time, these programs strengthen corporate reputations and make a company's jobs more attractive to employees, a company's stock more attractive to investors, and a company's presence more attractive to a community. Figure 1.1 diagrams the architecture of this concept of the good corporate citizen.

The Moral Pillar: Doing the Right Thing

What makes an action or decision morally defensible? Two criteria seem central: (1) moral acts have an imperative, almost sacred quality, and we defend them on the basis of general rules; and (2) moral acts are symmetrical; we expect the same rule to apply to all others facing comparable situations.

A moral approach to corporate citizenship therefore tries to articulate sacred and symmetrical duties and obligations that all companies have as institutions—their social responsibilities. It suggests that managers and their companies should act in particular ways simply because that is the *right thing to do*. Just as the Bible prescribes a code of conduct for

Figure 1.1.   Corporate Citizenship.

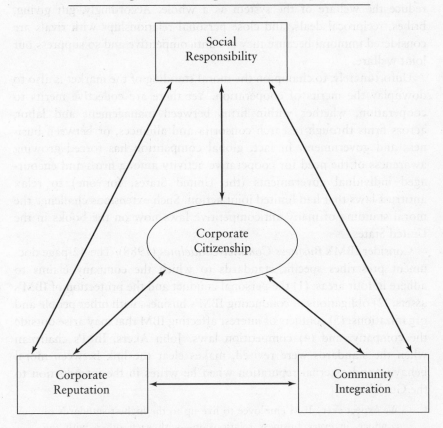

Christians, the Koran for Muslims, the Torah for Jews, the Upanishads for Hindi, so does a principled approach seek to enumerate the rules by which to judge the actions of a company.

Typically, initiatives are considered morally defensible when they protect basic rights, especially those of individuals. Some rules are granted moral standing, for instance, because they protect the property rights of shareholders to a company's assets. Insofar as companies own "soft" capital—assets that do not get reported in financial statements, assets as difficult to quantify as know-how or reputation—codes that regulate the dissipation of those assets are morally grounded in the property rights of shareholders. For instance, employees are routinely enjoined from disclosing proprietary information or from personally gaining from exploiting a company's intellectual property or confidential internal information.

Under capitalism, many laws governing competition derive from moral reasoning. Cartels, collusive agreements, and other attempts to restrict competition are considered immoral acts in the United States because they reduce the welfare of the system as a whole. Accordingly, gift giving, bribes, reciprocal deals, and close personal relationships with rivals are considered immoral because they are anticompetitive and so suppress our joint welfare.

Unfortunately, to champion the moral standing of the market is also to downplay the merits of cooperation. Yet there are collective merits to cooperation, whether within firms between management and labor, across firms through research consortia and alliances, or between business and government. In fact, global competition has forced growing awareness of the need for cooperative activity among firms and encouraged individual governments (the United States, for one) to relax antitrust laws that had limited joint action. Such extensions challenge the moral standing of many anticompetitive laws now on the books in the United States.

Consider IBM's *Business Conduct Guidelines* (1988). The 42-page document prescribes specific standards to which the company claims to adhere in four areas: (1) the personal conduct and the protection of IBM's assets; (2) obligations in conducting IBM's business with other people and organizations; (3) conflicts of interest affecting IBM that may arise outside the company; and (4) competition laws. John Akers, IBM's chairman when the standards were revised, makes clear the link between moral behavior and external reputation when he writes in the introduction to the Guidelines:

> We expect every IBM employee to live up to the highest standards of conduct, in every business relationship—with each other, with the company, with our customers, business partners, and competitors. Doing the right thing begins with the basic honesty and integrity of individual IBMers—you and your colleagues. More than ever, it also depends on your good judgment and sensitivity to the way others see us and how they may interpret our actions [p. 1].

Most large companies have defined codes of conduct similar in tenor to IBM's. A report produced by the high-powered CEOs who sit on The Business Roundtable (1988) documents how comparable practices are now in place in over 100 member companies, and highlights the ethical postures of prominent companies like Boeing, Champion International, General Mills, GTE, Hewlett-Packard, Johnson & Johnson, and Xerox.

Pragmatically, however, it would appear that taking the moral high ground produces mixed results at best. Daily we are bombarded with accusations and evidence of managerial and corporate behavior inconsistent with basic moral principles, be they insider trading, price fixing, or other infringements of individual freedoms, property rights, and social welfare. They give us pause to ponder whether relying on a principled approach can sufficiently discourage immoral acts.

In part, a principled approach fails to stimulate moral behavior because companies operate in a fragmented world of multiple cultures, each of which condones different standards of conduct. It becomes all too easy for managers to rationalize immoral behavior as a form of cultural relativism that states, "When in Rome, do as the Romans do." Multinational managers, hauled into court for paying bribes to local officials in other countries, often resort to this line of defense.

This weakness of a principled approach to corporate citizenship can also be traced to internal corporate diversity and weak control systems. Few companies can claim to screen and socialize their employees perfectly. Managers' core values ultimately derive from family and educational experiences acquired over years of upbringing and professional work. Given the disparate backgrounds of employees in multicultural companies, a morally based view of corporate social responsibility proves difficult both to endorse and to enforce.

We suggest, therefore, that moral principles alone constitute a relatively fragile defense for encouraging social responsibility. We propose instead that the argument for corporate citizenship is significantly strengthened when buttressed by two additional structural pillars: social integration and the long-term sustainability of the business enterprise.

The Social Pillar: Community Integration

According to Bell (1980), "What ultimately provides direction for the economy . . . is not the price system but the value system of the culture in which the economy is embedded" (p. 78). In this statement, penned at the start of the me-decade of the 1980s, social critic Daniel Bell warned of the implicit danger of reinforcing individual self-interest while neglecting to buttress the institutions that create shared values, be they the educational system or the activities that integrate individuals into social groups and organizations into communities.

All societies face a two-pronged threat. On the one hand, a philosophy of extreme laissez-faire that promotes individualism wears away the social fabric of shared values of a community. On the other hand, a philosophy of intensive socialization threatens individual liberties with totalitarian control of citizens' lives.

Sociologist Amitai Etzioni (1988) recognizes a middle ground between extreme individualism and the authoritarian community. As a compromise, he proposes the "responsive community" as a place where individuality is recognized and actively defended but where the benefits of community are also preserved. The responsive community champions individual liberties by recognizing that

> individuals who are typically cut-off and isolated . . . are unable to act freely, while . . . individuals who are bonded into comprehensive and stable relationships, and into cohesive groups and communities, are much more able to make sensible choices, to render judgment, and be free. . . . A responsive community is much more integrated than an aggregate of self-maximizing individuals; however it is much less hierarchical and much less structured and "socializing," than an authoritarian community. . . . *Individuals and community are both completely essential, and hence have the same fundamental standing* [pp. 8–9].

The social pillar of corporate global citizenship recognizes businesses as key players in building active, responsive communities. It also ascribes to profit-making companies a degree of responsibility for bonding and integrating individuals into the social fabric. The underlying justification for corporate involvement in community activities is the sense that so many of our daily activities and relationships are governed by the companies in which we work. Without a commitment to social integration by companies large and small, a community's infrastructure must inevitably collapse.

In *The Spirit of Community*, Etzioni (1993) proposes explicit pursuit of a "Communitarian Agenda," one that puts the spotlight on community relations. As he contends:

> America does not need a simple return . . . to the traditional community. . . . Such traditional communities were usually homogeneous. What we need now are communities that balance both diversity and unity. . . . Thus, we need to strengthen the communitarian elements in the urban and suburban centers, to provide the social bonds that sustain the moral voice, but at the same time avoid tight networks that suppress pluralism and dissent [p. 122].

A key aspect of corporate global citizenship, then, involves the protection of individual rights as well as the defense of community. Companies are not only bundles of resources or powerful political brokers, they are also vehicles of social integration, with the responsibility for maintaining the integrity of the communities in which they do business. Corporate citizenship means encouraging and sustaining full participation in the social and cultural life of local communities, recognizing and balancing institutional responsibilities that go beyond returning profits to shareholders.

Doubtless many companies have the wherewithal to provide financial support to communities. In 1992, charitable giving by corporations, for instance, accounted for a staggering $6 billion of $124 billion of total contributions made to philanthropy. Giving, however, accounts for only a small part of a company's responsibilities in building more responsive communities. Far more important is the support that comes from encouraging employee volunteerism and the transfer of skills from the corporate sector to nonprofit, educational, cultural, religious, and other community-based service groups. By intensifying the bonds between individual, organization, and community, benevolent activities both safeguard liberties against the authoritarian encroachment of powerful interests and weave whole cloth out of individual interests.

So, whereas a marketplace view of the world champions an individualistic concept of direct reciprocity between transacting parties—a philosophy of "scratch my back and I'll scratch yours"—our prosocial view of corporate citizenship calls attention to the more complex *web of exchanges* that glues together members of a thriving community in a multiplicity of ways. A company gives of itself, not for a direct return, but in the general expectation of receiving from the community a measure of good will. In fulfilling a social agenda, it is as if companies participate in a more dynamic, more generalized view of reciprocity in exchange relationships than the strictly dyadic market-based view adopts. These dense social ties within the community achieve two ends. On one hand, they sustain a shared understanding of the community's moral principles; on the other hand, they encourage managers to take a long-run view in making corporate decisions that sustain the viability and profitability of the enterprise.

The Economic Pillar: Long-Term Sustenance

At heart, no concept of social responsibility or corporate global citizenship proves defensible if, practically speaking, it only debits the liability side of a company's balance sheet. Discussions that reduce social responsibility to charitable donations, philanthropic activities, or to mere accommodations by firms to environmental pressures overemphasize the costs involved in acting responsibly, while undermining the returns. Our rationale for citizenship, therefore, sits squarely on a third pillar—the core idea that *citizenship practices, because they build reputational assets, stimulate long-term profitability and build economic value worthy of capitalization on the asset side of a company's balance sheet.*

In fact, critics of corporate behavior have repeatedly deplored managers' short-run outlook to decision making. A short-run orientation is typically traced to two sources: (1) an overriding concern with delivering a favorable near-term bottom line to shareholders, reinforced by financial reporting requirements and pressure to maintain stock market prices in order to protect credit terms; and (2) an incentive structure that encourages managers and employees to defend their self-interest, with resulting declines in employee welfare programs, in equipment maintenance, in product quality, and in research and development.

We suggest that to champion corporate global citizenship is implicitly to support policies that drive a long-run orientation to decision making. A citizenship outlook is consistent with *stakeholder* models that expect managers to balance the interests of all groups affected by the actions, decisions, policies, or practices of a company. Many of those interests, however, are incompatible in the short run. Only with a long-run view of a company's profitability and viability can these divergent interests be accommodated.

The vital link in establishing the mutual interests that bind all corporate stakeholders is a company's reputation. Reputational capital is built up from the quality and kind of repeated experiences a company has had with all of its stakeholders. Insofar as a company disregards the interests of a particular group of stakeholder interests, it loses credibility in the eyes of that group. If, as generally happens, miscreant companies get negative publicity from scorning stakeholders, their reputation suffers, with loss of good will from particular stakeholders and an attendant decline in employee morale, product image, and community prestige.

In our view, therefore, the long-term viability of a company requires *fulfilling expectations of all stakeholder groups.* By gratifying its publics, a company builds reputational capital that protects it from other less-deserving rivals, and so generates a relative competitive advantage in attracting and retaining consumers, suppliers, and employees. In turn, an advantaged position translates into greater stakeholder commitment to the products and activities of the company, and so confirms its long-term profitability and viability. Corporate global citizenship, therefore, constitutes *enlightened self-interest*—it enhances the long-run value of a company for all of its stakeholders.

Taken together, the three pillars that undergird this concept of corporate global citizenship lead to a formal definition: *Corporate global citizenship is a mindset according to which managers (1) make corporate decisions, design systems, and initiate programs according to prevailing moral principles; (2) encourage communitywide integration; and (3) build reputational capital wherever in the world they conduct business.*

ENLIGHTENED SELF-INTEREST

In March 1993, business students at New York University's Stern School of Business hosted the tenth annual Graduate Business Conference. Its theme? To identify emerging value systems in corporate America and explore the topic of corporate social responsibility. Discussion and interaction centered around successful companies that have woven social and environmental concerns into their corporate fabric through innovative practices. The keynote speaker was Anita Roddick, founder of the Body Shop, the 900-store chain of personal care products with a reputation for being both environmentally conscious and profitable in the long term. According to the *New York Times* (Hall, 1993) in her company:

> No animals are used to test products, bottles are refilled for customers who choose to bring them back, and most of the ingredients are gathered from natural sources. The stores are encouraged to participate in company-backed political programs, like a recent one in the United States to register voters [pp. C1, C8].

For many years, management training programs and business schools taught an undersocialized view of capitalism that championed the shareholder over other stakeholders; that stressed the bottom line at all cost; that scorned those who were concerned with more than the financial implications of corporate decisions. Strengthened by free market advocates, they encouraged narrow-minded, short-run thinking about self-interest that led to the design of reward systems that support individualism rather than teamwork and fragmentation rather than integration, with an attendant collapse of ethics and community.

Today we pay the piper as we tally the record of wrong-doing, infractions, and white collar crime, all of which can be traced to a loosening of attention to moral standards, social control, and reputational integrity. As a society, we define ourselves by the values we choose to emphasize. "Democracy means paying attention," as Bellah and his colleagues rightly conclude in *The Good Society* (p. 254). Throughout the 1980s, we endorsed individualism over community. Not surprisingly, therefore, the decade is best remembered for fostering speculative frenzy in the stock markets, merger mania on Wall Street—what political scientist Susan

Strange (1986) termed "the casino society," what observer John Taylor (1989) described as a "circus of ambition," and what was perhaps most realistically portrayed in Hollywood's production of *Wall Street* and in Tom Wolfe's novel, *Bonfire of the Vanities*.

In our concept of corporate citizenship are embedded interrelated themes of responsiveness, community, and reputation. After over a decade of me-isms, the pendulum, of necessity, must swing in the other direction. It pushes us to spotlight the long haul; to recognize and to disseminate an attention-based model of corporate behavior in which we, as individual stakeholders, jointly shape the values that companies attend to, and thereby encourage actions and decisions that not only make economic appraisals of firms but also assess their commitment to social responsibility, to community integration, and to political citizenship.

We therefore concur with the institutional view that economist Adam Smith ([1776] 1989) espoused when he wrote:

> When the institutions or public works which are beneficial to the whole society, either cannot be maintained altogether, or are not maintained . . . by the contribution of such particular members of the society as are most immediately benefited by them, the deficiency must . . . be made up by the general contribution of the whole society [p. 9].

In that direction, the cases in the second part of this book highlight companies that have done an exemplary job of making such contributions to society.

Figure 1.2 presents a summary model that regards citizenship activities as investments in reputation building. Through programs designed to integrate employees into the communities in which they work and to demonstrate responsiveness to investors and consumers, good corporate citizens build employee loyalty, community trust, consumer credibility, and investor confidence, thereby enhancing the company's reputational standing. Reputations, in turn, generate for well-regarded companies both greater economic performance and competitive advantage. The model provides the conceptual grounding for a growing movement in support of practicing a more caring form of capitalism.

CONCLUSION

According to journalists Mary Scott and Howard Rothman (1992), authors of *Companies with a Conscience*:

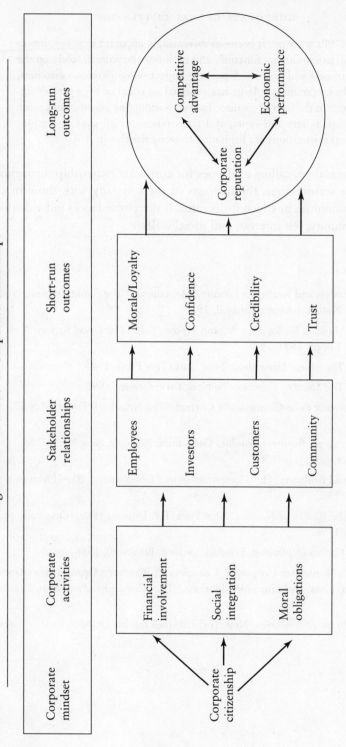

Figure 1.2. A Model of Corporate Citizenship.

Corporate mindset	Corporate activities	Stakeholder relationships	Short-run outcomes	Long-run outcomes

Corporate citizenship

Financial involvement

Social integration

Moral obligations

Employees

Investors

Customers

Community

Morale/Loyalty

Confidence

Credibility

Trust

Competitive advantage

Economic performance

Corporate reputation

As the '90s wear on, it becomes increasingly apparent that business in general can no longer function, and no longer be judged, solely on the basis of nets and grosses. A positive impact on employees, customers, and the community at large has assumed an equal or even greater significance in the overall picture. Today's bottom line encompasses more than just dollars and cents, and corporations of all sizes and philosophical orientations are beginning to recognize this [p. 16].

Such a mandate, calling as it does for corporate citizenship throughout the private sector, aligns the interests of the company with those of the wider communities in which it operates. It thereby balances individualism with community, self-interest, and social welfare.

REFERENCES

Bell, D. "Models and Reality in Economic Discourse." *The Public Interest,* New York: National Affairs Council, 1980.

Bellah, R., Madsen, R., Swidler, A., and Tipton, S. M. *The Good Society.* New York: Knopf, 1991.

Etzioni, A. *The Moral Dimension.* New York: Free Press, 1988.

Etzioni, A. *The Spirit of Community.* New York: Crown, 1993.

Hall, T. "Striving to be Cosmetically Correct." *The New York Times,* May 27, 1993.

IBM Corporation. *Business Conduct Guidelines.* Armonk, New York: IBM Corporation, June 1988.

Scott, M., and Rothman, H. "Companies with a Conscience." *World Monitor,* Oct. 1992.

Smith, A. *The Wealth of Nations.* New York: E.P. Dutton, 1989. (Originally published 1776.)

Strange, S. *Casino Capitalism.* London: Oxford, Blackwell, 1986.

Skrzycki, C. "Kudos for Corporate 'Conscience'; Watchdog Group Praises Good Deeds, Cites 'Dishonorable Mentions.' *The Washington Post,* Mar. 29, 1990.

Taylor, J. *Circus of Ambition.* New York: Warner Books, 1989.

2

THREE PILLARS OF RESPONSIBILITY

A Conversation with Amitai Etzioni About the Individual,
the Community, and the Corporation

Laurie Richardson

IN RECENT DECADES AMERICAN SOCIETY has been tilting too far in
the direction of letting everybody do their own thing or pursue their own
interests, and we have concerned ourselves too little with our social
responsibilities and moral commitments. It is time to set things right.

The nineties opened with a growing awareness that the previous
decades had left in their wake few firmly established moral positions. In
numerous surveys (Etzioni, 1993, p. 27; Patterson and Kim, 1991, pp. 66,
103, 155), almost half of all Americans surveyed report chronic malinger-
ing at work and calling in sick when they are not sick; one-sixth admit
that they have abused drugs or alcohol while at work. Six out of ten admit
to having used physical force against another person—and fewer than half
regret it. Twenty-five percent of Americans say they would abandon their
families for money, and 7 percent freely admit they would kill someone if
paid enough. The moral patrimony of the eighties has been the prolifera-
tion of cost-benefit analysis into realms in which it has no place; it has
devalued matters such as life, companionship, and integrity that ought not
to be subject to such superficial quantification.

This chapter is based on a series of discussions with Amitai Etzioni.

When social scientists ask what social forces have profoundly shaped and reshaped our values and social lives, their research regularly leads them to conclude: *social movements*. There can be no question that the environmental movement and the civil rights movement have changed the world around us and the way we live. What America needs now is a major social movement dedicated to enhancing social responsibilities, public and private morality, and the public interest.

The spirit of self-interest can be balanced by a commitment to the community without requiring us to lead a life of austerity, altruism, or self-sacrifice. Unbridled greed can be replaced by legitimate and socially constructive expressions of self-interest.

America needs a change in the way we approach things, in what we value, and in what we devalue—*a change of heart*. We need a new way of thinking, a reaffirmation of a set of moral values that we may all share. We need groups of people concerned with bolstering our families, schools, and neighborhoods to serve as the main conduits of a moral revival.

We must commit ourselves to recreating a new moral, social, and public order based on restored communities. We must work with our fellow citizens to bring about changes in values, habits, and public policies that will allow us to do for society what the environmental movement seeks to do for nature: to safeguard and enhance our future.

RIGHTS AND RESPONSIBILITIES, INDIVIDUAL AND COMMUNITY

A major aspect of contemporary American civic culture is a paradoxical demand that the community provide more services and strongly uphold rights, coupled with a rather weak sense of obligation to the local and national community. America's leaders have exacerbated this tendency in recent years. In 1961, President John F. Kennedy could still stir the nation when he stated, "Ask not what your country can do for you; ask what you can do for your country." But Presidents Reagan and Bush proposed a much less onerous course. They suggested that ever-increasing economic growth would pay for government services, and taxpayers would be expected to shell out less, implying that Americans could have their cake and eat it, too. But sooner or later, the responsibilities we load on the government end up on our shoulders or become burdens we bequeath to our children.

The eighties tried to turn vice into virtue by elevating the unbridled pursuit of self-interest and greed to the level of social virtue. But it has become evident that a society cannot function well, given such a self-centered orientation. The eighties was a decade in which "I" was writ large, in which the celebration of the self became a virtue. Now is the time to push back the pendulum. The times call for reconstruction through putting renewed emphasis on "we," on the values we share, on the spirit of community.

We aim for a judicious mix of self-interest, self-expression, and commitment to the commons—of rights *and* responsibilities, of I *and* we. A strong commitment to the commons must now be added to strong commitments to individual needs and interests. Balancing self-interest with a fair measure of resumed we-ness will bring our society closer to a balanced position, a society able to steer a stable course.

To take and not to give is an amoral, self-centered predisposition that ultimately no society can tolerate. Those most concerned about rights ought to be the first ones to argue for the resumption of responsibilities. Moral commitments can be strengthened in communities only when we shore up our responsibilities. Indeed, many of our core values entail concern for others and the commons we share. As we restore the moral voice of communities (and the web of social bonds that enables us to speak as a community), we will be more able to encourage one another to live up to our social responsibilities.

We must recognize that we have duties and responsibilities from which we derive no immediate benefit or even long-term payoff. Our commitment to a shared future, especially our responsibility to the environment, is a case in point. We are to care for the environment not only or even mainly for our own sakes. We have a moral commitment to leave for future generations a livable environment, even perhaps a better one than the one we inherited, not one that has been further depleted. The same holds true for our responsibility to our moral, social, and political environment.

In the early nineties, the waning of community that had long concerned sociologists is more pronounced and draws more attention. It is evident that the social environment requires fostering just as nature does. Responding to the new cues, George Bush evoked the image of a "kinder, gentler" society as a central theme for his first presidential campaign in 1988. The time was right for a return to community and the moral order it harbors. Bill Clinton made the spirit of community a theme of his 1992 campaign. In 1997, both joined forces to underscore the importance of community at a national conference to promote corporate voluntarism in the community.

The prolonged recession of 1991–1992 and the generally low and slowing growth of the American economy have worked against this new concern with community. Interracial and interethnic tensions have risen. This is one more reason why we will have to work toward a stronger, growing, more competitive economy. Interracial and ethnic peace are much easier to maintain in a rising than in a stagnant economy. However, this does not mean that community rebuilding has to be deferred until the economy is shored up. It does indicate that rebuilding the community will require greater commitment and effort from both the government and the people.

COMMUNITARIANISM: MORALITY AS A COMMUNITY AFFAIR

In 1990, a group of ethicists, social philosophers, and social scientists met in Washington, D.C. to explore problems that afflict our society. We were troubled by Americans' reluctance to accept responsibilities. We were distressed that many Americans are all too eager to spell out what they are entitled to but are all too slow to give something back to others and to the community. We adopted the name *communitarian* to emphasize our responsibilities to the conditions we all share, to the community. We suggest that *free individuals require a community*, which backs them up against encroachment by the state and sustains morality through the gentle prodding of kin, friends, neighbors, and other community members.

The mainspring of our values is the community or communities into which we are born, that educated us (or neglected to educate us), and in which we seek to become respectable members during our adult lives. We find reinforcement for our moral inclinations and provide reinforcement to our fellow human beings through the community. Communities are the most important sustaining source of moral voices other than the inner self.

The moral voice of the community does not merely censure; it also blesses. We appreciate, praise, recognize, celebrate, and toast those who serve their communities, from volunteer fire fighters to organizers of neighborhood crime watches. It is these positive, encouraging, yet effective moral voices that we no longer hear with sufficient clarity and conviction in many areas of our lives.

Communitarians are often asked which community we mean—the local community? The national community? The world community? Communities are best viewed as nesting boxes. Less encompassing communities (families, neighborhoods) are nestled within more encompassing ones (villages and towns), which in turn are situated within still more encompassing national and cross-national communities. Nongeographic communities criss-cross the others. When they are intact, they all lay moral claims on us by appealing to and reinforcing our values. However, societies in which different communities pull in incompatible directions on basic matters have moral voices that do not carry.

Nongeographic communities, which are made up of people who do not live near one another, may not have foundations as stable and deep-rooted as residential communities, but they fulfill many of the social and moral functions of traditional communities. Work-based and professional communities are among the most common of these. That is, people who work together often develop work-related friendships and community webs. Groups of coworkers learn to know and care for one another and to form and reinforce moral expectations.

Some critics have attacked these communities as being artificially constructed, because they are social networks without a residential concentration. But people who work every day in the same place spend more hours together and in closer proximity than people who live on the same village street. Most important, these nongeographic communities tend to have the moral infrastructure we consider essential for a civil and humane society.

THE ROLE FOR CORPORATIONS IN THE NINETIES

Too many businesspeople no longer accept the responsibility of *stewardship*, that is, at the very least to leave their communities no worse off than they found them. They no longer see it as their duty to reach beyond furthering their self-interest or corporate advancement to serve as trustees of a social undertaking. Speculation, cronyism, bribery, and raiding of corporate coffers have left numerous savings and loans, banks, insurance companies, and pension funds teetering on the brink of insolvency and have shattered public confidence, which in turn damages the country's economic performance. Deregulated airlines have become less safe and more monopolistic. Drug companies have continued to market drugs and devices such as silicone breast implants, artificial heart valves, and pacemakers long after they had found them to be unsafe. The list of examples is sadly long.

Traders have surely shortchanged customers, and merchants have tipped the scales in their favor from the first days bazaars were open. But no economy can thrive when greed is so overpowering that few have a motive to invest in the long run, and the highest rewards go to those who engage in financial manipulations rather than constructive enterprises.

Although it may be true that markets work best if everybody goes out and tries to maximize his or her own self-interest (although that is by no means a well-proven proposition), moral behavior and communities most assuredly do not. They require people who care for one another and for shared spaces, causes, and future. Here, clearly, it is better to give than to take, and the best way to help sustain a world in which people care for one another is to care for someone. The best way to ensure that common needs are attended to is to take some responsibility for attending to some of them. To strengthen the community requires changing the habits of the heart; working out conflicts between career needs and community bonds; and fostering volunteer endeavors that do not trivialize and squander our commitments to the commons.

We constantly, whether we are conscious of it or not, choose how to invest our energy, time, and resources. Some choose to invest ever more of themselves in the pursuit of "making it." To the extent that these efforts become their dominant pursuit to which all others are subordinated, making it becomes a self-defeating endeavor because it is an intrinsically unsatisfying activity. Regardless of how much you earn or gain, there are always higher salaries and ranks to aspire to, always some Joneses ahead of you in the race.

Genuine inner satisfaction cannot be attained this way. People are better off when they combine their self-advancement with investment in their community. Many young people view their alternatives as either a career of self-centered aggrandizement or a life of social service and self-sacrifice. The fact is that one's interests in developing a career and serving the community can be fused in many ways.

In general, there is a need for corporations to become not only more family-friendly but also more community-friendly. I do not mean merely contributing to the local Red Cross, children's museum, and chamber music society but to examine corporate policies from a community standpoint.

It has for some time been considered good corporate policy to move managers around frequently. Social bonds are disrupted to serve corporate and career needs. In recent years, however, it has become evident that many companies may do quite well, and perhaps even better, if they move their employees around less often and allow them to cultivate community roots. Moving corporate headquarters to another town 50 miles away may lower a corporation's office space costs, but it will severely disrupt the social bonds of many employees. And the savings in costs may well be less than the losses due to a decline in morale and increases in tardiness, absenteeism, and resentment that such disruptions often engender.

Closing plants that are the mainstay of a community sometimes cannot be avoided, but such closings should not be undertaken capriciously or abruptly. Affected communities should be accorded an opportunity to help the corporation solve its economic problems or to find buyers for the plant (including its workers), if it is to be sold rather than transferred. At least the employees should be afforded some time (and, if at all possible, financial aid) to help them and their community adapt. Even those who are opposed to government controls as a rule may see merit in new laws that slow plant closings by corporations that are grossly insensitive to community needs.

Much of what communitarians favor has little to do with laws and regulations, which ultimately draw on the coercive powers of the state, but with being active members of a community. Whether the activity is learning cardiopulmonary resuscitation or forming or joining a neighborhood crime watch, members of communities make them work for one another. Serious service activities nourish vital parts of the community, making its members true participants in its shared life and allowing them to draw significant inner satisfaction from serving one another and their common causes.

The best way to minimize the role of the state, especially its policing role, is to enhance the community and its moral voice. There are always some who violate what is right, and hence the state is unlikely to wither away, at least until very farreaching and fundamental changes occur in human nature. We must try to avoid relying on the state to maintain social order, which can be achieved more humanely and at less cost by the voluntary observance of those values we all hold dear.

THE LIMITS OF CORPORATE PURITANISM

Critics of the new morality evoke the specter of neopuritanism by pointing to corporations that use their economic power to force their employees to behave. Businesses, they say, are insisting that their employees refrain from smoking, avoid drug abuse, lose weight, exercise, and so on. Some of these measures may be prudent and hardly smack of neopuritanism. Moreover, corporations that explicitly inform persons who apply for jobs, before they are retained, that the job entails, say, drug testing, leave the choice up to the employee whether he or she wishes to join such a workplace. Economic coercion enters here only if there are no other jobs to be had, which is true only for a small proportion of the labor force.

True, according such a free choice does not automatically render ethical and proper all corporate requirements. The courts have already ruled that corporations may not impose conditions of employment that are unconstitutional. There is nothing in the U.S. Constitution to prevent companies from insisting that their employees be sober and not high on drugs. The Constitution bars unreasonable search and seizure, but drug tests for a large number of categories of employees have been ruled reasonable by the courts.

Some kinds of employee conduct have clear consequences for others, which corporations legitimately take into account. For example, smoking affects not merely the smoker but coworkers as well; drunken pilots endanger not only themselves but the lives of the airlines' passengers. Much more problematic is the question of whether corporations may ban behavior that occurs outside the workplace. As a general rule, these prohibitions are appropriate only if employees' private behavior significantly affects their on-the-job performance. For example, studies show that alcohol consumption impairs behavior for as long as 24 hours. Pilots may be expected not to drink for a given period before they come to work, even if it means placing restrictions on what they do in their free time. By the same token, private behavior that cannot be shown to affect on-the-job performance should not be corporations' business.

Finally, there remains the question of the propriety of corporations trying to control private behavior that affects only health care costs—a tab they pick up. For example, a small property development firm in Atlanta prohibits its employees from engaging in "hazardous activities and pursuits" such as skydiving, mountain climbing, and motorcycling. Best Lock Corporation of Indianapolis forbids alcohol consumption by its employees, even after work. The city of North Miami has a policy against hiring smokers. Fortunoff, a retailer, charges employees who smoke $12.50 more a week for health insurance costs. Some states have passed legislation prohibiting employer discrimination based on off-the-job smoking or other legal off-the-job activities.

Should corporations attempt to regulate this type of behavior? Probably not. In fact, this may be a good place to limit the reach of corporate morals. An important criterion for corporate intervention— protecting the life and limb of others beside the offender—is not met, and if we go farther down this road, there is no stopping. Most behavior affects health costs in some way, and if we endorse this kind of paternalism, soon we'll see corporations insisting that we go to bed early, floss and brush our teeth regularly, engage only in heterosexual intercourse with one partner, and meditate frequently to reduce stress.

In short, when private behavior directly affects job performance, corporations may step in. Otherwise, they should refrain from regulating the private affairs of their employees. This does not mean that anything goes after hours, only that the proper people to deal with private behavior are those who share in it: fellow family members, neighbors, and the community in which the behavior takes place.

THE COMMUNITARIAN FAMILY AND WHAT COMPANIES CAN DO TO SUPPORT IT

Parents have a moral responsibility to the community to invest themselves in the proper upbringing of their children, and communities to enable parents to so dedicate themselves. Throughout history, parents, especially fathers, have run off and left their children behind. But since the sixties we have witnessed a mass exodus, from the surge in single-parent households to the economic demand in two-parent homes that drives both from the home to the workplace. The younger generation cannot learn the difference between right and wrong if their parents are out pursuing their careers, whether for human fulfillment or economic necessity, and do not find the time required to educate them.

Consider for a moment parenting as an industry. As farming declined, most fathers left to work away from home. Over the past 20 years, millions of American mothers have sharply curtailed their work in the "parenting industry" by moving to work outside the home. By 1991, two-thirds of all mothers with children under 18 and more than half of women with children under the age of 3 were in the labor force. At the same time, a much smaller number of child care personnel moved into the parenting industry. If this were any other business, and more than half of the labor force had been lost and replaced with fewer, less-qualified hands, and we asked them to produce the same products of the same quality (with basically no changes in technology), we would be considered crazy. But this is what happened to parenting. The millions of latchkey children, who are left alone for long stretches of time, are but the most visible result of the parenting deficit.

Children require attention, time, energy, and above all, a commitment of self. Parenting requires physical presence. The notion of "quality time" presupposes that bonding and education can take place in brief time bursts, on the run. Quality time occurs within quantity time. With poor and ineffective community child care and ever more harried parents, if we both wish our children to grow up in a civilized society and seek to live in one, let's face facts. We must dedicate more of ourselves to our children's care and education. We need to return to a situation in which committed parenting is an honorable vocation.

Many parents argue that they both work because they cannot make ends meet otherwise. They feel that both parents have no choice but to work full-time outside the home if they are to pay for rent, food, clothing, and other basics. A 1990 Gallup poll found that half of those households with working mothers would want the mother to stay home if "money were not an issue." (The same question should have been asked about fathers.)

This sense of economic pressure certainly contains some reality. Many couples in the nineties need two paychecks to buy little more than what a couple in the early seventies could acquire with a single income. This problem will be with us at least until the American economy starts to grow faster. But at some level of income, lower than the conventional wisdom would have us believe, parents do have a choice between enhanced earnings and attending to their children. Several social scientists have shown that most of what many people consider to be essentials are actually things their cultures and communities tell them are essential, rather than what is objectively required. Although there may be conflicting notions regarding how high an income level is sufficient for people to satisfy their basic needs, there is clearly a level at which they are able to make choices.

We are not arguing that people should lead a life of denial and poverty, but that they have, and make, choices all the time, whether or not they are aware of this fact. They choose between a more rapid climb up the social ladder and spending more time with their children. In the long run, parents will find more satisfaction and will contribute more to the community if they heed their children more and their social status less. But even if they choose to order their priorities the other way around, let it not be said that they did not make a choice. Careerism is not a law of nature.

We return then to the value that we, as a community, put on bringing up children. Our society places more value on Armani suits, winter skiing, and summer houses than on education. Parents are under pressure to earn more, whatever their income. After two decades of celebrating greed and in the face of a generation of neglected children, we must recognize the importance of educating one's children.

Although the shift from consumerism and careerism to an emphasis on children is largely one of values, it has some rewarding payoffs. Corporations complain, correctly, that the young workers who present themselves on their doorsteps are undertrained. A good part of what they mean is a deficiency of character and an inability to control impulses, defer gratification, and commit to the task at hand. If businesses would cooperate with parents to make it easier for them to earn a living and attend to their children, the corporate payoffs would be more than social approbation: they would gain a labor force that is much better able to perform.

The community, too, would benefit by having members who are not merely more sensitive to one another and more caring but also more likely to contribute to the commonweal. Last but not least, parents would discover that, although there are some failures despite the best intentions and strongest dedication, by and large you reap what you sow. If people dedicate a part of their lives to their kids, they are likely to have sons and daughters who will make them proud and fill their old age with love.

The community—all of us—suffers the ill effects of absentee parenting. Gang warfare in the streets, massive drug abuse, a poorly committed workforce, and a strong sense of entitlement and weak sense of responsibility are, to a large extent, the product of poor parenting. True, economic and social factors also play a role. But a lack of effective parenting is a major cause, and other factors could be handled more readily if we remain committed to the importance of the upbringing of the young.

Given the forbearance of labor unions and employers, it is possible for millions of parents to work at home. Computers, modems, up- and downlinks, satellites, and other modern means of communication can now allow people to trade commodities worldwide without ever leaving the den, to provide answers on a medical hot line from the corner of a living room, or to process insurance claims and edit books from a desk placed anywhere in the house.

If both parents must work outside the household, it is preferable if they can arrange to work different shifts, to increase the all-important parental presence. These are not pie-in-the-sky, futuristic ideas. Several of the largest corporations already provide one or more of these family-friendly features. In 1992, DuPont had 2,000 employees working part-time and between 10,000 and 15,000 working flex-time. And corporations that now must compete for the most able workers are being rated in widely read books ranking the "best companies to work for in America," based on their family policies, flexibility, and social responsiveness.

Given increased government support and corporate flexibility, each couple must work out its own division of labor. The community's moral voice should fully approve of alternative arrangements to care for children, rather than expect that the woman be the parent who stays at home. At the same time, there should be no social stigma attached to women who prefer to make raising their children their vocation or career. We need more fathers and mothers who make these choices; stigmatizing any of them is hardly a way to encourage parenting. Reevaluating the value of children will help bring about the needed change of heart.

COMMUNITARIAN EDUCATION

If the moral infrastructure of our communities is to be restored, schools will have to step in where the family, neighborhoods, and religious institutions have been failing. Too many of our youngsters with underdeveloped characters and without a firm commitment to values are enrolled in schools. The basic reason is that the families have been dismembered or the parents are overworked or consumed by other concerns and ambitions. As a result, the children tend to be poor students. Moreover, if their lack of character and moral values are not attended to while at school, they will graduate to become deficient workers, citizens, and fellow community members.

Workers need self-control so that they can observe a work routine that is often not very satisfying in itself. Citizens and community members need self-control so that they will not demand more services and handouts but be unwilling to pay taxes and make contributions to the commons. And self-control, together with a growing sense of commitment to values, makes people more tolerant of those from different ethnic, racial, and political backgrounds. Such tolerance is a major foundation of democratic societies.

Education proceeds by tying gratification to the development of qualities that are socially useful and morally appropriate. By relating satisfaction to completing a task, taking other people's feelings into account, playing by the rules, and so on, one acquires the ability to abide by moral tenets and live up to one's social responsibilities.

To become committed to moral values, youngsters must acquire not only the capacity to commit but also the values that apply their moral capacity. To the extent that the family no longer provides these values, the community turns to schools to teach them right from wrong. Such moral education should be an integral part of all teaching.

The kind of value education our young people need is centered on the numerous values we all share as a community, such as the inappropriateness of racial and gender discrimination, the rejection of violence, and the desirability of treating others with love, respect, and dignity. If we would transmit to the young in schools only these shared values, our world would be radically improved.

Far from being necessarily controversial, values education may win wide support. The 148 public schools in Baltimore County, Maryland, teach a common core of 24 values, ranging from truth and responsibility to due process. A 1991 survey found that 98 percent of the district administrators, 85 percent of the parents, and 75 percent of the students believed that values education was a good idea.

OUTSIDE THE CLASSROOM: IS WORK EDUCATIONAL?

We must also look beyond the school itself to examine other opportunities for generating educational experiences that enhance character formation and moral education. Today's high school students spend much time outside the school and within the work environment. It would be short-sighted to ignore the educational effects of this context. Since work has become such an important part of many high school students' lives, it must be examined in this light: Is it educational?

About two-thirds of high school juniors and seniors these days have part-time paying jobs, many in fast-food chains. From lemonade stands to newspaper routes, it is a longstanding tradition that American youth hold paying jobs at which they learn the fruits of labor and trade and develop the virtue of self-discipline. Employment for teenagers in fast-food emporia seems to be nothing more than a vast extension of the lemonade stand, providing large numbers of steady jobs that test and reward their stamina.

Upon closer examination, however, this kind of work does not provide opportunities for self-discipline, self-supervision, and self-scheduling (like the old-fashioned paper route). It is highly structured and routinized. True, students must go to work, but once they don their uniforms, their tasks are spelled out in minute detail. There is little room for initiative or creativity. Fast-food franchises are breeding grounds for robots working for yesterday's assembly lines, not practice fields for committed workers in tomorrow's high-tech posts.

Today, fast-food chains and other such places of work keep costs down by having teens supervise teens, often with no adult on the premises. There is no mature adult figure for them to identify with, to emulate, or to provide a role model or mature moral guidance. Rarely is there a "master" to learn from; rarely is there much worth learning. Far from being places where solid work values are being transmitted, these are places where, all too often, teen values dominate.

It would be better for our children if corporations that employ teens would, in cooperation with schools, define what is the proper amount of gainful work, determine how late teenagers may work on school nights, and provide proper supervision. Schools might provide credit for jobs that meet specified educational criteria. Schools should be consulted by corporations on matters such as the nature of supervision and on-the-job training setups. School representatives should be allowed to inspect the students' places of employment. School counselors should guide students to places of work that are willing to pay attention to the educational elements of their jobs. Parents should encourage their children to seek jobs at places that are proper work settings and insist that teen employers shape up or find it harder to employ their kids. Parents should agree with their children, the young workers, that a significant share of earnings be dedicated to the family or saved for mutually acceptable items.

Above all, parents should look at teen employment not as automatically educational but as an activity, like sports, that may be turned into an educational opportunity or could just as easily be abused. Youngsters must start early to learn to balance the quest for income with the need to pursue endeavors that do not pay off instantly.

COMMUNITARIAN ACTION

Peter Drucker has made a strong case that in the nineties and beyond we will need to rely even more on voluntary efforts than in the past. He expects that attempts by governments to provide for numerous social needs will continue to suffer a shortage of funds and an increase in demand and what seems to be a congenital inability to provide services that match in quality those that voluntary associations regularly render.

Serious and useful community service provides a strong antidote to the ego-centered mentality, as people learn about and serve shared needs. Community service is an important community-builder because it acts as a grand sociological mixer. At present, America provides few opportunities for shared experience and for developing shared values and bonds among people from different racial, class, and regional backgrounds. Community service, if designed to enable people from different geographical and sociological backgrounds to work together, is an effective way for people to come together while working constructively at a shared task.

By encouraging and developing the virtues of hard work, responsibility, and cooperation, to name a few, community service would help the nation in its efforts to restore a climate of basic civility and improve economic productivity. Those involved benefit themselves and the community.

Each community, whether residential, work-related, monoethnic, or integrated, needs to work out its own agenda, depending on local circumstances and needs. However, some guidelines are clear. Communities need more people who dedicate more of their time and energy and resources—

more of themselves—to the commons. Young people and those who change jobs or retrain will do best if they seek to combine their career with pursuits that are supportive of the community.

REBUILDING COMMUNITY INSTITUTIONS

Just as American society since the fifties has been cannibalizing families and is now saddled with the dire moral and social consequences of their diminished capacity, so society has cannibalized communities, with similar antisocial consequences. The two often go hand in hand. As both parents commute to work in the big city, leaving the children without the educational presence of an adult, they abandon the streets, public spaces, and neighborhoods as well. Local governments must now hire police to patrol largely empty suburbs during the day, and there are fewer hands than before to serve the community. More and more people have been gobbled up by the economy, which is taxed to pay for hired hands to accomplish what people used to do as volunteers.

A return to family, which we argue is needed in its own right, will also help us shore up communitarian institutions. Thus, if more people work at home, there will be more hands for crime watches during the day. If people value children more, they will be more likely to find the time and energy to create (and pay for) public parks and help ensure their safety. If neighbors are more available to help one another, the pressure on public institutions will be alleviated. Community shoring up is of such import that we should draw on all available sources and let them strengthen one another as they combine to restore community.

The notion that the communitarian action par excellence is political participation is age-old. The implication is that the best community action is one long, nonstop town hall meeting. Although few members of most communities find public life that compelling, an important way to build community is to ensure that there are numerous occasions for active participation in its governance. This is achieved not only, or even primarily, by voting every few years to determine who will sit on the town's council. Participating in the governance of one of the town's schools, hospitals, and libraries is also participation in public life.

These activities have in common what has become fashionable to call "empowerment," that is, enabling people to participate openly and directly in making the decisions that govern their lives. Our ultimate purpose is to provide an opportunity for deep human satisfaction, the kind found only when we are engaged with one another, and to strengthen the community as a moral infrastructure.

PERSONAL RESPONSIBILITY, SELF-HELP, AND SOCIAL JUSTICE

A communitarian position on social justice for all groups includes the following elements. First, people have a moral responsibility to help themselves as best they can. The second line of responsibility lies with those closest to the person, including kin, friends, neighbors, and other community members. Every community ought to be expected to do the best it can to take care of its own. Charity—and more broadly, social responsibility—ought to begin but not end at home.

Each community must be expected to reach out to members of other communities that are less well endowed and hence less able to deal with their own problems. The ways are almost endless, from sending food, blankets, and volunteers when a neighboring community is overwhelmed, to housing refugees from a hurricane or earthquake, to sharing equipment such as snow plows. Societies (which are nothing but communities of communities) must help those communities whose ability to help their members is severely limited. Social justice is an intercommunity issue, not just an intracommunity matter. We start with responsibility to ourselves and to our community; we expand the reach of our moral claims and duties from there.

CONCLUSION

In the fifties we had a well-established society, but it was unfair to women and minorities and a bit authoritarian. In the sixties we undermined the established society and its values. In the eighties we were told that the unbridled pursuit of self-interest was virtuous. By the nineties we have seen the cumulative results. There is now near-universal agreement that the resulting world of street violence, the failing war against illegal drugs, unbridled greed, and so on—our well-worn list of ills—is not one we wish for our children or, for that matter, ourselves. Where do we turn from here?

Communitarianism is a social movement aimed at shoring up the moral, social, and political environment: part change of heart, part renewal of social bonds, part reform of public life. Change of heart is the most basic. Without stronger moral voices, public authorities are overburdened and markets don't work. Without moral commitments, people act without any consideration for one another. It is a mistaken notion that just because we desire to be free from governmental controls, we should also be free from responsibilities to the commons or indifferent to the community. More good people and leaders must join together to further develop these messages and form the basis of the social movement without which no basic change of direction is possible.

To shore up the foundations of society, we start with the family. Second in line are the schools. Third are the social webs that communities provide, in neighborhoods, at work, and in clubs and associations. These communities bind individuals, who would otherwise be on their own, into groups of people who care for one another and who help maintain a civic, social, and moral order. As our moral order is shored up, we need to concern ourselves with the civic order. Individuals' rights are to be matched with social responsibilities.

No community can long survive unless its members dedicate some of their attention, energy, and resources to shared projects. The exclusive pursuit of private interest erodes the social network on which we all depend and is destructive to our shared experiment in democratic self-government. The rights of individuals cannot long be preserved without a perspective that recognizes both individual human dignity and the social dimensions of human existence.

The preservation of individual liberty depends on the active maintenance of the institutions of civil society where citizens learn respect for others as well as self-respect, where we acquire a sense of our personal and civic responsibilities (our rights and those of others), where we develop the skills and habits of self-government, and where we learn to serve others. A responsive community is one whose standards reflect the basic needs of all its members.

The best place to start is where each new generation acquires its moral anchoring: at home, in the family. Fathers and mothers consumed by "making it" and consumerism, who are preoccupied with personal advancement, who come home too late and too tired to attend to the needs of their children, cannot discharge their most elementary duty to their children and their fellow citizens. It follows that workplaces should provide maximum flexible opportunities to parents to preserve an important part of their lives to attend to their educational and moral duties for the sake of the next generation, its civic and moral character, and its capacity to contribute economically and socially to the commonweal. Work-family experiments—with parental leave, flex-time, shared jobs, opportunities to work at home and for parents to participate as managers and volunteers in day care centers—should be extended and encouraged.

Above all, we need a change in orientation by both parents and workplaces. Child raising is important, valuable work—work that must be honored rather than denigrated by both parents and the community.

Unfortunately, millions of American families have weakened to the point where their capacity to provide moral education is impaired. By default, schools now play a major role, for better or worse, in character formation and moral education. Personal and communal responsibility come together here, for education requires the commitment of all citizens, not merely those who have children in school. We strongly urge that all educational institutions, from kindergartens to universities, recognize and take seriously the grave responsibility to provide moral education.

Education must be reorganized to achieve a better integration between work and schooling. Educators need to search for ways to connect schooling with activities that make sense to young people. Businesses that employ high school students part-time ought to recognize that they are educators, too. Early work experiences will either reinforce responsible habits and attitudes or will serve as lessons in poor civics and deficient work ethics.

The exclusive pursuit of one's self-interest is not a good prescription for conduct in the marketplace; for no social, political, economic, or moral order can survive that way. Some measure of caring, sharing, and being our brother's and sister's keeper is essential if we are not to fall back on an ever more expansive government and its bureaucratized welfare agencies.

No social task should be assigned to an institution that is larger than necessary to do the job. Government should step in only when other social systems fail, rather than replacing them. Vulnerable communities should be able to draw on the more endowed communities when they are truly unable to deal, on their own, with social duties thrust upon them. Moreover, many social goals require partnership between public and private groups. There is a great need for study and experimentation with creative use of the structures of civil society and public-private cooperation, especially where the delivery of health, educational, and social services are concerned.

Community service and volunteer work is desirable to build and express a civil commitment. Activities that bring together people from different backgrounds and enable and encourage them to work together build community and foster mutual respect and tolerance. Each member of the community owes something to all the rest, and the community owes something to each of its members. Justice requires responsible individuals in a responsive community.

Members of the community have a responsibility, to the greatest extent possible, to provide for themselves and their families. Honorable work contributes to the commonweal and to the community's ability to fulfill its essential tasks. Beyond self-support, individuals have a responsibility for the material and moral well-being of others. This does not mean heroic self-sacrifice; it means the constant awareness that no one of us is an island unaffected by the fate of others.

The multiplication of strongly democratic communities around the world is our best hope for the emergence of a global community that can deal concertedly with matters of general concern to the species as a whole: with war and strife, with violations of basic rights, with environmental degradation, and with the extreme moral deprivation that stunts the bodies, minds, and spirits of our children. Our concern may begin with ourselves and our families, but it rises inexorably to the long-imagined community of humankind.

REFERENCES

Etzioni, A. *The Spirit of Community*. New York: Crown, 1993.

Patterson, J., and Kim, P. *The Day America Told the Truth*. New York: Prentice-Hall, 1991.

3

A THREE SECTOR MODEL OF COMMUNITY SERVICE

*The Alliance of Business, Government, and
Nonprofit Organizations*

Mary Tschirhart

NO ONE ORGANIZATION CAN HOPE to solve the complex, pressing social problems of our time. Often community ills can be alleviated only through the cooperative involvement of business, government, and nonprofit organizations. Traditionally, it has been nonprofit and government agencies that have turned to business for support of community service projects. But today many corporations are seeking help from nonprofit and government agencies for their own service initiatives. The executives of these corporations are no longer content to take an indirect and relatively passive role in addressing community issues. They see benefits from doing more than responding to requests for donations. These executives, often encouraged and assisted by government and nonprofit agencies but sometimes acting alone, are asking their organizations to identify and proactively respond to community needs.

This chapter explores options for developing and delivering corporate philanthropy and citizenship programs by looking at the variety of relationships that corporations might form with nonprofits and government. By examining how corporations perform their philanthropic and citizenship work, the leverage of strengths and compensation of weaknesses by joint efforts among organizations in the business, nonprofit, and public sectors becomes apparent.

SHIFTING ATTITUDES TOWARD CORPORATE INVOLVEMENT IN IMPROVING COMMUNITIES

Businesses have long acknowledged some responsibility for the welfare of the communities in which they operate. Formalized corporate philanthropy in the United States can be traced to the turn of the century (Useem, 1987). The appropriate extent of corporate social responsibility and the best methods for achieving it have been debated for decades. We have moved from a society that once said any use of corporate funds for philanthropic purposes was illegal, to one where corporations are expected to be engaged in philanthropic activities (Sharfman, 1994). Many corporate annual reports now proudly report corporate community assistance projects.

A recent *Business Week*/Harris Poll found that 95 percent of Americans believe that corporations "should sometimes sacrifice some profit for the sake of making things better for their workers and community" ("America, Land of the Shaken," 1996, pp. 64–65). Building on this sentiment, U.S. President Bill Clinton invited corporate leaders to Washington in May of 1996 for a conference on corporate citizenship. As an outcome of the conference, private businesses funded a new award program to honor good corporate citizens, similar in design to the Malcolm Baldrige Award honoring innovative companies. To support this and other initiatives, the federal government established web pages devoted to corporate citizenship (http://ttrcnew.ttrc.doleta.gov/citizen/).

Further emphasizing his interest in community involvement, President Clinton, along with his predecessors George Bush, Ronald Reagan, Jimmy Carter, and Gerald Ford, put aside their political differences to convene a summit on volunteerism in Philadelphia in the spring of 1997. "Citizen service belongs to no party, no ideology. It's an American idea which every American should embrace," said Clinton. Added Bush: "When it comes to addressing many of the problems facing our nation, it isn't a question of partisan politics, one side against another. It's a question of all pulling together for the common good."

The summit is sure to intensify corporate action because it sought to encourage community activism among American corporations and individuals. Sponsors included AmeriCorps (Purdum, 1997), Points of Light Foundation, and corporations pledging to increase their efforts at volunteerism. Among those pledging action were Lens Crafters, which provided needy people—primarily children—with free vision care; Kimberly-Clark, which committed $2 million and the efforts of its employee volunteers to build community playgrounds in 30 cities; AT&T, which committed $150 million to connect 110,000 U.S. public and private elementary and secondary schools to the Internet; Columbia-HCA Healthcare, which will immunize 1 million children by 2000; and KPMG Peat Marwick, which pledged 160,000 hours and $20 million to paint classrooms, coordinate playgrounds, and tutor children in 1,000 U.S. communities (Carlson, 1997, pp. 28–29).

The shift in acceptance of greater corporate responsibility for the welfare of communities is not confined to the United States. Corporations in the United Kingdom and Germany, for example, are moving away from an emphasis on charitable donations to aid communities to more proactive approaches (Pinkston and Carroll, 1996). With the growth of multinational corporations, there is greater awareness of needs for assistance in the overseas communities where the corporations are operating. In undeveloped or developing countries, the complexities of working with relatively poor, unstable, or corrupt governments and weak service infrastructures have led some corporations to manage community service projects rather than send aid to government officials and hope it is used for desired projects. Merck & Co., Inc.'s experience with distributing medicine (see Chapter Seven) illustrates the challenges of corporate philanthropy in developing countries.

VEHICLES FOR CORPORATE ASSISTANCE TO COMMUNITIES

Corporate responses to community needs take a variety of forms. The most frequently used vehicle—corporate gift programs—keeps corporations at a distance from the communities and individuals being helped. The public and nonprofit agencies that apply for and receive gifts determine how the contributions are used. Other popular vehicles link corporations with nonprofit and government service providers to generate additional resources for service projects. Less commonly, a corporation forms a partnership with a nonprofit organization to offer new or advanced service projects. At the far extreme we find corporations that design and deliver their own community service initiatives. The next sections describe these approaches. Most of the examples are described in greater detail by Steckel and Simons (1992) or in later chapters of this book.

Transfer of Corporate Resources to Existing Service Provider

Most corporations, either directly or through a corporate foundation, contribute to nonprofit organizations and may be eligible to receive tax deductions in exchange. Corporate contributions rarely exceed more than 1 percent of pretax income for large firms, although deductibility limits are higher (Useem, 1987). Corporations provide approximately 5 percent of the charitable gifts received by nonprofits. This amounted to over $6 billion to U.S. charities in 1991 (Oster, 1995). Gifts may be for the general operating support of a nonprofit or a specific project and may take the form of financial contributions or donations of products or services. For example, IBM, Digital Equipment Corporation, Apple Computer, and Hewlett-Packard Company have all provided computers to schools and universities. In 1995, an estimated 80 percent of Apple Computer's donations were in the form of computer equipment (Gray and Moore, 1996).

Corporations vary in their interest in publicizing their giving activities. J.P. Morgan and Sara Lee Corporation, for example, have a policy of not seeking public attention for their philanthropic and citizenship activities (see Chapters Six and Ten). Other corporations are quite creative in seeking publicity. For example, Nike gained media attention by donating $1,000 to the Boys Club of America for inner-city youth programs for every point scored by Michael Jordan during the 1989 NBA All-Star game. Corporate gifts may be used to indirectly reach consumer targets, adding a marketing component to gift-giving decisions. Gifts to nonprofits may be allocated as part of corporate marketing or public relations budgets, not just community relations or philanthropic gift budgets. Sponsorship of nonprofit events can help corporations reach desired market segments. Corporate sponsorships are estimated to be a $2.9 billion-a-year industry (Steckel and Simons, 1992).

Gifts in Kind International helps businesses distribute their products to charities. It is one of the growing number of nonprofit organizations that matches needy charities with companies wishing to donate their manufactured products. Clients of Gifts in Kind International include IBM, Disney, Avon Products, Inc. and 75,000 charities providing housing, health care, emergency relief, education, and other services. Corporations participating in in-kind gift programs may gain tax deductions of up to twice the product's cost (Edelman, 1997).

Contract with Existing Service Provider Linking Donation to Sales

Corporations may promote sales of their products and services and, at the same time, help community nonprofits by associating the purchase with a social cause or nonprofit organization. Cause-related marketing was first seen in 1983, when American Express advertised that it would give a percentage of sales to the Statue of Liberty and Ellis Island Restoration Fund. Since then many corporations have tied sales to donations. Variations on this theme include linking donations to redemptions of coupons and proof of purchase seals.

Some cause-related marketing efforts tie corporate donations to sales of products that reflect a nonprofit organization's mission or are produced by the nonprofit. For example, Global Telecom prepared a recorded message from Pope John Paul II. The corporation sent the Vatican approximately one-third of what dialers paid to hear the spiritual message. The World Wildlife Fund distributed toys through Georgia-Pacific, with the corporation providing a donation for each toy sold.

Corporate Encouragement of Employee Donations to Existing Service Providers

Corporations may help nonprofit organizations and ultimately their communities by encouraging their employees to donate time and money to nonprofits. For example, employees may be encouraged to give financial contributions through workplace giving campaigns. While the United Way or other federated funding agents control the campaigns, corporation executives usually designate employees to assist with the campaigns, set contribution goals, and use presentations and letters to encourage employees to give.

Employees also may be encouraged to give through matching gift programs. At J.P. Morgan, if an employee financially supports a nonprofit, the bank will add its own contribution to the nonprofit (see Chapter Six). Some corporations also provide financial support to nonprofits that use employees as volunteers. For example, employees of Apple Computer who volunteer at a nonprofit for at least six months can request that Apple provide a $500 grant to the nonprofit.

Volunteering may be supported by allowing employees to use company time for their volunteer efforts. AT&T recently announced that it will give all its employees a paid day off to do volunteer work. The estimated $20 million cost of the program is justified as a way to raise employee morale, improve AT&T's image, and result in higher profits (Associated Press,

1996). Although AT&T is in the minority in allowing employees at all levels to be paid for volunteer time, many corporations expect and encourage upper-level executives to serve on nonprofit governing and advisory boards. Use of company time and resources to support this board work is expected. Some corporations even loan their executives to nonprofits. IBM employees can volunteer full-time at a qualifying nonprofit and maintain their pay and benefits for up to a year.

Some organizations have created a corporate culture that values employees' community outreach and service. Apple Computer announces local volunteer opportunities on its web page. The opportunities are found by a part-time employee of a nonprofit organization whose salary is covered by the computer company (Gray and Moore, 1996). Sara Lee demands high community involvement from its employees, listing the corporation's duty to society alongside obligations to stockholders, employees, and customers. Sara Lee even has a "volunteerism consultant" to help link new employees with nonprofit organizations (see Chapter Ten). Target Stores emphasizes volunteer teamwork, encouraging groups of employees to identify and get involved in community projects. By helping employees volunteer together outside the workplace, Target hopes to encourage a sense of community among employees.

Partnership with Existing Service Provider to Deliver Core Business Activity

Corporations have formed partnerships with nonprofit organizations to produce and deliver products. For example, Ben & Jerry's worked with HARKhomes, a homeless shelter in Harlem, to form a new business that would provide profits to the business's stockholders and employment opportunities and job training to needy Harlem residents (see Chapter Six). Vendor relationships with nonprofits may lead to customized, high-quality, credible products that carry the nonprofits' name and garner good will. For example, The Denver Children's Museum produced a booklet about pets for StarKist/9-Lives. The booklet increased awareness of the museum among pet owners, and payment for the booklet provided resources to the museum to use for its own programs.

Many of us know about the California Raisins and the Sesame Street characters. They were created by nonprofit organizations that licensed their use on commercial products. Nonprofit organizations can use corporations' manufacturing and distribution expertise and capacities to capitalize on nonprofit names, logos, and properties. These partnerships do not take corporations outside their core business activities; rather, they allow nonprofits to engage in profit-making activities without large investment costs.

Corporate Investment in Community-Based Projects

Corporations can assist communities by investing in community-based projects. This investment may take the form of purchase of stock in business ventures tied to nonprofit organizations. For example, J.P. Morgan invested in the HARKhomes partnership with Ben & Jerry's (see Chapter Six). Financial institutions may provide loans and other financial services at below-market rates and underwrite tax-exempt bonds. Unable to make loans itself, Upjohn recruited a nonprofit development corporation to its Kalamazoo, Michigan, location to make mortgage loans to city residents. The company financially supported the nonprofit's development efforts (Post, Frederick, Lawrence, and Weber, 1996).

Community development projects may require more than just financial backing. Corporations may be asked to provide expertise and strategic planning for new business ventures. For example, in 1990 the Cleveland Foundation successfully brought local corporate leaders together to study the city's poor neighborhoods and devise economic revitalization projects (Post and others, 1996).

Partnership with Existing Service Provider to Deliver Activity Outside Business Core

Corporations sometimes join existing providers in the design and delivery of community services. Corporate relationships with nonprofits to deliver services may take advantage of the corporation's expertise or contacts. J.P. Morgan was heavily involved in the implementation of the Professional Development Program in New York schools (see Chapter Six). In addition to providing funding for the project, Morgan's human resource department designed the procedure to select program participants and developed an outcome-based assessment system for teachers. Other departments were also directly involved in the provision of the program. Ameritech has used its technological resources in a variety of ways to help Focus: HOPE, a nonprofit organization in Detroit (described more fully in Chapter Seventeen) that has become a model for addressing poverty, racism, and injustice. But Ameritech employees (see Chapter Nine) also find value in helping paint apartments, deliver food, and carry out other projects in which they have no special competence.

Partnership programs may be short-term or one-time-only events. One innovative program, sponsored by Procter & Gamble (see Chapter

Eleven) but collaboratively developed and implemented by grocers and a nonprofit organization—Keep America Beautiful—involved a variety of educational programs about the environment. Events included a "Run for Recycling" in which shoppers had two minutes to fill their grocery carts with products in recyclable containers. Keep America Beautiful also worked with Kmart to develop a children's recycling kit that Kmart volunteers could take to schools as part of an environmental education program. Kmart did not have the expertise to develop the kit, and Keep America Beautiful did not have the community volunteers. By working together they were able to complement each other's strengths.

Corporate Establishment of a Nonprofit Service Provider to Implement Corporate Service Initiatives

Corporations may find advantages in carrying out their community service initiatives through a nonprofit firm. Within the nonprofit designation used by the Internal Revenue Service there are distinct categories. Depending on its category, a nonprofit may be eligible for tax exemptions, postal subsidies, tax deductibility of contributions by donors, freedom from lobbying restrictions, and other benefits. To deliver service activities, corporations have established nonprofit organizations in the form of foundations, direct service providers, and mutual benefit associations.

Sara Lee, American Express, General Electric, and Ameritech are among the many corporations that have established nonprofit foundations to carry out their philanthropic giving programs. In 1989, there were 1,587 corporate grant-making foundations in the United States with combined assets of $5.7 billion (Renz, 1991). The foundations operate under different rules than the corporations and are usually able to leverage corporate dollars and maintain consistent flows of contributions despite changes in corporate profit levels. The foundations' grant-making work reflects the values and service interests identified by their funding corporations.

In addition to foundations, the IRS also recognizes nonprofit social and recreational clubs as deserving special benefits. The nonprofit Elfun Society is one such social club composed of select General Electric employees who chiefly focus on volunteerism (see Chapter Eight). Originally the club was composed of senior managers but has expanded its membership roll to include 36,000 members in nine countries. The club performs service activities around the globe using corporate resources.

Corporations may choose to set up nonprofit organizations to serve as their direct service providers. For example, American Express established the National Academy Foundation to "advance student achievement and citizenship" (see Chapter Five). Southern Development Bancorporation spun off a nonprofit organization, The Arkansas Enterprise Group, to offer loan and equity investments, seed capital, small-business training, and short-term loans to rural areas with high poverty rates (Oster, 1995).

Corporate Service Initiative Within the Corporate Structure

Not all the direct service work of corporations falls under the auspices of a nonprofit organization or takes advantage of government support mechanisms. Many corporations reach out to their communities without formal or direct assistance from nonprofit or government agencies. For example, Sara Lee has an employee volunteerism committee to coordinate projects such as their Share Holiday program (see Chapter Ten). For Share Holiday, Sara Lee employees bring Christmas gifts to local children. The project is coordinated and presented as a corporate event.

Some might say that service initiatives that rely on only corporate resources are the purest demonstration of corporate citizenship behaviors. They exemplify the notion that corporations should actively work to forward the welfare of their communities, without the motivator of greater profits. Corporate service initiatives within the corporate structure may be the most path-breaking of the initiatives presented in this book. They present a new role for business as a community service provider.

Yet, no program operates in isolation from environmental influences, and no one program can hope to solve a complex social problem. It is best to view internal service programs as one option among many to help communities. They are one piece of a larger service network consisting of other businesses, nonprofit, and government organizations. For corporate employees and executives who wish to experience a project hands-on, these projects offer the greatest control and opportunity. They also demand greater understanding of community needs and accountability by the corporation. Without other partners whose sole purpose is to identify and improve the public good, a larger burden falls on the corporation to justify its work.

GOVERNMENT AND NONPROFIT ENCOURAGEMENT OF PHILANTHROPIC AND CITIZENSHIP ACTIVITY

That many corporations are finding ways to enhance the quality of their communities is clear. That this is in the company's interest is widely touted (Sharfman, 1994; Useem, 1987; Steckel and Simons, 1992). What motivates these philanthropic and citizenship efforts is less well known. Many factors, in addition to corporate self-interest, have been proposed as determinants of corporate involvement in community work. Government and nonprofit pressures and incentives are commonly listed as determinants.

Government policies and regulations play a role in setting expectations and encouraging practices that protect and promote the welfare of employees and communities. For example, The Community Reinvestments Act was the impetus for many of J.P. Morgan's community-based investments (see Chapter Six), and tax policies have been linked to corporate giving decisions. Corporations operating in the U.S. and abroad are subject to legal restrictions and political pressures, which influence their community involvement.

Government giving can affect corporate contributions. When governments provide nonprofits with grants that must be matched with private funds, nonprofits often turn to businesses for contributions. With declines in government support, nonprofits more aggressively seek funding from corporations and look to them for opportunities to make profits from activities unrelated to their missions.

Rhetoric and symbolic actions also can encourage corporate service initiatives. The Ron Brown Corporate Citizenship Award, developed by businesses with the persuasion of President Clinton, serves to remind corporations of their responsibility to their communities. Conferences, task forces, and commissions place attention on aspects of corporate citizenship. For example, the UN-sponsored Conference on Environment and Development, also known as the Earth Summit, publicly wrestled with the role of business in fostering economic growth without damaging the environment for future generations. At the state and local government levels, we see community leadership training and award programs. These activities offer role models, establish network ties leading to joint projects, support information sharing, and otherwise encourage desired community service by corporations.

Government is not the only actor that shapes opinions in favor of corporate service activities. Nonprofit organizations coordinate protests and boycotts and use other negative pressure tactics to convince corporations to respond to perceived community needs. Nonprofits may also approach business with a lighter hand, extending opportunities for collaborative projects that address mutual interests. By virtue of their presence and involvement in the corporation's community, nonprofits may be a ready source of information on community issues and serve as opinion leaders. They are often the first to identify a social problem and demand attention to it. Like government, they offer awards to good corporate citizens, convene conferences and task forces, and provide assistance to corporations engaged in community work.

WHY CORPORATE COMMUNITY SERVICE?

To varying degrees, the nonprofit and government sectors have embraced all the options outlined earlier that transfer corporate resources to service providers. Service providers are likely to try to maintain their integrity and image by not getting involved in projects that will reduce the public's trust. They may reject corporate support if there is a perceived conflict of interest between their service missions and the potential corporate donor (Lombardo, 1991). Ventures are unattractive if they take the provider too far afield from their mission or raise criticisms that the provider has become too commercial. For example, the National Archives experienced the danger of a corporate affiliation when it received negative publicity for allowing Philip Morris to celebrate the signing of the Bill of Rights in a sponsored ad. Acknowledging the dangers to nonprofits of mission drift, Ameritech makes a conscious effort not to overburden its nonprofit partners with administrative work and expenses. Ameritech believes that the nonprofits' most important obligation is to their clients (see Chapter Nine).

Corporations may have concerns about working closely with service providers. Some corporations have faced accusations that they took advantage of a nonprofit or a social problem to sell a product. For example, Burger King was criticized for using a disaster to advertise a product when it announced after the San Francisco earthquake that it would give a quarter for each sale of its new BK burger to the Red Cross for earthquake victims. U.S. Sprint used a television ad to address the cynicism that corporations may face when they promote their philanthropic activities. As part of their cause-related marketing campaign, one ad presented Candice Bergen saying, "Is Sprint doing this to get your business? What difference does it make? We're doing it."

Not all the approaches to community service outlined in this chapter involve corporate citizenship. Citizenship, as exemplified by the cases in this book, requires leadership of projects to improve community welfare that do not have direct profit-making purposes. It is not enough to distribute philanthropic contributions to nonprofits addressing community needs, encourage employees to donate time and money to these nonprofits, or even form partnerships with nonprofits for business ventures. Corporate citizenship involves the proactive devotion of financial and human resources to finding and implementing projects for the purpose of helping communities.

Corporate citizenship activities may be less likely to draw cynical responses than other activities that simply pass corporate resources to service providers. They also have the advantage of allowing employees to do the "real" service work in their community and experience any results. Employees who directly see how their work is improving communities are more likely to feel good about their organization and have a "stakeholder orientation" (see Chapter Four) than ones who only read about corporate contributions to good causes in company newsletters or annual reports. Also, corporations that design and implement their own citizenship activities are less dependent on other service providers' willingness to work with them.

CONCLUSION

Corporate global citizenship is more than just a new buzzphrase. It reflects awareness of the responsibility that corporations have as members, that is citizens, of their communities. It also helps us distinguish among the range of options for service activities that may or may not directly involve government and nonprofit partners. We have uncovered a rich pattern of connections in examining how businesses may work both independently and jointly with nonprofit and government organizations. Corporations have become integral parts of community service networks. Their place in those networks is no longer confined to funding roles. As corporations begin to fully accept their citizenship responsibilities, we are likely to see them engaged in more direct service activities, alone and in partnership with nonprofit and government agencies.

REFERENCES

"America, Land of the Shaken." *BusinessWeek,* Mar. 11, 1996.

Associated Press. "AT&T Invests in Volunteerism." *The Herald Times,* Nov. 16, 1996.

Carlson, M. "The General's Next Campaign." *Time,* Mar. 17, 1997.

Edelman, K. A. "Manager's Tool Kit." *Across the Board.* New York: The Conference Board Inc., 1997.

Gray, S., and Moore, J. "Big Gifts from Big Business." *Chronicle of Philanthropy,* July 11, 1996.

Lombardo, B., "Conflicts of Interest Between Nonprofits and Corporate Donors." In D. F. Burlingame and L. J. Hulse (eds.), *Taking Fund Raising Seriously.* San Francisco: Jossey-Bass, 1991.

Oster, S. M., *Strategic Management for Nonprofit Organizations.* New York: Oxford University Press, 1995.

Pinkston, T. S., and Carroll, A. B. "A Retrospective Examination of CSR Orientations: Have they Changed?" *Journal of Business Ethics,* 15, 1996.

Post, J. E., Frederick, W. C., Lawrence, A. T., and Weber, J. *Business and Society: Corporate Strategy, Public Policy, and Ethics.* (8th ed.) McGraw-Hill, 1996.

Purdum, T. S. "Clinton, Bush and Powell to Share Ideas About Volunteerism." *The New York Times,* Jan. 25, 1997.

Renz, L. *Foundation Giving: Yearbook of Facts and Figures on Private, Corporate, and Community Foundations.* New York: The Foundation Center, 1991.

Sharfman, M. "Changing Institutional Rules: The Evolution of Corporate Philanthropy, 1883–1953." *Business & Society,* 33 (3), 1994.

Steckel, R., and Simons, R. *Doing Best by Doing Good.* New York: Penguin Group, 1992.

Useem, M. "Corporate Philanthropy." In W. W. Powell (ed.), *The Nonprofit Sector: A Research Handbook.* New Haven: Yale University Press, 1987.

4

INSTITUTIONALIZING COMMUNITY ACTION IN CORPORATE AMERICA

A Road Map to Corporate Global Citizenship

Charles Kadushin and Lynda St. Clair

THIS CHAPTER ADDRESSES HOW corporate global citizenship activities can become institutionalized in organizations. We begin with a brief discussion of the concept of institutionalization. We then focus on different aspects of the process of institutionalization, that is, on how these types of activities come to be seen as part and parcel of corporate practice rather than as optional activities.

INTRODUCTION

Most major corporations in the United States engage in some corporate philanthropy; in addition, many have community action programs that call for personal involvement beyond check writing. Nonetheless, corporate responsibility for community and global citizenship is generally poorly instituted. That is, organized community action programs that require the organized time, energy, and commitment of corporate employees are not part of the regular day-to-day corporate activities in the same manner as activities that are seen as directly related to profits and productivity. Community action programs are a luxury, a happenstance, or an add-on in most settings—a nice thing, perhaps, but not an essential part of corporate life.

It is not surprising that for-profit corporations are, in fact, focused on making profits. What is surprising, however, is the lack of recognition of how dependent for-profit corporations are on the communities in which they operate. At a minimum, far too few corporations have engaged in the type of sustained efforts that would be consistent with a strategic view that took into account the vitality of the communities in which they operate.

The simplest means for convincing organizations that corporate global citizenship (CGC) activities should become a part of their everyday practices is to demonstrate their economic benefit. If CGC is economically profitable, then there is no reason for corporations not to engage in it. The problem lies, however, in demonstrating that economic benefit. Although, as discussed in Chapter One, companies often use economic rationales to justify their participation in CGC activities, empirical research to date has been inconclusive (see, for example, Arlow and Wogan, 1996; Ullmann, 1985). Even so, difficulties in accurately measuring the costs and benefits of CGC make it unlikely that these types of activities will ever be free from criticism by free market advocates such as Milton Friedman and the Chicago school of economists. Yet there is evidence (detailed in the Introduction section of this book) of at least a linkage between firms active in corporate global citizenship and superior financial performance versus their competitors.

Organizations, however, engage in much behavior that is not easily justifiable using purely economic arguments. Seventy-five years of organizational study and analysis have shown that much behavior in for-profit, nonprofit, or governmental organizations occurs because it is institutionalized or even ceremonial. That is, behaviors are enacted because conventional wisdom ordains the behavior. In turn, this wisdom is based on the fact that some other respected organization has successfully incorporated the behavior, or because the behavior is seen to help the organization fit into its environment. This is not to say that institutionalized practices are impractical. Most serve some directly visible, useful goal, which the organization believes helps it achieve its ends. As Powell and DiMaggio (1991) point out in their introduction to their book, *The New Institutionalism in Organizational Analysis*:

> The key thrust of institutional analysis is neither to expose the inefficiency of organizational practices nor to celebrate the non-optimality of institutional arrangements. . . . We rarely expect institutions to reflect current political and economic forces. The point is . . . to develop robust explanations of the ways in which institutions incorporate historical experiences into their rules and organizing logics [p. 33].

If CGC activities are not currently institutionalized in the majority of corporations, it is not because they are impractical or irrelevant. Rather, it is because they have not become incorporated into the rules and organizing logic of for-profit corporations. This chapter uses the insights of the "new institutionalism" to explore how organized, hands-on CGC activities can—and do—become part and parcel of corporate logic.

THREE REQUIREMENTS FOR INSTITUTIONALIZATION OF ACTIVITIES

There are three requirements for any activity to become part of the corporate organizational logic. First, corporations must believe that community hands-on programs are not only a morally good thing to do (are ethical and socially responsible) but that they in fact contribute to the internal welfare of the organization (are economically beneficial). In addition, corporations must feel that "everybody is doing it," that is, that admired and structurally similar corporations are engaged in the activity. Finally, the organization must develop a vocabulary and a set of common understandings about the activity. That is, they must socially construct a reality that includes corporate global citizenship as we define it.

These requirements can be accomplished to a large extent through corporate networks, through which information about corporate citizenship activities is diffused and interpreted. This process can be intentionally strategic, as when an organization sets out to create a norm for providing some type of community service such as release time for volunteers. Or it can evolve unconsciously, as organizational representatives meet and exchange stories about what they are doing and how it is working. Because the first of these three requirements was elaborated in detail in Chapter One, this chapter focuses primarily on the latter two requirements.

EVERYBODY'S DOING IT: LOOKING FOR EVIDENCE OF INSTITUTIONALIZATION

In this section we discuss the types of evidence that can be used to evaluate the degree to which corporate global citizenship has been institutionalized by an organization. This is, not incidentally, the same evidence that organizations seek to help them determine whether everybody is, in fact, doing it.

Institutionalization results in consistency in behavior across firms. Thus, to gain an understanding of whether or not corporate global citizenship activities have become institutionalized, it is necessary to determine detailed descriptions of the types of activities that competitor organizations are engaged in and how those activities are being carried out. That, in fact, was one of the underlying objectives that led to the preparation of this book. To develop the cases presented in Part Two, it was first necessary to collect detailed information about many corporations, including the selected companies. To provide some sense of how this research was accomplished, Exhibit 4.1 shows the contents of an initial document used to begin to collect data for these case studies.

FROM ACADEMIC STUDIES TO CORPORATE STANDARDS

The primary intent of such research on CGC activities is to monitor and measure those activities and/or to assess the degree to which those activities have become institutionalized. Such research, however, may also lead to the legitimation and further institutionalization of these types of practices. The questions that researchers ask and the questions that they fail to ask all become part and parcel of the gestalt of CGC. Although the impact of an academic survey on corporate global citizenship activities may not have the immediate impact of *Fortune*'s annual honoring of companies (see the discussion following), it serves a similar function by conveying the message that these types of activities are important. It also tends to imply that companies are engaged in these types of activities. This conveys the impression that everybody's doing it. The specific questions asked may also send signals about the types of activities in which organizations are currently engaging.

FROM CLASSROOM TO BOARDROOM

Another way that academe helps to institutionalize CGC is by influencing the attitudes of future generations of organizational leaders. For example, emphasizing the value of CGC in the classroom legitimizes those kinds of activities. How an academic institution goes about espousing its values related to CGC is also important. Classroom rhetoric is unlikely to have the same impact as actually getting students engaged in CGC activities. Thus, for example, the University of Michigan Business School includes corporate citizenship as part of its MBA program. The school has also created the MBA Domestic Corps program. This program, begun in 1992, provides summer internships for students to work with nonprofit

Exhibit 4.1.   Corporate Citizenship Cases: Information Requirements.

The context: company background and profile.

Why did the company get involved in community activities? What are the goals and motivations?

What is the range of activities they are engaged in?

How many people are involved in citizenship activities? What different businesses and units are involved? What is the network involved in citizenship within the company?

What is the structure and administration of community involvement programs? How is community involvement organized and institutionalized?

Where does community work "fit" in the organization. How are programs funded?

How are community needs assessed? What is the decision process for allocation of human and financial resources? Are employees and community representatives involved in management? How are programs evaluated?

What are the internal impacts? Are the participants "turbo-charged" through their involvement? Does the company include volunteer/community activity in job descriptions? What rewards or other incentive programs are used to encourage employee community participation?

What are the impacts on productivity, morale, turnover, image, sales? What value is added to the company and its participants and to the recipients/ partners? How are these effects measured? What does the company do to leverage impacts?

Does the company communicate citizenship values and practices internally and externally? How, and with what response?

How does the company justify its community involvement activities to its shareholders?

What do community stakeholders say about the company and its work? What impacts has the project had in the community?

Are they aware of and in contact with the network of organizations promoting increased corporate action in the community? What community organizations, government and non-governmental agencies does the company work with? What examples of best practices by other companies or organizations do they try to emulate?

What are the most important problems, obstacles and frustrations from the perspective of different participants? How could projects be improved and carried out more effectively, from the viewpoint of employees, managers, communities?

organizations throughout the United States. In addition to providing students with an opportunity to experience CGC work first hand, the existence of the MBA Domestic Corps program also provides an opportunity for corporations to demonstrate their CGC; corporate sponsors such as Ameritech, Union Pacific, and Whirlpool help fund the program.

THE CORPORATE DIFFUSION OF CGC: WHO'S TALKING TO WHOM?

Evidence that certain organizational practices exist across a number of organizations provides some support for the claim that those practices have become institutionalized. To understand how those practices became institutionalized requires that we step back and focus our attention on the diffusion of those practices. In order for these types of practices to spread across organizations, they must first be communicated. Network analysis can be used to learn more about how these ideas and practices become diffused both within a single organization and across multiple organizations.

Networks are critically important in the diffusion and institutionalization of new behaviors. To the extent that the behavior is novel, emotionally taxing, uncertain, and difficult to learn, direct social support and hands-on help are very useful. A network in which there is direct affiliation from one person to another—that is, it is a socially cohesive network—is very effective under such circumstances. If the behavior can be modeled merely by knowing about it or by reading about it, then structural similarity is very important (persons or organizations in a network are in a similar relation to others in the network, though they may not necessarily be connected), and the behavior is adopted essentially by persons or organizations who are keeping up with the relevant Joneses.

Internal Corporate Network

CGC is not an individual effort. The success of these types of activities often depends on broad participation by the members within the organization. The process begins when a member of the organization learns about other individuals within the organization who are involved in developing and implementing citizenship activities. Diffusion within the organization occurs if that organizational member begins to interact with those individuals involved with citizenship activities. As more and more individuals come into contact with people involved in developing citizenship activities, the network grows and the citizenship activities conducted within the organization typically expand.

External Corporate Networks

Without interaction between organizations, these types of citizenship activities tend to be isolated. Just as individuals communicate within their organizations, they also communicate across organizations. It is through this external network that CGC activities begin to diffuse throughout the business community. Just as individuals within the organization must act upon their new-found knowledge of citizenship practices, so, too, must individuals in other organizations act to implement those types of practices for CGC to become institutionalized. Helping this process along are media reports that praise organizations involved with CGC or that revile organizations that violate the current norms of corporate social responsibility.

Multisector External Networks

As discussed by Tschirhart in Chapter Three, nonprofit and public organizations also play a critical role in the diffusion of CGC activities. They often serve as boundary spanners in the network, bringing together multiple business organizations to allow for the creation of more ambitious projects than any individual corporation could undertake. Exhibit 4.2 contains a sampling of these types of organizations.

Networks are an excellent way for organizations to learn about how extensive CGC practices are. As an organization begins learning about and talking with other organizations that are involved in CGC activities, it is likely that its network will grow to include more and more organizations that are involved in similar types of activities. This adds to the perception that "everyone" is engaged in corporate global citizenship practices, thus encouraging that organization to adopt some such practices itself. As this process is repeated by more and more organizations, CGC practices become more and more institutionalized, leading to even more adoptions of those practices.

THE SOCIAL CONSTRUCTION OF CORPORATE GLOBAL CITIZENSHIP

As organizations seek out evidence to determine whether or not "everyone is doing it," they also begin to develop a vocabulary and a set of

Exhibit 4.2.   Some Organizations in the CGC Network.

Business Enterprise Trust   415-321-5100
204 Junipero Serra Blvd
Stanford, CA 94305
Promotes social responsibility; publishes educational materials.

Business Roundtable   202-872-1260
1615 L Street N.W., Suite 1100
Washington, DC 20036
Major U.S. corporations represented by their chief executive officers. An "influential lobbying force" representing the views of American business. Members
examine public issues that affect the economy and develop positions that seek to
reflect sound economic and social principles.

Business for Social Responsibility (BSR)   202-842-5400
1030 15th Street N.W., Suite 1010
Washington, DC 20036
Web address: http://www.bsr.org
National organization of businesses championing corporate social responsibility.
BSR develops, supports, advocates, and disseminates policies and practices in
four areas: workplace, marketplace, community, and sustainable development.

Center for Corporate Community Relations (Boston College)   617-552-4545
Bradley Googins, Director
Nancy Goldberg, Associate Director
Boston College
36 College Road
Chestnut Hill, MA 02167
Includes 155 corporate members. Provides training for community relations managers, research on corporate-community interaction, database on community
relations, monthly newsletter. Institutes and seminars on community needs and
corporate program development. Has a Globalization Council of senior managers of U.S. companies involved in overseas giving. Because of its academic affiliation, promotes involvement of business schools.

Center for Corporate Public Involvement   202-624-2425
1001 Pennsylvania Avenue N.W.
Washington, DC 20004
Corporate public involvement and activities of member insurance companies.
Sponsored for the purpose of assisting member life and health insurance companies to broaden their participation and improve their effectiveness in social
responsibility activities.

Conference Board   800-US-BOARD
845 Third Avenue   800-872-6273
New York, NY 10022
Publishes reports on topical business issues including some dealing with social
responsibility.

Council on Economic Priorities 212-420-1133
30 Irving Place
New York, NY 10003
Monitors social policies of large corporations. Publishes "Shopping for a Better World" and "The Better World Investment Guide." Publishes reports on corporate performance on social and environmental issues.

Council of Federations 703-222-3861
8608 McHenry St., Suite 1000
Vienna, VA 22180
Represents hundreds of local, national, and international charities organized to aid employees expand workplace giving campaigns.

Council on Foundations Corporate Leadership Project 202-466-6512
Dorothy Ridings, President
Fran Eaton, Director of Corporate Services
1828 L Street, Suite 300
Washington, DC 20036
Corporate Committee of 20 members guides programs for almost 200 member companies. Sponsors meetings, advocacy "to strengthen the giving function within the corporate culture," research on corporate philanthropy, the HBS case study on Dayton-Hudson, two corporate forums each year. Promotes private sector role in social problem solving, social policy making.

Franklin Research and Development Company 617-423-6655
711 Atlantic Ave.
Boston, MA 02111
Provides services for ethical investing; also publishes newsletters on socially responsible investing.

Gifts in Kind America 703-836-2121
700 North Fairfax St., Suite 300
Alexandria, VA 22314
Helps companies donate produces or services to non-profit organizations.

Healthy Companies 202-234-0100
1420 16th Street N.W.
Washington, DC 20036
Nonprofit organization dedicated to building networks and sharing information among government, labor, industry, and education to develop strategies for linking health and development of employees to health and productivity of companies.

Independent Sector 202-223-8100
Brian O Connell, President
Burt Knauft, Sr. Vice President
1828 L Street, 12th Floor #1200
Washington, DC 20036
National network of organizations promoting giving and volunteering. 800 members, including 150 corporate. Presents annual national conference to serve as meeting ground between corporate and nonprofit sectors. Sponsors annual Spring

Research Forum. Give Five Campaign promotes contributions of 5 percent of income and 5 hours per week of volunteer time to charitable organizations.

Initiative for a Competitive Inner City　　　　718–722–7376
One MetroTech Center North, 11th Floor
Brooklyn, NY 11201
Internet: initiative@aol.com
Started by Harvard Business School professor Michael Porter in 1994, ICIC has two primary objectives: to articulate and disseminate the new model for inner-city economic development and to be the catalyst in mobilizing the private sector in the inner city.

Interfaith Center on Corporate Responsibility　　　　212–870–2293
475 Riverside Dr., Rm. 550
New York, NY 10115

Investor Responsibility Research Center　　　　202–833–0700
Margaret Carroll, Executive Director
1350 Connecticut Avenue N.W., No. 700
Washington, DC 20036
The Center published a statistical summary of environmental performance of 500 S&P companies for investors concerned about the effects of environmental policies on the financial performance of companies.

National Alliance of Business　　　　202–289–2888
1201 New York Avenue N.W., Suite 700
Washington, DC 20005
Distinguished Performance Award to recognize excellence in job training and education programs aimed at helping structurally unemployed and other jobless people become productive citizens.

National Partnership for Social Enterprises　　　　201–540–1900
6 Brigade Hill Road
Morristown, NJ 07906
Helps establish businesses that deal with social problems.

Points of Light Foundation　　　　202–223–9186
Richard F. Schubert, President & CEO
Melissa Krinzman, Outreach Coordinator
736 Jackson Place
Washington, DC 20503
The Foundation's goal is "to help make direct and consequential community service aimed at serious social problems central to the life and work of every American and to increase the opportunities people have for that kind of service through their workplaces, schools, houses of worship and civic organizations."

Public Affairs Council/ Foundation for Public Affairs　　　　202–872–1790
Raymond Hoewing, President
Demetrius Parker, Manager, Program Support and Development
1019 19th Street, N.W., Suite 200
Washington, DC 20036
Over 400 corporate/association members. Offers counseling, workshops and sem-

inars, communications and publications, speakers bureau. Annual conference includes sessions on strategic uses of philanthropy, corporate community relations. Research carried out by affiliated Foundation for Public Affairs, Leslie Swift-Rosenweig, Executive Director. Tracks 2,000 activities groups and PACs.

Students for Responsible Business (SRB)/Tides Center   415–561–6400
Presidio Main Post, P.O. Box 29907
1014 Lincoln Blvd.
San Francisco, CA 94129–0903
Web address: http://www.srbnet.org
Promotes socially responsible business learning and networking among business school students and alumni. Sponsors internships, conferences, career networking.

United Way of America   703–836–7100
701 North Fairfax Street
Alexandria, VA 22314

Volunteer: The National Center   703–276–0542
National Center for Corporate Volunteerism
Mary Galligan, Deputy Executive Director
1111 North Nineteenth Street, Suite 500
Arlington, VA 22209
Has 108 company members. Conducts research on status of corporate voluntarism to advance concept of increased motivation and productivity—bottom-line impact—of employee voluntarism. Sponsors annual four–day institute to administrators of corporate volunteer programs. Annual conference includes a "corporate track." Volunteer steering committee of corporate executives advises companies, studies trends, and develops new strategies.

Walker Information   317–843–3939
P.O. Box 40972
Indianapolis, IN 46240–0972

---

common understandings about what corporate global citizenship is, its role in the corporation, and how that role can be fulfilled. Constructing a new reality of "what businesses do," for example, may begin with the codification of these common understandings in the company's vision statement. This symbolic act is important, but it is not sufficient to create that new reality. Companies must move beyond symbol to substance and begin engaging in partnerships to make that vision a reality. We discuss each of these issues in turn.

CREATING THE VISION

For many organizations, an important step is to build the idea of CGC into the mission or vision statement of the organization. This is important because it symbolically makes corporate global citizenship a central goal of the organization. It symbolizes the company's intention to create a more balanced and sustainable business vision. In the words of Edmund Burke of the Center for Corporate Community Relations:

> To achieve its business vision, a successful company must also have a social vision—an analytical understanding of societal and community issues, their impact on the company, and strategies for achieving that vision. The adequacy of housing in a community, public sensitivity to environmental damage, the status of race relations in a community, the inability of a local education system to meet a company's human resource needs, increasing community support for regulations that control business decisions, crime, drug abuse—these and dozens of other issues can interfere with a company's ability to grow and even survive.

As global business competition intensifies, corporations increasingly find themselves confronting new markets, new competitors, new cultures, and new people the world over. Along the way, many believe that to be a good citizen in all those diverse locales, business needs to give something back to the communities to which it belongs or is trying to belong to.

Traditionally, this "burden of guilt" often has been satisfied for many through charitable contributions in various forms—usually money. But such wholly mercenary answers did little to sensitize businesses and their leaders to the human problems that marred the underbellies of almost every community, did little to help those more fortunate give something back—in time and flesh—and be personally enriched in the process, and did little to bring both diverse groups together to discover that good citizenship can equal good business. As businesses have become more sensitive to these issues, CGC has begun to be viewed as an important part of the business. Making this a reality is facilitated by several concrete steps.

• The organization's social vision should be stated in the company's mission and corporate philosophy statement. It should be comprehensive, including contributions, volunteers, and partnerships. The vision should also be reflected in the company's internal policies on treatment of employees.

• The need for a social vision must originate from the CEO. The CEO should explain the relationship of the company's social vision to its business success. He or she should be personally committed to and involved in community affairs and communicate, by word and example, an embrace of the vision.

• A social vision must become an integral part of the company's culture. Business decision makers should review the societal and community consequences of all their decisions.

- A company's social vision must be individually tailored to the culture and environment of each company. Although many companies adopt similar programs, each company develops its own vision and methods for achieving it. Tailoring the social vision to the company's unique culture requires study and analysis to evaluate and incorporate employee interests and community needs.
- Companies must allocate adequate human and financial resources to achieve their social vision. A social vision cannot be implemented merely by increasing charitable contributions.
- Community affairs need to be decentralized and become a responsibility of general managers at the plant level. Community affairs staff need to identify and analyze community needs, put these issues into a planning framework, develop strategies for achieving the company's social vision, then in collaboration with other managers and employees, plan, manage, evaluate, and promote the social programs and image of the company in the community.
- The development and implementation of a social vision is the responsibility of a company's entire management team. Few managers are experienced in dealing with community issues, and they see these issues as unrelated to the success of the company. Corporations can no longer accept this attitude. By adopting a new role and integrating the social vision into the company's business vision, managers will learn important lessons on how to operate in turbulent times.

One example of an organization that has made its commitment to CGC visible by including a statement of that commitment in its mission statement is Ben & Jerry's. Their mission statement is shown in Exhibit 4.3.

A corporate social vision is an acknowledgment by the company that community issues are directly related to company success. Although it may be debatable whether or not the inclusion of issues of corporate global citizenship in the vision or mission statement of an organization should be considered a necessary condition for the institutionalization of those types of practices, there can be no question that it is not a sufficient condition. Words alone are no substitute for organized, intelligent, and practical action.

ESTABLISHING SOCIAL PARTNERSHIPS

Says Sandra Waddock of Boston College:

> Social partnerships are often built around such intractable issues as
> unemployment of the disadvantaged, economic or urban development,

Exhibit 4.3.   Ben & Jerry's Mission Statement.

MISSION STATEMENT

Ben & Jerry's is dedicated to the creation & demonstration of a new corporate concept of linked prosperity. Our mission consists of three interrelated parts:

To make, distribute and sell the finest quality all natural ice cream and related products in a wide variety of innovative flavors made from Vermont dairy products.

To operate the Company on a sound financial basis of profitable growth, increasing value for our shareholders, and creating career opportunities and financial rewards for our employees.

To operate the Company in a way that actively recognizes the central role that business plays in the structure of society by initiating innovative ways to improve the quality of life of a broad community—local, national, and international.

Underlying the mission of Ben & Jerry's is the determination to seek new and creative ways of addressing all three parts, while holding a deep respect for the individuals, inside & outside the company, and for the communities of which they are a part.

Reprinted by permission of Ben & Jerry's.

and improvement of the education system. Because these issues are so important, success is perceived as crucial to both participating organizations and society as a whole. Increasingly, public and private executives realize that these alliances have true "upside" potential for solving social problems that affect the firm and for achieving corporate, agency, or nonprofit goals. They also allow firms to behave in a socially responsible or responsive manner.

In Waddock's (1988, pp. 17–23) *Sloan Management Review* article, "Building Successful Social Partnerships," she addresses implementation issues and offers guidelines for successful partnerships. She concludes that public-private partnerships are inherently fragile. Managers must pay attention to keeping partners involved. As the previous examples suggest, some "best practice" ideas are to:

- Staff the partnership with the best people possible.
- Balance decision-making power. Work toward cooperation, but make sure that conflicts are aired and all points of view are heard.
- Hook partners by describing future benefits, areas of interdependence, and the importance of the issue. Pay attention to feedback and communication so that partners remain hooked. Provide infor-

mation and education about the issues and problems to be addressed.

• Realize that partnership does not happen overnight. Allow time for the partners to get to know and trust each other. Work on breaking down stereotypes.

• Understand the limitations as well as the potentials of partnership.

BEST PRACTICE EXAMPLES OF INSTITUTIONALIZED CORPORATE GLOBAL CITIZENSHIP

As corporate global citizenship practices become institutionalized, the programs resulting from those practices have blossomed. Part Two of this book provides detailed case studies on some of the programs that have been implemented to serve the needs of society. In the last section of this chapter, we provide several brief overviews of some of the other CGC activities that are taking place today.

Community leaders, business leaders, volunteers and staff from non-profit organizations, and individuals from America's small towns, inner cities, and rural America convened the first Citizen Service Summit in Philadelphia in 1997. With the support of the highest levels of government, those attending the summit asked that all Americans commit to working together to solve the serious social problems facing "our nation and our youth." Initiated by the Points of Light Foundation and the Corporation for National Service, the summit launched a new strategy for community service and leadership to "turn the tide" and connect people through volunteerism.

They agreed that millions of dollars and countless hours of volunteer service have produced model programs and helped individual people and groups throughout the world. But genuine change that will actually solve some of the problems facing us—hunger, homelessness, illiteracy, AIDS, and breast cancer, to name a few—cannot be achieved in isolation or by money alone. It takes coordinated and committed long-term strategies to achieve results. Corporate America must be part of the solution.

As *Fortune* noted in its annual bestowing of corporate community service awards, some corporations have been involved in the search for solutions for decades. Others are making new and enhanced commitments. Corporations are encouraging leadership and participation by all employees, from the executive suite to the copy room, and they are supporting volunteer activities with grants to organizations where employees volunteer. They are also asking families and friends to join in, so that, as one Allstate volunteer noted, children will be better able to "put their own problems in perspective and develop value systems."

The following best practice examples come from *Fortune*'s Fifth Annual Corporate Community Service special supplement (Gingold, 1997, pp. S1–S25), which appeared in the January 13, 1997, issue; it is used with permission.

BEST PRACTICE EXAMPLES

EDS: Connecting Volunteers with Community Partners

Electronic Data Systems (EDS) has pioneered new ways for corporations to serve communities where their employees and clients live and work, through programs like Education Outreach, Global Volunteer Day, and the JASON Project, which has reached more than 5 million students and teachers and helped change the way science is taught in the classroom. To guarantee productive community service programs, EDS evaluates and plans for the future as it would with any business unit.

"Business in the 1990s cannot operate as a unit separate from the rest of society," says John R. Castle, Jr., EDS executive vice president and Points of Light Foundation board member. "To be effective, we must connect all parts of the community into a cohesive unit working in collaboration." Applying these principles to community service means that businesses, nonprofit organizations, and recipients must individually and collectively identify the problems and set short- and long-term objectives. Business can bring its resources to the table—people, expertise, and business practices that are transferable to nonprofit organizations. To achieve systemic change, however, it is necessary to develop meaningful and sustainable collaborations directed toward solving existing social and educational challenges.

In 1989, Les Alberthal, EDS chairman and CEO, made education the company's No. 1 community priority. EDS's Education Outreach, which generates 125 school partnerships and more than 350,000 volunteer hours each year, requires that EDS and school representatives annually and jointly determine goals, evaluate existing school programs, and design the programs to meet critical needs. Because schools' needs are diverse, programs range from mentoring and tutoring to setting up an after-school educational facility to providing technology grants.

EDS's three-year-old Global Volunteer Day (GVD) designates one day a year when 95,000 employees in 42 countries, local business partners, and customers are invited to participate in community service projects. GVD, one of the first global programs of its kind, benefits both EDS and the communities in which it operates. Projects such as home building and cleanup, environmental activities, and working with children, seniors, and people with disabilities can all benefit EDS employees by providing fun and personally fulfilling opportunities for leadership development and team building. Some of the most innovative projects occur in places where corporate volunteerism is a new concept. For example, in Beijing, 73 employees, their family members, and friends had a real breakthrough for EDS China and for the Chinese-American relationship when EDS was the first American corporation ever to initiate a volunteer cleanup project at the Great Wall Museum.

"We are proud that EDS was one of the first corporations to promote global community service and that it has made a long-term commitment to public education," says Castle. "This investment in the future will have lasting value by connecting people and resources with those who are addressing our society's greatest needs."

SHELL INAUGURATES *CONNECT AMERICA* LEADERSHIP COMPANY

Shell Oil Company helped bring together the business community to establish the Corporate Volunteer Council of Greater Houston and helped establish the Volunteer Center of the Texas Gulf Coast. The 21-year-old SERVE program (Shell Employees and Retirees Volunteerism Effort) has contributed more than 2 million hours in Houston at a value of over $24 million. Its foundation, established in 1953, has contributed more than $325 million to worthy causes.

As a *Connect America* Leadership Company, Shell will help Points of Light mobilize people and resources through volunteer service and community involvement to address common problems—homelessness, drug awareness training and counseling, and educational mentoring. Shell's own history of involvement reflects the goals of *Connect America,* including:

- Education to achieve productive employment, economic fulfillment, and good citizenship for future generations through Shell Youth Training Academies in Los Angeles and Chicago.
- A healthy start in life and encouragement of healthy behavior by sponsoring a HealthAdventure trailer that has affected the lives of thousands of Houston-area school children.

- Safe and decent places to gather, learn, work, and play by rehabilitating classrooms, a crisis nursery center, and a senior citizen center.
- Caring and supportive mentoring relationships for young people through *Say Yes To A Youngster's Future,* a Shell mentoring program that promotes math and science to elementary school children and their parents.
- Time off from work to plan and attend departmental community service activities and to attend school functions involving employees' children.

Shell's vision reinforces its commitment to helping individuals "achieve their full potential" and ensuring the company is recognized in communities because of "our sensitivity and involvement."

AT&T STRENGTHENS COMMUNITIES THROUGH VOLUNTEERISM

Guided by a set of core values inspired by founder Alexander Graham Bell, AT&T has donated nearly $700 million in grants, sponsorships, and products to education, arts, health, and environmental programs.

AT&T Cares, the most recent addition to its community service programs, encourages AT&T's 127,000 employees worldwide to devote one paid workday to the communities they serve. According to the Points of Light Foundation, *AT&T Cares* is the largest publicly announced corporate volunteer program. On November 21, 1996, it was launched in 16 states and Washington, D.C., where AT&T volunteers helped Project Harvest collect food and set up a warehouse for its annual Thanksgiving food drive. It is estimated that *AT&T Cares* will represent a 1997 donation of 1 million hours, valued at approximately $20 million.

A complementary *AT&T Cares* grants program, initiated in 1994, reinforces employees' volunteer work. When an employee gives at least 50 hours of service annually to a nonprofit group, he or she can request a $250 *AT&T Cares* grant, and when four or more employees volunteer at the same organization, they can combine their requests for a maximum grant award of $2,500. "By giving our time and money, we demonstrate not only our commitment, but also our conviction," says Marcy Chapin, the AT&T Foundation's vice president of community service programs. For example, Jenna McCaffrey and 20 AT&T colleagues serve as literacy coaches for academically at-risk elementary students in Chicago's inner city. The program was in jeopardy, but the *AT&T Cares* group helped keep the tutoring project alive through an *AT&T Cares* grant.

Chairman Bob Allen believes, "A shared dedication to being the best at bringing people together will not only endure in the face of relentless change, it should flourish." To help achieve Allen's vision, AT&T launched the AT&T Learning Network in 1995, the most comprehensive technology donation ever made by an American company. It offers to connect all of the 110,000 U.S. elementary and secondary schools to the Internet by the year 2000 and, in doing so, fosters family involvement in education, provides professional development opportunities for teachers, and integrates technology training into the preparation of new teachers.

PFIZER: THE SPIRIT OF AMERICA

The Pfizer Community Ventures Fund supports local organizations that combat chronic poverty in economically depressed neighborhoods by creating jobs, commerce, and opportunity. Funding and in-kind support go to such grassroots groups as Harlem Textile Works, which trains young people for careers in textile design, and Catering with Conviction, a nonprofit catering business managed by former offenders.

Pfizer also has been innovative in bringing the benefits of its medicines to people most in need through *Sharing the Care*, a joint effort of Pfizer, the National Governors Association, and the National Association of Community Health Centers, which provides the company's major pharmaceuticals at no charge to low-income patients in more than 340 community, migrant, and homeless health centers nationwide.

The scientific expertise of Pfizer employees is the backbone of yet another unique effort, the Pfizer Education Initiative (PEI). It is designed to enhance precollegiate science education by providing science labs and equipment, hands-on science curricula, cutting-edge teacher training, and more than 750 Pfizer volunteers in the company's site communities. The PEI strives to build a scientifically literate public and develop the next generation of scientists.

The company's commitment to community service is clearest during Pfizer's annual United Way campaign. In 1995, the campaign reached a new high, with over 91 percent of the nearly 18,000 Pfizer employees in the United States giving a total of $5.6 million to their local United Way, a sum matched dollar for dollar by the company. And Pfizer employees logged countless hours as volunteer tutors, coaches, mentors, fundraisers, and board members with United Way agencies nationwide.

AMERICAN EXPRESS SUPPORTS EMPLOYEES' COMMUNITY INVOLVEMENT

Recently, American Express made a bold move by committing $5 million, its largest-ever single grant, to the World Monuments Fund to help create the World Monuments Watch. This is an effort to help restore and preserve many of the world's most endangered cultural sites, ranging from rock chapels in Bulgaria and the Temple of Hercules in Italy to ancient cities in Thailand and religious icons in Alaska. By creating a list of endangered sites, similar to the endangered species list, American Express and the World Monuments Fund hope to galvanize public support and raise additional funds to save these important sites.

To support the involvement of its individual employees, American Express created the Volunteer Action Fund (VAF) in 1994. VAF awards grants on a competitive basis to eligible organizations in which employees regularly volunteer their time. "The fund provides a vehicle to distribute more philanthropic dollars to projects that involve and concern the company's employees," says Mary Beth Salerno, president of the American Express Foundation.

VAF is employee-driven. Any employee or American Express financial adviser may nominate a nonprofit charitable, civic, health, social welfare, educational, cultural, or community organization or project where they volunteer. The grants awarded may be for up to $1,000 for an employee and $2,500 for teams of three or more.

Projects range from a summer camp in Arizona for children with cancer to the purchase of books for preschoolers in New York to funds for food for a homeless shelter in Budapest. Employee Nancy Garwick, the team leader for a grant made to the Minneapolis-St. Paul Meals on Wheels program, says, "The fund enables us to help smaller organizations both with our time and with financial support." The American Express grant helped Meals on Wheels produce a quality video to be used for volunteer recruitment locally.

STATE FARM EMPLOYEES AND AGENTS ARE "GOOD NEIGHBORS"

When third-grader Keagan Kertcher realized that her family's home was on fire, among her first thoughts was, "Follow the evacuation plan." After alerting her mother and sisters to the danger, Keagan, who has spina bifida and uses crutches to walk, urged them to use the evacuation route that the family had rehearsed the week after Keagan had participated in State Farm's *Smoke Detectives* program.

Keagan and her family are among the many beneficiaries of State Farm's community service programs. In 1971, after a half-century of community participation by agents and employees, State Farm officially adopted its well-known motto, "Like a Good Neighbor, State Farm Is There."

The company's Education Support Policy encourages all employees, whether they have a school-age child or not, to volunteer with pay one day per school year, to support local schools. As assistant vice president of public affairs, Dixie Axley remarks, "We are letting our employees, parents, and schools know we care about our youth and value education as the foundation for our shared future."

Videos and lesson plans on earthquake preparedness, health and safety, the use of 911, and character building are given to schools free of charge. To guarantee the programs' effectiveness and to extend outreach, they are developed with partners such as the National Association of Elementary School Principals, the International Association of Firefighters, and the National Coordinated Council of Emergency Management.

ELECTRONIC IMAGING DIVISION OF TOSHIBA HELPS FIND A CURE FOR BREAST CANCER

When the Electronic Imaging Division (EID) of Toshiba America Information Systems decided to increase its philanthropic giving and volunteer participation, it wanted to focus on one issue where its assistance could help solve a problem. Because employees supported the cause of finding a cure for breast cancer and additional monies for research were needed, this became the issue. EID knew that finding a cure would have a great impact because one out of eight women in the United States will suffer from the disease.

EID employees already were involved with the Susan G. Komen Foundation's *Race for the Cure,* an annual event in 64 cities that raises money to eradicate breast cancer as a life-threatening disease by advancing research, education, screening, and treatment. EID employee Donna Sutton led the way. "When I saw the *Race for the Cure* brochure, I suddenly knew that I, as an individual, could make a difference. Having recently lost my mother to breast cancer, I volunteered for the first time in my life because I wanted to raise awareness of breast cancer and empower women to take charge of their own health care. With the support of Toshiba EID as a corporate sponsor and the participation of increasing numbers of colleagues, I believe that there is a better chance for finding a cure."

EID decided that the best way to facilitate its philanthropic goals was to create partnerships with like-minded organizations. First, they contacted American Airlines, the organizer of the successful annual celebrity golf tournament that benefits the Komen Foundation and said, "We want to help; what can we do?" The result was increased participation as a presenting sponsor, a three-year financial commitment, and a promise to help increase participation and bring the message back to local communities through EID's dealers and customers.

Central to EID's community service endeavors are focused partnerships that will create a new synergy among employees, other corporations, nonprofit organizations, dealers, and customers.

NORTEL RECEIVES CED'S FIRST CORPORATE CITIZENSHIP AWARD

The first recipient of the Committee for Economic Development (CED) annual Corporate Citizenship Award, Nortel believes that corporations must uphold consistent standards of ethical business conduct and respect the culture and business customs in the communities in which they operate.

Ellen Gaconnier, a senior communications specialist in the community relations department at the company's Richardson (Texas) facility and coordinator for employee volunteers, exemplifies Nortel's volunteer leadership. Gaconnier, a recipient of the Texas Volunteer Leadership Award, has mobilized more than 1,200 employees to develop creative and successful solutions to community problems. This dynamic volunteer program won for Nortel the 1996 Volunteer of the Year Award (Large Business) from the Volunteer Center of Dallas. Nonprofit organizations in Richardson, Dallas, and surrounding communities know that they can count on Nortel employees to help with basic, ongoing needs—tutoring and mentoring, collecting food for the hungry, painting shelters for the homeless, and organizing fundraising events.

Ron Robinson, president of the Richardson Chamber of Commerce, summarizes Nortel's formula for success. "Nortel excels at providing assistance for immediate needs *and* understands conceptually the necessity of long-term community development. They always step forward and take action to fill the gap."

"READY TO LEND A HELPING HAND" CHARACTERIZES ALLSTATE EMPLOYEES

Ask an Allstate employee why he or she volunteers, and there will be a variety of responses such as, "Volunteering as a family brings us closer together" or "It helps you be less self-centered when you focus on the needs of others" or "The least I can do is try to give to those who are less fortunate than I am." More than 50 percent of Allstate's employees participate in volunteer activities because they want to give back to the community. Allstate makes it easier to do so through its Helping Hands program, one of the first corporate volunteer programs in the United States.

Helping Hands' goals are simply stated: (1) work with community groups to identify and address needs on a local basis; (2) involve employees at all levels in volunteer activities; (3) focus on activities that address issues in the areas of community and economic development, auto and highway safety, and personal safety and security; and (4) position Helping Hands both internally and externally with employees, key stakeholders, and the media to increase awareness of and participation in volunteer projects.

When Helping Hands celebrated its 20th birthday in 1996, it issued a new challenge for its employees: As a family, volunteer at least 20 hours during the year and help Allstate reach a new corporate goal of *1 million hours of community service in 1996*. For some 40 percent of the employees who already volunteer, it will be a goal easily met. Each of these individuals donated 100 or more hours to serving others in 1995.

The company understands that responsibilities of work and parenting often leave families with little time left for volunteering. Therefore, the family volunteer program encourages those employees with children to volunteer as a family. These hours can be a fun and educational experience for young people. One employee, whose family actively participates in volunteer programs, provides the following perspective: "It gives children the opportunity to share their talents and gain self-confidence. It also helps children put their own problems in perspective and develop value systems."

AMWAY DISTRIBUTORS HELP OTHERS HELP THEMSELVES

Imagine increasing your volunteer force overnight by as many as 35,000 people. When Amway and Easter Seals entered into a partnership in 1983, Easter Seals suddenly inherited a fundraising team of enthusiastic and energetic volunteers—Amway distributors who embraced the cause of helping people with disabilities achieve independence.

The National Easter Seal Society annually serves more than 1 million children and adults with disabilities through sites in the United States and Puerto Rico.

Amway Corporation supports the volunteer Easter Seal activities of its independent distributors with fundraising suggestions, support material, and recognition opportunities. Most importantly, the company provides a communications link—highlighting model programs, good ideas, and success stories. Since 1983, Amway and its distributors have contributed more than $18 million to support Easter Seals. But it doesn't stop there. A glance at Amway's home page on the World Wide Web reveals a plethora of programs in the United States and in some of the 75 countries and territories where the company has distributors. Partnerships and volunteer services with nonprofit organizations in arts and culture, education, the environment, human services, and athletics abound. Amway volunteers raise funds for diverse programs, including scholarships for orphans in Korea and Japan, a cardiac surgery unit in a children's hospital in Poland, and participation in "Look Good . . . Feel Better" hospital workshops for female cancer patients in Canada and Australia.

POINTS OF LIGHT RANKS PRUDENTIAL A LEADER IN COMMUNITY SERVICE

To understand Prudential Insurance Company's commitment to volunteerism and to building communities, tap into its World Wide Web site (www.prudential.com) and explore "community." Learn about the company's Social Investment Program, its Spirit of Community Initiative, its foundation, and local initiatives. Read about young people who have founded organizations like Stepp'n Up, which provides new shoes to needy children. See how Prudential volunteers help build affordable family homes. Or read about the Prudential Spirit of Community Youth and Adult Surveys, which reveal interesting facts about Americans and volunteerism. And employees can tap into volunteer opportunities through Prudential CARES.

Prudential's corporate involvement begins with its social responsibility mission statement: "To strengthen Prudential by investing financial resources, business expertise, and associate volunteer skills in programs that increase human potential and individual self-sufficiency through education, job skills, economic revitalization and basic community health." The company offers seminars to agents on how to mesh business success with community involvement and provides opportunities and training for employees who want to volunteer.

Ongoing programs include Prudential CARES (Community Action Relief Efforts), which enlists immediate companywide support when a natural disaster strikes; the 27-year-old Summer Computer Program for

High School Students; and the Community Champions Volunteer Recognition program, which financially supports the nonprofit organizations in which employees and retirees volunteer. These programs have been joined recently by the Corporate Retiree Volunteer Program and Global Volunteer Day.

Prudential assumed a leadership role in the development of the volunteers of the future when it launched the Prudential Spirit of Community Initiative. A long-term series of programs designed to rekindle America's community spirit, it helps young people become actively involved in making their communities better places to live by providing leadership training and recognizing their achievements through national and state awards.

CONCLUSION

The 12 companies profiled in *Fortune*'s Fifth Annual Corporate Community Service special supplement are outstanding leaders in corporate global citizenship. Corporate resources and volunteer service by employees and retirees have helped change the lives of those they have assisted as well as their own. It has been shown repeatedly that this combination can make a difference. Today, companies often are targeting specific issues to achieve measurable results. The Electronic Imaging Division of Toshiba America Information Systems, for example, wants to help find a cure for breast cancer. It is joining forces with other corporations and saying, "Let's support this cause until it is no longer a life-threatening disease."

Companies such as American Express, AT&T, EDS, and Prudential are taking the lessons learned at home and exporting them to an international community. Employees from the countries where global community volunteer days are being put into practice are identifying the needs and helping explain the American phenomenon of employee volunteerism and community service to their international colleagues.

As *Fortune* concluded, the needs are great. If systemic change is to be achieved so that solutions are permanent, it will take our commitment as a nation. Corporate global citizenship activities must become an intrinsic part of organizations in the future, just as the pursuit of profit has been an intrinsic part of organizations of the past. Only then will we all—businesses, individuals, and communities—reap the benefits.

REFERENCES

Arlow, P., and Wogan, T. D. "A Meta-analytic Review of the Relationship Between Corporate Social and Financial Performance." Paper presented at the National Academy of Management Meeting, Cincinnati, Ohio, 1996.

Gingold, D. "Corporate Community Service." *Fortune,* 1(135), 1997.

Powell, W. W., and DiMaggio, P. J. (eds.). *The New Institutionalism in Organizational Analysis.* Chicago: University of Chicago Press, 1991.

Ullmann, A. A. "Data in Search of a Theory: A Critical Examination of the Relationships Among Social Performance, Social Disclosure, and Economic Performance of U.S. Firms." *Academy of Management Review,* 10, 1985.

Waddock, S. A. "Building Successful Social Partnerships." *Sloan Management Review,* 29(4), 1988.

PART TWO

CORPORATE GLOBAL CITIZENSHIP IN ACTION

THE TEST OF A WINNING LEADER is authenticity in action. The first part of this book challenged readers to better articulate a teachable point of view on corporate global citizenship. This part is a benchmarking opportunity—a chance for readers to see best practices in action and to perform as these companies have.

In developing an action agenda, there should be a real-life interplay between one's teachable point of view and action. The action will, over time, modify the point of view as learning takes place. The opportunity in this part of the book is that as you, the reader, prepare your own global citizenship action agenda, you can see what others have accomplished.

Over the past decade, we worked with thousands of executives in our Global Leadership Program, with companies such as Sony, Hitachi, Honda, General Motors, Ford, General Electric, IBM, Shell, Nokia, and Citibank. After five weeks of spending 20 percent of their time examining and engaging in global citizenship activities in settings as diverse as drug rehabilitation and AIDS clinics in Washington, D.C., and hospitals in Bombay, Beijing, and Moscow, participants take a half-day for each executive to review his or her teachable point of view and, more importantly, develop an agenda for action.

The results have been very encouraging. Executives from Electronic Data Systems (EDS) have gone back to their company and engaged thousands of employees in community action projects. One of our Japanese executives got involved with the homeless in Tokyo. At Ameritech, a much deeper relationship with Focus: HOPE was developed, resulting in millions of dollars of support and hundreds of volunteers. The challenge is to use this part of the book to get involved—and formulate and make an action commitment of your own.

The companies you will read about have proceeded in the same way that you are about to proceed. Companies committed to corporate global citizenship put in place distinct practices to measure, monitor, and stimulate decisions and actions that produce beneficial consequences for their four generic stakeholder groups: employees, investors, customers, and communities. In this part of the book, the authors consider several large-scale citizenship efforts by leading U.S. companies. These cases provide a sense of the scale and scope of the movement for a more caring brand of capitalism, as well as lessons managers have learned along the way. The cases reveal many highlights:

The economic benefits of citizenship. A case study of the American Express company shows how an innovative educational program in travel and tourism helps both the company and the rapidly changing economy of Hungary as it shifts to capitalism. A review of banker J.P. Morgan's efforts to promote local entrepreneurship and development shows how a synergistic relationship can develop between a company and its community. Citizenship at J.P. Morgan is a complex intertwining of mutually beneficial practices.

The community benefits of citizenship. A case study of pharmaceutical giant Merck's decision to donate millions of doses of *Mectizan* to the diseased populations of developing nations highlights the unexpected problems that arise in carrying out charitable programs. The citizenship practices of the General Electric Company are highlighted in the activities of the company's Elfun Society. The case explores how Elfun Society members support the local communities in which GE operates, particularly in partnerships to improve public high schools. At Ameritech, involvement in citizenship activities focused on improving inner-city communities also served to inspire improvements in customer service within the organization.

The employee benefits of citizenship. A case study of Sara Lee identifies the company's citizenship practices as core aspects of its human resource systems and corporate culture. Not only does it mirror the decentralized philosophy of the company, it also defines for Sara Lee's managers and employees a moral and psychological context around which day-to-day decisions are made.

The customer benefits of citizenship. Environmentalism at Procter & Gamble has meant a complete overhaul of the company's practices in product design, manufacturing, and distribution. The case study of P&G demonstrates the implications of thoroughly linking citizenship and quality management. Similarly, Compaq's efforts to develop an environmentally responsible operation worldwide have not only resulted in reduced costs due to more efficient use of resources in production, but have also provided customers with products that can be upgraded rather than replaced. Compaq's lifecycle approach has had a major impact on how it designs and distributes its products.

The cases illustrate the strategic value to the corporation of community involvement. They also raise questions about and promote discussion of corporate social and environmental priorities and responsibilities: Why should and do companies become involved? How much inside and outside impact have their efforts had? What is needed to make them more effective? To help foster dialogue on these issues, key points are highlighted at the beginning of each case as a guide to thinking through the complexity of the interconnected issues raised in the case, particularly with respect to the employee, and economic, customer, and community benefits that result from these activities.

5

AMERICAN EXPRESS PHILANTHROPY

Developing an Academy of Travel and Tourism in Hungary

Michael Brimm

*Tourism is a major source of jobs and hard currencies for
Hungary as the country reshapes its economy. American Express
is a partner in helping turn the enormous potential to attract
foreign visitors into strong revenue-generating industries. This is
why we work hard through the [American Express] Foundation to
develop innovative programs that educate young people about
careers in the tourism industry and help enhance customer service.*

—Jurgen Aumueller, President, American Express Travel Related
Services for Europe, Middle East, and Africa

This case was written by Michael Brimm, Associate Professor of Organizational
Behavior at INSEAD. It is intended to be used as a basis for class discussion
rather than to illustrate either effective or ineffective handling of an administrative situation. It was funded primarily by a grant from the Commonwealth Fund
to the University of Michigan. The case data reflect the situation in American
Express in 1991. Reprinted with the permission of INSEAD. Copyright © 1994,
INSEAD, Fontainebleau, France.

PETER KRAFT WAS LOOKING FORWARD to the forthcoming visit of his chairman. In April 1990, he had been named vice president and country manager of American Express with the task of creating a new subsidiary in Hungary. In the following 18 months, he had developed an infrastructure in Hungary with a newly opened office in the center of Budapest that employed 14 Hungarians. The visit of James D. Robinson, III, chairman and CEO of American Express, was a recognition of the importance attributed to this new market in Central Europe, as well as an opportunity for Kraft to position the new subsidiary for senior management.

He had asked the head office for information that would help prepare the agenda for the chairman's two-day visit. The reply contained the usual suggestions for a presentation of current and projected financial results, as well as Robinson's desire to meet a number of key political and business leaders. In addition, there was a request to brief the chairman on the progress of the Travel and Tourism Academy, which had been funded by the American Express Foundation as part of American Express worldwide philanthropic activities simultaneously with the opening of the new subsidiary.

While American Express had committed $500,000 to a three-year philanthropic fund for Czechoslovakia, Poland, and Hungary, Kraft was not sure that this was really central to senior management's concerns for Hungary.

In addition, the Hungarian government had been pressing Kraft to use the name "American Express" on teaching materials for this program because of the positive connotation of pro-Western approaches. The current fascination with American management in the Central European countries presented a stark contrast to the negative image that once plagued American multinationals in the area. In other programs, the company had sought a low profile, with limited use of American Express as the public sponsor. Kraft had already agreed to have their name on certificates presented at the completion of the program, but he was hesitant to take the next step, as he knew the issue was currently under debate in the United States.

Kraft was also wary that the program might lose momentum. It had helped him introduce American Express into Hungary. Like himself, many of the others who had helped to establish the program from the hotel association and the government had already received much of the personal value they could achieve through association with this initiative. What, then, would be the motivation to carry it forward to successful implementation?

PHILANTHROPY AT AMERICAN EXPRESS

In 1991, American Express was one of the largest financial and travel institutions in the world. With revenues exceeding $30 billion and over 100,000 employees, the company had a global presence in a variety of financial services extending from its well-known credit cards and travel services to major involvements in banking, investment advisory services, and insurance.

In addition to the normal goals of business performance, American Express is a company that understands it has other responsibilities, too. This is reflected in initiatives in consumer affairs and volunteerism, and in advocacy on behalf of issues affecting the communities where its employees live and in which it does business. This orientation is also reflected in the funds committed each year to a broad range of cultural and philanthropic activities.

The particular initiative presented in this chapter is the development of a Travel and Tourism Academy in Hungary. It emerged from a context of the company's general approach to philanthropic activities and the history of other academy activities.

The American Express Philanthropic Program provides financial and organizational support to cultural programs, education and employment, and community service. This is organized mainly through the American Express Foundation, a nonprofit organization incorporated in 1954 whose only donors are the company and its subsidiaries. Similarly, the senior staff of the foundation are the same individuals who direct the philanthropic program, with trustees drawn from the senior management of the business. At the time of the case, this included James D. Robinson, III, the former chairman and chief executive officer.

American Express and its foundation together made an estimated $22 million in grants in 1990, rising to over $23 million in 1991. This represented a substantial increase over the approximately $5 million per year for these activities in the early 1980s. Approximately $4.5 million of the 1991 amount was spent outside the United States.

The rationale for this program is linked to the basic values espoused by the company: the "Blue Box Values," which are shown in Exhibit 5.1. This name is a reference to the square, blue box containing the words "American Express" that is the company logo and appears on all products and literature.

The philanthropic activities are closely tied by the company to the mandate of being good citizens in the communities in which American Express

Exhibit 5.1.   American Express Blue Box Values.

American Express
BLUE BOX VALUES

All our activities and decisions must be based on,
and guided by, these values.

Placing the interests of Clients and
Customers first.

A continuous Quest for Quality
in everything we do.

Treating our People with respect and dignity.

Conduct that reflects the highest standards
of Integrity.

Teamwork from the smallest unit to the
enterprise as a whole.

Being Good Citizens in the communities
in which we live and work.

To the extent we act according to these values, we believe we will provide outstanding service to our clients and customers, earn a leadership position in
our businesses and provide a superior return to our shareholders.

units operate. The initial communication of this "Blue Book" value
caused confusion in the organization. There was no clarity as to the
resources available. Was the company going to provide "release time" to
participate in community activities? Would there be financial support
available? Was the company dictating activity beyond the work role and
extending into the personal space of the individuals? A cross-unit, multi-
disciplinary task force was created to address these issues and suggest
clarification to the organization. Human resource professionals and
lawyers were involved to look at the legal implications of the "values"
that had been expressed. A brochure directed to employees outlined in
greater detail the rationale that emerged from this process. (See Exhibit
5.2. The document represents a clear statement of corporate intent in this
area.) It was a widely distributed, internal document that addressed the
issues of global citizenship. Because of the controversy that surrounded
this report, it is probably also a document that was widely read.

Exhibit 5.2. Philanthropy at American Express.

A philanthropic program reflects the values of the company that sponsors it. At American Express, our programs are as diverse as the people they serve. As a global company, we support programs around the world. The communities and the countries where our philanthropic program operates are where our employees and our customers live and work. We take philanthropy seriously. That seriousness is evident both in the level of financial resources we commit and in the personal involvement of management and employees. We take an entrepreneurial, creative approach to philanthropy, just as we do to managing our business. . . . We have found that partnerships work, and that the public and private sectors—profit and nonprofit—working together can develop new solutions to tough problems. . . . Our philanthropic activities focus on three themes: community service, education and employment, and cultural diversity and national heritage.

Answers to Your Questions on the Good Citizenship Value

American Express has a longstanding tradition of being a good corporate citizen. The company and its people contribute time, expertise, and resources to improve the welfare of the communities where we operate.

We do this because:

- It's the right thing to do.
- The health of our business and the well-being of society are interdependent.
- Our record in the community helps attract and retain the best employees, clients, and business partners.

Good citizenship is demonstrated in many different ways, across the company and around the world. The Philanthropic Program is one vehicle that helps the company address community needs locally, nationally, and internationally. American Express managers serve on regional philanthropic committees to help identify organizations and projects where company resources can be used best. Through wide-ranging employee giving-matching options, the Philanthropic Program supports individual employees who contribute their own money and time to nonprofit organizations in the United States.

Another way the company demonstrates good citizenship is by taking a leadership role on issues affecting our communities, such as:

- Championing education reform efforts and creating programs to directly address education issues affecting the work force, worldwide.
- Developing sound environmental policies and practices.
- Organizing nonpartisan voter registration drives at company facilities in the United States.
- Producing and distributing consumer education brochures.
- Helping local governments respond to fiscal and management challenges by volunteering our management and business expertise.

Senior Managers Have Special Responsibilities:

- To lead by example by personally representing American Express in the community.
- To build good citizen actions into strategic business plans and allocate adequate budget, resources, and time to support them.
- To encourage and facilitate good citizenship on the part of employees who want to be involved in volunteer and civic activities on their own time.

American Express encourages volunteerism as one way to practice good citizenship, and senior managers throughout the company have supported employee volunteer efforts in many ways, among them:

- Visibly demonstrating personal concern for and involvement in the community; sharing information about their activities, especially with direct reports.
- Finding out what types of volunteer activities are important to employees.
- Appointing a volunteer coordinator, setting up a volunteerism committee, and/or establishing a volunteer resource office.
- Encouraging employees to support Academies of Finance and Academies of Travel and Tourism (two-year programs that American Express has pioneered in more than 300 schools around the world) by serving on local Academy boards, enlisting additional business students, and volunteering to teach courses or mentor students.
- Developing a communication plan to inform employees about community needs, ways to address issues, and volunteer opportunities.
- Determining community needs by consulting with employees, United Way, public officials, community foundations, and civic organizations.
- Identifying and promoting training opportunities and other resources in our community that facilitate employee volunteerism.
- Recognizing individual and team volunteer activities by highlighting volunteer activities in internal and external communications, citing in performance appraisals volunteer activities that enhance job-related skills or support business goals, and creating an awards program for employee volunteers.
- Being responsive to employees' requests for alternate work schedules to participate in volunteer activities.

American Express Chairman and CEO Jim Robinson Responds to Employees' Questions

Q: "Being good citizens in the communities in which we live and work" is a Blue Box Value. Does that apply to me personally or to American Express as a corporation?

A: It applies to both. We believe in being a good corporate citizen because the health of our business and the well-being of society are interdependent. Setting a good example in the community helps us attract the best employees, clients, and business partners. It is also the right thing to do.

There are many examples of our corporate citizenship. They include our Philanthropic Program's activities, such as the creation of Academies of Finance and Travel and Tourism, and even to preserve places of cultural and historical importance around the world. The company's involvement in public policy issues, such as free world trade, is yet another example.

At the same time, it's important to recognize that American Express is first and foremost its people. Therefore, we encourage—and, wherever possible, facilitate the efforts of—employees to do whatever they can in their communities, each contributing in his or her own way.

Q: I don't have time to do volunteer work, but I still think I'm a good citizen. Will I be penalized in any way?

A: No. We respect individual choice and understand the time constraints many employees have in balancing their work and personal responsibilities. Managers whose jobs are highly visible, however, are expected to be actively involved in their communities as representatives of American Express.

We can all be good citizens without volunteering after-hours time to active community service. For example, an employee is a good citizen when he or she votes in every election, helps his or her children get a good education, and participates in recycling programs. Of course, those who have more time to give to help build a better world will definitely enrich their own lives by doing so.

A series of interviews with those involved in American Express activities yielded a reality that differed in some respects from the corporate rhetoric.

> Philanthropy is facing a major challenge these days in many departments within American Express. With downsizing, restructuring, and a difficult business environment, citizenship issues may be the first to go. This is even difficult in centrally sponsored programs as the future is so uncertain. It is very difficult to plan for the future when there is no certainty that the budget will remain. It has remained flat for the past three years. The "good news" is that it hasn't been reduced.

> These conditions also affect the non-financials. It is harder to get senior executives to sit on local boards for the philanthropy effort or to get involved with community groups. This calls for time, energy and commitment—resources which are also in short supply.

> Compensation and rewards are still based on the "bottom line." If you don't meet the business targets, you are gone! If you do reach those goals, the citizenship activities are well regarded and represent a real plus.

THE STRUCTURE OF PHILANTHROPY AT AMERICAN EXPRESS

At American Express, the audit and public responsibility committee of the board of directors has general responsibilities to oversee, among other things, the charitable contributions of the corporation. But the American Express philanthropic program actually coordinates both direct corporate and American Express Foundation giving. The foundation contributions total about twice the direct giving of the corporation. Both corporate and foundation giving go primarily to American Express operating locations.

Proposals originated from local and regional committees, which also participate in project development. In 1990 there were about 16 American Express philanthropic committees in the United States that were organized on a state or regional basis. Similar organizations were created in major international locations on a country or regional basis. In each case, the committees were made up of senior managers from the local American Express subsidiaries. Managers of these local committees completed the initial review of proposals and decided on any grants of less than $15,000. Proposals requesting more than this amount were forwarded to the trustees of the program for decision. Before being acted upon by the trustees, proposals were screened by the staff of the philanthropic program. In 1990 these numbered seven full-time professionals, seven full-time support personnel, and one part-time professional. This staff also served as the staff of the American Express Foundation. One such participant commented:

> Meetings of the statewide or regional philanthropic committees are well attended. I'd like to think that it is because of the "goodness" of the cause. The fact is that these are senior managers that use this as an excellent opportunity to network on a variety of issues. This is even legitimated as business and operational issues are placed on the agenda along with the philanthropic concerns.

Corporate departments also make contributions directly from their own funds. These are not included in the philanthropic program giving figures, which do include the American Express Foundation.

The stated philosophy of the philanthropic program is to leverage corporate giving through drawing upon the skills and financial resources of partners. American Express gives priority to funding specific projects rather than general support, to giving that includes more active involvement than simply grant support, and to high-profile projects that can demonstrate American Express's commitment to communities. The company attempts to provide a leadership role in the community through its citizenship activity and strongly encourages senior managers to actively participate in these endeavors.

EUROPEAN ACTIVITIES

In Europe, a major area of focus for this philanthropic activity has been the support of education and training programs for the travel and tourism industry.

In the United Kingdom, American Express Foundation developed a school course in tourism studies and worked with educational authorities to establish it as part of the school curriculum. Funded in conjunction with Forte Hotels, by 1995 the program was taught in 250 schools in England and Wales to students aged 14 to 16. It was replicated in Ireland and Mexico and was under development in Scotland and Hong Kong. This case focuses upon the development and introduction of such a course in Hungary.

Other activities include:

Education for careers in European travel and tourism. Finalized in June 1991, this study of industry experience and practice was written by the Paris-based European Institute for Education and Social Policy and sponsored by American Express Foundation. Travel and tourism companies in eight countries were interviewed for the study, which emphasized the need for close industry/education collaboration to prepare the industry's workforce. Another area of focus for American Express Foundation grants has been the preservation and management of the historical and cultural heritage that is one of Europe's major tourism assets.

Europa Nostra. American Express Foundation has sponsored Europa Nostra since 1986, primarily through an award scheme that encourages conservation projects to maintain Europe's architectural heritage. Europa Nostra is a confederation of over 200 conservation organizations from 23 countries in Europe. It plays a major role in promoting conservation projects, which maintain an equilibrium between the promotion and protection of European heritage.

World Monuments Fund. American Express Foundation has been a major source of financial support for this private organization dedicated to the preservation and promotion of historical monuments in Europe and around the world. Recent grants funded work at the Angkor complex in Cambodia.

Mozart's House, Salzburg. In 1990, an American Express Foundation grant inaugurated the fundraising campaign to restore Mozart's house in Salzburg as a museum and venue for concerts. American Express also supports a variety of programs designed to stimulate travel. The company's activities include marketing partnerships to promote particular destinations and the development of worldwide travel and tourism policy.

World Travel and Tourism Council. American Express has played a key role in the formation and funding of the World Travel and Tourism Council (WTTC). The WTTC is a global coalition of chief executive officers from all sectors of the industry. Its goal is to promote expansion of travel and tourism markets and encourage quality service to consumers. American Express CEO James D. Robinson, III, chaired this organization from its formation in 1989 to 1991.

Official card of tourism. American Express and the French Tourism Ministry developed a program to encourage American travelers to visit the regional areas of France. The program involves new telephone information services for travelers, a multi-million-dollar print advertising campaign, and customer service training for travel agents. A similar program was initiated in Spain, in partnership with Iberia Airlines and the Spanish Tourism Ministry.

THE ACADEMY PROGRAMS

"Finance, travel, and tourism are at the forefront of changes in the service and technological economies. These changes are every bit as dramatic as the earlier improvements in manufacturing and agricultural processes," noted Sven Groennings, then American Express's vice president for education. The National Academy Foundation is the company's effort "to meet real-world needs in global, technological, and service-oriented industries," he concluded.

Begun in the early 1980s, the National Academy of Finance, the first of four "academies" currently sponsored by the foundation, had somewhat more modest expectations. Ida Schmertz, then senior vice president for corporate relations, recalled that when Shearson became part of American Express, "we were not worried about recruiting, but we were extremely concerned about the difficulty in retaining young people in the Shearson back office. From the beginning, our objective was to work with the chancellor of the New York City schools to find the best way to use American Express and Shearson expertise to assist high school teachers in turning out students who were sufficiently motivated and able to work in a corporation."

THE ACADEMY OF FINANCE

The initial venture was the Academy of Finance pilot program that began in New York City in 1982 with 35 students. By 1990, the Academy of

Finance had an enrollment of 3,000 in 45 schools throughout the United States. Only 20 percent were New York City students. In addition, the Academy of Finance model was used to develop 14 Academies of Travel and Tourism, new programs on manufacturing in partnership with Ford Motor Co., and government-supported public service programs. The National Academy Foundation was founded in 1989 as an independent entity and began to attract the support of additional corporations. In 1990 NAF was an umbrella group for 61 U.S. programs in which 3,500 students were enrolled.

The first step in building the original Academy of Finance was to hire a director who could work with the public schools, universities, and the corporate community to develop a curriculum for the new venture. The money allocated to the project was small (less than $50,000), but the chief executive and top management in major departments were actively involved in putting the program together.

Discussions in which the executives described their work sites played a key role in giving the educators a realistic sense of their job responsibilities. Curriculum writers used this information to develop teachable subjects. Finally, as one participant recalled, "The program was developed so that it could be managed, monitored, and corrected. We had clear goals in mind, and we involved everyone in the process—including the teachers."

The blueprint that was devised for the first Academy of Finance contained three elements that have been key components in all subsequent academies:

1. *The program is embedded in the existing education structure:* students (usually high school juniors and seniors) take courses taught by teachers from a variety of traditional disciplines (for example, social studies, mathematics).

2. *Teachers receive special training:* business participants train academy faculty to adapt their knowledge of traditional subject matter and techniques to a specific, well-designed curriculum.

3. *Students gain experience as summer interns:* these summer jobs have guidelines and expectations that are related to the course work.

From the outset, American Express involved other companies in academy programs. Dow Jones and the New York Stock Exchange were early participants in curriculum development and sponsors of internship positions for the Finance Academy. National Academy Foundation (NAF) currently requires a minimum of three participating companies to start a new academy.

NAF programs also have procedural mechanisms for fine-tuning and program development and improvement. Project directors meet periodically to discuss issues of common concern. These sessions help to develop peer networks and are viewed by the NAF as a vehicle to improve program administration and management.

In addition, site visit reports solicit the views of the business community, school principals, teachers, and students regarding program effectiveness. These investigations also determine the program's impact on the community that is served by the project. Where possible, the NAF, in cooperation with its local partners, then seeks to remedy any deficiencies with financial or technical assistance as needed. (The Charter of the National Academy Foundation is shown in Exhibit 5.3.)

NATIONAL ACADEMY FOUNDATION

American Express is the creator and principal corporate supporter of the National Academy Foundation. The U.S. Department of Education awarded to NAF a four-year $380,000 grant to replicate academies of finance. Also, the Department of Education selected NAF as its illustration of a program that really works in advancing Student Achievement and Citizenship.

In 1990, NAF coordinated the activities of over 80 academies involving more than 3,500 students in four fields of study: finance, travel and tourism, public service, and manufacturing sciences (with Ford).

The American Express contribution to NAF was substantial. In addition to financial support of $2 million and additional funding of start-up projects, the company provided significant personnel assistance. Two board members are American Express employees. Other individuals who serve on local boards assist in curriculum development or teach special segments of courses in the classroom. The program has become a major focus for volunteer efforts by employees.

NAF has become a major node of networks both within the organization and with a client base in the communities. Other companies provide internships and develop both personal and business relationships with local American Express personnel.

PROGRAM EXPANSION AND IMPACT

Phyllis Frankfort, the then executive director of the National Academy Foundation, expressed the belief that academy programs have had a clear spillover effect in other areas within participating schools.

Exhibit 5.3.   National Academy Foundation Charter.

The National Academy Foundation has been established to encourage and support partnerships between business and education to strengthen the preparedness of the American workforce. It will enrich the resources and opportunities available to high schools and their students who are interested in emerging and expanding careers.

The Foundation builds upon the eight-year record of success of the Academy of Finance model by replicating it and applying it to professions and industries where rapid growth is anticipated.

The Academy of Finance, Academy of Travel and Tourism, and the Academy of Public Service offer a special two-year curriculum for public high school juniors and seniors, training for public high school teachers to teach the Academy courses, and, in the summer, on-the-job internships with businesses for Academy students. The National Academy Foundation will:

- Develop and maintain the quality of Academy programs.
- Foster the expansion of the Academy of Finance and the Academy of Travel and Tourism programs through partnerships between public school systems and national and local businesses.
- Provide technical assistance, curricula, and administrative materials for Academy programs.
- Through corporate sponsorships, develop new Academy programs in professions and industries which offer career opportunities.
- Maintain a national network among students, graduates, teachers, business participants, foundations, and public officials in order to facilitate the exchange of information and new ideas.
- Inform public policy makers and business leaders about the vision and effectiveness of the NAF Academies as educational reform models.

Benefits for Students, Schools, and Business

- Students receive practical and comprehensive classroom instruction and work experience for career preparation.
- Schools receive assistance for professional development of teachers, support staff and other program expenses, as well as comprehensive curricula and other contemporary learning resources to prepare and motivate students.
- Business has an opportunity to work closely with local schools using a successful national model program to assure a supply of qualified entry-level personnel matched to existing employment needs within the community.

They have helped to increase the self-esteem of young adults, built a bridge for them between school and work or work and college, and encouraged them to continue with their education. (Roughly 90 percent have eventually attended college.) Academy programs have also given company participants a more positive view of public school students.

Academy graduates have also gained a favorable impression of business institutions. For example, in a 1990 survey of 196 former Academy of Finance students, it was found that more than one-quarter (27 percent) were currently working in financial services or a related field. In addition, most (87 percent) working graduates with nonfinancial jobs preferred the financial sector, and almost half of the Academy of Finance alumni currently looking for work wanted a job in financial services. Thus, there appears to have been some movement toward the original objective of finding a dependable labor pool that could be *retained* by financial services organizations.

Finally, the list of cooperating institutions has expanded substantially since the first Academy of Finance project in 1982. In 1990, some 250 organizations sponsored internships in that program alone.

PHILANTHROPIC INITIATIVES IN TRAVEL AND TOURISM IN EASTERN EUROPE

The Creation of an Academy in Hungary

Of the various programs, travel and tourism academies have generated the most interest outside the United States. In 1991 the Travel and Tourism Program was already established in more than 250 schools throughout the United Kingdom. British educational authorities permitted students to take two-year comprehensive examinations in travel and tourism, and they were developing tests to certify 17- and 18-year-olds for more advanced training. In addition, travel and tourism academies existed in Ireland, Mexico, and Hong Kong and were in various stages of development in Brazil and France.

In developing its Academy of Travel and Tourism in Hungary, American Express sought to blend its approach to philanthropy and develop an in-depth, functioning academy program.

The American Express Fund for Central/Eastern Europe was established in 1991 to coincide with the opening of American Express offices in this region. It was a $500,000 philanthropic fund to be spent over three years, 1991 to 1993, to foster human resource development in the tourism sector in Czechoslovakia, Hungary, and Poland. The American

Express Fund will reinforce the company's commitment to support education and training programs that meet the needs of the tourism industry worldwide. The fund was administered by the American Express Philanthropic Program.

These countries in Central/Eastern Europe are facing major economic dislocations as they move toward market economies. American Express recognized the potential for their own business development upon the successful completion of this transition and pursued, as they have elsewhere in the world, a strategy of establishing a foothold in the countries as soon as possible.

"To American Express, the political and economic reforms in Central and Eastern Europe have generated new prospects for long-term growth in the travel and financial sectors," said Jurgen Aumueller, president, Travel Related Services for Europe, Middle East, and Africa. "We have chosen Hungary—an initiator of these processes—to be the country in which we will build up, step by step, an organization of our own," he explained.

This provided immediate service to existing clients from outside the region, who can use financial and tourism services while visiting Hungary for business or tourism. The new organization also served as a base for developing future business, as the economy expanded and government regulations permitted greater involvement in the local arena.

Peter Kraft, vice president and general manager of the operations in Hungary, stated at the opening of the American Express office in Budapest that he expected the company to play, "a key role in boosting Hungarian tourism." In 1990, 40,000 AmEx cardmembers visited Hungary and spent millions of dollars at the 1,500 service establishments then in the country.

"American Express shares a bit more than 40 percent of the total credit card turnover in Hungary, but we want to increase it sufficiently to boost Hungary's foreign currency income, reserves, and to provide jobs," Kraft said in 1991. The newly opened subsidiary was staffed by 14 Hungarians in January 1991.

Since tourism represents a potential source of jobs and hard currency during a period of difficult economic transition, governments are particularly responsive to initiatives that facilitate the rapid development of this sector and related industries. Particular challenges cited in Hungary by the minister of Industry and Tourism were to:

- Create the physical infrastructure necessary to attract tourists.

- Preserve and manage their tourism resources, both cultural and natural.

- Develop the human capital and tradition of customer service that will enable them to reach their potential as premier tourism destinations.

The third of these objectives tied closely to the successful experiences of academy projects in the United Kingdom, Mexico, Hong Kong, and Ireland. The Hungarian project aimed at the adaptation of these existing programs.

The initial proposals outlined plans for a travel and tourism curriculum that would not be a vocational training program. Rather, the objective was to offer an optional subject in academic high schools within the existing curricular framework for the two final years. The program would be available both in Hungarian and English. This would permit schools the choice of language for teaching either parts or the entirety of the curriculum. Two to six periods (45 minutes) could be assigned to this subject, depending on local schedule. Upon successful completion of the program, students would be provided an American Express diploma, and their grades would also appear in the official final report from the school.

THE STATED AIMS OF THE PROGRAM

The program aims to provide students with an overall picture of the possibilities and major problems of the international travel and tourism business; give students job orientation; increase the students' chances of finding first jobs (if they do not enter tertiary education); and to help Hungarian youth to become clever and quality-oriented customers in tourism.

THE STRUCTURE OF THE PROGRAM

Building on the earlier experience in the United Kingdom, the program would be developed in a modular structure. The whole program would consist of eight (four obligatory and four elective) modules. Obligatory modules would be taught in all participating schools, for all students in the first year of the program. The content of the second year would consist of the elective module(s) chosen by the teachers of individual schools (hopefully together with students). This program design was to maximize flexibility to respond to varying needs of different localities or schools. Each program would be partially individualized through a process that would further involve local teaching staff in the ownership and design of the program. A draft program for the Hungarian Academy is included as Exhibit 5.4.

Both the obligatory and the elective modules would be broken down into smaller elements. The objective was to give maximum curriculum flexibility to teachers. The sequencing of modules described is just one variation; the same content could be substantially rearranged to meet teacher preference or schedule.

The modular design of the program yielded additional benefits. Expensive textbooks subject to rapid obsolescence could be replaced by easily updated packages for each module.

The program should also develop contact between the schools and local tourism-related groups. American Express would develop a network of supporting business partners to help schools in this effort. This close relationship to *local* practice had been identified as a key to success in travel and tourism programs elsewhere.

This network facilitated the identification of summer internships. Such a work experience is central to learning about the actual workings of the tourism businesses while allowing the partners to meet prospective employees.

The Hungarian Project

The exploration of an activity in Hungary was initiated in 1989 by two American Express executives, Ida Schmertz, senior vice president for corporate affairs, and Connie Higginson, vice president, philanthropic program. Their goal was to determine the feasibility of establishing an academy-like structure in Hungary.

Higginson described their methods:

> Within our areas of focus, our approach is entrepreneurial. We see philanthropy as a form of R&D. We take risks, and trust that our successes will outnumber our failures. We constantly look for opportunities to leverage our successes by exporting them from one market to another, nationally and internationally. But we have learned by experience that there is no single simple formula that applies.
>
> There are markets, however, where curriculum content is still nationally controlled and where a travel and tourism-type program, while academic, would be seen as an unacceptable intrusion by business into the schoolroom. We are gratified to see this attitude is beginning to change, especially in Europe. But each opportunity must be assessed as an individual venture.

Their initial contacts with leaders of the tourism-related industries met with little enthusiasm, attributed in part to the general uncertainties in the political and economic situation in Hungary.

Exhibit 5.4. Draft Content for a Travel and Tourism Academy Program.

Obligatory Modules

1. *The structure of travel and tourism industry*
   - The international and Hungarian trends in tourism—analysis of statistical data. Tourism in national economies, its productivity, effects on employment.
   - Tourism and natural environment. The harmful effects of tourism on environment.
   - Nature friendly (green) tourism.
   - Tourism and social environment. The modernization and cultural effects of tourism.
   - The structural characteristics of tourism. Seasonal, active and passive tourism, mass and quality tourism.
   - The elements of tourist attractions. The image of a country's international tourism exhibitions and fairs.
   - Tourist bureaus. Their types, services, relationships. Reservation systems.

2. *The tourist—the user side of the industry*
   - Elements that influence choices of travelers. Political stability of a region. Buying potential, free time, interest, physical status, age, social status, etc.
   - Recreational tourism. Rural tourism, sport tourism, spas.
   - Religious tourism.
   - Health/medical tourism.
   - Business/congress tourism.
   - Incentive tourism.
   - Administrative element of travel. Embassies and consulates, passport and visa, customs, health regulations.
   - Insurance companies, forms of insurances.
   - Money management. Currencies, banks, accounts, convertibility, exchange rates.
   - Travelers cheques, plastics.

3. *Travel, accommodation, and board*
   - Air traffic. Services of airlines, tickets. Schedule. Operation of airports. Security measures.
   - Railways. International networks (Intercity, Eurocity). International tickets, passes. Schedules.
   - Ships and ferries. Seas, lakes, and rivers.
   - Hotels and hotel chains. Categories and services. Hotel operations.
   - Club hotels.
   - Campings and camping chains.
   - Youth hostels.
   - Private accommodation.

- Restaurants serving differentiated needs: fast-food chains, national restaurants, exclusive restaurants.

4. *Program organization*

- Needs and customs of various groups of tourists.
- Offerings of leisure centers and leisure parks.
- Expos, festivals, sports programs.
- Special experiences during traveling famous natural and cultural sites.
- Different offerings of casinos, clubs.
- The techniques of organizing programs.
- Information resources used for planning (journals, handbooks, maps, etc.).
- The souvenir business.

Optional Modules

1. *Tourism and environment*

- Facilities of tourism industry in the natural environment. Good and bad solutions.
- Relationships between tourists and local citizens in some specific tourist target areas. Possibilities of coordinating interests.
- Short- and long-range development strategies in tourism. Return time of environmentally friendly investments in tourism.
- Possible solutions to solve the contradictions between infrastructure investments and the seasonal nature of tourism.
- Small steps, new approach in developing an environmentally friendly tourism industry.
- The need for a clean, healthy, and untouched nature among certain groups of tourists.
- Possible ways of extending tourism to environmentally protected areas.
- Coordination of interests in tourism and environmental protection.

2. *Private enterprise in tourism*

- Forms of ownership in enterprises within the tourism industry.
- The investment need of different enterprises, the return rate and conditions of investments.
- Successful and unsuccessful enterprises. Hungarian and foreign case studies.
- Possible cooperative forms.
- The road from the idea to realization. Planning of the process.
- Legal framework of tourist enterprises, taxation.
- The optimal rate of growth—the pitfalls of too fast and too slow growth.
- From a one-man enterprise to an organization. The relationship of owners and employees. Loyalty. Organizational problems.
- Introducing the firm on the market. Planning the company image. Advertisement.

3. *Customer-oriented tourism*
  - Exploring the customer needs and satisfying those with services.
  - Customer-oriented company philosophies.
  - Customer-oriented behavior in direct human communication in the service industry.
  - The world of design in travel and tourism. Objects serving the customer.
  - The yields of reliability and stability of values for the owner. The direct and indirect losses resulting from insufficient quality of service.
  - The behavioral characteristics of the "smart" consumer.

4. *Advertisement and marketing in the tourism industry*
  - Complex exploration of possibilities offered by specific sites or regions. Targeting the potential group of customers.
  - Outlining the offerings for a specific group of customers.
  - The structure and mechanisms of the effective advertisement.
  - Printed, audio-visual, and other means of advertisement. Production from design to distribution.
  - The characteristics of the successful advertisement in travel and tourism methods used, time and timing, costs and return.

On this occasion, they also established contact with Attila Horvath of the governmental Center for School Development. His name had been suggested by a number of educators in the United States and Western Europe as a likely contact in Hungary. Horvath's spoken English was excellent and far better than that of other individuals encountered in the government education ministry—a consequence of his unique exposure through attendance at a variety of conferences outside Hungary. The resulting network of educators around the world created financing and further opportunities for foreign travel at a time when such movement was greatly restricted by the government. One interviewee noted, "Horvath's political connections were also instrumental in achieving the access to the West. Invitations alone were not enough to create travel opportunities in those days." While little progress was achieved in these early visits, Horvath emerged as a potential partner if American Express pursued the initiative.

Little further development occurred until 1991, when contacts were reestablished, and new energy was brought to the project by the foundation representatives. This new energy coincided with the designation of Peter Kraft, a Hungarian American, as the developer and future general manager of an American Express subsidiary in Hungary. Kraft noted the opportunity that a "philanthropic effort would have for the introduction and establishment of an American Express business in Hungary."

The idea of an Academy of Travel and Tourism was taken from the successful use of that idea in other European countries. In Hungary, the program was to include the design of curriculum concerning the economics and functioning of the travel industry, as well as a general orientation to the role of service. This would be integrated as a module in public school education. The initial grant was for the design of the curriculum, training of teachers, and the implementation of an experiment in three schools.

THE ADVISORY BOARD

An advisory board was constituted for the Fund for Central/Eastern Europe, a pool of funds to support American Express's philanthropic efforts in the region. Membership included the following.

In the United States: Tomasso Zanzotto, president, American Express Travel Related Services International; Colin Campbell, president, Rockefeller Brothers Fund; Frank Loy, president, German Marshall Fund; Marilyn Perry, president, Kress Foundation.

In Europe: Jurgen Aumueller, president, Europe/Africa/Middle East, American Express International; Adrian von Doernberg, board of management, Lufthansa; John Richardson, president, European Foundation Center.

The American Express staff: Ida Schmertz, senior vice president, corporate affairs; Connie Higginson, vice president, philanthropic programs.

The board brought together prestigious individuals from industry and the "charity" sector with the leadership of the American Express business in the United States and Europe. The first meeting of the U.S. members was held in November 1991. The European group met later after the program design had been established. No country-level management had attended these meetings.

Minutes of the meetings reflected a consensus of support for the recommendations of philanthropic program staff to launch the academy program as the initial activity in Hungary. Other activities were presented for the two other Eastern European countries and were accepted. One observer from American Express noted, "The meetings provide an opportunity for extending the network of key American Express executives. It serves to reinforce their commitment to philanthropic activities and may have immediate payoff in terms of other 'agenda' in relationships with key business and community leaders."

Statements from both American and European board members stressed the "philanthropic" nature of the activity. "Tourism continues to be a major source of jobs and hard currencies for Hungary as the country continues to reshape its economy," said Jurgen Aumueller. "American Express is a partner in helping turn the enormous potential to attract foreign visitors into strong revenue-generating industries. This is why we also work hard through the foundation to develop innovative programs that educate young people about careers in the tourism industry and help enhance customer service."

Connie Higginson emerged as the project director for creating the academy activities in Hungary. Her role as the vice president for the international activities of the American Express Foundation and her experience in establishing past programs made her the obvious and assumed leader. Her past investigations of prospective partners for the development of curriculum became the basis for the next steps of exploration.

FINDING A PARTNER

Higginson needed a Hungarian partner to prepare the necessary curriculum and pedagogical materials. Building upon her earlier contacts, she reestablished the dialogue with Attila Horvath. In the interim, he had become the director of the Foundation for School Development, a private consulting group consisting of three individuals from the government's Center for School Development. While the Center is a government agency for the creation of curriculum and pedagogical development, it paid low, government-level wages. A leader in the tourism industry also noted that:

> The government still has a legacy of bureaucracy. They move slowly and don't get much done. There is also some tension around who was a party member and who was not. It's not discussed, but it is there. This combines to make any innovation quite difficult when it concerns certain parts of the government. To the contrary, certain new ministers are fighting for the changes, but I'm not sure what luck they are having.

The "nonprofit foundation" was created to circumvent these issues by providing an alternative setting with an additional source of income to this group of younger professionals who wished to benefit from the opportunities for entrepreneurship in the new Hungarian economy.

As Horvath later recalled:

The Academy program is a unique opportunity for pedagogical innovation. This will both benefit the students in their general education and provide potential job opportunities.

I try to keep Peter Kraft informed, but my contact is with Connie and the American Express Foundation in New York. That's where the money comes from. Perhaps they want me to limit contact with the business here for tax reasons.

We needed a vehicle to supplement income outside the governmental structure. The academy provided funds to launch our consulting group and represents a model to allow us to benefit personally from the new economy. We have effectively avoided the government hierarchy through the Foundation and avoided any critique through the "philanthropic" character of the Academy project.

Through Attila Horvath, three pilot schools were enlisted in the project: in Budapest (Szilagyi Erzebet High School); in the countryside towns of Derecske (I. Rakoczi Gyorgy High School); and in Miskole (Avasi High School). The early involvement of the teachers from these schools was viewed as a key factor for the success of the program. Horvath noted:

With all of the changes taking place in Hungary, little attention has been given to restructuring the school curricula to reflect the new realities. The teachers, in particular, have received very little benefit. They greatly appreciate the program, as they would any serious attention to them and the development of their pedagogy and personal skills. The contact with local tourism businesses also gives them some benefits.

Parallel to the curriculum development and building an educational network, Peter Kraft arrived in Hungary from his previous posting as director of Travel Management Services for the Latin American and Caribbean regions. (This is basically the corporate credit card and business travel unit of American Express.) Kraft had risen quickly through the ranks of the American Express organization and was considered "one of the stars of Travel Related Services—a self-starter who always gets results quickly." He accepted the position of general manager, American Express, Hungary in March 1991 with the stated challenge "to develop a business quickly in a country where neither he nor the business had a network of contacts." His assets were his managerial experience in the United States and Latin America and some knowledge of the Hungarian language from his childhood in a family with a Hungarian background. Kraft said:

I accepted the job as an opportunity to help Hungary. Due to my ancestry, it seemed a worthwhile effort and leading the American

Express subsidiary in Hungary created a good opportunity to both develop business of the corporation and contribute to Hungary.

About 40,000 of AmEx's 37 million card holders visited Hungary last year. An AmEx-card tourist spends about $330 daily abroad, visitors to Hungary spend only a fraction of that. The challenge is to bring to Hungary more tourists who spend more money. Both AmEx and the Hungarian tourist industry will grow together if we can achieve this.

WINNING PROGRAM SUPPORT

While Higginson managed the development of the curriculum materials and the contacts with the educational establishment, Kraft launched an energetic campaign to solicit support from leaders of tourism-related industries and the relevant government ministries. His efforts were to enlist "business partners" who would cosponsor the program and provide summer internships for academy participants. These were two essential ingredients of the academy formula and foundation philosophy.

Kraft had little involvement in the design of the academy program itself. Some attributed this to a division of roles; others, to a difference in style between Kraft and Horvath that caused sparks to fly when they were together. Since their tasks and goals were not significantly interdependent, the project proceeded well without extensive interaction between Horvath and Kraft. However, Kraft noted:

> The Academy provided an ideal opportunity to meet people, to get to the minister of Industry and Trade and the offices of all business leaders in Hungary. It would have taken me years to make the contacts that I made in three months through this program. Now our business is in rapid expansion. I have little to do with the Academy effort.
>
> The opening will bring together everyone who is significant in Hungarian business. This will be the finishing touch to put American Express on the Hungarian business map.
>
> James D. Robinson, III, is visiting Budapest. He will meet every political and business leader in a two-day visit. The Academy certainly helped build the network for creating this schedule.

An early supporter was Andras Rubovsky, the president of the Hungarian Hotel Association and CEO of the Hotel Gellért. This government hotel, the site of world-famous therapeutic baths, is probably the best known hotel in Hungary. The Gellért's elegance has faded over time. Newer hotels managed and partially financed by international chains providing better location and modern convenience have become the stopping places for business leaders. Yet, the Gellert and its baths still remained prominent for Hungarians and those seeking a "classic" hotel. As with other major hotels, it was being considered for privatization and substantial renewal in the new economy.

Rubovsky had been trained as a lawyer but worked his way to the top managerial position in the hotel by moving through an apprenticeship as banquet manager, rooms manager, and eventually hotel operations chief. He achieved the top role following the demise of the Communist government.

In 1992, Rubovsky had just begun his tenure at the helm of the hotel association, a group that included 236 of the 370 hotels in Hungary. The association is the oldest hotel group in Europe and was the first socialist representative to the International Hotel Association. Commented Rubovsky:

> This is an excellent initiative for Hungary and its economic development. It provides an awareness of the potential for tourism as a major contributor to the economy and the trade balance. It would never have occurred without Peter Kraft and the American Express group. His enthusiasm and charisma generated the support because people were skeptical at first. They thought it was only a business deal.
>
> The Hungarian travel and tourism industry welcomes this pioneering joint venture between the public education sector and private business initiative. Both the philanthropic and financial support of American Express have enabled us to launch this strategic alliance, which will enhance the industry's international competitiveness and add to the attractiveness of Hungary as a tourist destination.
>
> American Express subsidizes the program, but they will benefit. This program trains the children to be tourists themselves. Hungarians don't have much experience with hotels and travel because of the past government. People were not allowed to travel. Visas were not available. People don't know how to get tickets or how to book a hotel. This is really creating customers for the industry as much or more than creating employment.
>
> The major challenge for the Hotel Association has been to produce programs that would benefit its members and build the allegiance to the association. The Travel and Tourism Academy is a basis for increasing membership and focusing energy on a task of common significance. Few would have been interested if they had to put up some money. So I have benefited by the growth of the Hotel Association.
>
> I could never have had this position in the old government because I refused to join the party. Since Hungary has not executed the party members as they have in Romania and other countries, I need allies to be able to build my role in Hungary. American Express and the

Academy have given me that opportunity to be legitimate and build a big network.

Kazmar Kardos was the president of the National Tourism Association, the governmental agency responsible for tourism in Hungary under the minister of Trade and Industry. The post is the equivalent of a senior civil service appointment, and appointment was supposed to be based on professional and technical expertise rather than political affiliation. Kardos had served as a director of a number of hotels prior to taking this position. He emerged as an important supporter to Peter Kraft in the development of a network. Kardos noted:

> The Academy is a prototype for the cooperation of private industry and government. American Express is taking the lead in promoting tourism in Hungary, creating the interest for jobs in this sector, and raising the possibility of travel for our citizens. Peter Kraft has enabled much of this to happen with his personal energy and capability.
>
> Tourism has never gotten the attention it deserves. Overall, it represents as much as 8–10 percent of the GNP of the country depending on how you add the figures, employing about 500,000 people.
>
> Their efforts are particularly welcome as they are financing development that I cannot afford in my budget. The real problem is that the Ministry of Industry and Trade has limited interest in my issues. I would like to be a separate ministry at some point. In the interim, it is useful to have the support of a powerful multinational company in dealing with my own government. In return, I can help American Express as they establish their business here. For example, they do not yet have the authorization to issue credit cards as Visa and MasterCard do. They will need some support to get that permission.

Ehrlich Da V. Lobo was the marketing manager for Delta Airlines in Hungary and the head of Delta's Budapest office operations. He was an early supporter of the academy and committed Delta to a role of "partner."

The Delta presence was the vestige of a longstanding Pan Am service to Budapest, which was obtained by Delta in the resolution of the Pan Am bankruptcy. Lobo had worked with Pan Am around the world, including assignments in Africa, Middle East, Europe, and the United States. He expressed frustration at the slow development of his own airline in Hungary, as well as their lack of understanding of these "developing markets." According to Lobo:

> The Academy has created an interesting network of people operating in the Hungarian tourist market. I enjoyed the meetings, particularly when they were more frequent at the beginning. It is difficult to move

into Hungary, and the Academy initiative coincided with my arrival. We are planning to provide a number of internships if students are interested.

Similar comments were obtained from other airlines and hotel groups operating in Hungary. The launch of the Academy appeared to provide a substantial contribution to the development of the Hungarian tourism industry, while providing benefit to the international organizations operating in this market and the individuals who managed the local units.

In return, business groups provided training opportunities, donated services, and assumed part of the financial costs of further developing the program. Thus, the initial effort and investment of the American Express Foundation was substantially leveraged by the contributions of other organizations. This support extended the opportunity beyond the resources of the American Express Foundation and its local operations, while promising a basis for continuing the program beyond the three years initially funded. A contribution equivalent to $20,000 by the Hungarian Tourism Board also indicated the successful integration into the existing tourism structure in the country.

On January 28, 1992, Budapest newspapers reported, *"Tourism is a Vital Source of Jobs and Hard Currency in Czechoslovakia, Hungary, and Poland.* American Express, together with more than 20 Hungarian and international business partners, announced today the 'Travel and Tourism Program.' The program is designed to strengthen the Hungarian tourism industry and to introduce young people and others to careers in travel and tourism. The program has been made possible by the American Express Fund for Central and Eastern Europe which is part of the American Express Foundation." The full report is contained in Exhibit 5.5.

CONCLUSION

Discussions with the people involved in the Hungarian program yielded a curious combination of self-interested behavior with socially and organizationally desirable outcomes. The American Express Foundation's funding mobilized a network of interested participants to achieve the goals of the program. American Express was able to effectively implement its philanthropic goals through this network. They have been equally successful in achieving business goals using citizenship as a vehicle.

The dual goals of citizenship are clearly recognized by key individuals directing the philanthropy program:

Exhibit 5.5.   Afterword.

Tourism Is a Vital Source of Jobs and Hard Currency in Czechoslovakia, Hungary, and Poland

Budapest, January 28, 1992—American Express, together with more than 20 Hungarian and International business partners, announced today the "Travel and Tourism Program." Developed by the Budapest-based IFA Institute, the Program is designed to strengthen the Hungarian tourism industry and to introduce young people and others to careers in travel and tourism. The Program has been made possible by the American Express Fund for Central and Eastern Europe which is part of the American Express Foundation.

The business partners include MAHART, Ibusz, Hotel Forum, the Hungarian Tourism Board, the Hungarian Hotel Association, Hotel Korona, Atrium Hyatt, Hotel Gellért, Delta Airlines, Taverna Rt., Lufthansa, Kereskedelmi Bank Rt., Budapest Tourist, OTP-Penta-Tours, Hungarian Chamber of Tourism, Café Gerbeaud, Hungarian Travel Agencies Association, Tourism Agencies Association, Hungarotours, Trade and Touristic Retrainer Company, Association of Village Farm Houses, College of Commerce and Hospitality among others.

Night-Time Explosion Damages Amex Bank Office in Athens: Incident Reported in Mexico City. No Injuries Occur.

Athens, Greece—The American Express head office here was damaged at approximately 1:30 A.M. on Monday, January 28, by an explosive device launched from an adjacent building. There were no injuries from the blast, but windows in the street-level office were broken and air ducts for heating and ventilation were damaged. No records or documents were destroyed.

The explosive device was timed to hit while the office was closed.

No one has really measured the effect of philanthropic efforts on the business. But, we do like to think that it helps the business in addition to simply "doing good."

We do this because it's the right thing to do. The health of our business and the well-being of society are interdependent. Our record in the community helps attract and retain the best employees, clients, and business partners.

The project was framed as a socially desirable effort to aid the economic development of the Hungarian economy. Thus, American Express has socially defined the nature of philanthropy for the organization. Drawing upon the legal definitions and structures that grant tax benefits to the foundation, philanthropy becomes situationally defined for the organization. The "philanthropy umbrella" is broad enough to shelter a number of different activities.

While each of the participants in the Hungarian Academy of Travel and Tourism accepts the notion of social desirability, they do not share a single value set. Thus, the project emerges equally as a "coalition of value-based action." Each set of individual objectives is validated by association with the socially desirable goal of Hungarian development. The "radiation effect" of philanthropy seems to bless all of the individuals and activities associated with the program.

The efforts of foundation personnel served to bring several disparate parts of Hungarian society into the network, rather than drawing on an existing coalition. The self-selection of network participants results in compatibility of personal interests and the project's goals. Variable levels of commitment are easily accommodated within this loosely structured coalition of partners. American Express through its foundation has normatively legitimated the program as a philanthropic activity. They have finessed the potential conflict between business and personal extracurricular motivations by defining activities that encompass both. Great subtlety and skill are necessary to maintain the balance of interests and achieve multiple goals.

The financial support provided by the foundation attracted the attention of potential participants and serves as a visible signal of American Express's citizenship values and commitment. Financial contributions also appear to have a secondary effect, which increases the value of corporate giving. Philanthropy can assuage the consciences of those who are not personally involved in citizenship activities but who can take pride in the policies and practices of the company. The importance of the good will associated with philanthropic activities is explicitly acknowledged by the American Express Philanthropic Program:

> Our integrity as a corporate citizen was tested last year when we discovered that our own code of conduct had been violated in a matter involving a private banking competitor. We promptly acknowledged the problem, and made a sizable charitable contribution as a gesture of conciliation and good will.

American Express's philanthropically defined academy activities yield identifiable business value to the company and, in this case, to the managers responsible for developing new business in Hungary. While cynics might be tempted to focus upon the self-interests of the participants in academy projects, foundation officials believe that, through these programs, American Express applies its unique corporate competence to citizenship efforts. The travel and tourism sector is one area where American Express philanthropy and skilled employee volunteers can make a significant contribution to economic development and employment.

6

DOING GOOD THE MORGAN WAY

Generating Economic Returns with Investments in Communities

Charles J. Fombrun

Our reputation rests on our ability to be an international leader in terms of both capability and character.

—Dennis Weatherstone, Chairman, J.P. Morgan & Co.

ON JUNE 11, 1992, 40 teachers and principals from two New York City public schools gathered at J.P. Morgan's headquarters to celebrate a major transition. The head of their Professional Development Laboratory (PDL), Mary Anne Walsh, was moving back to New York City's board of education to incorporate the laboratory's experimental program into the city's public school system. PDL had grown out of a private initiative begun in 1988 to improve public education by providing teachers with growth opportunities and peer feedback on teaching methods. J.P. Morgan helped found the program, with representatives from New York's central board of education, the United Federation of Teachers, the Manhattan borough president's office, and the city council president's office. Hildy Simmons, head of community relations and public affairs at Morgan, got the company to provide over $600,000 and mobilized Morgan human resources staff members to run intensive workshops in communication skills. Two city schools were selected as test sites; Morgan volunteers were picked as school liaisons, and groups of visiting teachers went through four-week training in teaching skills outside their classrooms. The PDL pilot program had been successful and would be replicated in other schools.

On July 25, 1992, in Harlem, one of New York's poorest neighborhoods, gourmet ice cream gurus Ben Cohen and Jerry Greenfield grinned proudly as news cameras rolled, music blared, children skipped rope, dancers frolicked, and everyone sampled free ice cream. The occasion was a block party to celebrate the opening of Ben & Jerry's first Partnershop, a revolutionary alliance between the ice cream maker, Harlem entrepreneur Joe Holland, and HARKhomes, a nearby homeless shelter. Joe Holland's idea was to create a viable business in a distressed neighborhood, in order to provide employment opportunities and job training for deprived residents. As Holland described it:

> The challenge is to meld the profit-making goals of a business enterprise with the social mission of HARKhomes and the economic development needs of a courageous comeback community. My greatest hope is that, by setting a sustainable example, we will encourage other companies and organizations to establish similar programs for doing well by doing good.

Oliver Wesson, president of the J.P. Morgan Community Development Corporation, had helped structure the deal and identify lending sources for start-up and operating expenses. In 1992, J.P. Morgan purchased $65,000 in preferred stock in the venture.

These events demonstrated the range of contributions that J.P. Morgan made in New York City, the community with which the company was most closely identified. As a company, J.P. Morgan had always taken corporate citizenship seriously because of an implicit recognition that doing good was good business. J.P. Morgan donated to nonprofit groups, supported local development by investing in community-based projects, and kept a close eye on its institutional mission. This case describes the characteristic ways Morgan implements its citizenship values.

- As a conservative financial institution with a long history of community responsibility, J.P. Morgan combines charitable giving with community investment to provide a balanced portfolio of corporate citizenship activities.

- Legislation requires that banks provide economic support for lower-income communities; for J.P. Morgan this legislative impetus led them to reevaluate how they were investing in their communities.

- J.P. Morgan has been very successful at generating business because of its emphasis on serving the not-for-profit sector as a financial institution as well as a benefactor.

J.P. MORGAN & CO.

Since 1933, J.P. Morgan has operated principally as a wholesale bank, providing banking services and loans to blue-chip corporations, governments, and prominent institutions throughout the world, as well as high net worth individuals. Its clients have been relatively few in number, distinguished not by size but by quality and scope of activity. The need for sophisticated financial services defined the market Morgan serves on a global basis. The company has grown largely by capitalizing on the skills and creativity of its employees.

In 1991, J.P. Morgan's 13,000 employees brought in over $8 billion in revenues. With $93 billion in total assets, the company ranked 70th among *BusinessWeek*'s top 1,000. Earnings rose by 44 percent, and investors bid up the price of the company's stock. Morgan's 1991 market value of $8 billion placed it No. 1 among commercial banks, ahead of Citicorp and BankAmerica.

J.P. Morgan operates as a holding company for a variety of subsidiaries. Its principal subsidiary is the Morgan Guaranty Trust Company, headquartered in New York City. Subsidiaries in London, Paris, Delaware, and Palm Beach are growing as the bank becomes more geographically decentralized. Although the bank has a global presence, it remains strongly committed to New York City. In 1989, Morgan moved into its newly built postmodern headquarters in downtown Manhattan. Over 65 percent of its 13,000 employees worldwide and 80 percent of its U.S. employees are based in New York City.

THE MORGAN WAY

J.P. Morgan is generally characterized as having a fortress mentality: a conservative, relatively low-risk posture in its lending practices; a cautious stance in investing its own portfolio; and a preference for maintaining a low profile in the media. Throughout the 1980s, it was frequently chastised by analysts and competitors for lacking aggressiveness. Morgan made few Third World loans; shied away from high-yield debt financing; and grew steadily, if somewhat unspectacularly. The bank's cautious style, however, proved highly effective, as more aggressive institutions like Citicorp faced the burdens of low-performing loans.

The Morgan culture encourages a broad recognition and interpretation of the company's public role. As one Morgan employee puts it:

> Our chairman has often quite explicitly said that we can't serve our shareholders without also serving other constituencies. There's no question that we have an ultimate legal responsibility to maximize value for the shareholders. But if you don't serve your clients well you can't serve your shareholders well. If you don't serve your people well, you can't serve your clients well. Serving your people well means being effective in the community that they work and live in. You have to think of the linkages to long-term shareholder value across all your stakeholder communities.

J.P. Morgan has a team-oriented culture. The bank recruits the best talent, trains them for specialized skills, and rewards professionalism. In contrast to the individualism stressed in many rival banks, the Morgan culture strongly supports cooperative relationships through team assignments. According to Chairman Dennis Weatherstone:

> Both creativity and common sense flourish when people with diverse points of view get together. We see it vividly working with people of different nationalities, because of our international orientation. We look for diversity of experience right up to the Corporate Office, the senior governing group at Morgan. But, as much as we believe in teams, we equally believe in getting the best and brightest *on* the teams. And we've got to have people who can balance sound principles with competitive drive and brilliance.

Morgan is well regarded for being fair in its dealings with clients, employees, competitors, and other stakeholders. Says one manager:

> We have a reputation for responsibility, international scope, integrity, long-term client-oriented focus, and quality in every possible definition of the word. We are a responsible participant in business finance, in the world monetary system, in communities, and in the way we deal with employees. And we care a lot about that reputation.

CORPORATE CITIZENSHIP AT J.P. MORGAN

The manager continues:

> Our overall philanthropic objective is to improve the quality of life in the communities in which we live and work. We focus our efforts on increasing the capacity of people and organizations to help themselves, and stress long-term solutions to problems rather than short-term remedies. We are often able to supplement and multiply the beneficial effect of our financial contributions in other ways.

At J.P. Morgan, corporate citizenship includes philanthropy, community development, and broad-based social responsibility demonstrated in far-flung projects to bolster global financial markets or sustain the environment. In 1988, upon receiving the Nichols Award at New York University's Graduate School of Business, then chairman Lewis Preston commented on the importance of doing good for both personal and institutional reasons:

> The drive to achieve, the accelerating pace of business life . . . are familiar features of our world. . . . One of their unfortunate effects, however, seems to be a diminished capacity to value and work for the greater good—whether that means pulling together within business enterprise for a common goal, as opposed to individual gain, or making time for service outside of work. I suspect that few people have ever struck an ideal balance between service and enterprise. But aiming for a better balance is a challenge we face as a civilized society.

The bank's senior executives exhort employees to get involved in their communities. A June 1992 memo from Sandy Warner, J.P. Morgan's president, reminded employees about the merits of corporate giving:

> A commitment to community responsibility and involvement is part of our institutional heritage; a similar personal commitment on the part of many of our people is one of the things that makes Morgan special. We support that personal generosity through the Matching Gifts Program. I salute those of you who have participated in this program in the past and urge everyone to consider taking advantage of it. It's a great way to make a difference and put Morgan's resources to work for the organization of your choice.

Corporate citizenship is rooted firmly in the tradition of "noblesse oblige" of the Morgan family. Laura Dillon, managing director of corporate communications, points out that:

There's a connection between quality, sense of responsibility, and doing the right thing. There are synergies between the values that have grown up in the business and what people do in their own lives, which come together in a sense of responsibility to the community.

Hildy Simmons, Morgan's patron of community development, adds, "We don't just write a check, however. We seek long-term solutions."

The Legislative Imperative

In 1977, the U.S. Congress passed the Community Reinvestment Act (CRA) in an effort to encourage banks to lend more to the poor and to minorities in areas in which they take deposits. J.P. Morgan was chartered as a commercial bank. This meant that, although it does not operate retail branches or make mortgage loans, it has to comply with the CRA, which requires financial institutions to abide by a specific set of regulations and to adhere to a broad mandate to look at lower-income neighborhoods as potentially profitable markets.

The Financial Institutions Reform, Recovery, and Enforcement Act of 1989 toughened the laws. Since July 1990, all regulated financial institutions subject to the CRA are monitored and assessed by examiners who visit the banks every 18 months and publish their assessment of performance in five categories. The categories are: ascertainment of community credit needs, marketing and types of credit offered and extended, geographic distribution and record of opening and closing offices, discrimination and other illegal credit practices, and community development.

Every 18 months, government evaluators visit J.P. Morgan and review the bank's compliance with CRA requirements. In its latest performance review, J.P. Morgan was assessed as having a "satisfactory record of ascertaining and helping to meet the needs of its entire delineated community in a manner consistent with its resources and capabilities. . . . Morgan has been able to establish a good working relationship with government and private sector representatives and to identify opportunities for becoming involved in community development lending programs." One manager notes that, in response to the CRA requirements:

> We're spending money differently, because the CRA has made us rethink how we could use our money. A lot of good has come from it. Would we have done all of this without CRA? Probably not, but I don't think a cynical view is warranted. It's not like we were doing nothing, and then suddenly everything. People like to see that Morgan is doing something responsible. We want to be effective in ways that build on our strengths. People feel good about it.

Citizenship Structure

Corporate citizenship at J.P. Morgan is carried out by two principal groups: the Department of Community Relations and Public Affairs (CRPA) and the Morgan Community Development Corporation (MCDC). Together, CRPA and MCDC work to fulfill the CRA mandate. Close contact is maintained with Chairman Dennis Weatherstone's corporate office. CRPA reports to the head of the legal/corporate staff group, who in turn reports directly to the CEO. As a separate corporation, MCDC is supervised by its own board of directors, whose president reports to the corporate office. MCDC is the principal way the bank formally demonstrates its fulfillment of CRA requirements to regulatory inspectors.

Citizenship activities of J.P. Morgan are coordinated by two interlocked committees. The advisory committee oversees charitable giving, while the CRA committee monitors community investments. The advisory committee to the charitable trust consists of the chairman, president, and three vice chairmen. According to Hildy Simmons:

> The advisory committee sets the tone for what we do, and makes the decision every year about how much we will give away. It's also a corporate decision whether to put money into the charitable trust, depending on earnings. Their input is crucial in terms of determining the pool of funds, and what we're going to do. They have a macro role.

Oliver Wesson, MCDC's president since 1990, explains the CRA committee's relationship to the Community Development Corporation:

> We generally go to them and say this is what we want to accomplish this year. For instance, we want to deal with entrepreneurs who want to open up businesses in Harlem and Bedford-Stuyvesant. We'd like to see $300,000–400,000 equity investments made in these firms, and we'd like to grow the assets by such and such an amount. We ask them if this makes sense for Morgan as a whole. After they give us their input and stamp of approval, we implement it through our own board.

Jack Ruffle, the head of Morgan's CRA committee, points out that the ground rules for success in community development require searching for committed individuals who will stay with a project:

> Successful community effort occurs only when the people themselves feel some kind of ownership in the process, and when we can encour-

age that, we can have an impact. The trick for us is to figure out how to do it intelligently and within our means. Again, it's consistent with the idea of adding value—just as we do for all clients.

J.P. Morgan formally demonstrates its corporate citizenship through a portfolio of activities that include charitable grant making, community development, volunteerism, networking, and communications. Through volunteer activities and board memberships, bank employees are networked into nonprofit organizations in the New York area.

Making Charitable Grants

Charitable contributions made by J.P. Morgan & Co. are channeled through the Morgan Guaranty Trust Company of NY Charitable Trust, which was established in 1961. Charitable grants are made by the CRPA department, staffed by five administrators and led by vice president Hildy Simmons. Grant-making decisions are made through team reviews by members of the CRPA staff of over 1,500 proposals received annually. Funding decisions for nonprofit groups are made by a contributions committee within the CRPA. Grants of $20,000 or less are decided at the contributions committee level. Grants of over $20,000 require approval of the general counsel and the chairperson of the bank's credit policy committee. Hildy Simmons explains the process:

> Other people get involved by suggesting organizations that ought to apply, or championing the cause of organizations that they are personally involved in. We set broad issues and goals. The task of this department historically has been to define the strategies we pursue and to fine-tune them every year.

Increasing geographic diversification encourages the decentralization of corporate giving in local communities. For instance, the bank's subsidiary in Delaware is becoming more active as the subsidiary grows in size; they have their own local contributions committee. No one there, however, is paid to do contributions work on a full-time basis. The CRPA in New York provides technical assistance on alternative approaches and strategies.

Decentralization means that subsidiaries set their own budgets. The $10 million annual grant-making budget of J.P. Morgan incorporates subsidiary contributions internationally. Historically, most subsidiaries set their budgets based on profitability. As Morgan grows more complex and diverse, profits are no longer counted in the same way, because the business units interact in different ways, and profits are difficult to identify narrowly within subsidiaries. Increasingly, subsidiaries set budgets based on the local management committee's views. They reflect a combination of history, community need, peers in the immediate community, and the gut feeling of local senior management, rather than precise formulas. "There's no real science to it," argues Hildy Simmons. "Nobody has ever been inclined to set a percent. They don't like formulas for those kinds of things."

J.P. Morgan makes charitable contributions consisting of grants, matching gifts, and volunteer funds. The CRPA in New York distributes 78 percent of the grant-making budget. The remaining 22 percent is given locally by subsidiaries located principally in London, Paris, and Delaware. The CRPA allocates its $6–7 million annual budget to nonprofit programs and projects of its choice. In 1991, funds were allocated to organizations involved in six principal areas: arts, education, health care, international affairs, urban affairs, and environmental issues.

Consistent with the needs of New York City, the largest number of grants are given to nonprofit groups involved in urban affairs, the arts, and education. Among the recipients of the largest grants made in 1991 were the N.Y. Downtown Hospital ($330,000), the Fund for Public Schools ($200,000), Lincoln Center for the Performing Arts ($100,000), and Educators for Social Responsibility ($100,000).

Assistance to Public Schools

Education receives a disproportionate share of Morgan's charitable grants. The Professional Development Program (PDL) received an extensive commitment from J.P. Morgan in terms of financial resources and involvement of Morgan employees. The program was launched in 1989 as a public/private collaboration with the goal of sharing skills that characterize excellent teaching practice across the public school system. In two different New York school districts, teachers volunteered for PDL "sabbaticals" of three to four weeks, which they spent in the classrooms of outstanding teachers. They observed their coaches in action, consulted with them, and practiced new skills in the classroom. Adjunct teachers were hired to replace teachers involved in PDL training.

The PDL program brought together Morgan's CRPA department, representatives of the Central Board of Education, the United Federation of Teachers, the Manhattan borough president's office, and the city council president's office. Morgan contributed $200,000 in the first year, and renewed its commitment for the second and third years. Morgan did considerably more than provide funding for the program. Morgan's human resources department played a key role throughout the program in helping to design an interviewing process to select the project coordinator and other project staff. The training department sponsored sessions in presentation, facilitation, and communication skills.

The human resource department also assisted in designing an outcome-based evaluation system for teachers. Morgan liaisons worked with teachers to design goal-oriented action-plan workbooks that encouraged individual accountability, and facilitated designing new performance appraisals that are now being used with teachers.

Another important resource that Morgan provided for PDL was the ability to network with relevant audiences. For instance, the adjunct teachers hired to substitute for those undergoing PDL training were hired from the financial services industry. Morgan invited representatives of the employment agencies they used to a luncheon, and the project hired a number of business people as adjunct teachers. Morgan also hosted luncheons for teachers and Morgan staff to share professional experiences. As a result, teachers from different schools formed networks to continue the process of professional development.

Two years after PDL was introduced, over 100 teachers had participated, and 5,000 students had been exposed to the program's results. Extensive evaluation indicated that PDL produced impressive results. Teachers had mastered more effective teaching strategies, and they learned to collaborate with peers. They also reported feeling increased confidence in themselves as professionals and closer rapport with students.

According to Mary Anne Walsh, the PDL project coordinator:

> A major reason PDL proved so successful was that, throughout the program, it never was Morgan doing for us, it always was Morgan doing with us—a really successful collaboration.

In mid-1992, with the program widely perceived as a success, PDL and its project coordinator moved under the umbrella of the Central Board of Education of New York's public school system.

Community Development Activities

The Bank Holding Company Act of 1970 allows bank holding companies to engage in activities that were not permissible for banks, including community development. It encourages the realization that a bank can make equity investments in community development projects that promote social welfare. Morgan's projects result from the company's commitment to helping low- and moderate-income neighborhoods improve. As MCDC's President Oliver Wesson points out:

> Bank holding companies started doing research on community development. At the same time, a housing act was passed that provided federally insured mortgages. People who knew something about real estate said, hey, this is a nice bet. We can set up a community development corporation, invest in real estate projects around the country, and be involved in building low-income housing, something that one would not identify with J.P. Morgan.

In 1971, J.P. Morgan became the first bank holding company in the United States to create a community development corporation. The subsidiary grew out of a Morgan study that suggested there was no necessary contradiction between making money and being a good citizen. Formed with initial capital of $1 million, the subsidiary's mission was to make equity investments in government-assisted housing for families with low and moderate incomes.

When the 1970 Bank Holding Act program was terminated a few years later, Morgan diverted resources from MCDC into public finance, and the subsidiary lay dormant for about ten years. It had a brief spurt of activity between 1977 and 1989 following passage of the CRA. Oliver Wesson points out:

> Some loans were made in community development during those years, but nothing really exciting. As the laws got tougher in 1989, the focus shifted to how we could become more responsive to the legislation but still do things in a Morgan-like way. It was decided that the focus should be to work with not-for-profits to get money out to the community. As a wholesale bank we don't have branches, but through the not-for-profits we could meet the community, find out what its needs were, and deliver products.

Since 1990, MCDC has provided debt and equity financing for community initiatives that improve New York City. It makes loans and investments for the construction or rehabilitation of low- and moderate-income housing, community enterprises and facilities, and related social services. Unlike CRPA, whose activities are heavily grounded in charitable donations, in MCDC the focus is on returns. "I don't believe in giving away money," says Oliver Wesson. "We're not a charity."

In addition to providing financial support, MCDC helps to promote community development by working in partnership with organizations that sponsored local projects. Morgan's financial resources, analytical skills, and expertise help MCDC turn community initiatives into reality.

According to Jack Ruffle, chairman of the CRA committee that over-sees MCDC's activities:

> Because we're not a retail institution with branches in those communi-ties, we find other viable alternatives, such as providing $250,000 in seed capital for the Community Capital Bank in Brooklyn, or lending $300,000 at below-market rates to the National Federation of Community Development Credit Unions, an umbrella organization for nonprofit, community-based credit unions that help provide capital and basic financial services in poor neighborhoods.

MCDC operates as a three-person corporation, distinct from its parent company, J.P. Morgan, with proprietary assets of some $25 million. Over the years, the subsidiary has leveraged those assets and made more than $60 million in loans, investments, and commitments to finance commu-nity development ventures. In addition to financial advice, MCDC draws on other Morgan departments for *pro bono* support, particularly the legal department, the corporate trust department, and CRPA.

Rather than fund programs directly, MCDC makes loans to intermedi-aries with more intimate knowledge of the local area and the skills needed to deliver and monitor programs. For instance, through MCDC Morgan pledged $10 million to the New York Equity Fund, a limited partnership jointly funded by Morgan, Banker's Trust, and Republic National Bank. The purpose of the Equity Fund is to revitalize neighborhoods by financ-ing rehabilitation and providing low-cost housing. "The Equity Fund's commitment to New York City," says Ruffle, "goes well beyond bricks and mortar, and reaches into the community."

An example of the kind of venture support MCDC favors is the Ben & Jerry's Partnershop in Harlem. In 1990, Joe Holland, a New York entre-preneur, approached MCDC. He wanted to open a Ben & Jerry's fran-chise in Harlem next to the homeless shelter he operated there. Ben & Jerry's was interested in donating a franchise near 125th Street. Holland presented MCDC with his projections. MCDC knew that the state Urban Development Corporation (UDC) provided low-cost capital to minorities and franchise businesses. But they would only leverage equity, so MCDC provided $65,000 as an equity investment. Holland was able to get a $100,000 loan from the UDC, and the Community Capital Bank (which Morgan funded) gave him a construction loan.

On July 25, 1992, Holland opened the Ben & Jerry's Partnershop to a barrage of local publicity. Although present, Oliver Wesson adhered to Mor-gan's traditional low profile, avoiding press interviews. J.P. Morgan was not mentioned in the press releases distributed to reporters and officials.

Communications

Morgan employees are inclined to be very low-key and reserved in dealing with the public. "That stance suits our institutional character, with its stress on discretion and seriousness of purpose," says Jack Morris, head of public relations in the corporate communications department. Public reticence carries over from the business side to how the bank publicized its community development efforts. As Laura Dillon, Morgan's managing director of communications, explains:

> I think we haven't communicated our efforts quite as aggressively as we could have. It's part of a natural reticence about blowing one's own horn about doing good things. We've built relationships in the community the way we deal with clients, building on a corporate tradition of privacy, without much fanfare. We approach it the same way we approach other things, which is not to broadcast or say that we're doing it better than other people. We want to get our fair share, but we don't want to overstate.

Morgan relies on internal brochures to communicate both with employees and outside publics. Internally, these communications help to build a common bond among employees. Laura Dillon adds:

> Once an organization gets to be as large as ours, you have to communicate what the organization does so that people who work for you identify with your approach. So part of our communication efforts are focused internally to help people understand what the company does to be responsible in the community.

The principal newsletter circulated throughout the bank, the monthly *MorganNews,* announces ongoing events and activities, including requests for volunteers. In 1990, the CRPA launched a specialized biannual publication called "Capital Ideas: How J.P. Morgan Invests to Strengthen the Community." Each newsletter focuses on particular grant recipients and describes their progress. It is distributed to all of Morgan's U.S. employees, community groups, and interested government officials.

Externally, these brochures help the bank fulfill the CRA regulation that required publication of activities. Other brochures describe Morgan's citizenship activities. One entitled "Community Development Initiatives" explains the credit and investment products of MCDC and the grants provided by CRPA. It is widely distributed to Morgan employees, not-for-profit community groups, and public and elected officials in New York City.

The Rewards of Citizenship

Morgan employees are proud of their community involvement and corporate citizenship. Morgan is often thanked by politicians, educators, hospital administrators, artists, and community organizers. In July 1991, a multicolored quilt was presented to J.P. Morgan at a reception that marked the end of the first full year of the Professional Development Laboratory School—the teacher training program J.P. Morgan assisted. The quilt was sewn by appreciative students and teachers of elementary schools in the two districts in Manhattan where the program was piloted. The teachers were so enthusiastic about the program that they wanted to give something back to J.P. Morgan. The quilt hangs in a prominent place at Morgan headquarters, where employees pass every day for lunch. It is a constant reminder, symbolic of Morgan's good works.

Capitalizing on Good Will: Opening New Territory for Citizenship

A pervasive belief among Morgan employees is that corporate citizenship, as one employee puts it, "is not merely a charitable act, but is a form of enlightened self-interest." The convergence of good will and good business is manifested in the bank's efforts to extend its business into the not-for-profit domain. By marketing its services to nonprofit groups, Morgan can capitalize on a heretofore untapped source of potential synergy between its line activities and its good-will-generating citizenship efforts.

In August 1990, Morgan underwrote $54 million in tax-exempt bonds for the renovation of the Guggenheim Museum in New York. Coming after a similar $20 million tax-exempt financing for the new headquarters of the National Audubon Society, it pointed to Morgan's entry into a new and promising line of business: the financing of not-for-profit companies. The Not-for-Profit group (NFP) was formally constituted in early 1991 to assist in marketing Morgan's asset and liability management services to not-for-profit groups such as foundations, health care institutions, and educational, environmental, religious, and cultural organizations. According to Sandy Smith, NFP's manager:

> The purpose of the NFP group is to enhance the efforts of several parts of the firm that have significant relationships with not-for-profit organizations, such as Private Banking, Public Finance, and Community Relations.

The NFP group's explicit strategy is to identify the not-for-profit clients served by various Morgan business groups, determine which products and services those clients used, and expand these relationships into new areas.

The group also identifies key prospects and develops new client relationships with them.

Through the NFP group, not-for-profit organizations gain access to the same broad range of Morgan financial products and services available to major corporations, governments, and wealthy individuals. The NFP group develops financial plans for not-for-profit organizations and their donors. Through Morgan's Fiduciary Services group, the bank helps wealthy individuals identify philanthropic objectives, establish appropriate legal and accounting structures for charitable trusts and foundations, and make long-term commitments of assets. Morgan acts as the trustee or investment adviser for charitable accounts totaling over $3.1 billion.

In May 1992, the NFP group sponsored a seminar entitled "Philanthropy and the Family." Some 60 clients and wealthy prospects came to hear experts in philanthropy, including CRPA chief Hildy Simmons, outline strategies for effective giving. The NFP group has also tried to generate marketing contacts within Morgan itself. Employees who participate as volunteers in the management of not-for-profit organizations are encouraged to contact NFP if their group could benefit from Morgan's services. Sandy Smith describes these efforts as:

> Nothing fancy, just basic relationship management. We want to make the organization as seamless as possible to clients so that we can capitalize on business opportunities that otherwise might fall through the cracks.

This is doing good, the Morgan way.

CONCLUSION

In the tradition of its founders, J.P. Morgan demonstrates strong institutional and social responsibility—donating money and technical expertise to nonprofit organizations, supporting local development by investing in community projects, and working as a leader within the banking industry to protect the world monetary system. Corporate citizenship is rooted firmly in the tradition of noblesse oblige that grew up in the Morgan family. The company uses its core competencies in the delivery of financial services to both promote community improvement and develop new business opportunities.

Citizenship and community involvement is also mandated and legitimated by legislation that requires banks to be more responsive to all of the communities where they take deposits. Though Morgan does not operate retail branches or make mortgage loans, as a commercial bank it is required to comply with the Community Reinvestment Act (CRA). The official CRA mandate is "to ascertain community funding needs and implement community development lending, investment and charitable programs appropriate to the activities of a wholesale bank."

Morgan's Department of Community Relations and Public Affairs (CRPA) and the Morgan Community Development Corporation (MCDC) work to fulfill the CRA requirements. Both groups focus their activities on New York City, where 80 percent of Morgan's U.S. employees are based. The CRPA makes grants to and provides personnel as volunteers in organizations in the areas of education, health care, urban affairs, and the arts. The MCDC works with organizations that sponsor local development projects, providing financial support and investments, as well as analytical and technical expertise. The CRPA is explicitly involved in charitable giving, and the MCDC president says, in so many words, "We are not a charity."

Both the CRPA and MCDC benefit the community by applying the unique resources and competencies of a premier financial institution. But is Morgan merely complying with the provisions of the CRA, and not involved in the community because it is the right thing to do? Does the CRA provide Morgan's main motivation, and if so, does this represent a dilemma for citizenship? Does the rationale for citizenship matter? Does citizenship change when community involvement is required by law? Would the Morgans of the world make investments in the community without the CRA?

MCDC makes money on its community investments, and Morgan gets a tax deduction for charitable donations made by CRPA. Morgan also benefits from improved employee morale, loyalty, recruitment advantages, development of employees' skills and experiences. Good citizenship enhances the firm's reputation in the community. And the communities it serves benefit, regardless of the rationale behind Morgan's citizenship.

7

MERCK & CO., INC.

From Core Competence to Global Community Involvement

Jane E. Dutton and Michael G. Pratt

ON OCTOBER 21, 1987, Dr. Roy Vagelos, then CEO of Merck & Co., Inc., the fourth-largest pharmaceutical company in the world,[1] announced that Merck would donate a drug that combats river blindness[2] to all affected populations in developing countries until it is no longer needed for treating the disease. There had never been a pharmaceutical donation program of this scale, let alone one aimed at delivering a product to such inaccessible and poverty-stricken areas.

The announcement of the donation followed from a series of events that had begun almost a decade earlier. Dr. William Campbell was involved in the parasitology research program at the Merck, Sharp and Dohme Research Laboratories (MSDRL, later Merck Research Labs) animal health division in Rahway, N.J. In 1978, he and his colleagues discovered that an antiparasitic compound they were testing against animal parasites could also treat river blindness in humans without side effects. The veterinary drug posed few problems. It was effective and could generate substantial revenues. But its counterpart for humans raised many difficult issues.

Millions of people who needed the drug to combat river blindness were impoverished and could not pay for the product. What were the benefits, tangible and otherwise, of developing such a product? Merck's executives never hesitated in the decision to develop the drug for human use. But, once it was developed, they had to figure out how to market and distribute it. Many complications arose along the way.

This case will summarize the story of Merck and *Mectizan*. Key points that will be elaborated include the following critical factors.

- Merck's core competence (Prahalad and Hamel, 1990, pp. 79–91) in the development and distribution of pharmaceuticals played a critical role in the company's choice of citizenship activities.

- The culture of the organization not only supported but practically demanded Merck's decision to develop *Mectizan* and make it available in the marketplace.

- Merck could not simply view the decision to donate *Mectizan* as an act of good corporate citizenship. The complexity of the relationships of Merck with its many constituents made it necessary to provide multiple accounts for the donation that would satisfy people's expectations about the company's economic responsibilities as well as its social responsibilities.

AMERICA'S MOST ADMIRED CORPORATION

Merck & Co., Inc., headquartered in Rahway, N.J., employed 37,000 employees worldwide in research and development, manufacturing, marketing, and distribution of pharmaceutical products for humans and animals. In 1991, sales totaled over $8.6 billion, 12 percent higher than 1990. With over $2 billion in profits in 1991, Merck ranked No. 6 in *Fortune*'s Global 500. The company had 5 percent of the worldwide prescription drug market—the largest world market share of any pharmaceutical company.

Merck's product lines included human and animal health products, crop protection products, and specialty chemicals. In 1992, Merck had 19 products in 9 therapeutic classes, each with worldwide sales over $100 million. In prescription medicines, Merck held over 9 percent of the U.S. market.

Merck's commitment to research and development drove its strong financial performance. In 1991, Merck spent $1 billion on research, representing 10 percent of total U.S. pharmaceutical companies' expenditures on research and 5 percent of the industry's expenditures worldwide.

Three traditions defined Merck's culture: innovation, global enterprise, and service to society. Merck was also known for social responsibility. Merck had been named "America's Most Admired Corporation" by

Fortune magazine for six consecutive years, and in 1992 received the highest overall ranking of any company in the ten-year history of the survey.

Steve Darien, vice president for human resources, explained:

> People who come here are basically very socially minded. They like to be associated with an organization that produces products that are beneficial to mankind. Merck has always been known for taking the high ground. We're here to do something beneficial. Ultimately that will be recognized financially, but that comes second to human life.

Originally founded in Germany, Merck was incorporated in the United States over 100 years ago. George W. Merck, the son of the founder of Merck in the United States, originally expressed Merck's commitment to social responsibility. "We try never to forget that the medicine is for the people. It is not for the profits. The profits follow, and if we have remembered that, they have never failed to appear."

THE SCOURGE OF RIVER BLINDNESS

River blindness (*onchocerciasis*) was a leading cause of blindness in the developing world. In 1990, the World Health Organization (WHO) estimated that 340,000 individuals had been blinded by *onchocerciasis,* and about 17 million people were afflicted with the parasites, many with visual impairments and all at risk of becoming severely incapacitated or blind. *Onchocerciasis* was prevalent in river basins in tropical areas of Africa and Central and South America. WHO called the disease "a scourge of humanity" throughout recorded history, and estimated that 90 million people were at risk of contracting it.

Onchocerciasis was known as river blindness because the black flies that transmitted the disease to humans bred in fast-flowing rivers. Black flies picked up skin-dwelling microfilariae (tiny worms) by biting infected human hosts. While in the fly, the microfilariae grew into larvae and were deposited into other human beings. Since humans in infested areas could get thousands of black fly bites each day, river blindness reached epidemic proportions.

Within infected individuals, the parasites' larvae grew into adult worms that lived for 10 to 15 years, gathering under the skin to create nodules. Other signs and symptoms included acute and chronic skin rashes, severe itching, and weight loss. Adult worms produced millions of microfilariae in their human hosts. These tiny worms colonized the eyes and caused lesions, which could result in permanent total blindness.

In parts of West Africa, as many as 15 percent of the population, and 65 percent of people over age 55, were blind. Most people in affected villages believed that blindness was simply part of growing old. It was common to see young children leading old blind people around with sticks. People marked with the characteristic skin discoloration of the disease—often weak and unable to do productive work in their communities—were frequently ostracized. In extreme cases, the severe itching caused by the parasites led some sufferers to commit suicide. The river basins in which the black flies bred were often extremely fertile agricultural lands, but when villagers abandoned these areas, they disrupted their communities and experienced food shortages.

IVERMECTIN AND *ONCHOCERCIASIS*: FROM HORSES TO HUMANS

In 1975, Dr. William Campbell and his colleagues at Merck discovered a new antiparasitic compound that was effective against a number of animal parasites and was also safer than similar veterinary drugs currently on the market. They synthesized the active ingredient—ivermectin. Ivermectin became one of Merck's largest-selling veterinary pharmaceuticals, with annual sales of around $500 million.

In 1978, while testing ivermectin against parasites in horses, Dr. Campbell noticed that it was effective against a parasite that resembled the one that caused river blindness in humans. To test the hypothesis that ivermectin could provide a treatment for river blindness, he sent a sample of the drug to an Australian colleague, Dr. Bruce Copeman, whose tests confirmed that the drug acted against a similar parasite in cattle. The news that ivermectin worked against two related strains of parasites prompted Dr. Campbell to approach management in the research lab about developing an ivermectin-based drug to combat river blindness in humans.

On December 20, 1978, Dr. Campbell reported to the research lab management that an ivermectin-based drug could become the first satisfactory means of preventing the blindness associated with *onchocerciasis*. He recommended that Merck contact the WHO to discuss the most appropriate method for distributing the drug. Dr. P. Roy Vagelos (later CEO, but then president of MSDRL) gave strong support to Dr. Campbell.

Dr. Vagelos encouraged Dr. Campbell to learn as much as possible about potential human applications for ivermectin, and by the end of 1978 he approved initial funding for research on the use of ivermectin as a treatment for river blindness. The roots of the decision to develop a treatment for river blindness lay in Merck's historical mission to alleviate human suffering. But, there were other motivations too. Dr. Vagelos was acutely aware that refusal to fund research and testing of new drug discoveries could demoralize Merck's scientists. He also recognized that development of the drug could contribute to Merck researchers' basic knowledge and understanding of parasitology—a priority field for future product development.

CLINICAL AND OTHER TRIALS

By January 1980, clinical trials of an ivermectin-based drug for humans, called *Mectizan*, began under the direction of Dr. Mohamed Aziz. Dr. Aziz, a native of Bangladesh and an expert in tropical diseases, quickly became the principal champion of the *Mectizan* program. His passion for the potential treatment came from firsthand familiarity with river blindness. He had worked on public health programs with WHO in Sierra Leone, West Africa.

In 1980, Dr. Aziz began exhaustive studies of the drug, which continued over seven years. Merck's high standards for safety and effectiveness required extensive testing. Safety was of particular concern because other drugs used to combat *onchocerciasis* had serious side effects, including blindness and death.

Merck faced challenges in the development of *Mectizan* beyond ensuring the drug's safety. First, there was the tremendous cost of testing any drug and bringing it to market. Second was the high risk of failure common to clinical testing. Even after millions of dollars were spent in development and testing, a very small percentage of drugs passed the medical and regulatory hurdles to receive approval. A third challenge involved finding suitable test sites. River blindness was endemic in inaccessible areas. Most governments of the affected countries lacked the resources to provide even basic health care. Merck executives decided to try to forge an alliance with WHO, which had an ongoing *Onchocerciasis* Control Program (OCP). This proved unexpectedly difficult.

Merck Attempts a Partnership with WHO

While Merck scientists were developing *Mectizan,* which attacked the young parasites in the human body, WHO/OCP staff were attempting to control the spread of river blindness by attacking the black fly with aerial spraying of insecticide. The OCP program also included research on a drug to kill adult *onchocerciasis* worms without harming their human hosts.

When Merck first approached WHO officials about *Mectizan,* some officials expressed skepticism about the idea of a drug aimed at killing the microfilariae, since the WHO's program was tied to finding a drug that would affect adult worms. Convinced of the enormous potential of *Mectizan* to fight river blindness, Merck executives and scientists persisted in their support of the drug. By the end of 1981, Merck was working closely with WHO to gain access to remote countries for clinical trials of *Mectizan.*

A Misinterpreted Memo

Given the poverty of the afflicted communities, Dr. Vagelos knew that development of the drug was at best a "borderline economically viable project." Merck executives hoped governments, international health agencies, or charitable foundations would come forward to purchase *Mectizan* and fund its distribution. This would enable Merck to sell the drug and provide for it to be distributed at no cost to the people who required it but couldn't pay.

In July 1985, Merck issued a statement:

> It has always been the Company's intention to make appropriate arrangements to supply (ivermectin) in sufficient quantities for use in the public health sector of affected countries. Merck will provide, either through separate arrangements which the Company will make or directly to the WHO, sufficient quantities of the drug to satisfy the needs of such programs.

Some Merck employees interpreted this statement as a commitment to donating it. Their misinterpretation sparked debates within the company about the pros and cons of donation. The debates lasted for two years.

Finding Money for the Miracle

Even though there did not seem to be a conventional market for the drug, Merck developed *Mectizan* in the hope that funding would materialize. As late as 1986, Merck executives expected donors to finance the supply of the drug to those affected countries that could not pay for the drug. Dr. Vagelos made several trips to Washington, D.C., to seek funding for the purchase and distribution of the drug, even though such negotiations were normally handled by regulatory affairs and marketing staff.

His meetings took place among the highest levels of U.S. government policy makers. He approached the deputy secretary of state, John Whitehead, the White House chief of staff, Donald Regan, and Peter McPherson, the head of the U.S. Agency for International Development (the organization responsible for grants and loans to international development projects). These talks all ended in a similar way. No one offered monetary support. Appeals for funds from African health ministries and private charitable foundations also ended in failure.

Debate on the Dangers of Drug Donation

Merck executives faced the prospect of not being able to sell a wonder drug that its scientists had developed at a cost of several million dollars and which the company had committed to make available. Once again, senior staff debated the idea of donating the drug. These executives devoted enormous time and energy to resolving the question of what to do with *Mectizan*. Charles Fettig, senior director of marketing, remarked, "In my first year in this position I spent more time in executive conferences than I had in five years before—all on the *Mectizan* project." Mr. Fettig went on to explain the position Merck's executives found themselves in:

> Early on we knew that the people who needed the drug would not be able to pay for it, so we had to work out a scheme to make the drug available at no charge. That was where the misinterpretation that we were going to donate it started. Because of this situation, we had to look at ways we could raise funding for distribution and purchase of this drug.

Some argued that donating the drug might create an expectation that all other drugs created for developing countries should be donated. Since pharmaceutical companies were in business to make profits from selling drugs, such a precedent could discourage research and development of drugs for diseases plaguing developing countries.

Albert Angel, vice president for public affairs, thought about the potential for demands for other product donations. "The first question is always, Well, if you're doing it there, why aren't you doing it everywhere else? If you can donate *Mectizan,* then why can't you donate hypertensive drugs in the Los Angeles area? It's tough to work out where the line is."

Donating the drug would be tremendously costly. In addition to manufacturing and administrative costs, Merck risked legal liability if *Mectizan* caused adverse reactions (Weiss, 1990). At the same time, some Merck advisers suggested that health workers and recipients might question the value of a product provided for free.

Dr. Campbell recognized other problems of motives and medical credibility. "You always have people who are going to ask, What is their real reason?" If Merck decided to donate the drug, would the company be accused of attempting to unload a "useless" drug on a needy populace? Would people understand the difference between *Mectizan* and the veterinary drugs, or think that Merck was distributing animal drugs to humans? Would someone allege that Merck was using people in developing countries as guinea pigs?

The Decision

The donation decision did not come until almost nine years after the drug had been approved for clinical testing. When Merck's scientists started work on the development of *Mectizan* in 1978, the company's executives did not foresee donating the drug, much less donating it for as long as it was needed. Dr. Edward Scolnick, Dr. Vagelos's successor as head of MSDRL, believed:

> We should donate *Mectizan* because we can afford to donate it. We're fortunate. If we weren't so successful, we might not be able to donate it. Other companies have to make their own decisions.

This simple justification was enough to convince many that donation was the best way to achieve Merck's overriding mission to improve human health. Few could argue with the rationale: "Donate because we can afford to." The veterinary drug was reaping more than $300 million a year, with sales growing by 15 percent annually (Weiss, 1991).

Charles Fettig remembered the period of internal debate as a struggle. "At that time, there was never a clear answer. We got to the point where we said, How can we be involved in fundraising? We're a pharmaceutical manufacturer, we do great research and great marketing; that's where our expertise is."

Even though there was still some hope that WHO or another organization would buy the drug for a minimal price, Merck went ahead with its decision to donate. As Dr. Vagelos told the story:

I said to the deputy secretary of state, "Think what it would mean if the United States went into Africa and wiped out a devastating disease for $20 million. You would be the hero." He said, "Yeah, we've got to do it." But they didn't do it. So after a year, it was getting very close to approval of the drug, and we at Merck said, "Okay, goddamn it, we'll do it."

Mectizan Free and Forever: One Decision Leads to Another

The public greeted Merck's announcement of the donation with some initial skepticism. One reporter asked Dr. Vagelos how long Merck intended to donate the drug. Dr. Vagelos answered, "for the foreseeable future." The reporter pressed him to explain what he meant by the "foreseeable future." Did Merck plan to discontinue the donation and demand payment once villagers came to know the drug's effectiveness? Dr. Vagelos replied that Merck would donate the drug "wherever it's needed, for as long as it's needed."

Years later, Art Kaufman, director of public affairs, had an experience that became one of his favorite stories about *Mectizan*:

In one African village, the chief came out to talk to us. I wanted to get him on videotape telling how important this drug was for his village, but no matter what I asked, I couldn't get him to be really enthusiastic. When we started to leave, a local field doctor came over to me. He had been talking to the chief, and he was laughing. He told me the chief was really very enthusiastic about *Mectizan,* but the chief had told him, "I really didn't know how to answer. I certainly don't want this drug company to know how good this drug is because they might start charging for it."

Redefining Business as Usual

When Merck developed a drug, its standard marketing approach had been traditionally to achieve three objectives: reach the customer, make a profit, and educate the customer. For the marketing and distribution of *Mectizan,* those responsible for the program had to find a way to tailor these objectives to the unique target population in developing countries. Since they would not be distributing the drug in traditional, fully developed markets, Merck's marketers first had to educate international health organizations—and later tribal villagers—about *Mectizan*'s usefulness.

Due to the difficulty of delivering the drug to the areas where the affected populations lived, the first objective—getting it to the most people—was vital. Now that the decision had been made to donate *Mectizan*, distribution posed unprecedented and difficult challenges and responsibilities. Dr. Vagelos's view of the problem was, "The limiting factor is the ability to distribute the drug. We can manufacture all they need."

Facing the Distribution Challenge

Once committed to donating the drug, Merck was faced with the Herculean task of distributing it in inaccessible areas with poor infrastructures. Early in 1988, Merck's management came up with the idea of forming a committee of experts in tropical medicine to review applications for donations. The *Mectizan* expert committee (MEC) included experts from a variety of well-respected organizations who gave the program immediate legitimacy in the international health arena. The MEC was headed by Dr. William Foege, executive director of the Carter Center in Atlanta. Dr. Foege had been a leader in the fight to eradicate smallpox throughout the world. Merck and WHO had nonvoting representatives on the committee, who served as advisers.

The committee's task was to ensure the appropriate distribution of the drug by developing guidelines for distribution, monitoring, and record keeping. As an independent committee, the MEC could bypass the internal politics and bureaucratic delays of organizations like WHO and government agencies. The MEC, not Merck, had authority to turn down applications from organizations that had not developed adequate distribution plans. Because the MEC would set its own rules for distribution, Merck's executives believed they would ensure that *Mectizan* was supplied quickly and efficiently (Weiss, 1990).

Running the Mectizan Donation Program

The creation of the MEC did not end Merck's involvement with the program to donate *Mectizan*. Merck remained responsible for manufacturing, marketing, and public relations, but no central authority in Merck oversaw all of the activities associated with the drug donation.

Merck's corporate division incurred many *Mectizan*-related expenses, such as staff salaries in a number of departments and business units. The public affairs department was responsible for public education on *Mectizan* in the United States and abroad. Corporate contributions, a unit of public affairs, dealt with the tax implications of the donations, and paid shipping costs. The human health division paid the expenses of the expert committee. Two European business units were also involved, because Merck manufactured *Mectizan* in Holland and packaged it in France.

The people involved in the *Mectizan* donation could not specify the number of divisions affected, the number of people working, or the costs of the program, because, while manufacturing costs were meticulously tracked, other ancillary costs were not. If management had wanted to quantify the costs of the program, estimates would probably have been unreliable. The corporate contributions staff estimated the market value of the donation by multiplying the number of tablets shipped by $3, but this estimate did not include the costs of staffing, shipping, or the expert committee. Merck accountants did not keep a full balance sheet on the donation program. Top management was more concerned with achieving its primary corporate objective for the drug donation: getting *Mectizan* to the people who needed it.

Albert Angel described wrestling with these dilemmas:

> Corporate giving is a real conundrum. Who decides what is to be counted and how you count it? Do you count it at market value? Or at the IRS's value of two times the material cost? Or at inventory cost? Even if you want to keep score, it's very interesting to try to figure out how you get the right sort of score.

Measuring Success One Tablet at a Time

Though Merck did not track the dollars spent on the drug donation, it did keep records on the number of *Mectizan* tablets distributed and the number of people treated. From 1988 to 1991, the *Mectizan* expert committee approved treatment plans in 28 countries where the disease existed. By the end of 1991, more than 6.7 million tablets had been shipped, including over 5.3 million for community-based treatment and almost 1.7 million in a companion effort.

Charles Fettig considered it imperative to market *Mectizan* the way Merck marketed other drugs.

> People in the company constantly ask, "What can we do to build these numbers?" We handle this just like we were getting two dollars a tablet

or whatever dollar you want to put on it. We have plans. We have people assigned to it. We have expenses, and we set goals just as we do for our marketed products.

Morale at Merck

Charles Fettig looked at the decision to donate *Mectizan* this way: "We didn't go into this saying, 'Well gee, what kind of benefits can we get if we do this donation program?' It was kind of the other way around."

Many people at Merck believed the company reaped a variety of benefits. Employee morale seemed to be higher. Dr. Vagelos said, "The effect this had on morale was absolutely electric. Here was a drug we developed that would sit on the shelf if we didn't go forward with it, because no government was willing to pay for it. Yet the company announced that we would donate it worldwide. It was the most positive thing."

Steve Darien remembered the reaction of employees when the *Mectizan* program was announced:

It was one of the highlights of my career here. The reaction of people was very, very positive. They understood that it was a unique thing to do. I think these things provide a reservoir for us to draw on when we ask people to work very hard for protracted periods of time. When people feel positively about the company they work for, you can get them to do things with a positive attitude.

Response from the Public

Charles Fettig described the feeling Merck employees got from learning about the favorable public response to the donation of *Mectizan*:

We're a very successful company because we make a lot of money and we do a lot of good things. There's no direct return on it, and I don't know that there will be any. Maybe this will help governments accept our products, but no one really knows. But it does make us a company worth dealing with. If people will go to the trouble of writing us a letter because they feel this is a wonderful company, we love it. It makes us feel warm and fuzzy.

At least one person who wrote a letter to Merck congratulating the company for the donation program promised to use the company's products in the future:

I've just read in *Time* about the wonderful thing that you decided to do for the people of the world by donating your entire production of Ivermectin to prevent the spread of *onchocerciasis*. I'm just an ordinary citizen, not a doctor or a health worker. Anytime I need a prescription from now on, I'm going to ask my pharmacist to fill it with one of your products. God bless you. Not many companies would put people before profits. I'll be proud to use your products the next time I need a prescription filled.

Running the Mectizan Program

Five years after the announcement of the donation, Albert Angel talked about some of the real difficulties of a program of this size and scope. "Consumer activists ask, 'Why can't you make a drug less expensive for the Third World?' Now we have a drug that costs zero, but the real problem is that in the Third World, infrastructure problems, government priorities and limited resources prevent it from getting to as many people as it should."

By 1992, it appeared likely that controlling river blindness would require the drug donation program to continue well into the first decade of the 21st century. Merck's commitment to donating *Mectizan* wherever and whenever it was needed was being tested.

Dissenting Voices

Along the way to reaching the decision to donate *Mectizan* and during the first years of the distribution program, there had been some dissenting voices—not expressing disagreement or disenchantment but hard-headed awareness of the practical challenges involved. Charles Fettig described Merck's experience with the program. "We knew we were going to have difficulty, but it was more difficult than we thought."

Dr. Campbell was one of the first Merck employees to visit the countries where river blindness was endemic. He witnessed that: "The communities that receive the drug are in the very poorest, most remote areas that I have ever been in. You wouldn't be able to get to these places unless somebody familiar with them was there to show you the way. If you tried on your own it would be very risky."

As Albert Angel saw it, "It's just not good enough to do good."

Doing good requires as much business skill as making profits in terms of planning, objective setting, resource allocation, stick-to-itiveness, evaluation, assessment, and reassessment. If you apply less than good solid quality standards, you're not doing a quality job of social responsibility. We have to do more than just give the drug away—that's not good enough.

Charles Fettig reflected on some of the pitfalls encountered in implementing the program: "In Liberia, where much of the early work was done and where we had a very good program, there was a civil war and the people working on the program had to leave. The program was decimated. It's caused all kinds of frustrations. Even when you're donating, it's tough."

Still, Albert Angel maintained, "It's important to carry it through. I think it is very good business. I also think it's very good ethics."

On September 23, 1992, the *Wall Street Journal* carried an article that seemed to capture many of Merck's executives' fears.

Merck's 'River Blindness' Gift Hits Snags
By Elyse Tanouye
The Wall Street Journal
September 23, 1992

Five years ago, Merck & Co. stunned the pharmaceutical industry with a promise to give away millions of doses of a drug to treat a Third World disease called "river blindness."

Accolades and great publicity followed. But for Merck, a marketing giant, giving a drug away proved to be tougher than selling one.

To date, the drug has reached about 5 percent of the more than 100 million people who either have, or are at risk for, the disease. An inadequate health care delivery infrastructure, coups d'etat, and rough terrain have presented big roadblocks to the giveaway.

River blindness, or onchocerciasis, afflicts 17 million people and threatens an additional 90 million, primarily in Central and West Africa and in limited areas of Central and South America, according to the World Health Organization. An estimated 350,000 people are already blind from the disease, and up to one million more have lost much of their eyesight. Researchers have estimated that more than half the inhabitants of some hard-hit areas will become blind before death.

River blindness is caused by a parasite, onchocerca volvulvus, carried by black flies. It burrows under human skin, growing as long as two feet and causing severe itching. An adult worm, which may live for 10 to 15 years in a human host, produces millions of offspring, or microfilariae, that migrate through the body. Those that invade the eye cause a slow deterioration of eyesight that can lead to total blindness.

According to Merck, the disease has also taken a social and economic toll by forcing entire communities to abandon fertile lands near rivers to flee black-fly infestation.

Merck's drug, ivermectin, is one of the company's biggest-selling products, with estimated annual sales of $500 million—for the treatment of parasites in animals. But when its use against river blindness in humans was discovered, the company faced the problem of how to get the drug to people who live in some of the world's poorest regions without the means to buy it at any price.

Merck's solution was simply to donate the drug. But that turned out to be complicated.

The Rahway, N.J., company had to figure out how to transport the medicine to remote villages where the disease has hit hardest, said Philippe Gaxotte, Merck's medical director responsible for overseeing part of the drug's distribution.

At the time, Merck decided it must place restrictions on the drug's distribution out of concern that incorrect use of the drug could induce unnecessary side effects, and taint the medicine's success in treating animals.

Company officials also were concerned that if the drug weren't properly distributed, it could fall into the hands of black marketeers.

Once approvals were granted, distribution remained a daunting undertaking. Many villages are accessible only by foot. To send a vehicle requires hiring laborers to clear the brush, said Ebrahim M. Samba, director of the World Health Organization's Onchocerciasis Control Program, which distributes Merck's drug in 11 West African countries. Without bridges and often without boats to cross the fast-flowing rivers, health care workers must use hollow logs to float across water. Two physicians died last year while trying to cross a river to deliver the drug, he said.

Although Merck is giving the drug free of charge, some countries still can't afford to deliver it to those in need, Dr. Samba said. "How do you do it?" he asks. "They don't have the staff, they don't have the vehicles, they don't have the fuel."

Civil strife has also snarled distribution of Mectizan (Merck's brand name for ivermectin for humans) in key countries such as Ethiopia, Liberia, Sudan and Zaire. "It's been frustrating for us," said Michael Heisler, secretariat manager of the Mectizan Expert Committee, an organization funded by Merck to review applications from voluntary organizations and governments to distribute the drug. "There are people at risk who oughtn't to be" because of political instability in their countries, he said.

Civil strife has even endangered Merck officials. Dr. Gaxotte, for example, was forced to flee Zaire last year because disorder erupted in its capital, Kinshasa, where he was meeting with health officials in hopes of setting up a treatment program. And he barely missed another outbreak of violence in Nigeria, where he was attending a meeting.

Even though the vast majority of those infected with the disease haven't received the drug, people who have long worked in the developing world are pleased that the medicine has reached as many sufferers as it has, Dr. Heisler said.

P. Roy Vagelos, Merck's chairman, argued that Mectizan's penetration is high, considering that it will have reached, by the end of this year, six million of the 17 million infected people.

Rene Le Berre, who headed the World Health Organization's filariasis disease unit until his recent retirement, said he doesn't see a comparable program for other common diseases in Africa. For example, although yellow fever vaccines are very cheap, many people in Africa still die from the disease. "It isn't only a question of money; it's a question of willingness to spread the treatments into the bush. There's no organization to distribute it."

Dr. Vagelos said Merck's experience shows how difficult it would be to distribute drugs to treat other diseases in the developing world. "It gives the lesson of how difficult it is, a lesson we learned pretty fast," he said. "It's a learning process that is going to facilitate the next time this happens."

"All of the work to set up the network and relationships has taken a long time," said Dr. Heisler, noting that the effort is paying off with an acceleration in drug distribution.

But, he cautioned, "The tasks in front of us are greater than the ones behind us." In the next five years, the committee hopes to reach all of the six million people at the highest risk of the disease. In addition, it hopes to start reaching those at the next level of risk, perhaps treating 10 to 12 million people overall in the next five years.

The program must be sustainable, because people must take the drug every year for 10 to 12 years, Dr. Heisler said.

Merck plans to celebrate the fifth anniversary of the drug-donation program today with a scientific symposium and dinner at the United Nations, where former President Jimmy Carter; Hiroshi Nakajima, director general of WHO; and Dr. Vagelos, will speak.

CONCLUSION

The Merck case illustrates that community involvement is not peripheral to an organization but is central and closely integrated with the way the organization does all of its business. It provides a clear example of the relationship between corporate citizenship and core competence: An organization's core competencies—the corporationwide skills and values that allow an organization to adapt to its ever-changing environment—

determine which communities organizations target for their citizenship activities, and what form these citizenship activities take.

Corporate interest in community social and environmental problems now goes beyond traditional definitions of corporate philanthropy. It is taking the form of large-scale, strategic projects like the *Mectizan* donation. The Merck case moves beyond viewing citizenship as a matter of business ethics or social responsibility in theory, and instead concentrates on understanding the dynamics, motivations, strategies, and forms of corporate citizenship performance.

Merck's corporate citizenship activities are central and interconnected to its ways of thinking about and doing its major business. The two processes—thinking about and doing—are closely intertwined, and both have their roots in the traditions, values, and practices that have been part of the organization since its inception. Moreover, the way the organization thinks about corporate citizenship undergirds the way it conducts its citizenship activities; and the way Merck does corporate citizenship sustains and commits Merck members to the way they think about corporate citizenship.

Merck blurs the boundaries between the company and its community constituencies through participation in citizenship activities that draw upon its core traditions, values, and practices. In analyzing Merck's corporate citizenship as a boundary-transcending activity, we see how a leading global organization constructs the strategies it uses to manage and transcend external horizontal boundaries, by reaching out to community groups.

The *Mectizan* donation story includes decision-making dilemmas faced by the company over years of developing, testing, donating, and distributing the drug. The case raises real-world questions about what one Merck executive describes as the "conundrum" of doing good. "It's not enough to do good," and "even when you're donating, it's tough."

Do the benefits outweigh the costs? Can the costs even be accurately measured? Once embarked on a citizenship program that has received substantial public recognition, does the firm have the option of curtailing it, given the difficulties encountered? What might be the effects, both internally and externally, of doing so?

REFERENCES

Prahalad, C. K., and Hamel, G. "The Core Competence of the Corporation." *Harvard Business Review,* May-June, 1990, pp. 79–91.

Weiss, S. *Merck and Co., Inc..* Stanford, Calif.: Bunnen Enterprise Trust, 1990.

ENDNOTES

1. Ranked by 1991 sales in *Fortune*'s Global 500.
2. River blindness is a debilitating and disfiguring parasitic disease that often resulted in blindness among residents of river basins in tropical countries in Africa, and in Central and South America. In the early 1990s, 18 million people were infected with the disease. The World Health Organization (WHO) estimated that as many as 90 million people were at risk to contract river blindness.

8

THE GENERAL ELECTRIC ELFUN
SOCIETY

Leveraging Employee Volunteerism with Foundation Dollars

Jeannette L. Jackson

OVER THE PAST 12 YEARS, the Elfun (Electric Fund) Society, a volunteer organization of General Electric Company leaders, has applied the skills and energies of its members to social problems by developing partnerships with public and nonprofit organizations in their communities. Elfun Society members mobilize, support, and lead effective large-scale employee volunteer efforts to assist public schools and community groups around the United States. Under the society's auspices, thousands of GE employees volunteer in schools as mentors and advisers to students, faculty, and administrators. The General Electric Fund's College Bound Program provides grants to high schools serving minority and low-income students to complement Elfun volunteer efforts.

In 1990, General Electric received the George S. Dively Award for Leadership in Corporate Public Initiative from Harvard University. Accepting on behalf of the company, CEO Jack Welch praised his employees' achievements. "I'm here today because in the mid-eighties people in local chapters of the Elfun Society began to try to change things in their local schools—one kid at a time. And they did." Welch gave an example of the Elfun Society's work:

One of the first high schools they tackled, in Cincinnati, Ohio, the home of our Aircraft Engines business, was sending three students a year to college out of a graduating class of 324. But it has a zealot as principal, who is committed to improving things. With his support over 200 people—longtime employees, new hires, retirees, and interested community leaders—linked up with students who wanted help and acted as mentors and advisers. They were a window into a world these kids had never really experienced—a world of work, study, achievement, and success. . . . One statistic tells the story. The school that in 1985 sent 3 to college, sent 82 this year from a class of 208— from 4 percent in 1985 to 44 percent in 1992—to 56 percent in 1996.

He explained GE's special power to achieve this sort of social benefit. "A company as diverse as ours—from jet engines to NBC—yet as integrated in the transmission of ideas, [can] scan the global landscape for new ideas, best practices, and share them with each other almost in real time. This normally applies to business practices . . ., but in this case, the experience at the Cincinnati school and the lessons learned from it spread quickly among the leaders of the local Elfun chapters."

Welch continued. "As efforts began to make a difference, we added money to expand the scope of work. But money is the least important element in this program. The people, the mentors, are the key. We seldom send money without them." And he speculated about the future impact of these programs. "Within five years there will be more than 2,500 students—almost all minorities—who will have gone on to college and who would not have gone without the guidance and help of our people. Perhaps of equal importance are the thousands more who will make it through high schools made better by our people, our equipment, and our financial aid. We have over $20 million earmarked for this effort, but it's the people who really make it work."

GE'S PHILANTHROPIC TRADITIONS

The Elfun Society was founded in 1928 as a leadership recognition, investment trust, and social organization for GE managers. Since 1981, when CEO Jack Welch challenged the society to examine its role for the 1980s and beyond, it has become a vigorous organization emphasizing community service and volunteerism. The society has over 70 local chapters, which focus the resources of GE businesses in communities where the company operates. The society provides organizational structure and leadership for most community activities undertaken by GE employees. A number of other companies have expressed interest in emulating its structure and activities.

GE established the GE Foundation in 1952 to fund philanthropic activities. The foundation emphasizes education in the belief that a capable workforce, competitive economy, and compassionate society depend on a well-educated citizenry. It typically directs grants to educational programs that serve women and minorities. The GE Fund[1] and the Elfun Society cooperate to leverage the effects of Elfuns's volunteer work with foundation financial resources.

This case will describe two examples of the Elfun Society—the GE Fund model partnership at work with the Aiken High School in Cincinnati and the Manhattan Center for Science and Mathematics in New York City. The cases fall against this backdrop:

- The Elfun Society evolved from an organization designed to foster socializing among GE managers to an organization that provides extensive volunteer support that takes advantage of the expertise of GE's elite personnel.

- The breadth of GE's operations, across industry and national boundaries, provides a unique opportunity for the company to disseminate exemplary practices to aid a myriad of important social institutions in the communities in which they do business.

- GE's focus on education, particularly in the areas of science and mathematics, reflects a long-term investment that will pay off for the company with a much larger pool of highly qualified employees in the future.

GE Corporate Context and Culture

By any standards, GE is a giant. In 1997, the company, with 239,000 employees worldwide, had revenues in excess of $79 billion. It ranked No. 7 in the overall 1996 *Fortune* Global 500 and No. 1 in the electronics and electrical equipment industry. If ranked independently, eight of GE's businesses would be on the *Fortune* 500 list. The total value of GE's stock makes the company first on the *Business Week* 1000 and *Financial Times* 500 lists.

The principle of "Integrated Diversity" links GE's 12 businesses: Aircraft Engines, Appliances, Financial Services, Industrial and Power Systems, Lighting, Medical Systems, NBC, Plastics, Electrical Distribution and Control, Information Services, Motors, and Transportation Systems.

These diversified businesses exchange information, innovations, and ideas to capitalize on the value of a multinational, multibusiness company.

GE's technique for strengthening global competitiveness relies on strategic alliances and worldwide investments. With presence in Europe, Japan, Canada, Korea, and Taiwan, the company is expanding in Southeast Asia, China, and Mexico, pursuing export opportunities in the Middle East and Turkey, and laying the groundwork for markets in Eastern Europe, Russia, and India.

In recent years, GE has been clearing away bureaucracy, management layers, and functional boundaries, and breaking down horizontal and vertical barriers within and among businesses. The "Work-Out" process brings GE employees from all ranks and functions together with customers and suppliers to analyze and take action to increase teamwork and productivity.

The GE culture reflects these values, as do its volunteer and philanthropic activities. Jack Welch highlighted GE's commitment to social involvement in the 1991 Annual Report:

> The spirit of boundarylessness is nowhere more evident than in the renaissance of volunteerism that is bringing GE talent and enthusiasm to bear on the problems and potential of the communities that the Company's hundreds of plants and installations call home . . . [It] has spread to work on environmental cleanups and beautification, homeless shelters, wildlife conservation, blood banks, and scores of other projects. GE retirees have been drawn back into active volunteer service alongside veteran employees and new hires. GE businesses, and the communities in which they are citizens, have never worked together so closely and so well.

Welch noted another benefit of employee volunteerism: "It has become one of the best things that's ever happened to the volunteers themselves. Many who were in the middle of predictable, routine careers have become more outspoken, innovative, and productive. . . . Volunteerism has become a winning experience for our communities, our employees and our Company."

The Elfun Society

Gerard Swope, GE's CEO in 1928, founded the Elfun Society to foster loyalty, fellowship, cooperation, innovation, and resourcefulness among GE's managers. Swope said, "If people can relax together and enjoy each other's company, they can work together efficiently and profitably." The society is organizationally and financially independent of the GE company. Its purposes are to promote the interests of its members and the company, and to make a difference in local communities.

In 1981, when Jack Welch challenged the society's leadership to evaluate its goals, the society redefined its purposes as community service, volunteerism, and communication. Welch endorsed the re-dedication. "Rallying Elfun around the concept of volunteerism and taking advantage of the tremendous GE retirement team can truly make a difference in each community where we live and work. A healthy, strong GE and a healthy, strong Elfun Society go hand in hand."

Elfun Society membership is open to GE employees in responsible positions who meet service and salary requirements. Joining the society is considered a major career milestone. Of Elfun's 36,000 members, nearly 44 percent are retirees. Eligibility requirements are currently becoming more open; criteria are broader, including nominees regardless of position who demonstrate sustained contributions to volunteerism.

The society offers its members opportunities for community outreach, as well as business, social, and cultural programs. Community activities involve schools, hospitals, public television, mental and physical rehabilitation centers, youth and senior citizen groups, service clubs, environmental improvement, and dozens of other local causes. Business programs range from presentations by corporate executives to personal financial planning seminars. Social and cultural programs include dinner dances, sports outings, and cultural events. Local chapters of the Elfun Society provide a broad spectrum of activities to match members' skills and interests with community needs.

The society offers members both tangible and intangible benefits. Tangible benefits are investment opportunities in a variety of no-load funds and IRAs, supplemental medical insurance for over-65 Elfuns, a no-fee credit card that returns royalties to Elfun community projects, and financial planning seminars. Intangible benefits include opportunities to develop relationships across company components, job ranks, and age boundaries; improved communications among employees; contact between employees and retirees; self-development through leadership responsibilities in the society and community; relaxation and social opportunities; and a network of community leaders and society members.

The Elfun Society benefits GE in a variety of ways. As Jack Welch put it, "Elfun's emphasis on being a communications link for management can be very helpful. The more [employees] who understand what a healthy General Electric can mean in terms of public and social responsibility, the better off we all will be." Members' involvement in their communities enhances the image of the company in the eyes of the public, customers, and government. Elfun membership promotes strong ties to the company and improves recruitment and employee development. The society contributes to an atmosphere of integrity, social awareness, and excellence.

Two full-time Elfun Society staff members—the executive director and an administrative project leader—are based at corporate headquarters. They provide outreach and communications support to the society president, board of directors, and chapters. They help set up new chapters and programs or revitalize existing chapters, advise chapters on planning and executing activities, and organize an annual meeting of chapter leaders.

GE sanctions the use of company office space, facilities, telephones, and equipment by members. Local managers often permit flexible scheduling to allow volunteers to participate in community activities during normal working hours. Volunteers are not, however, given paid time off for their Elfun Society activities. All society officers and chapter leaders are volunteers, and do their society work in addition to everyday business responsibilities.

The Elfun Society is decentralized, reflecting the overall GE business strategy. Local chapters, each with their own organization and by-laws, implement society policies autonomously. A chapter leader explained, "Whatever you do for your community should be appropriate for the chapter and the business group in that community, so it's a win-win for the community and for the business." Chapters learn from one another's experiences through communications and training seminars. The Elfun board promotes the flow of information about successful projects between chapters.

The society recognizes its members for outstanding performance in the areas of community service, government, education, or any company or public service activity with "Elfun of the Year" awards, based on nominations from each chapter. Awards consist of a contribution to the charitable organization of the winner's choice. Golden Elm Awards go to the Elfun chapter whose programs excel at fulfilling the purposes of the society.

The Elfun Society reflects the GE corporate culture, even though it is independent and autonomous. The organization and activities of the Elfun Society rest on the same principles of self-direction, action, service, and change that distinguish GE as a company.

The GE Fund's Pre-College Programs

In 1952, GE established the GE Foundation to fund philanthropic activities focused on making GE business communities better places to live and work. In 1994, the foundation became known as the GE Fund. The board of directors of the GE Fund includes officers of the GE company, and it is chaired by the chief financial officer. The foundation emphasizes grants to education, especially in science and engineering. In 1992, it made grants totaling $24.7 million, including $2.8 million to pre-college programs. The foundation's program areas are pre-college and higher education, public policy, arts education, international, United Way, and matching gifts.

The foundation's program manager for pre-college programs believes that corporations must help improve America's schools in order to increase competitiveness and develop a well-prepared workforce. The foundation does this by meshing financial resources with the volunteer efforts of GE employees, whose close ties with their local school systems allow them to have a significant impact on the quality of pre-college education.

In the early 1980s, the foundation recognized the need to fund programs to improve pre-college education; in 1987, the foundation began to combine its financial resources with Elfun Society and other GE employee community service volunteer efforts to support pre-college education. Foundation leaders believed that their collaboration would enhance the effectiveness and visibility of both foundation and employee activities.

One collaborative activity is the GE Fund's Elfun Challenge Grant Program. Since 1987, a total of $250,000 a year in foundation grants of $5,000 or more has gone to over 40 schools where Elfun volunteers make hands-on contributions—mentoring, tutoring, conducting science demonstrations, developing math curricula, offering reading programs, and conducting teacher training.

In 1989, the foundation initiated the College Bound Program, a $20-million, ten-year commitment to double the number of college-bound students from selected disadvantaged schools. Communities with a major GE operation, a potentially large pool of GE volunteers, and a school with a large disadvantaged population are eligible, if there is a low rate of graduates going to college and a desire to improve this situation. The foundation makes grants of $250,000 to $1 million to individual public schools in such areas, and commits itself to a three- to five-year support program.

Together, the foundation and the Elfun Society support College Bound Programs in more than a dozen high schools around the United States: Albuquerque, New Mexico; Cincinnati and Cleveland, Ohio; Erie, Pennsylvania; Durham, Hendersonville, and Wilmington, North Carolina; Florence, South Carolina; Lynn, Massachusetts; Louisville, Kentucky; Lowndes County, Alabama; New York City, Ossining, and Schenectady, New York; and Parkersburg, West Virginia. Each school tailors a program to its unique needs. Programs include improvement in core subjects, SAT/ACT preparation, enrichment activities, motivation programs, staff development, curriculum development, parent guidance, career and college advice, college visits, incentives, and scholarships. As part of the College Bound Program, the foundation brings staff members from involved schools together with Elfun leaders each year to share best practices and meet with business leaders and the superintendent of schools.

According to the foundation's pre-college programs manager:

> Experience clearly demonstrates that [the education] issue will not be resolved with large expensive national programs, but with school-by-school changes tailored to meet local needs. . . . GE has learned that the most effective resource it has is its large number of employee volunteers.

The foundation hired the Rand Corporation to evaluate the College Bound Program. Findings suggest success in achieving permanent systemic change in the site schools. The GE Fund also created the College Bound Plus Program—a new initiative to provide additional funds for staff development and teacher training to the College Bound schools where the foundation has existing programs, established relationships, and has seen a strong record of achievement.

The College Bound Program has taught the GE Fund and the Elfun Society valuable lessons about the importance of dynamic school leadership, high expectations, teacher involvement and training, parent involvement, full course loads for students, real partnerships, and long-term commitment. They and their school partners are committed to helping disadvantaged students realize that higher education is obtainable.

TWO EXAMPLES: CINCINNATI AND MANHATTAN

The Cincinnati Chapter

GE-Aircraft Engines (GEAE) is the primary GE business located in the Cincinnati area, and GEAE employees make up the majority of the Cincinnati Elfun chapter membership. The Cincinnati chapter is one of the largest chapters, with approximately 3,200 regular and senior Elfuns and an Elfun Spouse Organization of 2,900 members. The chapter, which recently celebrated its 40th anniversary, won the National Elfun Society's Golden Elm award for community service in 1986, 1989, 1991, and 1992.

Community service project responsibilities are divided between two chapter officers—the director of educational involvement and the director of community involvement—who coordinate programs with project team leaders. The chapter's community activities have increased from 5 projects in 1985 to 26 in 1992. Educational involvement activities include 10 projects in schools and universities. Community involvement activities include 16 projects, from a talking books repair program run by retired

GE Elfuns, to walk-a-thons and other fundraising programs for nonprofit organizations, and housing reconstruction.

Cincinnati chapter board members describe their roles and the purpose of the chapter in the following words:

> I'm serving as a leader of a chapter with 3,000 members, and if I can touch each one of those people in some way, then I've served the purpose.
>
> I think that I'm serving the society in two ways: the individual and the community.
>
> It would be great to have everybody doing something, but you have to be able to leverage what you've got.

The chapter's community activities are open to all interested GE employees; Elfun members provide program leadership and management. Non-Elfun employees, spouses and, in some cases, non-GE volunteers, participate in Elfun activities. Many retired Elfuns are actively involved. As one board member comments, "We are constantly encouraging more on-going involvement with projects and a campaign that will keep people pumped up."

Each year, GE employees who meet the eligibility requirements are invited to join the society. In 1992, the chapter's new member nominations doubled to over 300 due to changes in eligibility requirements. New members are encouraged to undertake at least one community service project, to engage new members' active participation, and to develop their experience and skills.

The Cincinnati chapter sends a questionnaire to its members to determine which activities interest them, and keeps this information in a database. According to the chapter's educational involvement director, approximately 10 percent of members are active in Elfun-organized education and community programs.

The Aiken High School Partnership

In 1979, a GE program called "Educators in Industry" began the relationship between the Elfun Society and the Aiken High School. Aiken and GE established the first high school mentoring program in the Cincinnati Public Schools in 1985. The mentoring program developed into a $1 million College Bound grant from the GE Foundation to double the number of Aiken students who go to college by providing expanded services to help them gain acceptance to college.

Aiken, a neighborhood school, has a large number of students who move into and out of the school throughout the year. The student body is 78 percent African American, 21 percent white, and 1 percent other. Approximately 40 percent of the students live at or below the poverty level. Aiken received one of the GE Foundation's first College Bound Program grants to develop Project Continued Success (PCS). PCS improves college preparation by focusing on college entrance exams, the college selection and admission process, financial aid awareness, and strategies for success in college. Mentoring has been effective in helping accomplish the program's goals by making students aware of expanded educational opportunities and possible future careers, and assisting them in making the transition to higher education. Currently, 131 mentors are working with 11th and 12th graders in the PCS program, and 31 mentors are helping 9th- and 10th-grade students in the GE-sponsored Minorities in Mathematics, Science, and Engineering Project.

GE Fund grant resources enhance the Elfun-Aiken relationship. With GE Fund grant money, Aiken has developed a new pre-college curriculum. The grant is used to fund a full-time secretary and a part-time career counselor, and provides funds for overtime pay for teachers. The PCS director assists in the planning, management, preparation, and direction of a special year-long college preparation course for students in the program.

School counselors, teachers, and peers refer students to participate in PCS. The PCS staff reviews referrals and applicants using an inclusive process to select students who meet minimal academic, attendance, and interest requirements.

The PCS College and Career Center is an inviting, dynamic environment filled with college and career information resources. PCS staff members and mentors work with students to evaluate educational choices and possible careers. The College and Career Center is a frequent meeting place for mentors and students.

The Elfun-Aiken partnership defines mentoring as providing a role model, being a motivator, adviser, resource, and friend rather than a tutor, a "bank," or a replacement for parents. Mentors must have either been to college themselves or sent someone to college. Mentors include GE employees (Elfun members and non-Elfuns) and some non-GE volunteers. Participation is solicited through GE in-house publications, as well as civic, church, fraternal, and technical organizations.

The rise in Aiken graduates' college attendance—from 4 percent in 1985 to 56 percent in 1996—demonstrates the impact of Project Continued Success. Other programs in the GE Fund College Bound initiative have been modeled on the Aiken program.

The New York Chapter

The organization and activities of the New York Elfun chapter differ markedly from those of the older, larger Cincinnati chapter. The New York chapter has approximately 600 active members, including around 250 senior Elfuns, and includes employees of NBC and other GE businesses represented in Manhattan.

The chapter chairman estimates that between 10 and 15 percent of members volunteer in community activities sponsored by the society. Despite the contrasts between the New York and Cincinnati chapters, they have about the same level of participation in community activities.

Jack Welch's endorsement of Elfun and his belief that Elfun's community service "reflects glory" on GE, as well as the endorsements of local GE business leaders, have encouraged employee involvement. The New York chapter chairman educates employees about the dual benefit of membership—to employees and to the company—by pointing out its opportunities for networking and learning about other businesses, as well as serving the community. The chapter uses a variety of approaches to get new members to join, then attracts them to join in community activities.

The chapter's community involvement focuses on the Manhattan Center for Science and Mathematics. The chapter leaders made a deliberate decision to focus, strengthen, solidify, and expand the Manhattan Center mentoring program rather than diversify and spread their efforts among other programs and organizations. They give money to Meals on Wheels, Cornell Children's Hospital Emergency Fund, and other city causes, and individual chapter members participate in activities such as work in homeless shelters. But the chapter neither initiates nor officially sponsors these other activities. When approached to participate in other community service programs, chapter leaders generally decline in order to focus on improving and expanding the Manhattan Center program. The only exception is "Everybody Wins," a lunchtime, once-a-week reading program at PS 111. More than 75 NBC volunteers participate.

A past chapter chairman is responsible for the mentoring program at the Manhattan Center and for other community programs the chapter sponsors.

The major obstacle to increasing community participation by New York chapter members, according to a past chapter chairman, is geography. Most members live outside of Manhattan and prefer to take part in activities in their home communities. People who live outside Manhattan prefer not to return to the city after their long work days or on weekends. This represents a serious problem for Manhattan, like other urban communities with severe social problems. People who can afford to live elsewhere do not feel part of the urban community where they work, and they are often reluctant to play an active role in improving it.

The Manhattan Center for Science and Mathematics Partnership

The Manhattan Center is a public high school established in 1982 to provide the community of East Harlem with a school designed to prepare students for college and careers in math, technology, and science. Since the first class graduated in 1986, over 95 percent of the center's graduates have gone to college.

The GE Foundation made its first major three-year grant to the Manhattan Center to fund the GE Foundation Scholars Program in 1985. The foundation learned about the school from GE employees who volunteered there. The school's emphasis on preparing selected students in science and mathematics, and the foundation's policy of responding to needs identified by involved GE employees, made this grant a high priority for the foundation. Students participating in the GE Scholars Program, paired with GE mentors with science and engineering backgrounds, took part in special college preparation activities. Another GE Foundation grant sponsored teachers to help students improve their writing skills.

In 1987, 25 11th-grade students were selected for the GE Scholars Program. Each year since then, juniors have been selected for the program based on their interest in careers in math or engineering, and in their college potential. In 1991–92, there were 33 seniors and 27 juniors in the program, with GE mentors who provided college counseling and career role models. Mentors and students developed their own activities, meeting at least once a month for career-oriented or social meetings.

Often students come from high-risk families, with language problems, financial constraints, and inadequate role models. The program provides extra nurturing and support to increase their chances of success. An important message of the program is dispelling the myth that college is only for certain people.

The chapter's Mentoring Program at the Manhattan Center began in 1987. The program involves 60 GE mentors, both Elfun and non-Elfun employees, who work with juniors and seniors. Enthusiasm about mentoring has been so high that there have been more mentor volunteers than students in the program. The chapter is working with the school principal to expand the program.

A steering committee meets monthly to plan mentor-student events. They have devised a questionnaire to match mentors and students, and started a mentoring newsletter. They have talked about extending the program to sophomores but plan to take this step only after they have solidified their work with the juniors and seniors.

The chapter sponsors career days at the different GE businesses in Manhattan, and organizes cultural and sports programs for the mentors and students. Group events provide structured opportunities for mentors to meet with their students.

The chapter renovated and replanted a greenhouse on the roof of the school. This event was televised on NBC News, and GE made a video on the greenhouse project to use in recruiting Elfuns. The chapter also provided funds for professional production of a video on the school and its students called "A Beacon of Hope," to be used to raise additional private sector funds and recruit students.

Pre-College Program grant funds are used for schoolwide initiatives such as staff development, classroom activities, and purchases of equipment. The GE Fund subsidizes teachers' attendance at workshops, conferences, and seminars; additional math teaching hours; and a tutoring program for 9th graders taking advanced math. An SAT preparatory course is given each spring. The school also purchased computer research indexes and networks, CAD equipment and software, and equipment to upgrade the electronics and computer labs. The GE and NBC offices in New York donate used furniture for school classrooms and offices.

PROGRAM SIMILARITIES

The College Bound Program has made longlasting investments in infrastructure and faculty development. The fund's support helps the schools achieve institutional gains that go beyond the one-to-one benefits for students and mentors. The PCS director at the Aiken School in Cincinnati has adopted the same strategy to maximize the benefit of volunteer mentors and foundation support.

Through the school's connection with GE, the principal has access to other organizations that might not otherwise have worked with the school. The GE Fund's arts education program manager's contacts with arts organizations have helped the school develop cultural enrichment activities for students.

Future goals of the program include setting up an alumni association to track the students' progress in college and careers, and expanding the staff development program. The school anticipates that increasing budgetary constraints will require GE funds to support after-school tutoring and support programs.

The principal of the Manhattan Center firmly believes that, "This school would not be what it is without GE's support. . . . The program is blossoming. . . . It extends well beyond simply mentoring to be a more global involvement with the school."

The integrity of the GE volunteers and the relationships developed contribute greatly to the program's success. The schools, the foundation, and Elfun members are true partners in the design, planning, and implementation of the program. The principal attributes the atmosphere of "constant renewal" at the school to GE's involvement.

The Manhattan Center principal feels that it is unrealistic for schools to operate in isolation from the world of business. He believes that the GE volunteer mentors also benefit because participation fulfills a basic human need to be involved in something important outside of their normal work life. He sees tremendous potential in the involvement of businesses in schools, particularly in areas like curriculum planning to meet workforce training demands, and on program assessments where corporation personnel have special competence. He sees the resulting improvements in education as a factor in increasing the relevance of what the schools are doing. The School-to-Work initiative promoted by President Clinton in his Goals 2000 is the prime example of what GE volunteer mentors are trying to accomplish.

THE FUTURE

A significant trend in the society, reflecting the culture of the GE Company as a whole, is globalization. Since 1992, Elfun has expanded globally, forming new chapters in Japan, Singapore, Malaysia, Mexico, Brazil, United Kingdom, the Netherlands, and Hungary, joining previously established chapters in Puerto Rico and Canada. The society anticipates further expansion, as GE businesses increase their operations and staffing around the world.

The GE of the future is expected to embody the concept of boundary-lessness—a new organizational style designed to do away with internal barriers of hierarchy, geography, and function, while moving into closer partnerships with customers and suppliers. This goal is mirrored in the citizenship work of the Elfun Society and the GE Fund, especially in successful partnerships with public schools and other community service organizations in the United States and, increasingly, around the world.

CONCLUSION

The Elfun Society and the GE Fund have accumulated valuable experience in partnerships with schools and community organizations. The lessons relate to leadership, management, communications, relationship-building, volunteer recruitment and retention, private-public partnerships, and the use of core competence. As the foundation's Pre-College Program manager summarized their experience:

> The critical ingredient for success is a combination of people who truly care: a dynamic principal committed to turning around a troubled school; dedicated teachers and motivated parents; excited and ambitious students who, often for the first time in their lives, know that they can control the future; and volunteers who contribute their time, their energy, and their hearts as mentors, tutors, planners, advisers, and friends. Their personal attention and encouragement can make all the difference.

Another key factor in the success of GE's community service efforts has been the close alignment between corporate goals and community needs. Roberta Trachtman (1988) points out that "GE and the GE Fund are committed to quality science and mathematics education for reasons that combine a strong sense of corporate social responsibility with a large measure of enlightened self-interest. It may just be that such a combination is the requisite for success" (p. 173).

Projects need champions from the business and the community organization partners. Leaders from the Elfun Society and the community organization must work together as a team. Successful trust-building relationships are critical to partnership success. Flexibility and adaptability are key success factors. Program design should be tailored to partners' needs, with partners' participation in program design.

Employee morale is boosted by the satisfaction of successful new relationships. The company can attract better people due to the image of a caring company. Employee volunteering provides opportunities to interact with people from different layers and businesses working together outside the corporate hierarchy. Community service activities reinforce the boundarylessness of the organization, allowing for linkages across different functions, levels, and businesses, with the communities. Corporate community involvement strengthens the corporate identity. GE executives talk about "basking in the reflected glory" of corporate good works.

REFERENCES

Trachtman, R. "Strategies for Business Involvement." *American Business in the Public Schools.* New York: Teachers College Press, 1988.

ENDNOTE

1. In 1994, the GE Foundation became The GE Fund.

9

AMERITECH

The Community Service Link in Organizational Transformation

Jeannette L. Jackson

IN MARCH OF 1993, 48 Ameritech executives entered Cabrini Green, a Chicago inner-city housing project known for its poverty and violence. As they descended from the buses to gather in the community church, silence fell on the group. They moved instinctively and silently toward the church building that serves as the headquarters for Cabrini Green Alive, a program working to revitalize the Cabrini community. The level of discomfort among the group was extremely high; many had never been in this part of town, and recently a young child had been shot to death (a highly publicized story in Chicago), which had been the subject of hushed conversation on the bus trip to Cabrini. Once inside, the group was immediately introduced to the families with whom they would be working side-by-side to refurbish family apartments—apartments that had not seen a fresh coat of paint in over 20 years.

In the next eight months, over 10,000 Ameritech employees (executives, managers, and union members) would take part in similar community service activities as a part of Ameritech's transformation process. Ameritech's philosophy of community service is that since the community is the bedrock of where Ameritech gets its customers, it makes sense for Ameritech to get involved to make a difference in the communities in which it does business. Thus, one of the goals of community service in the transformation process is to connect Ameritech to its communities and customers and to start to build longer-term relationships with those community service agencies that have a positive impact on the quality of life within the communities in which Ameritech does or will do business.

- In contrast to Merck, whose citizenship activities reaffirmed the existing organizational culture, Ameritech used its involvement in citizenship activities to help transform the culture of the organization.

- Ameritech tied its choice of citizenship activities to its organizational strategy. Engaging in citizenship activities where employees literally got out and worked with people in the community was entirely consistent with its strategy of becoming more competitive by excelling in direct customer service.

- Because the type of community service activities that Ameritech employees were participating in were not necessarily related to the core competencies of the organization, Ameritech leveraged its contribution by working in partnership with agencies that were experienced in those types of projects.

AMERITECH—NO LONGER JUST A TELEPHONE COMPANY

Ameritech is a leading information services company that primarily provides advanced telecommunications technologies and networking capabilities to the upper midwestern portion of the United States—the midwestern off-shoot of the AT&T divestiture. It consists of what used to be Michigan Bell, Ohio Bell, Indiana Bell, Wisconsin Bell, Illinois Bell, and other information businesses. As a result of the transformation process, Ameritech is now organized in the following customer segment-specific units: Ameritech Consumer Services, Ameritech Custom Business Services, Ameritech Enhanced Business Services, Ameritech Small Business Services, Ameritech International, Ameritech Telephone Industry Services, Ameritech Information Industry Services, Ameritech Long-distance Industry Services, Ameritech Pay Phone Services, Ameritech Long Distance (global), Ameritech Cellular Services, Ameritech Advertising Services, Ameritech Leasing Services, and Ameritech Network Services.

In 1993, Ameritech generated over $11 billion in revenues and employed over 67,000 people (down from 71,000 people in 1992). Ameritech's competitive direction is best described in its vision statement:

Ameritech will be the world's premier provider of full-service communications—for people at work, at home, or on the move. Our goal will
be to improve the quality of life for individuals and to increase the
competitive effectiveness of the businesses we serve.

As we move and manage information for our customers, we will set
the standards for value and quality.

Ameritech's competence will be worldwide, building on our strength
in America's vibrant upper Midwest. Customers can be assured that we
will assume no task that we cannot do exceedingly well.

How Community Service Works at Ameritech

The three vertices in the Ameritech community service triangle are money,
volunteers, and the change process. Money flows to various community
service projects through corporate contributions and the Ameritech
Foundation. Volunteers are managed through the business entities and the
Pioneers, an organization made up of volunteers from the Bell System,
which means that Ameritech, AT&T, and the other regional Bell companies are involved. "Breakthrough!" is Ameritech's organizational change
process of which community service is a cornerstone element.

Breakthrough!: The Transformation of Ameritech

Ameritech started its transformation process—Breakthrough!—in 1991
with the top team of executives. The increasingly competitive telecommunications industry required that Ameritech change quickly. Ameritech's
culture was a relic of the old AT&T system, characterized by hierarchy,
bureaucracy, and life-time job security. To succeed in the new environment, the top team decided that Ameritech needed to focus the company
around customer needs and replace the old culture with a team-based
approach in which performance determines job security. In addition,
senior management put a stake in the ground that the success of
Ameritech depends on the success of the communities in which it does
business. Consequently, community service is considered to be an integral
part of the change process.

The structural elements of the change process are new management,
new business unit structures (now focused on customer needs across the
region rather than operating as state telephone companies), and a need to
change Ameritech's culture to match the competitive environment. The
primary elements of the change process are developing an understanding
of the environment in which Ameritech does business, identifying the
levers for making money, and focusing on customer service while working
on action-oriented change projects using high-performance teamwork to

get business results. The change process started with the top of the organization and cascaded throughout the organization.

THE IMPORTANT LINK TO COMMUNITY

Community service is a catalyst to the change process in several ways. Community service work takes a team out of its comfort zone in a regular business environment and gives people real work to accomplish in a limited time frame. Working on community projects creates a realistic environment for teams to get a sense of how they might perform with a work-related task and customers with whom they are not familiar. Community service, if orchestrated appropriately, connects employees to the customers in their communities face-to-face. Oftentimes, because the areas where the community service agencies are located are in rougher parts of town, many of the employees have never been to these locations—where they have customers and where Ameritech service technicians do business every day. Finally, Ameritech's involvement in the community demonstrates to employees the positive side of change. The early stages of change and transformation tend to be associated with layoffs, confusion, high levels of ambiguity, and a tremendous amount of anxiety on the part of people working in the organization. Even though the other side of change is exciting in that it means long-term viability for the company, the transition to this state is often long and painful.

The work done in the community gives people an immediate way to get involved in larger issues both emotionally and tactically. This experience often leads people to a personal vision that they can make an impact on a seemingly insurmountable problem, which can be a tremendous psychological boost in a time associated with layoffs.

The community's primary reaction to working with Ameritech in the context of the company's change process is one of renewed hope. Christiana Williams, a resident of Cabrini Green who worked with Ameritech employees to paint her apartment, expressed her feelings about the experience. "It was a ball. They just opened their hearts and filled our home with warmth. These people could be doing something else, but they chose to take the time to help us. They can come again and paint my apartment any time, even just to keep me company." Henrietta Johns, president of the 1015 and 1017 buildings in Cabrini Green and who has been instrumental in working with Ameritech, said, "We were amazed that a big company would come to reach out and give us a hand. We need help; it is great to get the help. We are poor here and in come these Ameritech people with good jobs to work with us. We just can't get over that."

The most important result of the work Ameritech is doing in the Cabrini community, according to Reverend Infelt, the pastor and leader of Cabrini Alive, "is the uplift in our community that comes from Ameritech taking on a honest and caring role in its community. This experience is unusual; no one else has tried it this way." When asked about the importance of the volunteer work versus the potential money from corporations such as Ameritech, he said, "Monetary donations from companies are important, but they are not as powerful as the memory that people with good jobs come to help our community."

AMERITECH MOVES BEYOND CABRINI GREEN

In the context of the change process, at least one community service agency in each state was carefully selected to work with Ameritech in the formalized portion of the change process. This process started with the top 1,000 managers, who then had the responsibility to replicate the experience with teams working under them. The selected agencies received attention from both the corporate and local leadership to capitalize on the relationship building that had already taken place and to ensure a long-term commitment to these agencies.

For example, Ameritech's first experience working with Cabrini Green so moved some Ameritech individuals that they took up a collection the very next day to buy educational games for the Cabrini Green children. This group also made time to go to Cabrini to work with the children and teach them how to play the games. Some Ameritech employees made personal connections with individuals from Cabrini, and continue to stay in contact. In addition, as a part of the Breakthrough! workshops, several groups of 50 or more Ameritech managers have returned to Cabrini to continue working with families as they revitalize their apartments. From the corporate side, Cabrini Alive has applied for and received a sizable corporate grant to support two pilot projects, one to promote better health care and one to develop parenting skills.

Several of the business units have adopted these agencies to provide ongoing support. "Focus: HOPE" in Detroit, Michigan, is another example of building relationships with community agencies through the Breakthrough! process. Focus: HOPE is an agency dedicated to the eradication of racism, poverty, and injustice and takes a holistic approach to its clients. (See Chapter Seventeen for a detailed description.) It operates a food program, a high school math program, a technical training program, an engineers training institute, and the Center for Advanced Technologies—a fully operational educational and manufacturing operation that showcases state-of-the-art technology. As a result of working in the food distribution program, at least one Ameritech group has adopted a group of seniors to whom they delivered food.

When Ameritech first began to work with Focus: HOPE, it was in small steps, primarily helping to distribute food in the food program. As the relationship developed, Ameritech was able to help Focus: HOPE with some immediate short-term as well as some longer-term needs. Short term, Focus: HOPE found itself significantly understaffed in the food distribution program when a company that had been supplying a steady stream of paid volunteers to deliver food unexpectedly discontinued their support due to issues internal to that company. Ameritech was able to step in with a group of volunteers from the Pioneer network to fill the gaps. Ameritech facilitated the sale of a Michigan Bell building to Focus: HOPE to house people involved with the Center for Advanced Technologies. Ameritech has also provided technical assistance on the Focus: HOPE phone system and donated some of its computer equipment to help Focus: HOPE expand its high school math training program. Ameritech has provided some of its state-of-the-art technology developed through the Super School project (see end of chapter) to an elementary school in Focus: HOPE's community.

St. Agatha's is another community service agency working with Ameritech. St. Agatha's is working to revitalize a community on the south side of Chicago. In the context of the change process, Ameritech has painted many apartments, landscaped, and worked with the children in the community in several different capacities. In speaking with several residents of this community, they are most touched and impressed by the work Ameritech is doing with the people in the community, particularly the children.

According to Kathryn Harris, "I have lived in this community all my life, I've seen it wonderful, I've seen it terrible, and now it is just so-so. Ameritech's most important work is connecting with the kids. It helps to raise their self-esteem and opens up avenues to see how to change some of the negative aspects in their lives. Some of the kids are still in contact with the Ameritech folks (after their community experience)."

Father Mike Ivers, the leader of the St. Agatha's parish, remarked on the significance of Ameritech making it a point to "stick with selected agencies to develop long-term relationships," because the more sustaining the relationship, the more commitment on both sides (corporate and community) to success. Father Ivers indicated that he is much more used to the "in and out kind of experience," where a corporation comes in for a quick project and then leaves—rarely to be heard from again. Ameritech continues to work with the St. Agatha's community on its project needs, and St. Agatha's has recently been the recipient of a grant from the Ameritech Foundation.

Each community agency was subjected to rigorous selection criteria in order to be a part of the Breakthrough! change process. The initial selection was based on the impact Ameritech could have on the social issues in the communities where it operates. After spending considerable time getting to know the agency and making telephone calls and several site visits, the determination was then made as to whether the agency had the impact, vision, and leadership qualities necessary to work with Ameritech in the Breakthrough! process.

There is no corporate social vision statement indicating how and what should be done. Each business unit is left to wrestle with its concept of social vision and to define its appropriate role in the community. The rationale is that each business unit knows what is most needed in its own community, and given Ameritech's overall vision, each team should be able to determine the appropriate course of action. Perhaps more importantly, if the commitment to action comes from the team's own social vision, it will be personally meaningful to the individuals who are part of the team. Unlike the "old" Ameritech, in which people were told what to think and how to act, this "new" Ameritech encourages the integration of personal and corporate social vision.

Charitable Giving

Ameritech contributes to the communities in which it does business through the Ameritech Foundation and corporate contributions. The Breakthrough! process resulted in a significant shift in the way contributions are managed. It used to be that Ameritech companies and the state organizations of Michigan, Ohio, Indiana, Wisconsin, and Illinois managed contributions. Now they are managed at a corporate level in order to avoid duplications and to focus the impact of contributions through the business units. Ameritech companies contributed more than $25 million in cash contributions—.91 percent of pre-tax net income—to more than 2,000 organizations in 1996. The Ameritech Foundation works on larger initiatives that are regionwide, countrywide and/or international in scope. In terms of Ameritech's total contributions, approximately 50 percent come from the Ameritech Foundation, and 50 percent come from corporate contributions.

Ameritech contributes to education, to economic development, to health care and to overall "quality of life." While customers are paramount to

Ameritech, and Ameritech invests billions of dollars each year to provide them with high-quality, state-of-the-art communications products and services, Ameritech also invests a portion of its earnings in selected educational, civic, community, health, and cultural organizations. In 1994, priority was given to those requests that improve *education, economic development, quality of life,* and *relationship building.*

A new addition to Ameritech's corporate giving policy is that foundation dollars will follow volunteer hours in the community agencies where the volunteers work.

VOLUNTEERS

Volunteers are orchestrated by business units and the Pioneers (see the next section). Generally speaking, community activities fall under the aegis of public relations, although this is changing as Breakthrough! cascades through the organization and management takes on a more significant role in managing the community relationships. The business units operate under the philosophy that dollars should follow employee interest. Some business units are proactive and seek out community organizations that are setting standards for improving the environment and/or quality of life, while others operate in a reactive mode, whereby community service organizations approach them. Each business unit is different in terms of who volunteers. In some cases, management and nonmanagement volunteer together, while in others only management participates in community service projects.

THE AMERITECH PIONEERS

Ameritech has a significant history of community service starting back to the days of the old Bell system. In 1911, a few employees attempted to organize people from all around the nation. Initially, it was for the purposes of having fun, a social organization "to perpetuate friendships, to encourage such other worthy and appropriate purposes as may from time to time be suggested and approved." Individual Pioneers were active in many community causes, and during World War II, for example, the Pioneers developed a coordinated program of visiting employees who were hospitalized during military service. The first Pioneer group community service activities probably began in 1948, when a unit was organized to make bandages for the Red Cross. During the next ten years, new service projects were begun in the fields of hospital volunteer work, as well as various services for the blind and handicapped. In 1958, the new role of community service called "the New Tradition" was officially adopted as an associationwide goal.

At the point of divestiture, there was a conscious decision by its sponsor companies to keep the Pioneer organization together, which meant that when there is a Pioneer general assembly or gathering of any kind, all of the sponsoring companies are represented. Currently, there are approximately 800,000 Pioneer members from the regional Bell companies, AT&T, and 22 sponsoring companies in Canada. Ameritech's Pioneer membership is approximately 85,000, of which about 15 percent participate in community service. Of the 85,000 current members, 49,000 are retired. Ameritech Pioneers currently donate about 1 million hours a year to community service.

Just as Ameritech is undergoing a major change, so is the Pioneer organization. All employees are now encouraged to be Pioneers, whereas before it was primarily for long-service employees. The Ameritech Pioneers are working to be consistent with Ameritech's new business unit structure and culture. The Ameritech Pioneers are focusing on each business unit as they identify the areas on which they wish to focus their attention in order to make an impact in the communities in which they do business.

FOCUS ON EDUCATION

Ameritech's focus on education has a community service as well as business growth dimension. Ameritech developed the Super School concept, which is designed to show how telecommunications can improve education. It includes distance learning using interactive video, voice, and data lines, education hot lines, technology for the handicapped, automating school systems in a "feature-rich telecommunication network," and multiple-location networking. Ameritech has installed distance learning networks in Northern Michigan, Wisconsin, and Indiana. Estimated annual revenues to Ameritech from education are over $100 million. Ameritech's motives are clear; technology drives the bottom line, and they can make the lives of parents, students, and teachers better.

BEST PRACTICES IN DEVELOPING
COMMUNITY PARTNERSHIPS

Working community service into the Breakthrough! change process was a learning experience. It took some time to refine the best practices that really leverage the value of community service to both Ameritech and the communities in which it does business. Outlined next are some of the key learnings that were integrated into Ameritech's way of working in its communities:

Focus and leverage the company's resources on a few selected agencies. Select agencies that are making a difference in the community using specific criteria. Then focus the organizational resources, both human and financial, on these agencies. By targeting the organization's resources in a few well-defined areas, the potential to make a lasting impact is greater than the scattershot approach of working with multiple agencies.

Establish clear goals. Prior to getting into the details of a relationship, make sure the agency understands what you want to accomplish. It is important to be clear about what each party will both give to and get out of the experience. For example, you are exploring the possibility of establishing a long-term relationship with the agency and, as a part of this process, you want to set up a work activity whereby the clients of the agency and Ameritech employees work side-by-side. Establishing clear goals should be continuous as the environment and organizational needs may—indeed, probably will—change at any time.

Achieve socialization. This means talking through with the organization what exactly you plan to do with them and how you will interact with their clients. Community agencies are most concerned about the way a group of executives might treat their clients. They need to know that their clients will be treated with dignity and respect and will never be embarrassed or belittled.

Connect the community agency clients with Ameritech employees. The most powerful experiences came when Ameritech employees worked with community agency clients in a joint effort. Often when groups of business executives go to do "good work" at an agency, it is by themselves; they never have to interact with the clients of the agency, never have to put themselves in the shoes of those they are "helping," never have to face the issues faced by the clients. When you connect people-to-people, working on a community project becomes much less of a technical project and much more of a personal growth experience. Although this is often difficult to arrange, it has proven to be a powerful experience for both the Ameritech employees as well as the community agency clients.

Recognize the time it takes to develop meaningful community partnerships. One of the key lessons is that you don't rush into a community partnership activity (that is, don't expect to call an agency and plan an activity that same week). Partnerships require cultivation. There are suspicions on both sides—"What do nonprofits know about real work?" and "What do companies know about the problems we face?" It takes time to break down the barriers to establish a solid working relationship.

Take responsibility for all arrangements when working with an agency. Ameritech takes the stand that it can ill afford to burden the community service agency with whom it is partnering. Recognizing that the agency's first order of business is its clients, Ameritech takes care of all arrangements such as procuring and paying for any materials that will be used in the projects. Ameritech has even gone so far as to pay for community service administrative time used to set up the work experiences.

THE FUTURE

Community agencies selected to work with Ameritech are now able to take advantage of the leadership and business skills training available to Ameritech employees. The decision to invest in the community agency development came from the lessons learned as Ameritech grows closer to the community agencies with which it works. There are many parallels between community agencies' needs and the transformation process ongoing at Ameritech. Community service agencies (particularly the large ones), on the whole, have not recognized the need to change the way they work, and yet they are often hierarchical and bureaucratic organizations. Ameritech recognizes that such agencies might benefit from some of the leadership tools used to accelerate transformation and that the more the community service agencies speak the same language as Ameritech, the easier it will be for both parties to take full advantage of the partnership. As a result of the work done developing community partnerships through Breakthrough!, the following next steps have been identified:

Invest quality time to work with the agency to give them the benefits. One of the key benefits for the agency of working with Ameritech is that both Ameritech and the agency employees are teaming to become change agents. Continuing to invest in the development of the community leadership may help to accelerate the good work they are already doing.

Strategically set goals jointly with the agency. Often an agency has a priority list of things it wishes to accomplish. That list, however, may not connect with Ameritech's vision of what needs to be accomplished. For example, the agency is most interested in serving its clients and consequently sees all other activities as relatively inconsequential, such as billing Ameritech for services it provides, ensuring the availability of clients to work with Ameritech managers on projects, and procuring materials. Ameritech can work with them to show how and why these activities are important—that is, the agency loses money that could be applied to serve clients if it doesn't bill Ameritech; or the clients lose a potentially valuable interaction with Ameritech managers if they don't show up, or projects don't get completed without the appropriate materials. In essence, Ameritech can help facilitate the agency's understanding of how to work most effectively with a business to nurture an ongoing relationship.

Formally debrief with community service organizations. Formally debrief with community service organizations after every activity. Make it a disciplined activity, one wherein Ameritech and the agency examine how they are working together, identifying best practices, and fixing what is broken. The goal is to develop a healthy, open process whereby the community agency pushes Ameritech to achieve more, and Ameritech in turn inspires the community agency to achieve more.

Leverage the experience. Develop a mechanism to leverage community activities for employees, retirees, and employees affected by downsizing. All three of these groups have tremendous skills to offer community agencies, and the goal is to capture them in the most effective way possible.

Continue institutionalization. The process of integrating the teamings from working with community service in the Breakthrough! change process into day-to-day practices has really just begun. While there have been significant changes in the way community projects are utilized, the way contributions are handled, and the way Ameritech is now focusing its efforts in a few key areas, there is still a lot of work to be done. As with most transformations of large entities, some areas of the business "get it," in that they have a vision for community service, and others don't. Ameritech Pioneers is one of the ways that the Breakthrough! learnings around community service are becoming institutionalized.

Since 1993, Ameritech has focused and refined its commitment to community service. The intensity of the projects is less now than in the earlier stages of the transformation, but Ameritech's community service activity and financial contributions are more focused to increase the potential impact in the community. Corporate contributions are now linked directly to the agencies where Ameritech employees volunteer their time in their communities. Long-term relationships have been built with several agencies that were part of the initial launch of Ameritech's transformation.

For example, groups of employees continue to do work in Cabrini Green community in Chicago. In some cases the Pioneer volunteers became more involved with the community agencies that helped to launch

Ameritech's transformational efforts. The Ameritech Institute, which was
established to help institutionalize the transformation at Ameritech, continues to implement community service projects as part of its programs.
The initial burst of energy in working with specific designated community
agencies has translated into a more cohesive link between volunteer time
and corporate contributions, as well as ongoing support for the agencies
involved with Ameritech's transformational efforts.

WHY COMMUNITY SERVICE IS GOOD BUSINESS FOR AMERITECH

Community service is good business for Ameritech because if the communities in which Ameritech does business thrive, then there is a healthy
environment for existing and potential customers—the life blood of
Ameritech's success. Focused community service contributes to the quality
of life in Ameritech's communities, provides a venue for building teamwork, and connects employees to customers. When asked why community
service makes sense in the context of a transformation process, the
response is that transformation is an emotional, gut-level process, and the
community experience has the power to transform individuals at an emotional level. Many of the people who are going through the transformation process at Ameritech have never experienced anything like the
magnitude of change that is currently taking place. This produces stress
and anxiety in the system, and very few apparent release valves are in
place. The community experience in the transformation process "cracks
the code" by opening people up in a way that enables them to deal with
their anxieties and emotions around the transformation.

CONCLUSION

The Ameritech case demonstrates how corporate global citizenship activities can benefit the companies that engage in them, while at the same time
serving the community. As a result of its community service programs,
Ameritech has created a more competitive and closely knit corporate culture. Just as importantly, its efforts to revitalize communities have resulted
in more profitable markets for their information and telecommunication
services.

Ameritech was faced with a tremendous need to change its organizational culture. Emerging from the protective cocoon of a regulated
monopoly, the company discovered that it was ineffective in competing in
a world that demanded customer service. Only by coming to understand

the needs of its customers could the company hope to compete. Ameritech's strategy for developing the necessary understanding was to become directly and deeply involved in the communities that it served.

That strategy has served the company well. As employees began to serve the needs of their communities, they began to build the type of service culture that was critical to the continued success of Ameritech. In addition, community service activities also brought employees together in a meaningful way that helped to create closer bonds among the employees, facilitating their efforts to work in teams in the organization.

Just as Ameritech was changing its corporate culture as a result of its participation in community service programs, the communities in which these programs were being implemented were also changing. Because revitalizing a community doesn't happen overnight, Ameritech focused on committing to long-term relationships with selected agencies to ensure that their efforts would have a lasting impact. Although Ameritech's investment in these communities may not have a quick, direct financial payback, the company has already benefited from establishing a more responsive and cohesive organizational culture.

10

SARA LEE CORPORATION AND CORPORATE CITIZENSHIP

Unity in Diversity

Ann E. Tenbrunsel, Zoe I. Barsness, and Paul M. Hirsch

WHAT DO THE FAMILIAR brand names Hanes, Bryan Meats, Kiwi, Hygrade, Jimmy Dean Meats, Coach Leatherware, L'eggs, and Champion all have in common? Their parent company is the Sara Lee Corporation, which has come a long way since 1939, when it began as a small wholesale sugar, coffee, and tea distributor in Chicago. One of the world's largest diversified consumer products companies, with sales of approximately $12 billion, Sara Lee today has over 110,000 employees in more than 30 countries.

Most of the firm's growth has occurred in the last decade, a fact that could lead one to expect a host of management problems—lack of coordination and accountability across diverse business lines, a discordant organizational culture, and no distinct corporate identity or graspable hierarchy. On the surface, Sara Lee's large size, wide array of products, and number of divisions suggest just such problems. But senior management at Sara Lee has adopted a cohesive philosophy that is expressed in a unified, specific business methodology across all product lines and divisions. As a result, Sara Lee has forged a distinct corporate identity and gained a reputation for good management and high-quality products.

Three critical components define the management philosophy that enabled this potentially unwieldy conglomerate to market itself and its products effectively. The first is management's consistent dedication to being the premier brand in all its product and service categories. Second is the CEO's strong leadership and hands-on involvement. Last, and perhaps most important, is a unique decentralized structure and grassroots approach that promotes employee participation. Sara Lee encourages employee entrepreneurship in support of corporate goals at all levels of the company, from the corporate offices to divisional headquarters to local plants. This grassroots approach, coupled with a clear corporate vision, helps resolve potential tensions between the divisions and the corporate level.

Sara Lee's products are known for strong market performance and consumer brand recognition. Yet, many of Sara Lee's brands were acquired, and growth through acquisition always presents a further challenge to management. Local and division managers, who seek to maintain the integrity of their own brands, must simultaneously work to develop and maintain the corporate image. Sara Lee executives have chosen to create a decentralized organizational structure to accomplish this goal. This decentralized structure lets each division decide how to achieve corporate goals while serving its own needs. Divisions have the authority to meet market challenges quickly and effectively, implement innovations, and respond to customers quickly. Decentralized structure allows this corporation to maintain a seemingly effortless balance among competing demands that a more tightly structured organization might find impossible to manage.

Taken individually, each of the three essential factors of Sara Lee's management philosophy would be insufficient to achieve the success for which the corporation is known. But integrating them makes Sara Lee a uniquely agile giant.

- The structure of Sara Lee's organization provides the framework for how the company carries out its citizenship activities.

- The diversified nature of Sara Lee's business is also reflected in the diverse array of accounts that are used to justify the company's participation in citizenship activities, reflecting moral, social, and economic arguments.

- Sara Lee's attitude toward continuous improvement in its products and services is also reflected in the company's attitude toward its citizenship activities. Thus, the company has a system that measures and tracks the impact of philanthropic activity on employees, with a particular emphasis on turnover.

COMMUNITY INVOLVEMENT MIRRORS BASIC BUSINESS PRACTICES

The ways Sara Lee implements its strong commitment to community involvement mirror its diversified approach to business. Community involvement, like any other business activity at Sara Lee, conforms to the firm's strategic mission. In fact, meeting high standards of social responsibility in employee and community relations amounts to a fourth element of the company's basic management philosophy. Despite the striking differences in Sara Lee's business lines and the communities and countries in which it operates, a single cohesive approach to philanthropy shapes the firm's community involvement. Officers, managers, and employees at the corporate and local levels assert that the company's duty to society is equal to its obligations to stockholders, employees, and customers.

As John Bryan, Sara Lee's CEO put it, "Serving society is the reason business exists." The firm applies the same high performance standards to community involvement as to manufacturing products and delivering services. The corporation requires that each of its facilities—whether corporate headquarters, a division office, or a local plant—hold a leadership position in its community's civic and cultural life.

The firm's decentralized structure provides the skeleton upon which its community activities are organized. Each division manages its own corporate citizenship programs. This grassroots approach ensures that contributions reflect and quickly respond to local community concerns. Although each division approaches corporate citizenship differently, all units adhere to the corporate philosophy that Sara Lee should help others help themselves. Company literature states that the firm thinks of itself as a "partner in community progress," not merely an indiscriminate benevolent dispenser of dollars and good will.

CEO Leadership

The CEO's role is crucial. John Bryan, the firm's very visible top manager, sets the tone. He is philosophically devoted to the community and, by extension, to corporate social responsibility. Bryan feels strongly that corporations have internal and external obligations to their many stakeholders, including the community. Bryan contrasts this belief with the actions of companies that do not seem to honor any obligations to the community. He believes responsible companies must do more than provide jobs. They must get involved in the communities where they operate.

Why Get Involved?

The explanations for Sara Lee's ambitious citizenship and philanthropic agenda are as diverse as its product lines. Many tangible benefits accrue to the firm because of its community involvement. As one division manager reports, "It's good business to be a good corporate citizen." The most apparent benefit is the tax savings the firm achieves by its corporate contributions. Current U.S. tax law allows firms to deduct donations of up to 5 percent of their pre-tax income. Bryan claims therefore that tax benefits are a "major inducement" for Sara Lee to contribute. They allow the firm to avoid capital gains taxes on its real property by making contributions to its foundation. But tax savings represent only the tip of the iceberg.

Community involvement is also recognized as an effective public relations technique. While the firm did not pursue its citizenship activities expressly for marketing purposes, officers and managers realize that visible corporate citizenship activities enhance the corporate image and brand-name recognition.

But mostly, Bryan asserts, community involvement helps support the communities from which Sara Lee draws its workforce. "Every company recognizes that making its community a healthier, safer, and more pleasant place to live pays real dividends." This attitude harmonizes with Sara Lee's interest in retaining employees by creating an appealing work environment. Management believes that the firm possesses many attractive qualities for employees: its decentralized structure, thin management layers, entrepreneurial atmosphere, and open-door policies. These attributes, coupled with high-quality products, enhance employee pride. In addition, management believes that the firm's reputation for community activism helps attract and retain desirable employees. Moreover, participation in community service activities improves employees' administrative skills and leadership qualities—thus improving the quality of the corporation's pool of managerial talent.

Beyond these tangible economic benefits, a moral motivation also drives Sara Lee's corporate citizenship activities. Many employees simply believe that community involvement is "the right thing to do." Bryan argues vigorously that corporations have a moral obligation to serve their communities regardless of the reciprocal benefits.

At face value, economic and moral rationales for corporate community involvement might appear to be contradictory. At Sara Lee, managers and employees often use both of these arguments in combination to endorse corporate community activism. Managers and employees agree that it is both ethical and smart business practice to be a good corporate citizen.

Philanthropic donations and community activities are integral parts of Sara Lee's corporate strategy, and wholly consistent with its identity as a profit-making corporation. As its citizenship activities improve the community, they enhance the business environment and the company's image. In John Bryan's philosophy, Sara Lee's mission is "to serve both the community and company interests simultaneously."

MAKING CORPORATE CITIZENSHIP WORK AT SARA LEE

What is characteristic about corporate citizenship at Sara Lee? At first glance, not much. No one program is closely identified with Sara Lee. Rather, the firm has myriad commitments to a wide variety of nonprofit organizations and community concerns. Instead of concentrating its efforts on developing one program as a corporate showcase, the firm focuses on a specific approach and applies it to all citizenship endeavors at all company levels and locations. The approach is procedural rather than structural.

How Decentralization Works

Consistent with its general grassroots management philosophy, the organizational mechanisms that make corporate citizenship work at Sara Lee are dispersed throughout the company. The firm's commitment to community involvement relies on employee initiative, entrepreneurship, and autonomy. Employees, managers, and officers at every organizational level—corporate, divisional, and local—define and participate in the firm's citizenship and philanthropic activities. Responsibility for corporate social activism in the communities where Sara Lee operates, therefore, resides with the divisions and local plants.

At the corporate level, three groups oversee the firm's philanthropic activities: the Sara Lee Foundation, the employee volunteerism committee, and the Office of Public Responsibility. The CEO established the Sara Lee Foundation in 1981. Its staff consists of five people: the foundation director, the assistant director, two consultants, and a receptionist. The management contribution committee—a senior management group that includes the CEO—oversees the foundation. The foundation's primary functions are to make corporate grants and to structure programs for corporate employees. Its secondary function is to be an intermediary between the community and the corporation. It is the clearinghouse for corporate donations and grants to nonprofit organizations. Lastly, although the management contribution committee has ultimate authority over the foundation and establishes its broad goals, the foundation staff bears responsibility for all charitable giving and citizenship operations.

The employee volunteerism committee (EVC) is a volunteer group at corporate headquarters. Directed by the assistant director of the foundation, the EVC consists of ten steering committee members and another five or six members who belong to a special projects subcommittee. Membership in the group crosses all levels of employment, as does participation in EVC-sponsored activities. The committee's mandate is to develop and organize corporate-level volunteer activities. Its primary purpose is to provide opportunities and make information available so that busy people who might otherwise not have the time can get involved in community volunteer activities. As one steering committee member indicates, "The EVC committee provides a smorgasbord of volunteer opportunities for employees, and gives them the information they need to participate."

Corporate Volunteerism Projects

For example, the committee coordinates corporate projects like the Share Holiday (a Christmas wish list for local children), Earth Day projects, and an on-going program that provides opportunities for employees to donate to homeless shelters in the Chicago area. The EVC does not seek to compete with employees' existing loyalties to churches, schools, or other interests. Rather, as one EVC member notes, "Our goal is to create new outlets for employees to participate in the community."

The third administrative body that directs a portion of corporate-level citizenship activity is the Office of Public Responsibility, designed to play both an internal and an external role in Sara Lee's community involvement process. Headed by the vice president of public responsibility, the office focuses primarily on national issues that affect all of the company's divisions. The Office of Public Responsibility has three key goals: to attract and retain new employees, given changing workforce demographics; to demonstrate Sara Lee's commitment to greater corporate responsibility; and to interpret, define, and manage awareness and perceptions of Sara Lee's public interests. For example, this office is involved in Sara Lee's efforts to meet the high standards on corporate social responsibility published by the Council on Economic Priorities for concerned consumers and investors.

The committee on public responsibility, the largest board committee, was established in 1972. Backed by this committee, the Office of Public Responsibility acts as a catalyst and a corporate resource. Although the vice president of public responsibility and her staff work with the foundation, they are the "big picture people," addressing more global and national concerns such as women's issues, the environment, and the relation between work and family. Internally, they seek to create synergies by coordinating foundation, EVC, and programs at divisions and plants. Externally, they try to ensure that Sara Lee's public image accurately reflects the company and its goals. The office also oversees connections among Sara Lee's divisions and the local branches of the many nonprofit organizations with which the company works. The office focuses on human resource issues because of the changing workforce demographics that the company expects to face in years to come. Unlike the foundation, the office does not simply disburse funds. It supplies labor as well as material support to citizenship efforts throughout the organization.

Although the Sara Lee Foundation is responsible for overall corporate donations, the company promotes a localized approach to corporate giving at the division level. Company literature strongly emphasizes this point. For example, a publication describing corporate philanthropic activity highlights Sara Lee's unique approach:

> The corporation employs a grassroots strategy that is as decentralized as its business operations. Each of the company's divisions manages its own giving program, and since many divisions are based in small towns, they often become leading corporate citizens, providing support that is not available from any other source [*Partners in Community Progress*, Sara Lee Corporate Affairs Department, 1992, p. 2].

Senior managers trust the divisions to act appropriately, confident that each division is well-positioned to assess pressing community concerns, and come up with ways to address them. Consequently, plants vary in their approaches to community service. A unifying theme, however, is that all employees are encouraged to volunteer time and talent to community endeavors. By delegating responsibility for community involvement to the lowest level—the plants—the firm can maximize employee involvement and reach all communities where the company operates.

Local employee volunteer groups inform management at the plants about which programs to implement or support. These community action teams are characteristically independent. Organized along lines similar to the EVC, these groups include interested employees who determine which projects Sara Lee will undertake in their local communities.

What results is a wide array of community activities, from aiding children by adopting their school, to preserving the environment through Earth Day efforts, to helping and providing role models for disadvantaged women.

Funding

Company policy dictates that the firm donate at least 2 percent of its U.S., pre-tax income to nonprofit organizations. In 1991, the company exceeded this goal, as it has done each year since the early 1980s, contributing $11.7 million. While the foundation disburses the majority of the corporate giving budget, it also supports projects proposed by the Office of Public Responsibility if these meet its grant criteria. The board's committee on public responsibility channels funds for the Office of Public Responsibility to support functions that the foundation legally cannot. The EVC, by contrast, requires little funding; most of its activities require donations of employees' time and effort rather than money. The foundation provides funds when necessary to support EVC activities.

Each division has its own pool of money for citizenship activities, separate from funds budgeted by the foundation. Division managers determine the size of this pool based on a percentage of their division's operating budget and allocate them to each of the division's plants in local communities. Plant managers are responsible for the disbursement of these funds at their discretion and are accountable for these monies. Often, community action teams decide how to distribute these funds.

Program Implementation

The approach that Sara Lee uses to market its products effectively also shapes the implementation of its citizenship and philanthropic agenda. Many of the same integral aspects of Sara Lee's business strategy—CEO leadership and involvement, extensive employee participation, and decentralized management—also characterize the way in which Sara Lee manages community involvement. Whether in the initiation, recruitment, or execution phase of a community project, these factors come into play in all citizenship efforts.

Project Initiation

Employee activism and decentralized management show up in the project initiation phase, including idea generation, development, and approval. Sara Lee officers claim they are unconcerned about whether the firm acts alone or in concert with other firms when engaging in citizenship undertakings. Sara Lee collaborates with philanthropic groups, including the Council on Foundations, the Donors Forum, the Affinity Group, and various other local groups in Chicago. However, most of Sara Lee's ideas have grassroots origins. Sara Lee tends to favor projects that have percolated up through the corporation from employees at the local level.

This approach typifies the style of both the Office of Public Responsibility and the EVC. The Office of Public Responsibility gets ideas from many sources, including word of mouth, publications, shareholder letters, and shareholder meetings. In addition, it solicits employee suggestions through a variety of mechanisms such as opinion surveys, programs that encourage anonymous recommendations, and meetings that bring corporate officers into contact with employees. Similarly, the EVC acts as a clearinghouse for employee recommendations. Although the committee receives notices of opportunities from nonprofit and community organizations, Sonya Jackson, assistant foundation director and EVC coordinator, states that, "It truly is an employee committee. The largest source of new project ideas is employees."

Division-level projects also originate at the company's grassroots. Community surveys assess local issues, and employee input is strongly encouraged. Like the foundation, the divisions do not rely on corporate role models. Rather, they act independently, often donning the mantle of leadership in community programs.

Project Approval

The project approval process takes project ideas through both formal and informal filters. Following its decentralized management approach, each philanthropic group defines its own project approval criteria. Contributions made through the foundation follow a formally defined giving agenda: 50 percent of all corporate donations go to the disadvantaged, 40 percent to the arts, and 10 percent to all other programs.

These guidelines reflect the imprint of a specific corporate strategy. Robin Tryloff, foundation director, explains that Sara Lee's focus on women in the disadvantaged category recognizes the fact that "women constitute over half of the firm's employees and more than 80 percent of its customers. In fact, we are the largest company in the world named after a woman."

Moreover, within the categories established by its giving guidelines, Sara Lee attempts to determine which nonprofit organizations are really making a difference in the community, and to support those. The company does not lightly drop a nonprofit organization, but if a cooperating group ceases to fit the firm's grant criteria, or if the foundation feels that the organization no longer serves the best interests of its constituents, funding will be stopped.

In contrast to the formal, predetermined guidelines of the foundation, those of the Office of Public Responsibility are more dynamic, as fits the specific mission of this office: projects must respond to current issues. This means that the office's current attention to human resource issues will change as the company confronts new global and national challenges.

The EVC applies a different set of criteria, determined more by employee interests than foundation guidelines or national concerns. As a steering committee member indicates, "Judgments are made more on interests rather than value. But, there are times when proposals are denied because we feel that they won't fit with the committee's mission. If people on the EVC are divided, we feel that that means others will be divided as well."

Thus, although the committee does not formally sponsor projects that it believes may offend certain employees (such as projects dealing with abortion), it posts information about a variety of projects on bulletin boards where interested employees may inform themselves.

At the division level, foundation guidelines for giving serve as models, subject to modification to fit local community needs. Divisions, for example, tend to emphasize help for the needy and contribute less to the arts than the foundation. Although guidelines vary by division, many divisions use teams of employees to determine the appropriate mix of projects to support. Like the employee volunteerism committee, divisions avoid supporting controversial issues that may blemish the company's image in the community.

Approval for foundation projects comes from the director of the foundation. The management contribution committee reviews the foundation's activities four times a year, but this formality is usually directed toward larger issues rather than individual project approval. Similarly, the EVC reviews and approves its own philanthropic activities. Divisions prepare annual contributions budgets and, upon approval, receive free reign to implement local community projects. Ad hoc requests to any of the philanthropic groups are handled individually by whichever committee or individual is responsible for approving the group's overall budget.

Recruitment for Citizenship Activities

A variety of encouragement mechanisms help guarantee the success of citizenship activities at Sara Lee. One such mechanism was an unintended consequence of the CEO's beliefs and values. While numerous employees at different levels stress the importance of the CEO as a role model, as Eleanor Williams, vice president of public responsibility, sums it up, "The chairman is personally involved and has a high profile himself. His support is a key success factor. We couldn't do it without the CEO, and our efforts wouldn't look like they do without his support." His beliefs show in the way the company supports employees who volunteer, not only allowing time off from work but also by making company resources such as electronic mail and meeting space available.

At corporate headquarters, employees at all levels are encouraged to participate through informal employee networks. Members of volunteer groups invite their peers to join, and the employee volunteerism committee uses innovative techniques such as "Bring a Friend" meetings to increase employee participation.

Sara Lee also uses more direct mechanisms. For example, it retains a "volunteerism consultant" whose sole responsibility is to match corporate employees with nonprofit organizations. To ensure that all employees have opportunities to participate, the human resource department gives this consultant the names of new employees when they join the firm.

The most direct mechanism, however, is the incorporation of public service objectives into the annual performance reviews of middle and senior managers, who are required to document their records of public service. As Bob Warren, employee relations director for Sara Lee Knits, explains, "Managers work with their supervisors to set their own standards of performance. These standards include those related to actual job performance and commitments to specific community service activities. These criteria are then incorporated into the individual's performance review."

Evaluation of actual citizenship activity, as it relates to performance objectives, is then linked to the bonus and compensation system. The incorporation of public service responsibility into performance objectives is also apparent at the division level, where each division president reviews standards of performance. In addition, division managers attend seminars that address corporate ethics in the community.

Project Execution

The Office of Public Responsibility and the EVC tailor project execution to specific needs and goals. The Frontrunner Awards, sponsored by the Office of Public Responsibility, reward outstanding women. To select the recipients, a committee chooses four applicants from over 350 candidates. The Office of Public Responsibility performs its duty to promote a positive corporate image by advertising the awards in leading magazines and newspapers.

By contrast, the EVC sponsors events that vary in magnitude and scope. Some projects, such as Earth Day, may only involve a handful of employees who volunteer their time. Others, such as Share Holiday, involve over 300 employees at corporate headquarters. Although attendance varies, all projects involve employees from a wide variety of levels, working side by side. Participants do not remain constant across projects but follow their interests and contribute their time to projects that are near and dear to their hearts.

At the division level, project execution matches the individual community and project. For example, a majority of Sara Lee divisions sponsor Adopt-a-School programs, designed to improve the quality of local public schools. Each Adopt-a-School program is designed to respond to local needs. As Bob Russ, human resource manager at Sara Lee Knits puts it, "We'd be crazy to dictate a cookie cutter approach." A majority of the suggestions for services—mentoring, fundraising, buying computers, instructing, tutoring, career counseling, mock interviewing, and teacher training—come from the employees themselves. Employees also contribute their time, often during company hours, in areas that match their skills and abilities.

Thus, Sara Lee uses the same skills necessary to market an individual product to implement its citizenship and philanthropic programs. All phases of project implementation, from idea generation to recruitment to execution, involve employees from various corporate levels working together. Both the CEO's highly visible role model and the autonomy and responsibility of each individual employee are vital. As Bob Warren states, "All the corporation expects is that the divisions be perceived as good corporate citizens in our community. We have lots of latitude to decide ourselves how to accomplish this goal."

Reporting

Sara Lee details the progress of citizenship activities by requiring each corporate philanthropic group to make direct formal reports up through the hierarchical chain. In addition, a variety of informal mechanisms provide information to the company at large. The Sara Lee Foundation provides an oral and written report to investors at the annual shareholders meeting, and bi-annual reports to the management contribution committee. The Office of Public Responsibility provides periodic reports to the committee of public responsibility. Divisions send annual reports describing the status of corporate citizenship activities to the foundation. In addition, each division, as part of a report on employee indicators, sends monthly reports on its community involvement to the CEO.

All Sara Lee employees get information on philanthropic activities through a variety of company publications. The *Leeway Magazine,* a vehicle for company news, is one forum for reporting and promoting citizenship activities that occur throughout the company. Information on philanthropic events is also posted on company bulletin boards and published in company newsletters.

At the division level, each facility receives the newsletter, "Partnerships," which details the division's philanthropic activities. A variety of communication tools send information within and across divisions. Each division sends regular newsletters to each plant, to division headquarters, and to individual employees. Although these newsletters are prepared separately and focus on a variety of topics, community activity is consistently mentioned.

As a rule, however, Sara Lee, does not promote its citizenship activities directly to the general public, preferring to let its actions speak for themselves. As many officers strongly assert, the foundation is not a marketing department, and corporate citizenship is not just another promotional activity.

ASSESSING BENEFITS: IS IT DONE?

The company makes no attempt to measure levels of employee participation or assess the internal or external effects of its corporate citizenship activities, even though managers and employees frequently mention that community involvement brings a variety of benefits to the firm. What little systematized assessment there is happens at the division and corporate levels. The foundation evaluates each division president's contributions to the community and presents Community Service Leadership awards in recognition of outstanding efforts. Similarly, the foundation reviews the achievements of its grant recipients and annually awards four $25,000 Chicago Spirit Awards to exemplary nonprofit organizations.

The benefits that result from Sara Lee's citizenship activities are assessed at an intangible level. Sara Lee managers do not attempt to quantify, but they firmly believe that the firm's citizenship programs produce rewards. One perceived reward is an enhanced company image, although the firm does not survey public perceptions of Sara Lee before and after a publicized citizenship event. Managers instead cite the local and national awards that Sara Lee has received (such as recognition from Gifts in Kind America and Second Harvest) as benchmarks of its success. Managers suggest that these awards may indirectly promote the company's products. For example, they perceive that programs directed toward women, such as the Frontrunner Awards, enhance Sara Lee's image and its products' appeal to women.

In addition to external awards, managers see internal rewards such as increased employee morale coming from corporate citizenship involvement. To determine what these internal effects are, divisions survey employees to determine their perceptions of the company and its activities in their communities. As an EVC steering committee member puts it, "Participation in corporate-sponsored volunteer activities affects employee morale positively but not directly. They don't necessarily become Sara Lee cheerleaders; rather, they make friends, have fun, develop pride in the company. Participation makes it a nicer place to work."

Involvement in community volunteer activities appears to increase networking among employees and foster relationships among employees and between the company and its communities that might not otherwise have developed. The results—increased integration and pride in the company's achievements—build loyalty to Sara Lee.

Managers also believe that the firm's public service record helps their recruiting efforts. Without having formally assessed the accuracy of this perception, managers argue that recruiting has been easier since Sara Lee became a visible household name. The firm's rank as one of America's most admired corporations in the *Fortune* magazine survey "definitely makes recruiting much easier," says one division human resources manager. Since John Bryan instituted the Sara Lee Foundation in 1981, this manager finds it easier to recruit because of the company's increased recognition. Interviewers no longer have to focus on defining who and what Sara Lee is. Managers assert that Sara Lee's increased involvement in philanthropic activities has helped to create this increased visibility.

WHO'S WATCHING?

Given Sara Lee's diverse concerns, one might be surprised that the company has not had to defend its philanthropic programs to any audience, including special interest groups, shareholders, and investors. Although Sara Lee's philanthropic activities might engender controversy among special interest groups in some communities, the company does not seek to tailor its programs to the vagaries of public opinion. As Robin Tryloff asserts, "A company as large as Sara Lee can't follow a knee-jerk policy. Our base of consumers is too large, and if you tried to jump around you would drive yourself crazy."

Company officers are adamant that the firm follow a proactive policy on corporate citizenship and philanthropic activities that transcends particular consumer concerns. In addition, Sara Lee managers feel confident that if any special interest group did clamor for support, they can produce examples to satisfy critics, principally because of the wide range of activities and nonprofit organizations served by the corporation's diversified, grassroots approach to philanthropy.

Shareholders rarely write to question the firm's community involvement. When they do, any potential concerns are countered by the argument that donations are tax deductible. Moreover, the largest shareholders of the company are descendants of the founders and espouse many of same beliefs as the founder. If current and former trustees feel that the foundation is not addressing a particular issue, they are encouraged to bring this to the foundation's attention. These issues usually fit the foundation's guidelines and become part of its budget allocations. In addition, the corporation extends matching grants to these individuals so that they can partially direct corporate donations.

In terms of the wider investment community, the vice president of investor relations claims that stock market analysts are indifferent, although not necessarily positive, about the extent and character of Sara Lee's charitable contributions and community service programs. Aside from mutual funds with a social responsibility mandate, which Sara Lee meets in terms of most criteria, members of the investment community do not look closely at the firm's philanthropic activity. They focus on the bottom line.

Because Sara Lee has consistently surpassed its growth goals over the last decade, the firm encounters few arguments that it is wasting money. Officers speculate, however, that the corporation might have to answer questions about its use of funds for philanthropy if the firm's performance disappoints the investment community over a number of years. In general, the investment community believes that Sara Lee is well managed; therefore it must be doing something right, including its community service.

THE FUTURE

Senior management expects continuous improvement in all products and services, including community involvement. At the corporate and division level, these expectations translate into objectives for assessing both inputs and outputs of citizenship activity. This may include developing a system to track employee involvement through entrance and exit interviews, maintaining formal records on project participation, and measuring the impact of philanthropic activity on employee turnover.

In addition, Robin Tryloff indicates that the foundation hopes to expand its activities internationally. Currently all divisions, domestic and international, are involved only as much as they choose to be. Foreign subsidiaries, however, take their own initiative in developing and maintaining local philanthropic programs. As a result, international philanthropic activities are not as sophisticated as domestic ones, especially since other societies exert less pressure on their business communities than does the American culture.

It is difficult to assess the reputation of a nonprofit organization abroad, so the company often finds it difficult to sponsor activities internationally. It is hoped, however, that corporate contributions in other countries where Sara Lee operates will become more formalized through the development of written giving guidelines for foreign subsidiaries. Sara Lee also hopes to establish communication with foreign nationals who might serve as liaisons between Sara Lee and local nonprofit organizations. Finally, the Sara Lee Foundation plans to host annual meetings for all foreign subsidiaries active in their local giving communities to promote the exchange of ideas and methods.

Sara Lee faces a unique set of challenges. The breadth of its services, diversity of its products, and autonomy of its divisions are enormous. Whether in its core business or its citizenship activities, the firm has applied a consistent set of values and a philosophy to meet these challenges. By providing a unifying theme for its business and corporate citizenship activities, senior management at Sara Lee has been able to manage effectively what might otherwise be perceived as a large conglomerate with no clear purpose, culture, or values.

CONCLUSION

This case illustrates how citizenship can be made to work in a highly diversified, decentralized company. The management philosophies and policies that emanate from the core corporate culture provide a framework for and support decentralized decision making and action throughout all of the parent company's subsidiary businesses. Accountability and reporting are clearly defined by the head office, and all of the divisions and units must be involved. But each unit defines and implements its actual citizenship practices at the local, grassroots level. Employee involvement at all levels is expected and encouraged. Managers are responsible for and evaluated on their citizenship efforts. Citizenship is carried out the same way as any other business priority.

The case also brings out the seemingly paradoxical arguments for being a good corporate citizen. In the same breath, people at Sara Lee, starting from the top with John Bryan, espouse their corporate self-interests and economic benefits of citizenship, and they explain that they do citizenship because of moral obligations. In a speech to the annual conference, Bryan discussed these rationales and interests and justified them by saying, "Given our strong obligations to our shareholders, it is indeed proper for us to require that our businesses benefit from community involvement."

The Sara Lee example provides discussion material for both philosophical arguments about the nature of and reasons for corporate citizenship, as well as the practicalities of organizing to support and institutionalize the decentralized implementation of citizenship.

11

THE EVOLUTION OF PROCTER & GAMBLE'S ENVIRONMENTAL PROGRAM

Paul Shrivastava

SINCE THE EARLY 1970S, the degradation of the world's natural environment has been a serious public concern. Increasing awareness of dangers to the environment has raised public alarm and outcry and prompted regulatory action. Manufacturers of consumer products like detergents with phosphates, which were widely used in the 1970s, have been criticized for a number of major environmental problems such as water pollution. In the 1980s, the accumulation of packaging materials and disposable diapers in landfills became a national concern. Similarly, plastics, metal, and paper contributed to the nation's garbage crisis.

Procter & Gamble (P&G), the world's No. 1 soap and cosmetics manufacturer, recognized the importance of ecological concerns to its business early on. Since the 1980s, P&G has been establishing itself as a world leader in environmental management through a corporationwide transformation of its environmental policies and manufacturing and marketing processes.

- Environmental activities are only one in a diverse array of citizenship activities that P&G engages in, consistent with the values of the founders of the organization.

- P&G leverages its standard business processes by using them not only for improving manufacturing and packaging efficiency but also by using them to improve its environmental performance.

- P&G's emphasis on environmentally conscious manufacturing also
  serves as a foundation for partnerships with other organizations
  around the world to provide education and foster legislation
  designed to protect the environment.

In the early 1980s, P&G adopted a total quality management (TQM)
program. In the late 1980s, P&G extended TQM into management of the
environment and embarked on a systematic process of environmentally
conscious management that made it a leader in its industry. P&G has
adopted environmental quality management in all of its manufacturing
and packaging processes to implement its commitment. It builds partnerships with its stakeholders through community environmental programs.
It joins with local partners such as city governments, school boards, individual schools, suppliers, and customers. It gives financial support to
organizations like the Solid Waste Composting Council. It works with
existing groups like the Coalition of Northeastern Governors. And P&G
pioneered the Global Environmental Management Initiative, a partnership among 20 leading companies for business-to-business exchange of
environmental management practices.

Citizenship at P&G is considered to be synonymous with good business
practice. In many of the communities where P&G operates, the company
is known for setting the standard in citizenship through employee volunteerism, corporate giving, and environmental responsibility. This aspect,
above all, distinguishes citizenship at P&G. In addition to being a good
community citizen, P&G strives to be a good environmental citizen. Since
P&G made the decision to be pollution-free, it has applied sound environmental policies throughout the company. From environmentally friendly
products to zero waste discharge plants, P&G has changed its ways of
operating at all levels and has become an environmental leader among
consumer products companies.

THE COMPANY

In 1991, with $27.4 billion in revenues, P&G ranked No. 1 worldwide in
the soap and cosmetics industry. P&G's operations in 53 countries employ
over 100,000 people. Its products are found in almost every household in
the developed world. In 1992, the annual *Fortune* magazine survey rated
P&G No. 9 among America's most admired corporations.

P&G manufactures paper, health care, food and beverage, laundry and
cleaning, and beauty care products. It produces reliable, well-known
products such as Bounty, Metamucil, NyQuil, Folgers, Tide, Cheer,

Cascade, Cover Girl, and Oil of Olay. Half of P&G's products are No. 1 in their market, and the majority of its other products are in the top three. P&G's goal is to have the largest market share for each of its products.

P&G's corporate Statement of Purpose reads:

> We will provide products of superior quality and value that best fill the needs of the world's consumers.
>
> We will achieve that purpose through an organization and a working environment which attracts the finest people; fully develops and challenges our individual talents; encourages our free and spirited collaboration to drive the business ahead; and maintains the Company's historic principles of integrity, and doing the right thing.
>
> Through the successful pursuit of our commitment, we expect our brands to achieve leadership share and profit positions and that, as a result, our business, our people, our shareholders, and the communities in which we live and work, will prosper.

PUTTING P&G'S CORPORATE CITIZENSHIP VALUES INTO PRACTICE

The P&G Statement of Purpose applies to every aspect of its business, including corporate citizenship. Former chairman and CEO Howard J. Morgens summed up Procter & Gamble's corporate citizenship beliefs. "We do not and should not mistake business for an end in itself. It is only a means to an end, and the end is a constantly improving society." This sense of social responsibility drives the company to participate in community interest programs, philanthropic activities, and corporationwide environmental programs. By putting its beliefs into action, P&G is striving to become a model of corporate environmental and social responsibility.

At P&G, the tradition of corporate citizenship rests on the values of its founders. Both William Procter and James Gamble strongly believed in helping the community through their business. This value has become a part of the corporate culture, institutionalized in corporate policies, donations, and community programs. P&G's Beliefs Into Action statement provides the company's rationale for involvement in the community:

> Corporations have a responsibility beyond their basic economic function, just like any U.S. citizen. Their success in achieving their economic goals not only makes it possible for corporations to create jobs, pay taxes, provide a return to shareholders and develop new and better-performing products, it also helps them support other broad needs of society such as education, the arts, and health and social programs.

P&G's community involvement rests on four pillars. The first pillar is the company's purpose—the *betterment of society*. Its goals are to satisfy the needs of the human and natural environments in which it operates. P&G's environmental orientation focuses on all its stakeholders—customers, employees, shareholders, communities, and the environment. The second pillar is *direct financial support for community programs*. The company provides funds primarily through the P&G Fund to support numerous citizenship activities. The third pillar is *volunteerism*. The company encourages its employees to get involved in community programs by recognizing and symbolically rewarding employees' volunteer activities. The P&G Fund often provides grant support to nonprofit and community organizations where its employees volunteer. Finally, and representing the fourth pillar: although P&G's corporate citizenship takes shape from a global vision, *its solutions are implemented locally*. The corporation as a whole values responsiveness to community concerns and encourages each operating unit or division to identify opportunities to serve the needs of its local community.

A senior manager at P&G headquarters relates that, "P&G is a very ethical company; it's part of our culture. 'We do what's right' is a phrase you hear from day one when you come into this company. It's inbred in all of us. It's no different from all of the other parts of our business."

CREATING AN ENVIRONMENTAL QUALITY POLICY

P&G's original environmental initiatives, beginning with pollution control efforts in the 1960s, came from middle management. One manager who has been involved in environmental efforts since the beginning recalls that in the early 1980s, "some of us began to see a crisis coming that was going to impact our business in the plastic packaging area. The public's perception that plastics were evil was an early sign that we were on a collision course, because at the same time our company and others were moving toward plastic packaging. We put together an ad hoc work team to wrestle with the solid waste issue facing our country."

At their urging, and with the approval of then CEO John Smale, the company adopted an institutionalized environmental quality policy, which makes environmentalism central at P&G. The P&G Environmental Quality Policy, formalized in 1989, provides the guiding framework for greening. The policy states, "Procter & Gamble is committed to providing products of superior quality and value that best fill the needs of the world's consumers. As a part of this, Procter & Gamble continually strives to improve the environmental quality of its products, packaging, and operations around the world."

At P&G, there is a strong belief that "it is possible for humankind to progress without damaging the earth." The company does everything possible to support this belief and carry out this commitment. Procter & Gamble's stated policies are to:

Ensure our products, packaging, and operations are safe for our employees, consumers, and the environment.

Reduce or prevent the environmental impact of our products and packaging in their design, manufacture, distribution, use, and disposal, whenever possible.

Take a leading role in developing innovative, practical solutions to environmental issues related to our products, packaging, and processes. We support the sustainable use of resources and actively encourage reuse, recycling, and composting. We share experiences and expertise and offer assistance to others who may contribute to progress in achieving environmental goals.

Meet or exceed the requirements of all environmental laws and regulations.

Use environmentally sound practices, even in the absence of governmental standards. We cooperate with governments in analyzing environmental issues and developing cost-effective, scientifically based solutions and standards.

Assess continually our environmental technology and programs and monitor progress toward environmental goals.

Develop and use state-of-the-art science and product lifecycle assessment, from raw materials through disposal, to assess environmental quality.

Provide our consumers, customers, employees, communities, public interest groups, and others with relevant and appropriate factual information about the environmental quality of P&G products, packaging, and operations.

Seek to establish and nurture open, honest, and timely communications and strive to be responsive to concerns.

Ensure every employee understands and is responsible and accountable for incorporating environmental quality considerations in daily business activities.

Encourage, recognize, and reward individual and team leadership efforts to improve environmental quality. We also encourage employees to reflect their commitment to environmental quality outside of work.

Have operating policies, programs, and resources in place to implement our environmental quality policy.

IMPLEMENTING P&G'S ENVIRONMENTAL VALUES

P&G's decentralized business unit structure facilitates implementation of its environmental policies. Top managers in each business unit or profit center are responsible for developing their own environmental programs. Decentralized decision-making authority empowers lower and middle managers, and encourages and motivates the entire organization to take action to combat environmental problems. Most employees are aware of the environmental problems facing their communities. P&G's environmental thrust gives them opportunities to help alleviate some of these problems through their work. Senior managers learned from employee surveys conducted in the late 1980s that, "Our employees are no different than the people in the rest of the community. They want to feel good about their company. They want to be part of something, and they don't want to feel guilty about where they work or that they have to live by two standards."

Top management support, coupled with lower- and middle-management enthusiasm for implementing environmental policies and programs, has helped make the entire company environmentally responsive.

Other corporate strategies—a strong brand management system, commitment to product excellence through R&D, and globalized management structures—also support its environmental programs. Brand managers are responsible for all aspects of their brands' performance, from product design, packaging, and advertising to pricing and distribution. The brand management system fosters inclusion of environmental criteria in all brand development strategy decisions. Research and development investments also facilitate the environmental performance of the company. Scientific and technological solutions to environmental and health concerns are continuously developed in company laboratories. Using its global management structures, the company communicates and re-applies the most effective environmental solutions to operations around the world.

In recent years, environmental responsiveness has taken on increasing importance throughout the company. Once P&G decided to be responsive to consumers' and other stakeholders' demands for environmental quality, having "green" products and packaging was not enough. P&G began to make environmental responsiveness the cornerstone of its strategy. The company does not exploit consumers' environmental concerns for short-term competitive gains, although business gains are an expected long-term outcome from systematically improving the way it uses natural resources, its production processes, and its products and packaging.

P&G is a world leader in developing partnerships with trade organizations, government regulators, environmental public interest groups, and its suppliers and retailer partners. The company undertakes environmental education programs aimed at its employees, customers, the general public, and other companies.

Reducing the Use of Natural Resources

P&G attempts to reduce the amount of resources used in its production processes as much as possible. The company was once undoubtedly one of the world's largest consumers of forest resources. The wood pulp used in the packaging of hundreds of P&G products worldwide in one year— one and one-half billion paper cartons—requires enough trees to cover the Great Sahara Desert. But P&G's reforestation and forest management programs returned to the earth each year enough trees to cover the Great Sahara three times over. P&G harvested less than 3 percent of its forest resources each year.

P&G scientists developed disease-resistant, faster-growing seedlings to rebuild its forest resources. P&G used tree-to-tree cycling so that any wood pulp products not completely recycled were returned to the earth as compost to fertilize seedling trees. P&G researchers also continually studied ways to protect and preserve water supplies and wildlife on P&G-owned lands.

P&G works with a number of groups in its efforts to preserve forests and wildlands. It is a member of the American Forest and Paper Association, a round table of consumer and forest product companies working for ecologically sustainable forestry. P&G sold over 97,000 acres of wilderness along the Gulf of Mexico in southern Florida to the Nature Conservancy at a great discount. It also has been involved in Nature Conservancy efforts to preserve lands and wildlife along the Gulf Coast of Florida, in the Suwannee River National Wildlife Refuge, and in wetlands east of Tallahassee, and has set up a wildlife preserve in western Florida.

Programs in Holland and Switzerland encourage private citizens to contribute to public tree planting drives by offering to match their donations. The French division of P&G participates actively in the Foundation for Environmental Action's reforestation programs and serves as a role model for other European corporations.

Conserving Energy Resources

Since the oil crisis in the 1970s, P&G has encouraged energy conservation programs such as co-generation, maintenance, and waste-burning furnaces. Paper and dry detergents—two of P&G's major products—are highly energy-intensive to manufacture, so initial energy conservation programs targeted these products. A P&G engineer describes how their conservation programs developed. "We took learnings about ways to use alternative fuels from our paper business, and extrapolated them so that today we actually fuel a plant in Georgia with peanut shells from farmers. Our coffee plants burn spent coffee grounds from the instant coffee process."

Another innovative program converted waste pulp from paper mills into pellets, which can be burned as fuel. All of P&G's paper plants are now largely energy self-sufficient, using biomass from waste bark, wood chips or other fuels that come from the logging process, or co-generation. Though P&G's energy conservation projects were initiated to reduce costs in an era of high fuel prices, the programs carried on after fuel prices came down. Its engineers continuously seek opportunities to reduce energy use; P&G's energy costs are now about 2 percent of total production costs.

Greening Production Processes

Industrial production technology has undergone a sea change brought about through improvements in environmental controls. Twenty years ago, there was little concern about the environmental effects of industry. In the 1980s, environmental management became a functional staff responsibility. Staff persons were assigned at plants and headquarters to design and implement environmental programs.

George D. Carpenter, P&G's director of environment, energy, and safety systems, explains the evolution of environmental management to a plant level responsibility:

> What's changing right now is that we have learned this cannot be handled at the corporate staff level. With the current stringency of regulations and the expectations of society, it has to become part of everyone's job, or it won't happen. At the plants that are our best performers—they are driving awareness, training, and accountability

down to the operators on the lines—people feel accountable at the operations level for what happens environmentally.

Plant-level environmental improvement practices are shared and transferred to other plants worldwide. For example, a P&G soap plant in Venezuela devised a zero-discharge production process to manage water shortages in an arid environment. Plant workers designed water recycling systems to conserve water, and over the years improved their use of water to create a zero-discharge plant. The Venezuelan innovations have been widely shared and adopted in other plants in South America. A plant in Mexico was designed for zero-discharge, using the model from Venezuela.

P&G creates "industrial ecologies" around its plants wherever possible. Waste from one plant is used as raw material for another. Quality improvement engineers at all P&G plants look for opportunities to sell their wastes, help to create new markets for their plant's wastes, and reuse recoverable wastes from other facilities.

Designing Green Products

P&G's new product and packaging development processes address environmental needs in addition to more conventional ones. The process begins by identifying consumer needs and preferences through surveys and focus groups. Product designers identify functional, aesthetic, and environmentally desirable attributes of products and packages, and base new product and packaging designs on this analysis. Pre-testing of products and packages in test markets provides data that is used to modify designs. Product specifications are finalized only after several iterations of design, prototype development, and pre-testing. The entire development process can take as long as five years.

Because P&G manufactures a wide variety of products, it does not have a single materials requirement policy. However, it discourages the use of controversial materials when alternatives are available and encourages the use of recycled inputs. P&G's efforts to design environmentally sound products and packaging methods have resulted in many successful innovations without compromising safety and functionality.

Promoting Composting Projects

The P&G Environmental Quality Policy is based on a vision of producers and consumers cooperating to reduce waste to an absolute minimum. The policy encourages recycling, reusing, and composting through integrated solid waste management. Landfills are to be used only as a last resort. Taking its cue from successful European programs, P&G promotes composting as an important part of municipal solid waste management programs. P&G educates the public about the benefits of composting, alerting them to the fact that up to 60 percent of the material in landfills is compostable. P&G invested $20 million in solid waste composting projects worldwide to help communities adopt composting as part of integrated solid waste programs. When P&G first got involved in composting activities, there were only ten municipal composting facilities in the United States. Plans for 150 more facilities might not have materialized without P&G's community education programs.

P&G is involved in end use research for composted materials. With the U.S. Bureau of Mines, P&G scientists are investigating the use of compost to recover stripped lands. P&G also works with agricultural researchers at universities in the United States and Europe on the use of compost as a soil additive for corn and barley crops. P&G's research shows that using compost as topsoil reduces the need for chemical fertilizers. In addition, because it increases soil drainage capability, compost reduces the loss of valuable topsoil caused by erosion.

For years, consumers have demanded biodegradable disposable diapers. Even though P&G diapers were up to 90 percent biodegradable, P&G brand managers knew that biodegradability meant virtually nothing in air- and water-tight landfills. Instead of merely responding to consumer demands for biodegradable diapers, P&G researchers developed a disposable diaper that was 80 percent compostable. Rather than simply marketing the diapers as biodegradable, P&G also educates consumers about the greater environmental advantages of compostable diapers. To provide more facilities for composting the new diapers, P&G works with waste management officials in New York, Boston, and San Francisco—three of the largest solid waste producers in the nation—to plan composting sites.

Creating Partnerships with Stakeholders

P&G works in partnerships with its stakeholders and other global corporations to disseminate and leverage its environmental programs. The company is involved in environmental education programs in schools and cooperates with governments to develop environmental legislation. It promotes sound environmental management policies and programs to its business networks of suppliers and retailers and to other companies in its industry.

In the area of environmental education, the company works in close partnerships with schools. For example, in one program, P&G specialists designed an innovative environmental awareness curriculum about rain forests to increase students' awareness of important rain forest products that could be lost forever. The program educates students about ways to preserve forests and other precious environmental resources.

P&G works with its suppliers to ensure a continuous supply of high-quality recycled materials. It helps to establish stable markets for recycled plastics and supports research on plastic reprocessing technology. P&G encourages its suppliers to develop recyclable and recycled plastic packaging. P&G maintains open communications and mutual learning relationships with its similarly environmentally conscious suppliers. Successful supplier relationships allow P&G to use recycled fiber for 80 percent of its paper packaging.

P&G works with retailers and wholesalers to create environmentally sound distribution systems, including energy-efficient warehousing and systems to minimize damage losses in transportation. It promotes clear product labeling, customer education, and truthful advertising about the environmental attributes of its products and packages. P&G believes that successful long-term environmental solutions require changes in consumers' buying habits, consumer participation in recycling and composting, and consumer support of solid waste disposal infrastructure. P&G and its retailers contribute to educational programs like "Keep America Beautiful" and "Let's Not Waste the 90s" to inform customers about waste management methods.

P&G works with state and national legislators to promote sensible environmental legislation. Since 1988, P&G has been active in the Coalition of Northeastern Governors (CONEG) and the Source Reduction Council. CONEG's Heavy Metals bill was derived directly from P&G policies. The company shares its scientific and technological knowledge base to help create implementable regulations. Its managers work closely with legislators, participate in public-private discussions, and encourage environmental groups to participate in creating regulations. In fact, P&G's success in the legislative arena has attracted some criticism from other companies, who feel that P&G "collaborates with the enemy" to regulate industry.

P&G uses its influence in its industry to encourage other companies to adopt strong environmental policies. P&G works with the Food Manufacturing Institute, the National Food Processors Association, and the Grocery Manufacturers Association to develop environmental guidelines and standards for the industry. P&G joined with other companies to create the Solid Waste Composting Council. The Global Environmental Management Initiative is another example of P&G's leadership in promoting environmental management globally.

Leading the Global Environmental Management Initiative

The Global Environmental Management Initiative (GEMI) is a collaboration among 23 leading companies to promote a worldwide business ethic for environmental management and sustainable development and foster environmental excellence among businesses. GEMI member companies collectively set an example of business's environmental responsibility. George D. Carpenter, P&G's director of environment, energy, and safety systems, is the founding chairman of GEMI. Since GEMI's inception in 1990, P&G has played an integral part in the organization, taking the lead through demonstrating environmentally sustainable policies and management.

GEMI's goals are to:

Stimulate, assemble, and promote worldwide critical thinking on environmental management.

Improve the environmental performance of business worldwide through example and leadership.

Promote a worldwide business ethic for environmental management and sustainable development.

Enhance the dialogue between business and its interested publics such as nongovernmental organizations, governments, and academia.

Forge partnerships around the world to encourage similar efforts in other countries.

GEMI members share state-of-the-art environmental codes of conduct and adapt them to the needs of multinational and multisector industries. GEMI coordinates and supports research and disseminates reports on successful environmental management practices developed in industry and academia. The organization is a center of corporate leadership on environmental management and has helped to create a proactive worldwide business ethic on the environment.

In May 1990, the International Chamber of Commerce announced that world businesses were creating a "Charter for Sustainable Development" to guide decisions in environmental management. GEMI members participated in the development of the charter, which was unveiled at the second World Industry Conference on Environmental Management in April 1991. GEMI also coordinates with other international organizations working on environmental management, including the United Nations Environment Program.

Applying Total Quality Management to Environmental Practices

Many GEMI member companies have total quality and continuous improvement management principles as central elements of their corporate strategies. The practice of these principles has resulted in significant breakthroughs in production processes and management systems, including environmental management. Shortly after GEMI's inception, George Carpenter and a colleague from another major global corporation decided to try to adapt these ideas to their companies' environmental work. Carpenter said, "After we created GEMI, Tom Davis from AT&T and I tried to figure out how to put the organization on the map, how to live up to GEMI's purposes. We thought, 'What if we tried to develop ways to apply total quality to the environment?' The reception we got with this idea was incredible."

GEMI activities emphasize the applications of TQM to environmental problems. Members are adapting the techniques, tools, and measurement systems of TQM to enhance the effectiveness of environmental management. They are pioneering in the application of corporate management systems to track and improve performance in environmental areas.

Through total quality environmental management (TQEM), companies relearn that "the customer is always right," redefining "customer" to include all individuals and organizations to whom the companies answer on environmental issues: local, national, and global environmental rights groups; environmental regulatory agencies; concerned consumers and stockholders; and employees educated to understand the necessity for environmental responsibility. The most important customer in this definition is the earth's environment. The demands and needs of the environment are top priorities for any company embarking on a TQEM program.

Continuous improvement is an important element of the TQEM system. "No matter how good you are, you can always be better," is one of the themes of GEMI. Member companies constantly make efforts to improve, despite their already leading status. Corporate policies motivate employees to always seek innovative solutions and alternatives, knowing that there is no end to the total quality process and unlimited potential for environmental improvement.

Another critical element of the TQEM system is demonstrated by the GEMI group's interaction and teamwork, which is essential to the achievement of the group's objectives. Companies in the network learn from one another by benchmarking, sharing ideas and information within corporate partnerships, and adopting best practices as goals.

As George Carpenter puts it, "In GEMI we're starting to see the light, not only about using the tools of total quality, but also, how do you communicate this? How do you begin to share with other people the progress you're making?"

Wrestling with Environmental and Community Responsibilities

George Carpenter recounts a revealing story about the dilemmas involved in trying to meet conflicting business and environmental goals:

> In Florida we had a plant that was built in the late 1940s, 20 years before the clean air and water legislation. This was in a county that was destitute—high unemployment, no economic base. But we recently had problems with groundwater contamination and the safety of drinking water in this area.
>
> A plant in a rural community like that is the main source of jobs. The company is in the role of a figurehead. Our people are leaders in the community, involved in local councils and things like that. We want to do what's right. We're in the middle now, trying to understand whether the water problem is related to our plant. In the meantime, we're spending a lot of money to run city water out to the people while we figure out what's going on technically.
>
> It's a very tough issue. Do we throw away millions of dollars of investment and jobs and everything else the plant represents? I don't know what the answer is, morally, ethically, responsibility to P&G's shareholders. . . . I'm not really sure what the right answer is.

Such dilemmas will become commonplace as more and more such conflicts emerge in the future.

HOW TO BE GREEN

What can other companies learn from P&G's example? Although each company's circumstances are unique, companies should strive to make what is good for the environment good for their business and what is good for their business good for the environment. Other transferable lessons include:

- Do not have a single focus. Address all types of community and environmental problems in plants and offices using a systems approach to environmental management.

- Assess progress on environmental performance through periodic appraisals and evaluations. Urge each plant and office to move forward with environmentally sound policies and actions.

- There is no acceptable level of pollution, waste, or any other environmental degradation. Zero waste discharge should be the goal of all plants and offices.

- Community awareness is a key to success. Support environmental education at all levels of the education process.

- Assist communities to establish the infrastructure for environmental activities (for example, recycling and product awareness).

- Form partnerships with other corporations, government agencies, and community groups to share information and resolve problems cooperatively.

- Educate employees to be environmentally responsible and contribute to the company's goals.

- Carefully and consciously think through all plans and do projects right the first time, to eliminate waste from faulty products.

- Strive for continual improvement by applying total quality management principles to environmental management programs. Never be satisfied with the status quo.

CONCLUSION

Citizenship at P&G is not seen as different from good business practice. It is part of the overall professional management paradigm. Citizenship programs work because managers at P&G are bright, well educated, well trained, and motivated to excel.

People are a key ingredient of success in P&G's citizenship activities. The company hires the brightest and the best, then gives them discretion to act and expects involvement and participation. Programs are analyzed by several committees before they are implemented. The company encourages employees to engage in community projects by providing structured opportunities, infrastructure, and financial support, and by acknowledging employees' work with symbolic nonmonetary rewards.

The company strongly believes in "doing the right thing." It is committed to doing right by its customers and communities. "Right" is judged by scientific and technological standards. The company makes enormous efforts to be scientifically grounded. When science is inadequate to make the right decisions, as with many environmental problems, "right" is judged by a fuzzy sense of consensus among selected stakeholders. P&G managers consult with many constituencies in their decisions to meet the needs and serve the best interests of all parties.

P&G is renowned for good management, with highly developed systems and routines for virtually all activities. It uses the same systems approach to organize its environmental programs. Systematic environmental audits, needs assessments, environmental impact assessments, risk/benefit analyses, project planning, and pilot programs are used to develop environmental programs. The matrix structure ensures both line and functional oversight over environmental activities.

Top management does not dictate environmental programs, but when top management hears about good ideas, it nurtures them, sanctions resources for them, and gets out of the way of implementors. Top managers set an example for the organization. Top management commitment to the environment is reflected in the appointment of top management people to focus on important environmental issues. Notable is the appointment of a vice president for environmental affairs and a director of environmental engineering and quality programs.

Changes in corporate behavior are most effectively driven from inside the corporation.

12

COMPAQ COMPUTER CORPORATION

Maximizing Environmental Conscientiousness

Around the Globe

The Employees of Compaq Computer Corporation
with Lynda St. Clair

MOST EXAMPLES OF CORPORATE global citizenship are tied primarily to single geographic areas. Even in those localized instances, however, it is apparent that coordinating corporate citizenship activities requires a massive effort. When global companies begin to think about expanding their citizenship activities throughout their organizations, the complexity increases a thousandfold. Consider the activities of Compaq Computer Corporation, which has extended its corporate citizenship activities, especially those related to environmental responsiveness, throughout its global operations.

This case study includes interview data from key members of Compaq's organization and draws heavily on material from Compaq's 1995–96 Environmental Report. The company's Environmental Report is distributed widely within Compaq and is also made available to visitors to the company as well as news agencies and other interested organizations. Consistent with their concern for the environment, copies are typically available on the Internet. Individual copies are available upon request. Three key ideas form a foundation to ensure that Compaq's activities are environmentally responsible:

- Environmentally sound design means not only producing less waste and using less energy in the initial manufacturing process, but also producing products that can be reused or recycled to minimize their impact on the environment after they leave Compaq's possession.

- Rather than adopting the least common denominator in their operations around the globe, Compaq's internal environmental standards determine its operating practices in all of its facilities worldwide.

- Compaq balances its worldwide policies for environmental standards by also focusing on specific environmental issues that are particularly important in the local areas where they operate.

THE COMPANY

Compaq Computer Corporation, founded in 1982 in Houston, Texas, achieved phenomenal success in the highly competitive computer industry. The company grew from an idea sketched on a place mat in a pie shop into a global company whose products are sold and supported in more than 100 countries and generated revenues in excess of $18 billion in 1996. The company's rapid growth is the stuff of legends (it made the *Fortune* 500 in only four years), making it a staple in business school curricula. Competitive success, however, is only one of Compaq's achievements. A less-known but perhaps even more inspiring story relates to Compaq's efforts to make environmental leadership a cornerstone of its global operations.

From its beginnings as a manufacturer and seller of portable IBM-compatible computers, Compaq has taken advantage of being on the cutting edge of technology. That emphasis served Compaq well not only in terms of its core products but also in terms of its core processes. The willingness to accept technological challenges as opportunities rather than as obstacles has helped to make Compaq's environmental programs exemplary.

In 1997, Compaq was selected as the recipient of the World Environment Center (WEC) Gold Medal for International Corporate Environmental Achievement. The WEC Gold Medal is presented annually to a multinational company that has an outstanding, sustained, and well-implemented worldwide environmental, health, and safety program. Compaq was selected from a record number of multinational corporate nominees by an independent, international jury, which consists of distinguished environmentalists from government, academia, nongovernmental organizations, and industry. The WEC Gold Medal jury bases its decision on a corporation's establishment of an exemplary environmental program, globally uniform application of a corporate policy, and international environmental leadership extending beyond traditional corporate boundaries.

Another accomplishment for Compaq was being named "PC Partner of the Year" two years in a row by the U.S. Environmental Protection Agency (EPA) in 1996 and 1997. The award recognizes the advanced nature of the environmental features of Compaq's products, as well as its promotion of the Energy Star program and provision of Energy Star-compliant computer products. The EPA's Energy Star program consists of voluntary partnerships with the private sector to encourage the production and use of energy-efficient equipment. One component of that program, the Energy Star Computers program, works with manufacturers and end users to bring more energy-efficient personal computers, monitors, and printers to market in an effort to reduce air pollution caused by power generation.

Although Compaq had won several other Energy Star awards from the EPA in the past (including Highest Percentage of Sales and Most User Friendly Power Management Interface), the PC Partner of the Year award represented a significant achievement. Underlying that success are a number of specific accomplishments that are the direct result of the company's Design for Environment (DFE) program. For example, in 1995 100 percent of Compaq portable products offered were Energy Star-compliant. In addition, energy saving features were included in 100 percent of its desktop products and 100 percent of Compaq's monitor products were Energy Star-compliant. The impact of the types of features that Compaq has been building into its computers may seem to be small, but they are not. According to EPA figures, the power management features on the desktop PCs and monitors Compaq shipped in 1995 could lead to worldwide energy savings of as much as $60 million and reduce CO_2 pollution by as much as the emissions from 150,000 automobiles.

CORPORATE ENVIRONMENTAL PHILOSOPHY

Hans Gutsch, senior vice president for human resources and environment at Compaq says:

> Our goal is a leadership position in all aspects of our business, including environmental performance. Customers expect Compaq to deliver quality products and services in an environmentally sound manner. Our employees play a critical role in the success of environmental programs. We will continue to use employees' innovative ideas and initia-

tive to benefit our customers and the environment. We will also continue to work with our suppliers to facilitate environmental improvements in their operations, while continually improving the efficiency of our own manufacturing operations.

The lifecycle philosophy is driven at the highest levels of the corporation and linked with business strategy at every level of management. We believe this philosophy will secure our position as the industry leader. We recognize that operating a company in a manner that is compatible with the environment is good for our community, employees, customers, and business. Our efforts will continue.

As companies move toward the 21st century, their businesses must be competitive in global markets. Compaq Computer Corporation believes that the same can be said for their environmental programs. They must be integrated with the business, applicable on a global basis, and focused on the entire lifecycle of a product. Accomplishing such a lofty goal is far from easy, as the above quote suggests, but with the hard work of its leaders and employees, Compaq is blazing a trail for other organizations with their exemplary environmental programs.

One leader in that regard has been Hans Gutsch, senior vice president for human resources and environment. Gutsch's personal interest in environmental responsibility, combined with his international experience, made him a respected advocate for global environmental responsibility throughout the organization. But, as he himself admits, it took a lot of time and effort to convince skeptics that environmental responsibility was not only the right thing for the company to do but also the competitive thing for the company to do.

Today at Compaq, the appropriateness of environmental responsibility is no longer questioned. Compaq continues to integrate environmental concepts into each of its business strategies, making them integral to the operation of the organization rather than add-ons that can easily be disregarded. More than ever, Compaq feels that its customers seek environmental assurance regarding manufacturing processes, products, energy conservation, and recycling programs. Compaq's strength lies in its ability to satisfy customer requirements and simultaneously minimize the impact of their operations on the environment. In this way, Compaq serves as a leadership example in the industry.

Compaq takes that leadership role very seriously. The company integrates numerous features into the product design and manufacturing process that reduces the environmental impact over the lifecycle of their products. This is not something that focuses on a single product or process, but something that Compaq is working toward across its entire business. Compaq's philosophy is that environmental responsibility begins with the design of its products and carries through the manufacturing process and continues to the end of the product's life. (See Exhibit 12.1 for a copy of Compaq's Environmental Policy.)

To live up to this philosophy, Compaq products are currently designed and manufactured to meet a variety of the world's environmental standards and expectations. Lifecycle design principles that reduce the environmental impact of products are already incorporated into many of Compaq's products.

WASTE MINIMIZATION

Waste minimization is a manufacturing company's single most important environmental concern. Since the company's inception, Compaq has been a strong proponent of waste minimization and recycling programs. In 1989, Compaq solidified its commitment to waste minimization by announcing a plan to reduce CFC emissions from its manufacturing processes by 50 percent by 1993 and to eliminate CFC emissions in manufacturing entirely by 1995. Compaq exceeded its goal by eliminating CFCs in 1993. Also in 1993, to monitor environmental performance on a worldwide basis, Compaq developed a process for tracking and communicating worldwide environmental performance metrics. On a year-to-year basis, this performance measure quantifies the materials and resources used in their worldwide operations, allowing Compaq to develop a strategy for source reduction, waste minimization, and recycling. Each facility within the organization can use this measure to plan improvements.

The results of Compaq's focus on environmental responsibility have been impressive. Through process improvements, the company has reduced its total emissions of CFCs and volatile organic compounds by more than 82 percent in its manufacturing operations since 1989. By implementing inert nitrogen gas processes, the company was able to reduce soldering by-products by over 70 percent on a per unit produced basis. Waste minimization outside of the manufacturing area has also been substantial and has not gone unnoticed. Waste reduction efforts such as placing the bi-weekly employee newsletter and bulletins on-line (saving approximately 2 million sheets of paper per year) and switching from a paper purchasing system to an electronic order system were just some of the activities that led the EPA to select Compaq as a recipient of a Waste Wi$e Comprehensive Program Award in September 1996.

Exhibit 12.1. Compaq's Environmental Policy.

Environmental Policy

Compaq is committed to conducting its business in a manner that is compatible with the environment and protects the quality of the communities where we operate. We believe that business must work in partnership with suppliers, government, community and industry groups in an effort to protect the environment.

Compaq fosters openness and dialogue with employees and the public anticipating and responding to environmental concerns in a timely manner. Compaq is dedicated to integrating sound environmental practices in our products and services.

Compaq will continue to develop and implement programs that meet or exceed compliance with country, province or local regulatory requirements. We will continue to develop long-term plans that identify and manage environmental issues, even though the issues may not be regulated.

Key groups within the company have clearly defined roles and responsibilities for the environmental program. In addition, each employee has a responsibility to follow environmental procedures and to participate proactively in our environmental programs and committees.

Our goal is to operate our facilities in a safe and environmentally sound manner. We integrate environmental considerations into our products via the business planning process and by using innovative engineering controls, proactive programs and the creativity and ingenuity of our personnel. Through the efforts and teamwork of all employees, Compaq will continually review product designs, processes, materials, recycling and treatment technologies to reduce our chemical usage, waste production and impact on the environment.

LIFECYCLE STRATEGIES

Compaq's environmental programs extend beyond manufacturing operations. By working with worldwide recycling companies, Compaq is able to gain insight into design features and materials that are best suited to disassembly and to the recycling of the products that it manufactures. In 1994, engineering guidelines were developed that take into account a product's impact on the environment throughout its lifecycle. Called "Design for Environment," these guidelines focus on technologically advanced products that are energy-efficient and easy to disassemble and recycle.

A product's life begins with design, continues through the manufacturing process, and extends beyond the company's operations when the materials are recycled into other useful products. Between these stages lie challenges and opportunities that allow the company to minimize the environmental impact of their products, processes, and services.

Compaq's strategy in this regard is simple: "Consider the lifecycle impact of everything we do." One example of this type of lifecycle thinking is a line of desktop personal computers that Compaq introduced in 1995. Exemplifying the relationship between technology and the environment, the new Compaq Deskpro was designed to be a high-performance, energy-efficient, desktop personal computer that is easy to service, upgrade, and eventually recycle.

BOUNDARYLESS ENVIRONMENTAL RESPONSIBILITY

Compaq believes that for environmental programs to be successful, they must extend beyond their own operations. For example, Compaq expects its suppliers to be environmentally responsible. In 1995, Compaq expanded the environmental requirements of the supplier selection process. From waste minimization to CFC-free processes, Compaq expects suppliers to provide cost-competitive, defect-free, environmentally superior components. Although this might appear to be an effort to shift costs to suppliers, Compaq contends that it has demonstrated through its own programs that most environmental programs will actually reduce costs, as well as the risks and liabilities associated with future pollution problems. Including an environmental assessment in the procurement process also helped Compaq to improve its own assessment mechanisms, according to David Lear, environmental program manager. He noted that initially the requirements were less international in scope but that questions and feedback from suppliers helped the company broaden its scope to better reflect Compaq's global perspective.

ENVIRONMENTAL PROGRAMS AROUND THE GLOBE

Worldwide Direction

The global business market provides tremendous opportunities for Compaq. That opportunity, however, is accompanied by increased complexity and varied regulatory requirements. To compete on product quality, Compaq ensures that its manufacturing operations are certified to the Organization for International Standards (ISO) 9000 series quality standards. With respect to global environmental standards, ISO 14001 is becoming popular and may become the standard of choice in the future. Compaq is aligning its current Environmental, Health, Safety, and Security management system to be consistent with ISO. Compaq has developed a uniform expectation for all of its operations around the world and routinely conducts audits to ensure that sites are meeting or exceeding those high standards.

In keeping with Compaq's role as an international leader, its environmental programs are expected to evolve and expand globally. Underscoring the fundamental dedication to continuous improvement, Compaq's environmental programs are regularly reviewed and modified to maintain state-of-the-art leadership. Due to differences in infrastructure and support systems globally, the environmental programs focus on the needs of their customers in various regions of the world. The following sections describe activities in the major regions that Compaq serves.

North America

The Compaq North America geographic region consists of Canada and the United States, with corporate headquarters located in Houston, Texas. Environmental issues continue to grow in North America as people become more sensitive to the use of natural resources.

With waste reduction and energy conservation as a goal, the development of environmental performance measurements have helped the company devise a strategy for source reduction, waste minimization, and recycling throughout the manufacturing process. At the Houston manufacturing operations, Compaq has developed innovative process changes that have reduced CFC and volatile organic compound emissions by 82 percent since 1989, with even greater reductions expected in the future. New technologies are tested in Houston and then shared with Compaq's worldwide operating facilities. In keeping with their objective of minimizing waste and conserving energy, the Houston operations reduced electricity use per PC manufactured by 39 percent since 1993.

In addition to reducing the amount of waste produced, Compaq has also focused on recycling; Compaq currently recycles 80 percent of its waste. In 1992, Compaq North America implemented a battery recycling program for customers to recycle rechargeable batteries from their portable computers. Compaq's efforts were recognized by the Houston Corporate Recycling Council with awards for recycling, waste minimization, and use of recycled products.

Innovative product design earned Compaq an invitation to participate in the Energy Resource Center (ERC), a public education project of the Southern California Gas Company. Established to demonstrate recycling and conservation technologies in industrial and residential applications, the ERC is constructed from recycled warehouses, wrecked airplanes, an old Navy submarine, and many other recycled materials. Compaq contributed Energy Star-compliant desktop computers for teaching the latest resource conservation technology.

Compaq has also carried its environmental concerns outside the business arena and into the community directly. For example, the company sponsored a "Recycling Computers Contest" along with Champion Recycling Corporation. The contest involved over 1,100 Houston area schools and resulted in over 6,400 tons of paper being collected for recycling over the course of the two-month contest. Eleven area winning schools were awarded over $50,000 worth of Compaq personal computers for their stellar efforts in the project. Nearby Brazos Bend State Park also has reason to be grateful to Compaq, which provided the park a state-of-the-art computer system for its headquarters.

To celebrate Earth Day, displays and other communication tools help update employees on Compaq's progress and reinforce the need for employee participation to make further environmental improvements. Compaq's employees continue to be their most avid supporters and active participants in environmental leadership.

Latin America

The Compaq Latin America geographic region includes subsidiaries in Argentina, Brazil, Chile, Colombia, Mexico, and Venezuela; sales offices in Ecuador and Puerto Rico; a manufacturing operation located in Jaguariúna, Brazil; and a network of over 4,000 re-sellers throughout the region.

Environmental issues are growing in importance throughout Latin America, as efforts are increased to protect the vast natural resources in that region. Much of the attention has been focused on protecting the rain forest and cleaning up the rivers and waterways.

Compaq's manufacturing site in Jaguariúna, Brazil, operates a wastewater treatment facility that minimizes the impact on Brazilian waterways. Opened in October 1994, the manufacturing plant has implemented numerous programs to measure and track environmental performance. Waste generation measures are used to identify priorities and targets for waste minimization. The first Corporate Environmental, Health, Safety and Security (EHS&S) audit of the Jaguariúna site was completed in August 1995. The audit assisted site management in assessing the status of programs and processes with Compaq EHS&S Minimum Standards.

In keeping with the worldwide Compaq philosophy of proactive environmental protection, the Jaguariúna manufacturing site has established recycling bins for office wastes and provided for employee residential waste recycling. A compost area has been constructed to produce the 114-acre site's fertilizer needs.

The Jaguariúna plant has embarked on a bio-remediation plan to clean up diesel-fuel-contaminated soils on the site, the result of practices by the previous owners. The clean-up is not regulated by Brazilian environmental law. Under the bio-remediation plan, the site will be restored to its original condition.

In various parts of Latin America, Compaq is investigating the recycling of portable notebook batteries for its customers. Although the recycling infrastructure is not well developed, Compaq is evaluating alternatives for collection and shipment to various recyclers. Throughout Latin America, Compaq's energy-efficient products help their customers reduce electrical usage, thereby reducing power plant emissions and air pollution.

Europe, Middle East, and Africa

In Europe, the Middle East, and Africa (EMEA), environmental issues are taken very seriously. Compaq's worldwide corporate policy regarding meeting regulatory requirements is treated as merely the minimum acceptable standard in EMEA. This division works with governments, universities, and research centers to facilitate environmental improvements. All employees are encouraged to play their part, as are suppliers who are asked to meet specific environmental criteria.

Although responsibility for protecting the environment extends throughout the organization, because of the breadth of this region, environmental activities are overseen by an environment team at EMEA Headquarters. This team is led by the EMEA vice president of human resources and environment. Thus, environmental programs are supported by top management and implemented by individual champions and teams throughout the region. For example, at the Erskine, Scotland, manufacturing site, a plantwide team established in 1993 addresses environmental concerns. As part of the continuous improvement process, health, safety, and environmental procedures are being integrated into the Erskine Quality Management System.

During personal computer (PC) production, EMEA works to minimize emissions, waste, and energy consumption. Scotland operations continue to recycle office material and timber pallets. Electronic production by-products are disassembled and recycled. The total amount that can be recycled is as high as 80 percent by weight. Energy use has declined significantly in the production process, falling 30 percent per PC manufactured between 1993 and 1994. Product take-back programs are in place in Germany and Switzerland, with additional programs to be piloted in other European countries.

EMEA reaches outside the organization by sharing ideas and concepts for improving their products and services with environmental associations. With respect to overall results, comparison tests carried out by Bund and consumer magazines indicate that EMEA's results are exceptionally good.

Japan

Japan is considered one of the most environmentally conscious countries in the world. Because of the country's unique geographic location, the conservation of land, space, and natural resources has always been a priority with the people, industry, and government of Japan. The Environment Agency and the Ministry of International Trade and Industry (MITI) have developed numerous initiatives that encourage industry to incorporate sound environmental practices in their products and services. As a result, industry initiatives have been ahead of legislation in Japan.

The electronics industry has taken a leading role in developing designs that incorporate environmental features into products. For example, in spite of the government's active role in developing initiatives for sound environmental practices, the worldwide Compaq Design for Environment Engineering Guidelines are actually ahead of guidelines being developed by the Environment Agency.

Currently, recycling of old computer products is not widely practiced in Japan. Japan's take-back and recycling infrastructure is in its formative stages, creating an opportunity for Compaq Kabushiki Kaisha (CKK). Compaq Japan is evaluating several options for recycling used computer equipment and is confident it will be able to provide some recycling solutions for its customers in the near future. As Compaq sales continue to grow in Japan, computer recycling will take on greater importance to customers and should help to facilitate a shift toward recycling practices.

Energy use is another important environmental issue in Japan due to its effect on cost to consumers and businesses. Electricity costs in Japan are about three times the costs in North America. With the energy conservation features of Compaq products, Compaq Japan provides its customers with products that minimize the impact on the environment and reduce operating costs.

Compaq Japan incorporates conservation practices into all of its operations. For example, at the configuration center in Atsugi, where computers are inspected and tailored to meet customer needs, there are a number of recycling programs in place. These programs include office paper and packaging materials. Also, at Compaq Japan's Tokyo head office, employees practice office recycling. In an effort to expand these ideas, Compaq Japan is developing employee education programs focused on waste reduction, energy conservation, and recycling.

Asia Pacific

The Compaq Asia Pacific Division (APD) is a geographically and culturally diverse region that extends north to China, south to Australia and New Zealand, and west to India, with manufacturing locations in Singapore and Shenzhen, China. APD's stated aim is to be a leader in environmental protection through its commitment to practices that will improve the quality of life in the region. In support of that goal, "Green Kits" were distributed to managers throughout the region in 1995. The Green Kit materials help managers communicate the division's environmental goals to their colleagues and staff. APD believes that building a successful environmental program requires changes in attitudes that can best be achieved by communication and education. Steering committees have been instrumental in communicating environmental information and soliciting new ideas for environmental improvements. Some of the improvements include use of recycling bins, use of recycled paper, and elimination of the use of polystyrene cups. Suppliers are being encouraged to use environmentally friendly alternatives. A significant improvement has occurred among employees who encourage each other to, for example, switch off lights not needed, recycle paper, and use double-sided copying.

The impact of encouraging these environmentally responsible attitudes has been paying off handsomely. For example, at the manufacturing facility in Singapore, recycling of manufacturing by-products has risen more than 850 percent since 1993. In this region, the introduction of inert gas soldering in production processes reduced the amount of solder by-product by about 50 percent.

Concern for the environment also influences strategic decisions such as where to locate facilities. For example, the manufacturing site in Shenzhen, China, began operations in 1994. Prior to opening that plant, a comprehensive environmental survey of the site in Shenzhen was conducted to determine if there were any preexisting environmental concerns. The development of the corporation's worldwide environmental performance measures has been initiated and will be used to evaluate opportunities for waste minimization and recycling.

APD's initiatives are not only directed internally. APD sponsored numerous activities for World Environment Day, including a community clean-up day at a nature preserve. By extending its efforts beyond the walls of the organization, APD is helping to change attitudes toward environmental responsibility throughout the community. In concert with APD's own environmental programs, this bodes well for safe and sustainable development in the Asia Pacific region in the years ahead.

LEADERSHIP IN BUSINESS AND ENVIRONMENT

Compaq has set a goal of being in a leadership position in all aspects of its business, including environmental performance. Customers expect Compaq to deliver quality products and services in an environmentally sound manner. Employees play a critical role in the success of their environmental programs. For example, Compaq uses employees' innovative ideas and initiatives to benefit its customers and the environment. They work with suppliers to facilitate environmental improvements in suppliers' operations and continually work to improve the efficiency of their own manufacturing operations. The lifecycle philosophy is driven at the highest levels of the corporation and is linked with business strategy at every level in management.

The complexity of Compaq's environmental efforts is greatly increased by the number of different regions in which the company operates. Compaq has addressed this complexity with a two-pronged strategy. First, the company has developed worldwide measures and guidelines to ensure that operations in different regions meet the minimum standards of the organization. To ensure compliance with those corporate standards, performance reviews and bonuses are linked to meeting standards and routine audits of compliance are conducted. The second prong of Compaq's strategy is to focus its operations in different locations on the specific environmental issues that are most prominent in those regions. For example, when employees in Brazil began bringing in items from their homes into the plant to be recycled, the company provided funds to help the local municipality set up a recycling program.

In sum, Compaq has been very successful at developing a program of environmental responsibility that serves both the company's needs by providing cost savings as well as society's needs for waste minimization and reduced energy usage. Compaq's actions are not bounded by geography but are built around its global operations. In addition, Compaq's efforts have also resulted in more environmental responsibility on the part of its suppliers, further extending the impact of Compaq's corporate global citizenship activities.

CONCLUSION

The Compaq case demonstrates the power of taking a unified approach to environmental activities. The concept of unity can be seen in the company's lifecycle strategies for its product, its worldwide standards for environmental responsibility, its relationship with its suppliers, and its efforts to involve the communities in which it operates in environmentally responsible activities.

Compaq's use of lifecycle strategies explicitly recognizes the importance of approaching the entire design, manufacture, and eventual recycling of its products in a unified way. Unity is also demonstrated in the company's decision to meet the highest global standards for environmentally responsible behavior, even when less onerous standards are required by local regulations.

Compaq's relationships with its suppliers reflect the concept of unity in two ways. First, by requiring its suppliers to meet strict environmental standards, Compaq demonstrates the importance of environmental responsibility during the entire range of the manufacturing process, not just in Compaq's own operations. Second, the company reinforces the idea that environmental responsibility must be an integrated effort by working with suppliers to meet Compaq's environmental standards.

Finally, Compaq has gone beyond the confines of its own operations and worked to engage communities directly in activities such as recycling. By supporting activities such as the Recycling Computers Contest with companies such as Champion Recycling Corporation, Compaq has brought its environmental activities full circle.

Compaq's decision to continually integrate environmental concepts into its business strategies and to encourage communitywide environmental responsibility has brought the company economic benefits as well as social recognition. The real reward for Compaq, however, is in seeing the positive impact that its conscientious environmental leadership is having on the global environment.

PART THREE

THE FUTURE OF CORPORATE GLOBAL CITIZENSHIP

THE LAST PART of this book challenges both your teachable point of view as a leader and your action agenda by looking into the future and stretching your thinking, your values, and your ways of energizing others.

One of the key goals of the Global Leadership Program has always been to help executives develop a global mindset—an intelligent framework that enables leaders to understand geopolitical economic and cultural issues so as to make business decisions in the context of these macro forces. One set of issues that cuts across these areas clearly involves global citizenship issues embedded in one's view of the world.

This last part challenges your assumptions and beliefs at multiple levels—from the planetary to the individual. As a leader who has a teachable point of view, this part provides a way for challenging your thinking and assumptions and, we hope, helping you walk away with a renewed and enhanced teachable point of view.

The final part should be studied with your teachable point of view deeply in mind—even though it is only a work in progress at this stage. As you read, you should come across new ideas, values, ways of energizing people, and positions requiring edge. At the end of this part you should be able to pass the "elevator test"— what we sometimes describe as running into a journalist such as Tom Brokaw as you get off an elevator. Imagine that he's doing a documentary about you, and his first question is, "What is your teachable point of view about corporate global citizenship?" You then have five minutes to share your teachable point of view. Your response must be simplified and crisp, personal and provocative, backed by strong logic and examples, based on a vision about how things interconnect in the world. When you complete this part—indeed, this book—you should be able to complete this exercise.

To spark your thinking, recall that, as demonstrated in Part Two, the choice of corporate global citizenship activities is greatly influenced by an organization's competitive strength and expertise. That, however, is just one side of the equation. Equally important are the needs and cultures of the local areas where corporate global citizenship is to be practiced. In the third and final part of the book, we consider in some detail the implications of local characteristics on successful corporate global citizenship practices. In particular, we address four different levels of analysis:

The Planet. Beginning at the broadest level, Stuart Hart takes as his locale the planet Earth, and provides a general discussion of sustainable development. Rather than viewing the need for moving toward sustainable development as a threat as many organizations seem inclined to do, Hart proposes that the imperative for sustainable development actually provides extraordinary opportunities for corporations in the future. To capitalize on those opportunities, however, companies will need to educate customers about the advantages or products and services that are consistent with sustainability.

The Nation-State. Next we narrow our focus to the national level. Chapters on China, Russia, Ukraine, Kazakstan, and India provide a more fine-grained view of the specific challenges associated with corporate global citizenship practices in these countries. In addition to outlining some of the pressing problems in these countries, authors Erik Olson and Ben Goldsmith provide insight into the complex historical, cultural, and political issues that make successful corporate global citizenship interventions especially challenging. First and foremost, organizations interested in engaging in citizenship activities must come to understand the specific local context. Failure to take cultural differences into account may undermine even the best-intentioned and best-planned citizenship efforts.

The City. Moving from nation to city, we next look at the impact of a masterpiece of citizenship activities that have been orchestrated in Detroit, Michigan, by an organization called Focus: HOPE. Consistent with the recommendations of Olson and Goldsmith, the founders of Focus: HOPE started with a solid understanding of the specific needs of their community. Beginning as a provider of food to prevent brain damage due to malnutrition in young children, Focus: HOPE has become a powerhouse in education and training to help members of the Detroit community become self-reliant. Along the way, this organization has provided a blueprint for successful corporate citizenship activities.

The Individual. After recapping key issues discussed throughout the book and recognizing some of the challenges of corporate global citizenship, our final chapter closes with a call to individual action. The final success of corporate global citizenship is dependent upon the individuals who make up those corporations. Each of us needs to look at ourselves and ask what we have done to make the world a better place. Have we encouraged our organizations to engage in corporate global citizenship activities? Or have we subtly resisted committing to these kinds of endeavors?

One clear theme that runs through each of the chapters in this section of the book is the importance of education, not only as a form of citizenship activity that corporations can engage in but also as a critical prerequisite for successful corporate global citizenship programs. Organizations must first learn about the locales in which they wish to become responsible corporate citizens before they can successfully implement effective programs that serve the needs of their communities in culturally acceptable ways.

13

FROM GLOBAL CITIZENSHIP TO SUSTAINABLE DEVELOPMENT

Stuart Hart

TODAY MANY COMPANIES have accepted the responsibility to be good corporate citizens. Many firms now actively contribute to society in the form of grants and gifts to a range of deserving programs and institutions; employees volunteer their time to important community concerns and serve as mentors to underprivileged youth; pollution control has become a priority with companies, many of whom now recognize that poor environmental performance is bad for business in the long run; products and production processes are becoming cleaner; and where such change is under way, the environment is on the mend. We have come a long way.

To date, however, corporate citizenship has been framed as an activity separate and differentiated from the company's core purpose. It has been premised upon the notion that a profitable business must "give back" to society. In this sense, citizenship occurs as an afterthought—after the firm has successfully formulated and implemented its business strategy, it seeks to mitigate social and environmental effects through corporate citizenship activities. In this view, citizenship is an obligation, not an opportunity, and can continue only as long as the underlying business concept remains profitable. Few executives realize that citizenship might actually become a major source of *revenue growth*. Rarely is citizenship linked to mission,

---

This chapter draws heavily from an article by the author, "Beyond Greening: Strategies for a Sustainable World," *Harvard Business Review,* Jan.-Feb., 1997.

strategy, or technology development and, as a result, most companies fail to recognize opportunities of potentially staggering proportions.

Seen in this light, the real challenge is to create *sustainable development*—to create an economy that the planet is capable of supporting indefinitely. Although signs of improvement abound in the developed world, the planet as a whole remains on an unsustainable course. Those who think that sustainability is only a matter of philanthropy are missing the bigger picture. Increasingly, the scourges of the late 20th century include depleted farmland, fisheries, and forests; choking urban pollution; poverty; infectious disease; and migration—all are spilling over geopolitical borders. The simple fact is that in meeting our needs of today, we are destroying the ability of future generations to meet theirs.

The roots of the problem—explosive population growth and rapid economic development in the emerging economies—are political and social issues that exceed the mandate and the capabilities of any corporation. At the same time, corporations are the only organizations with the resources, the technology, the global reach, and, ultimately, the motivation to achieve sustainability.

It is easy to state the case in the negative: faced with impoverished customers, degraded environments, failing political systems, and unraveling societies, it will be increasingly difficult for corporations to do business. But the positive case is even more powerful. The more we learn about the challenges of sustainability, the clearer it is that we are poised at the threshold of a historic moment in which many of the world's industries may be transformed.

WORLDS IN COLLISION

The achievement of sustainability will mean billions of dollars in products, services, and technologies that barely exist today. Whereas yesterday's businesses were often oblivious to their negative impact on the environment and today's responsible businesses strive for zero impact, tomorrow's businesses must learn to make a positive impact. Increasingly, companies will be selling solutions to the world's environmental problems.

Envisioning tomorrow's businesses, therefore, requires a clear understanding of those problems. To move beyond greening to sustainability, we must first unravel a complex set of global interdependencies. In fact, the global economy is really three different, overlapping economies.

The *market economy* is the familiar world of commerce comprising both the developed nations and the emerging economies. About a billion people—one-sixth of the world's population—live in the developed countries of the market economy. Those affluent societies account for more than 75 percent of the world's energy and resource consumption and create the bulk of industrial, toxic, and consumer waste. The developed economies thus leave large ecological *footprints*—defined as the amount of land required to meet a typical consumer's needs.

Despite such intense use of energy and materials, however, levels of pollution are relatively low in the developed economies. Three factors account for this seeming paradox: stringent environmental regulations, the greening of industry, and the relocation of the most polluting activities (such as commodity processing and heavy manufacturing) to the emerging market economies. Thus, to some extent, the greening of the developed world has been at the expense of the environments in emerging economies. Given the much larger population base in those countries, their rapid industrialization could easily offset the environmental gains made in the developed economies. Consider, for example, that the emerging economies in Asia and Latin America (and now Eastern Europe and the former Soviet Union) have added nearly 2 billion people to the market economy over the past 40 years.

With economic growth comes urbanization. Today one of every three people in the world lives in a city. By 2025, it will be two out of three. Demographers predict that by that year there will be well over 30 megacities with populations exceeding 8 million and more than 500 cities with populations exceeding 1 million. Urbanization on this scale presents enormous infrastructural and environmental challenges.

Because industrialization has focused initially on commodities and heavy manufacturing, cities in many emerging economies suffer from oppressive levels of pollution. Acid rain is a growing problem, especially in places where coal combustion is unregulated. The World Bank estimates that by 2010 there will be more than 1 billion motor vehicles in the world. Concentrated in cities, they will double current levels of energy use, smog precursors, and emissions of greenhouse gas.

The second economy is the *survival economy:* the traditional, village-based way of life found in the rural parts of most developing countries. It is made up of 3 billion people, mainly Africans, Indians, and Chinese who are subsistence-oriented and meet their basic needs directly from nature. Demographers generally agree that the world's population, currently growing by about 90 million people per year, will roughly double over the next 40 years. The developing nations will account for 90 percent of that growth, and most of it will occur in the survival economy.

Owing in part to the rapid expansion of the market economy, existence in the survival economy is becoming increasingly precarious. Extractive industries and infrastructure development have, in many cases, degraded the ecosystems upon which the survival economy depends. Rural populations are driven further into poverty as they compete for scarce natural resources. Women and children now spend, on average, four to six hours per day searching for fuelwood and four to six hours per week drawing and carrying water. Ironically, those conditions encourage high fertility rates because, in the short run, children help the family to garner needed resources. But in the long run, population growth in the survival economy only reinforces a vicious cycle of resource depletion and poverty.

Short-term survival pressures often force these rapidly growing rural populations into practices that cause long-term damage to forests, soil, and water. When wood becomes scarce, people burn dung for fuel, one of the greatest—and least well-known—environmental hazards in the world today. Contaminated drinking water is an equally grave problem. The World Health Organization estimates that burning dung and drinking contaminated water together cause 8 million deaths per year.

As it becomes more and more difficult to live off the land, millions of desperate people migrate to already overcrowded cities. In China, for example, an estimated 120 million people now roam from city to city, landless and jobless, driven from their villages by deforestation, soil erosion, floods, or droughts. Worldwide, the number of such "environmental refugees" from the survival economy may be as high as 500 million people, and the figure is growing.

The third economy is *nature's economy,* which consists of the natural systems and resources that support the market and the survival economies. Nonrenewable resources such as oil, metals, and other minerals are finite. Renewable resources such as soils and forests will replenish themselves, as long as their use does not exceed critical thresholds.

Technological innovations have created substitutes for many commonly used nonrenewable resources; for example, optical fiber now replaces copper wire. And in the developed economies, demand for some virgin materials may actually diminish in the decades ahead because of reuse and recycling. Ironically, the greatest threat to sustainable development today is depletion of the world's *renewable* resources.

Forests, soils, water, and fisheries are all being pushed beyond their limits by human population growth and rapid industrial development. Insufficient fresh water may prove to be the most vexing problem in the developing world over the next decade, as agricultural, commercial, and residential uses increase. Water tables are being drawn down at an alarming rate, especially in the most heavily populated nations such as China and India.

Soil is another resource at risk. More than 10 percent of the world's topsoil has been seriously eroded. Available cropland and rangeland are shrinking. Existing crop varieties are no longer responding to increased use of fertilizer. As a consequence, per capita world production of both grain and meat peaked and began to decline during the 1980s. Meanwhile, the world's 18 major oceanic fisheries have now reached or actually exceeded their maximum sustainable yields.

By some estimates, humankind now uses more than 40 percent of the planet's net primary productivity. If, as projected, the population doubles over the next 40 years, we may outcompete most other animal species for food, driving many to extinction. In short, human activity now exceeds sustainability on a global scale.

As we approach the 21st century, the interdependence of the three economic spheres is increasingly evident. In fact, the three economies have become worlds in collision, creating the major social and environmental challenges facing the planet: climate change, pollution, resource depletion, poverty, and inequality.

Consider, for example, that the average American today consumes 17 times more than his or her Mexican counterpart (emerging economy) and hundreds of times more than the average Ethiopian (survival economy). The levels of material and energy consumption in the United States require large quantities of materials and commodities, sourced increasingly from the survival economy and produced in emerging economies.

In the survival economy, massive infrastructure development (for example, dams, irrigation projects, highways, mining operations, and power generation projects), often aided by agencies, banks, and corporations in the developed countries, has provided access to raw materials. Unfortunately, such development has often had devastating consequences for nature's economy and has tended to strengthen existing political and economic elites, with little benefit to those in the survival economy.

At the same time, infrastructure development projects have contributed to a global glut of raw materials and, hence, to a long-term fall in commodity prices. And as commodity prices have fallen relative to the prices of manufactured goods, the currencies of developing countries have weakened and their terms of trade have become less favorable. Their purchasing power declines while their already substantial debt load becomes even larger. The net effect of this dynamic has been the transfer of vast amounts of wealth (estimated at $40 billion per year since 1985) from developing to developed countries, producing a vicious cycle of resource exploitation and pollution to service mounting debt. Today developing nations have a combined debt of more than $1.2 trillion, equal to nearly half of their collective gross national product.

FROM CITIZENSHIP TO SUSTAINABILITY

Nearly three decades ago, environmentalists such as Paul Ehrlich and Barry Commoner made this simple but powerful observation about sustainable development: The total environmental burden (EB) created by human activity is a function of three factors: population (P); affluence (A), which is a proxy for consumption; and technology (T), which is how wealth is created. The product of these three factors determines the total environmental burden. It can be expressed as a formula: $EB = P \times A \times T$.

Achieving sustainability will require stabilizing or reducing the environmental burden. That can be done by decreasing the human population, lowering the level of affluence (consumption), or changing fundamentally the technology used to create wealth. The first option, lowering the human population, does not appear feasible short of draconian political measures or the occurrence of a major public health crisis that causes mass mortality.

The second option, decreasing the level of affluence, would only make the problem worse because poverty and population growth go hand in hand. Demographers have long known that birth rates are inversely correlated with level of education and standard of living. Thus stabilizing the human population will require improving the education and economic standing of the world's poor, particularly women of childbearing age. That can be accomplished only by creating wealth on a massive scale. Indeed, it may be necessary to grow the world economy as much as tenfold just to provide basic amenities to a population of 8 billion to 10 billion.

That leaves the third option: changing the technology used to create the goods and services that constitute the world's wealth. Although population and consumption may be societal issues, technology is the business of business.

If economic activity must increase tenfold over what it is today just to provide the bare essentials to a population double its current size, then technology will have to improve twentyfold merely to keep the planet at its current levels of environmental burden. Those who believe that ecological disaster will somehow be averted must also appreciate the commercial implications of such a belief: over the next decade or so, sustainable development will constitute one of the biggest opportunities in the history of commerce.

Nevertheless, as of today, few companies have incorporated sustainability into their strategic thinking. Instead, environmental and social issues remain differentiated from core operations, often in the hands of engineers, lawyers, or public affairs specialists. Focusing on sustainability requires putting business strategies to a new test. Taking the entire planet as the context in which they do business, companies must ask whether they are part of the solution to social and environmental problems or part of the problem. Only when a company thinks in those terms can it begin to develop a vision of sustainability—a shaping logic that goes beyond today's differentiated view of corporate citizenship.

THE FUTURE

Companies with their eye on the future can begin to plan for and invest in tomorrow's technologies. The simple fact is that the existing technology base in many industries is not environmentally or socially sustainable. The petroleum industry, for example, is constrained by its current technology base. Must the industry be oriented around extracting and refining fossil fuels from the earth's crust (unsustainable), or is it possible to envision an industry that produces, refines, and distributes biofuels from the earth's surface? Sweden's OK Petroleum, for example, has come to the conclusion that its core competence need not be tied to fossil fuels but to its skills in refining and distributing liquid fuels. As a result, the company has taken a leadership position in lobbying in favor of carbon taxes on fossil fuels, and it is aggressively pursuing alliances and joint ventures with the players necessary to create the new system.

The chemical industry, as another example, is similarly limited by its dependence on petroleum and the chlorine molecule. (Many organochlorides are toxic or persistent or bioaccumulative.) As long as the industry relies on its historical competencies in petroleum feedstock and chlorine chemistry, it will have trouble making major progress toward sustainability. Monsanto is one company that is consciously developing new competencies. It is shifting the technology base for its agriculture business from bulk chemicals to biotechnology. It is betting that the bioengineering of crops rather than the application of chemical pesticides or fertilizers represents a sustainable path to increased agricultural yields.

Such thinking can even extend to the financial and service sectors. The Grameen Bank in Bangladesh, for example, was founded with the idea that making financial resources available to the poor can make not only social but also economic sense. Over the past decade, Grameen Bank has demonstrated that poor people can be viable customers, achieving a better than 98 percent repayment rate on loans. In an effort to spread the impact even wider, Grameen has begun several spin-off companies to facilitate economic development in more remote villages. Through its Grameen Phone, Grameen Energy, and Grameen Cybernet subsidiaries, the bank is seeking to interconnect remote villages with a cellular phone network and Internet services so as to reduce the need for time-consuming travel for villagers seeking economic opportunities. By putting communication technology in the hands of the poor, Grameen facilitates entrepreneurship and economic development while simultaneously reducing the need for expensive and polluting bus and automobile transportation in rural areas.

Companies selling social and environmental solutions are desperately needed in the emerging economies of Asia and Latin America. But precisely because economic growth is so high—capital stock doubles every six years in Southeast Asia—there is an unprecedented opportunity to replace current product and process technologies with new, cleaner, more sustainable ones.

Japan's Research Institute for Innovative Technology for the Earth is one of several new research and technology consortia focusing on the development and commercialization of clean technologies for the developing world. Having been provided with funding and staff by the Japanese government and more than 40 corporations, RITE has set forth an ambitious 100-year plan to create the next generation of power technology, which will eliminate or neutralize greenhouse gas emissions.

SUSTAINABILITY VISION

A vision of sustainability for an industry or a company is like a road map to the future, showing the way products and services must evolve and what new competencies will be needed to get there. Few companies today have such a road map. Ironically, chemical companies, regarded only a decade ago as the worst environmental villains, are among the few large corporations to have engaged the challenge of sustainable development seriously.

Companies can begin by taking stock of their own missions and strategies. Is there an overarching vision of sustainability that gives direction to the company's activities? Consider the auto industry. During the 1970s and 1980s, government regulation of tailpipe emissions forced the industry to focus on pollution control. The 1990s are witnessing the first signs of product stewardship. In Germany, the 1990 "take-back" law required auto manufacturers to take responsibility for their vehicles at the end of their useful lives. Innovators such as BMW have influenced the design of new cars with their *design for disassembly* efforts. Industry-level consortia such as the Partnership for a New Generation of Vehicles are driven largely by the product stewardship logic of lowering the environmental impact of automobiles throughout their lifecycle.

Early attempts to promote clean technology include such initiatives as California's zero-emission vehicle law and the U.N. Climate Change Convention, which ultimately will limit greenhouse gases on a global scale. But early efforts by industry incumbents have been either incremental—for example, natural-gas vehicles—or defensive in nature. Electric-vehicle programs, for instance, have been used to demonstrate the infeasibility of this technology rather than to lead the industry to a fundamentally cleaner technology.

Although the auto industry has made progress, it falls far short of sustainability. For the vast majority of auto companies, pollution prevention and product stewardship are the end of the road. Most auto executives assume that if they close the loop in both production and design, they will have accomplished all the necessary environmental objectives.

But step back and try to imagine a sustainable vision for the industry. Growth in the emerging markets will generate massive transportation needs in the coming decades. Already the rush is on to stake out positions in China, India, and Latin America. But what form will this opportunity take?

Consider the potential impact of automobiles on China alone. Today there are fewer than 1 million cars on the road in China. However, with a population of more than 1.2 billion, it would take less than 30 percent market penetration to equal the current size of the U.S. car market (12 million to 15 million units sold per year). Ultimately, China might demand 50 million or more units annually. Because China's energy and transportation infrastructures are still being defined, there is an opportunity to develop a clean technology yielding important environmental and competitive benefits.

Amory Lovins of the Rocky Mountain Institute has demonstrated the feasibility of building hypercars—vehicles that are fully recyclable, 20 times more energy-efficient, and 100 times cleaner and cheaper than existing cars. These vehicles retain the safety and performance of conventional cars but achieve radical simplification through the use of lightweight, composite materials, fewer parts, virtual prototyping, regenerative braking, and very small, hybrid engines. Hypercars, which are more akin to computers on wheels than to cars with microchips, may render obsolete most of the competencies associated with today's auto manufacturing, for example, metal stamping, tool and die and making, and the internal combustion engine.

Assume for a minute that clean technology like the hypercar or Mazda's soon-to-be-released hydrogen rotary engine can be developed for a market such as China's. Now try to envision a transportation infrastructure capable of accommodating so many cars. How long will it take before gridlock and traffic jams force the auto industry to a halt? Sustainability will require new transportation solutions for the needs of emerging economies with huge populations. Will the giants in the auto industry be prepared for such radical change, or will they leave the field to new ventures that are not encumbered by the competencies of the past?

CONCLUSION

A clear and fully integrated environmental strategy should not only guide competency development, it should also shape the company's relationship to customers, suppliers, other companies, policy makers, and all its stakeholders. Companies can and must change the way customers think by creating preferences for products and services consistent with sustainability. Companies must become educators rather than mere marketers of products.

For senior executives, embracing the quest for sustainability may well require a leap of faith. Some may feel that the risks associated with investing in unstable and unfamiliar markets outweigh the potential benefits. Others will recognize the power of such a positive mission to galvanize people in their organizations.

Regardless of their opinions on sustainability, executives will not be able to keep their heads in the sand for long. Since 1980, foreign direct investment by multinational corporations has increased from $500 billion to nearly $3 trillion per year. In fact, it now exceeds official development-assistance aid in developing countries. With free trade on the rise, the next decade may see the figure increase by another order of magnitude. The challenges presented by emerging markets in Asia and Latin America demand a new way of conceptualizing business opportunities. The rapid growth in emerging economies cannot be sustained in the face of mounting environmental deterioration, poverty, and resource depletion. In the coming decade, companies will be challenged to develop clean technologies and to implement strategies that *drastically reduce* the environmental burden in the developing world, while simultaneously increasing its wealth and standard of living.

Like it or not, the responsibility for ensuring a sustainable world falls largely on the shoulders of the world's enterprises—the economic engines of the future. Clearly, public policy innovations (at both the national and international levels) and changes in individual consumption patterns will be needed to move toward sustainability. But corporations can and should lead the way, helping to shape public policy and driving change in consumers' behavior.

The era of corporate citizenship, where companies made amends for the problems created by their activities, is drawing to a close in favor of the era of sustainable development, where companies integrate social and environmental objectives into the fabric of their mission, technology, and strategy. This transition holds great potential for those interested in being both business people and agents of social change at the same time. With sustainable development, citizenship is the core business.

14

CHINA

Opportunities and Constraints for Corporate Citizenship

Erik C. Olson

AS WITH MOST THINGS RELATED TO CHINA, the logic of corporate global citizenship, ably defined by earlier contributors to this volume,[1] takes on enormous proportions in the world's most populous country. This chapter aims to place those conditions, issues, and opportunities in China in some perspective—assuming that, for a variety of reasons, some foreign enterprises operating there will wish to better China's environmental or human welfare conditions. Even purely self-interested companies can find reason to act, if only to avoid the growing threat of litigation in Chinese courts.

But larger incentives also exist. For, as with most of the world's populous nations, the consequences of China's environmental and human welfare policies and practices often reach well beyond its borders. Take China's policies and practices on energy, for example. Its choices about fuels, fuel processing, investment in energy-efficient technologies, and the like, powerfully affect global levels of greenhouse gasses. Or consider its rural development and labor migration policies. If mishandled, these policies could induce mass migrations with serious international spillover effects.

Businesses can find useful ways to help, but they should not proceed naively. There are bright spots, including measurable improvements over the last few decades in nutrition, health, education, and living standards, as well as the recent awakening to the serious state of China's environment. To be sure, the challenges are huge; many problems are not subject to enterprise-level solutions, and there are important political constraints.

CHALLENGES: POVERTY AND POLITICS

According to recently revised estimates, over 300 million Chinese live below the poverty line of $1 a day.[2] That is more people than live in any other country of the world except India, and the vast majority of these live well outside the spheres in which foreign businesses have yet operated or made an impact. China's environment, meanwhile, is under assault from extremely serious pollution, biodiversity loss, and natural resource degradation—some of it irreversible.

Another difficulty companies face is that many root causes are simply not subject to enterprise-level remedies. With soil erosion, for example, some existing damage can only be fixed by massive intervention, and new damage will be avoided only if, among other things, certain property rights rules are rewritten.

Politics also presents difficulties because many demonstrably effective socially or environmentally oriented action plans that a foreign business might wish to undertake are, politically, not options in China; reasons include the high premium China's leadership places on face-saving self-reliance, its historically rooted suspicion of foreigners' actions in China, and its opposition to organizations and institutions outside the direct control of the Communist Party.

Despite the sometimes narrow scope for foreign firms' global citizenship actions in China, real opportunities exist, particularly on the environmental side. Some actions will have an immediate or direct impact; other effects will be delayed or indirect. Some actions will tangibly affect many; others will be more symbolic. Some will provide visible leadership, thereby raising the standard or providing inspiration for others—domestic and foreign—to follow, while others will make their impact tangibly but quietly.

CHINA'S HUMAN WELFARE SCORECARD

China's human welfare scorecard is mixed. On the plus side, basic indicators compare favorably both with other developing nations and with China's own conditions at mid-century. Despite China's relatively low GNP per capita (in 1994, US$490 in exchange-rate terms versus US$871 average for developing countries [see Table 14.1]),[3] note some current conditions in China versus current averages for developing countries generally:

- Life expectancy: 68 years versus an average of 61.
- Under-five mortality rate: 43 per thousand versus 101.
- Adult literacy rate: 78 percent versus 67 percent.[4]

China's rate of improvement also has been impressive:

- Life expectancy: up from 49 years in 1960.
- Under-five mortality rate: down from 209 per thousand in 1960.[5]
- Medical infrastructure: in the last 20 years, the number of doctors per capita has nearly doubled, and since 1949 the number of hospital beds has increased by a factor of 15.[6]

But there are serious problems on China's human welfare scorecard. One is that, particularly since 1985, most of the gains are concentrated in coastal and urban areas. In rural areas, particularly in interior provinces, poverty is often serious.[7] Income disparities, contrary to expectations, are comparable to those in developed countries and are growing. Housing is frequently old, small, and—particularly in rural areas—without plumbing or electricity. Unemployment and underemployment—formerly hidden in cities by guaranteed job schemes and in the countryside by tight limits on rural-to-urban migration, but now accelerated by market pressures in agriculture and industry—are rising at politically worrisome rates. Medical services and schooling are being commercialized, even if only informally, faster than wages are growing among the poor.[8] Furthermore, many social norms and human welfare structures—some constructed by the Communists, others of more ancient origin—are collapsing. New epidemics of crime, drug abuse, prostitution, kidnaping, and so forth are rapidly rising. And demographic changes induced by China's widely varying birth rates over the last 50 years, coupled with new mobility and new norms among the young, have undermined the former structures of care for the elderly.

KEY HUMAN WELFARE ISSUES

Consider four key human welfare issues.

Nutrition and Health

China's nutrition and public health pictures are best summarized in the life expectancy, child mortality, caloric intake, and medical access data.

Table 14.1. Comparative Statistics on Developing Regions.

Comparative Numbers (1994 est. unless noted)	China	East Asia & Pacific	South Asia	Developing countries	Developed countries
Income & its distribution					
GNP per capita (US$)	490 (1800 PPP)	987	309	871	23,195
Percent share of household income, lowest 40 percent	17	18	21	..	18
Percent share of household income, highest 20 percent	42	44	41	..	41
Nutrition					
Percent born underweight	9	19	33	11	6
Percent children underweight, moderate & severe	17	35	64	23	..
Calorie supply as percent of requirements	112	107	99	112	134
Health					
Life expectancy at birth	68	66	59	61	77
Under–five mortality rate (per 1000)	43	56	124	101	9
Percent with safe water access	67	66	80	70	..
Health care access (percent)	92	89	77	80	..
Education					
Adult literacy rate (percent) (1990)	78 (82 overall)	80	46	67	95
Percent enrolled in primary school	121	116	91	99	103
Percent reaching grade 5, primary school	88	87	59	74	98

Note: China's purchasing power parity (PPP) income data from Poverty in China: What Do the Numbers Say? (World Bank, 1996), cited in "How Poor Is China?," The Economist, 12 October 1996, p. 35. China's overall literacy rate data from the 1990 census, since published annually in State Statistical Bureau, China Statistical Yearbook, cited in Economist Intelligence Unit (EIU), 1996, "Education," Country Profile—China, 1995/96, p. 25. All other data from UNICEF, 1996, The State of the World's Children 1996 (New York: Oxford), pp. 81ff.

These indicators have all improved considerably over the last 45 years. But, again, conditions are changing, and some may prove problematic.

On the nutrition side, as incomes have risen, nutrition generally has improved. And, assuming incomes continue moving upward, the picture will remain positive. Several conditions merit watching, though. First, many in the remote rural areas are not yet experiencing the dramatic income gains seen elsewhere. They, therefore, depend nutritionally on their own subsistence agriculture. Unfortunately, these extremely poor people are often located in the very places where agricultural conditions are worst. This is in a country already badly endowed agriculturally: 22 percent of the world's people must survive off only 7 percent of the world's arable land. Second, though technological solutions, certain property rights and policy shifts, or changes in relative prices for agricultural products could work to reverse this, China's arable land quality and quantity has been declining. Problems include rapid loss of some of the best farmland, as urban and industrial development gallops forward in China's coastal provinces, serious erosion from cultivating lands of marginal quality, salinization from improper irrigation and net depletion of soil fertility—the latter largely due to property-rights structures that discourage farmers' long-term investments in soil quality. Third, while China can import food, worldwide growth in demand is outstripping growth in supply. Hence, in the short term at least, prices will rise, and any serious global food shocks (for example, from particularly bad weather in the world's biggest grain-growing regions) could have unexpectedly serious consequences.

Housing

China's housing picture has two main faces—urban and rural. China's farmers have been largely responsible for their own housing. During the early 1980s, China's liberalized agricultural policies boosted many farmers' real income, particularly in the most fertile provinces. Some had enough to build improved housing, but many areas were unaffected. In the most impoverished interior areas, some people live in caves.

Housing in cities, on the other hand, had long been provided as part of a worker's basic employment package. Although wages were low, rents were held correspondingly low. Unsurprisingly, artificially low rents were matched by relatively short supply. Hence, two newly married workers at, say, Wuxi's No. 1 Cotton Factory would normally join a years-long queue for one of the cramped apartments on the factory grounds. In the meantime, each would often continue to live with his or her parents.

Recently this has begun to change. State enterprises' financial woes have made it tough to meet their comprehensive social service obligations (housing, medical care, retirement, and education, and so forth). Hence, the Chinese leadership has sought to relieve these enterprises of at least some obligations by, among other things, marketizing and privatizing housing. Problems, though, primarily with pricing, have slowed the transition. Furthermore, although the urban housing stock is expanding, it has not been sufficient to match soaring demand driven by China's population growth and the staggering influx of former rural dwellers. For the majority of city dwellers, then, housing remains extremely tight.[9]

Education

China's record in basic education has been impressive, as China's roughly 80 percent adult literacy rate (up from about 70 percent in 1982) shows.[10]

There is more to the story than just the numbers, though. First, primary and secondary school class sizes are often in the 40- to 60-pupil range; education budgets—and hence teachers' incomes—are falling far behind; and teachers are widely dispirited.[11] Second, to make up their budget shortfalls, many schools, particularly rural ones, are imposing unauthorized "fees" on already poor parents. Third, with new pressures and opportunities in marketized local economies, some parents are holding children out of school to work and help boost family income. Fourth, China's college graduates are probably too few to support its still-ambitious long-term development aims, though, in the short term, the shift away from the old system of assigning jobs is leaving many college graduates without means of applying their skills.[12]

Distribution of Wealth

Since great accumulated personal wealth is still uncommon in China, *wealth* distribution among individuals is primarily an issue of *income* distribution. Per capita GDP for 1996 is estimated at $687.[13] However, the distribution of this income—although roughly comparable with developed- and developing-country averages—is increasingly unequal. Though inequality shrank early in the post-1978 reform era, the trend since the mid-1980s has reversed.[14]

The most serious is the urban/rural disparity. Incomes of urban dwellers (about 30 percent of the population) are on average over twice that of rural dwellers, exacerbated in part by urban subsidies on food, housing, medical care, and so forth.[15] For example, Shanghai's GDP per person of $2,084[16] is roughly three times the national average.

Coastal-inland differences are also serious. As of March 1995, of China's 11 coastal provinces and municipalities (excluding Guangxi), all but 2 had incomes above the national average, while among the 19 inland provinces and regions, all but 3 were below the national average[17] (China's provinces are shown in Figure 14.1). And this disparity has been growing since 1990.[18] Foreign direct investment has been reinforcing this disparity. Of the $37.2 billion of foreign direct investment China absorbed in 1995, 88 percent went to the 12 coastal provinces and municipalities (including Guangxi), though they are home to only 41 percent of China's population.[19]

The joint significance of these differences is more than just economic. Central government officials worry that resentment among rural residents of China's interior may translate into rebellion. Not surprisingly, the latest five-year plan (1996–2000) pledges to address income disparities.

Perhaps the one bright spot is the reduction in income inequalities between men and women. Initially, it appears that post-1978 reform-era opportunities for earning nonfarm income were seized largely by men, leaving women with the less-rewarding farm incomes.[20] More recently, it appears the pendulum is swinging back. Reportedly, rural women have come to dominate the livestock and poultry industries and have grabbed opportunities in the rapidly expanding township-and-village-enterprise (TVE) sector. Moreover, with men constituting the vast majority of the over-100-million internal migrants searching for work in cities, rural women now account for over half of farm output.[21] Thus women on average earn 40 percent of household income, up from 25 percent before 1978.[22]

Interestingly, with this last arguable exception, increasing income inequality is largely a product of post-1978 policies of domestic economic reform and of "opening to the outside world."[23] This is in part because reform has enriched those it has touched, though not all places have been included equally.[24] It is also in part due to different local policy emphasis given to agriculture versus rural industry, with stress on the latter increasing inequality.[25] Ironically, the prescription for this inequality is still more reform. Measures could include:

Figure 14.1. China's Provinces.

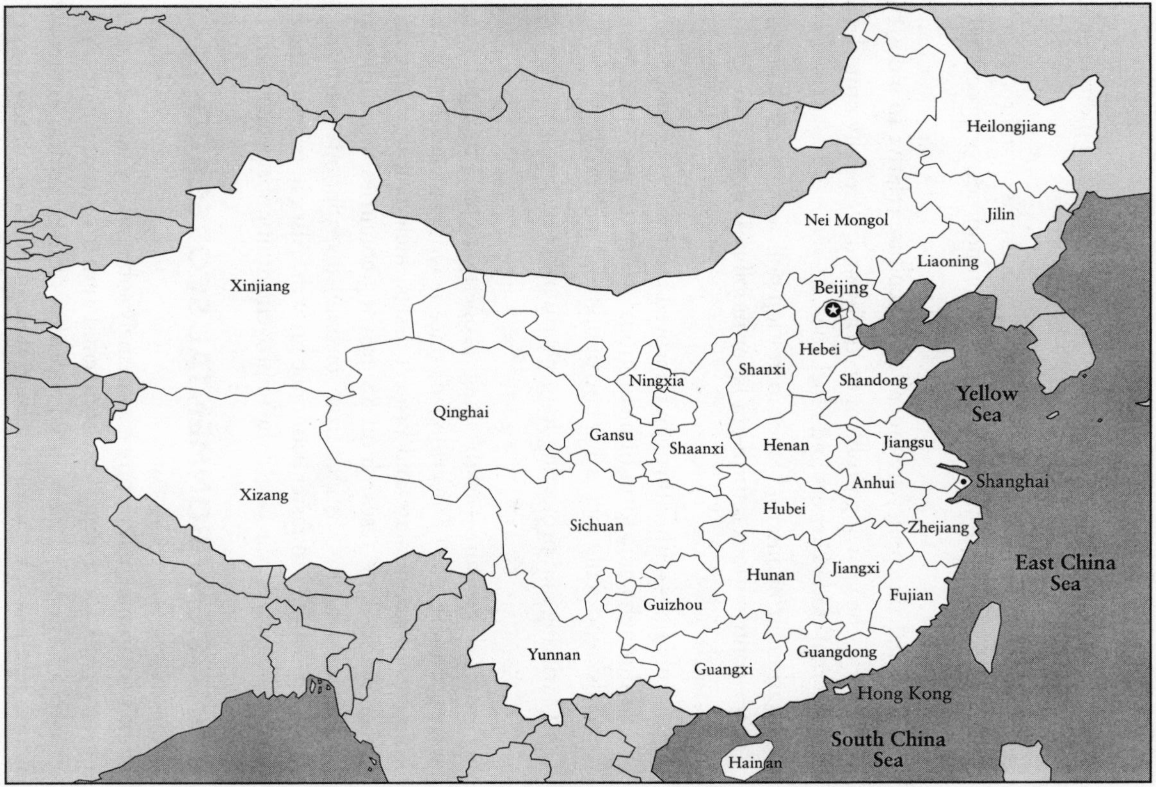

- Permitting interior provinces and rural areas the same economic freedoms as the coastal provinces and urban areas have enjoyed, including equal openness to foreign trade and investment.

- Rationalizing tax rates across farm (lower-earning, yet higher-taxed) and nonfarm activities in the rural areas.

- Trimming or eliminating urban dwellers' direct and indirect subsidies.[26]

- Permitting further rationalization of procurement and retail prices, whether for natural resources, farm commodities, or processed items.

- Rationalizing policy treatment of agriculture relative to industry.

- Ending the growing problem of locally and regionally imposed internal trade barriers and blockades.

- Rationalizing internal labor migration policies in accordance with the contributions reform-era labor mobility is making to economic growth.[27]

- Combating—either through improved monitoring and enforcement or through some form of institutional restructuring—local rural officials' reportedly increasing corruption and malfeasance.

- Clarifying and protecting longer-term property rights.

This final measure—establishing property rights—though seemingly esoteric, should not be overlooked, since it would strengthen individual incentives to accumulate and protect assets, including farmland fertility. Recent World Bank research on 88 growing countries found that greater equality of *asset* (as distinct from *income*) distribution—particularly of land—contributed to faster economic growth. Also, in general, the higher the rate of growth, the larger the improvement in poor people's incomes.[28]

CHINA'S ENVIRONMENTAL SCORECARD

China's environmental picture is extremely sobering. By most any measure, the prospects for a rapid environmental turnaround are dim. Problems include: a huge population; rapid depletion of some critical nonrenewable natural resources (fresh groundwater, topsoil) that are already in very limited supply; breakneck development; distorted incentives, both institutionally and economically; very low levels of implemented technology that can benefit the environment; relatively low political understanding of or commitment to environmental protection; and improving environmental laws but weak legal, monitoring, and enforcement institutions.

Pollution

China's pollution affects several parts of the biosphere: air, water, and soil. This section will give some attention to soil and water pollution—the latter arguably the most serious form of pollution facing China today—but first a look at air pollution. Examining one area in greater detail will illustrate the complexity of the problems, causes, and prospects for improvement that foreign firms should understand if they wish to effectively target their global citizenship activities.

China's air pollution is serious, worsening, and unlikely to be overcome in the short term, though some solutions are being tried, and foreign companies could be of further help in a variety of ways.

How bad is it? As one measure, in 1992 daily particulate levels in China's northern cities averaged 403 micrograms per cubic meter (g/m3), and in southern cities 243 g/m3. Compare London, normally at about 48 g/m3 and the World Health Organization's recommended limit of 90 g/m3.[29] Sulfur dioxide (SO_2) levels are similarly excessive and climbing, putting certain major northern cities in the ranks of the world's worst and making China one of the few developing countries with a major acid pollution problem.[30] Indeed, in Sichuan province, massive forest demise was being reported as early as the mid-1980s.[31] Nitrogen oxide (NO_2), desert dust, coal ash and methane gas emissions are also problems.[32]

The leading sources of these problems are:

- China's heavy dependence on coal, which supplies about three-quarters of China's energy needs[33] and accounts for 69 percent of its particulate pollution.[34]

- The very high sulfur content of China's coal, which contributes to high SO_2 levels.

- The low level of China's installed combustion technologies, whose inefficiency (by world standards) greatly increases both the total amount of coal that must be burned and the ratio of pollutants to energy output.

One company attempting to make a difference in conservation and energy consumption is Owens-Corning, which hopes to attack pollution by manufacturing and selling insulation in China.

By way of background, people who live north of the Yangtze have central heating in their homes, switched on by the government in mid-November and off again in February. Those who live south of the Yangtze have no central heating. They must make do in drafty apartment blocks with electric radiators, gas heaters, and air-conditioning units.

Ben Yau, managing director of the Asia Pacific building materials group for Owens-Corning, the U.S. maker of construction materials, points at the walls and ceiling: "The potential market in China is residential houses—insulation in the attic, in the partition walls, and between the floors. These are just huge opportunities." This growth potential has outweighed the current insulation oversupply problem for Owens-Corning, which opened a 12,000-ton-a-year insulation plant in Shanghai in early 1997.

In 1996, China had introduced its first energy conservation code, requiring new buildings to meet energy savings targets using insulation materials. Ministry of Construction officials were persuaded by tests in Beijing, where temperatures can drop as low as 20 degrees below freezing in the winter, showing that 50 percent of household energy can be saved using two inches of fibreglass insulation—or an eight-foot-thick brick wall.

Insulation makers are now lobbying Beijing to introduce a second energy conservation code for southern China. "Along the Yangtze River, the winters are very cold and the summers are very hot—a lot of energy is lost from electric heaters in the winter and air conditioners in the summer. It is a great potential market for insulation," says Mr. Yau.

Instructions by the Construction Ministry to use light-weight materials on partition walls—typically, plasterboard with glass fibre acoustic insulation—have been accompanied by financial penalties for builders who continue to use bricks. So, at least some efforts at tackling the problem[35] have begun.

Air pollution is serious in rural areas, also. This is due in part to coal, both because it provides the chief energy source for the rapidly growing township-and-village enterprise sector and because the TVE sector's installed pollution control technologies and procedures are worse than the already low levels (by world standards) in the largely urban state-owned-enterprise sector.[36] But this rural air pollution is also due to the burning of biomass fuels—crops, dung, and wood—which are used for heating and cooking and which supply about 80 percent of rural energy.[37]

The causes of this air pollution are many—complex, typically interacting, and in many cases jointly responsible for other forms of pollution. A short list of causes includes political emphasis on economic growth over the environment, still-weak monitoring and enforcement institutions, extremely inefficient combustion technologies, and low or limited pollution abatement technologies.

Several major effects of this air pollution include effects on the ecosystem (vegetation damage), health (increased morbidity and mortality), and the cost of living (more frequent cleaning and washing)—effects that cause major and unsustainable economic losses.[38] The health effects particularly warrant mention. In 1988, 26 percent of all deaths were attributable to chronic obstructive pulmonary disease (COPD), which is linked to exposure to particulates and SO_2, though cigarette smoking (widely practiced in China) is also closely identified. That 26 percent COPD death rate is five times higher than in the United States. Costs stemming from air-pollution-related morbidity (disease) in urban areas have been estimated to approach $1 billion.[39]

Various technical and policy solutions are available, though sometimes at a very high price. Technical solutions, for example, include (1) conversion to cleaner fuels such as natural gas, hydroelectric, and solar forms, (2) installation of more efficient combustion devices in both commercial and residential settings, (3) wide-scale adoption of coal cleaning and processing techniques,[40] (4) installation of post-combustion filtering/cleaning technologies, and (5) addressing the rural fuelwood shortage. Policy solutions include (1) rationalizing energy prices (coal and natural gas are priced well below their equilibrium market prices) to make investment in more efficient technologies attractive and (2) strengthening not just relevant laws and agencies through bureaucratic power realignments and institutional restructuring but actual *implementation* of environmental protection laws.

The prospects for reversing this pollution in the near term are mixed. On the one hand, marginal gains are being made as various localities' leadership gets serious about cleaning up their jurisdictions. Examples include massive shifts to cleaner fuels or requiring enterprises to post sizable bonds before constructing new factories—bonds that are returned only when environmental protection compliance has been assured.[41] In addition, due to (1) mild movement toward more rational energy pricing, (2) a shift in industry structure somewhat toward less-energy-demanding light industry, (3) gradual investments in improving the energy efficiency of state-owned heavy industrial enterprises, and (4) centralized administration of environmental regulations, there has been at least one important favorable trend: a reduction in energy intensity over the 1980s of about 37 percent.[42] Nevertheless, particularly outside the state-owned enterprise sector, penalty-free circumvention or subterfuge of environmental rules is the rule not the exception, and local authorities often turn a blind eye. And, in both rural and urban settings, though scrubbers and electrostatic filters have been installed in the smokestacks of most coal-burning plants, frequently many of the devices are turned off or broken.[43] In sum, the compelling desire for economic growth usually overrides concerns about environmental protection.

Against such a backdrop, what can foreign enterprises with corporate citizenship goals do? One important option now is to provide novel and affordable pollution-control or environmental-repair technologies, as Owens-Corning is doing with building insulation. With China's high-sulfur-content coal presenting a major problem, affordable and effective desulphurization technologies would be an especially welcome addition. Firms outside the environmental technologies industry could help simply by complying with existing (and foreseen) regulations. Note that such compliance is also rational, since compliance failures among foreign firms are targeted before those among domestic firms.

WATER POLLUTION Now that many of the complexities of China's environmental problems have been illustrated in the air pollution discussion, even more potentially troublesome topics can be raised.[44] In fact, China's most serious pollution problem may be its water. The reasons and possible solutions—demographic, geographic, economic, technological, bureaucratic—are much the same as with its air. Consider data about urban water pollution. In 1992, 87.5 percent of river sections running through cities failed to meet China's own safety standards; ammonium nitrate, volatile phenol, and oxygen-consuming organic matter were commonly the chief offenders.[45] A late 1980s study found that only 6 of 27 major cities could provide safe drinking water. As late as 1992, fully 32 percent of industrial wastewater and 81 percent of municipal wastewater entered rivers, lakes, and seas without treatment, exacerbating the already severe harm to human health and marine life. As an example of the latter, between the 1970s and early 1990s, fry production among the Changjiang (Yangtze) River's top four fish species fell from 20 billion to 1 billion. And pollution of various estuaries, bays, and even coastal portions of the East China Sea has been alarming. Still, China has dramatically improved its treatment of industrial waste water (from 13 percent in 1981 to 82 percent in 1993),[46] but that touches only a small portion of the problem. For the vast majority of China's people, clean water is "accessible" only after they boil it.

As for human health, this widespread boiling of drinking water helps contain the incidence of illness from drinking contaminated water, but cases of uncontrolled irrigation of market crops with raw sewage have been thought responsible for intestinal worm disease among children. One dramatic case in Shanghai of seafood being contaminated by untreated water led to some 300,000 people contracting hepatitis A. Moreover, boiling does nothing to eliminate the industrial toxins, including carcinogenic compounds, in urban water.

Rural water is declining, too, with some small rivers now no longer able to sustain aquatic life.[47] As mentioned earlier, TVEs tend to use outdated technology and are not well designed or built. Operation and maintenance are below standard, and pollution abatement equipment is lacking or ineffective. Moreover, TVEs are difficult to regulate because they are dispersed and small, and regulation is divided between the Ministry of Agriculture and the National Environmental Protection Agency.[48] And, though some rural locales have had moderate success controlling water pollution recently,[49] in 1989 only 14.8 percent complied with water discharge regulations.[50] Because they are concentrated in light industry, TVEs produce less pollution than their share of economic output, yet several industries are serious offenders: food processing, textiles,[51] brick and tile, porcelain and pottery, cement, and pulp and paper. The latter accounts for nearly 44 percent of wastewater discharge.[52] The health consequences are compounded because these enterprises' effluents contaminate drinking or irrigation water near food-growing areas.[53]

As with air pollution, China has developed standards for the discharge of pollutants and has a variety of policy mechanisms to combat this pollution. One notable tool is the pollution levy system, which imposes a fee on violators. But, again, levies are so low that most firms have chosen to pay them rather than invest in pollution control equipment.[54]

SOIL POLLUTION China's soil pollution[55] is less serious than its soil degradation, and neither has yet so constrained China's food production capacity that immediate disaster looms, despite arguments about the longer-term prospects.[56] Indeed, 1996 saw another bumper crop in China, with about 485 million tons harvested, bettering even 1995's total of 465 million tons.[57]

Yet soil pollution is serious enough. The Ministry of Agriculture's crude estimates are that 10 million hectares (or a square about 200 miles wide on each side) are polluted, with grain losses of 12 billion kg/year (or about 22 pounds per person annually). The chief culprits are increased and improper use of chemical fertilizers (consumption tripled from 1978 to 1988 and was then estimated at twice the world average per hectare)[58] and pesticides. Integrated pest management (IPM) had been widely used before the reform era, but the shift from communal to family agriculture worked against this, since IPM must be used over a wide area to succeed. On the plus side, there are soil improvement efforts at various levels of government, though bridging the gap from the research farms to everyday farms is proving a challenge. Also, there is a reported return to organic fertilizers,[59] presumably among farmers whose soil fertility has so decayed that even short-term returns require the extra investment. Yet the amounts used and acreages covered today are only a shadow of pre-reform levels.[60]

Beyond the obvious use and promotion of pollution control equipment, good operations, and management, foreign enterprises interested in global citizenship in this area could seek advances in appropriate agricultural technologies (for example, seeds, fertilizers, pest control, equipment, soil-repair, soil-replenishment) or could develop and affordably market other indirectly supportive advances (for example, marketing, distribution, finance) that would boost farming incomes, making it easier for motivated farmers and farming communities to undertake local soil protection or reclamation measures.

TOXIC AND SOLID WASTE Prior to economic reforms launched in 1978, China's solid waste situation would not have been considered a problem by world standards.[61] Industry waste was not necessarily well handled, but the absolute size of the industrial sector was smaller then. And house-hold waste consisted largely of kitchen scraps and coal ash. Few homes had indoor plumbing, so human wastes were collected for transformation into "night soil" organic fertilizer.

With rapid reform-era economic growth, though, several things changed. For one, the industrial sector grew in absolute terms, producing correspondingly more waste. Household income also grew, spawning con-sumer patterns that increased nonorganic household wastes, including more heavy metals. Chemical fertilizers were widely substituted for night soil, so collection efforts decreased. And some of this untreated matter was added to the solid waste channels. The basic unit of rural organization shifted from communes to households, weakening previous economies of scale in collecting and transforming crop wastes and human and animal excrement into bio-gas. Absolute consumption of coal increased, produc-ing still greater quantities of poorly managed mine tailings, especially in rural areas, which generated their own new water pollution problems.

Current challenges therefore include discovering and implementing ways to process and haul waste, as well as burial and incineration processes, that best match China's conditions. Expansion of toxic waste storage capacities and elimination of radiation exposure risks near nuclear-testing and nuclear-energy-producing areas is also recommended. There is some good news: treatment and recycling rates of industrial solid wastes are on the increase, rising from 33 to 64 percent between 1985 and 1990.[62] Nevertheless, potential for technological or operations/managerial contributions from foreign enterprises remain in several of these areas.

GLOBAL WARMING AND CLIMATE CHANGE Even though as late as 1990 the average Chinese household used only 0.03 percent of the energy used in the average American home,[63] China as a whole is the world's third largest emitter of carbon dioxide (CO_2), behind the U.S. and Russia.[64] China is responsible for about 11 percent of global CO_2 emissions (1989), up from just over 1 percent as recently as 1950.[65]

And with China's already mammoth population, economy, and energy consumption growing at faster rates than the developed world, China's share of world *growth* in energy use is expected to be about 25 percent, with even greater growth in CO_2 output, due to the extraordinarily high share of coal in China's energy mix.[66] China could, therefore, be the world's largest CO_2 emitter within 20 years.[67]

Carbon dioxide is the major, but not the only, concern. So are methane and various ozone-depleting substances (ODS), chiefly chlorofluorocarbons (CFCs). Methane comes from China's wet paddy rice farming cultivation and from venting of subterranean pockets opened during coal mining. CFCs are released both during manufacturing of certain foams and plastics and in mishandling of previous-generation refrigerants, the very sort in use during the 1980s rapid introduction of household refrigerators. CFCs use has been growing dramatically: China had only 0.2 refrigerators per 100 households in 1981 but 42.3 per 100 households in 1990,[68] while production of CFC-12, an aerosol, grew ten times between 1988 and 1990.[69] The Chinese government estimated that, unless demand were restrained, production of all ODSs would rise from 48,000 metric tons in 1991 to 117,000 metric tons by 2000.[70]

Various solutions have been proposed. To reduce CO_2 emissions, for example, China could rationalize energy prices and reduce or eliminate subsidies for energy-intensive industries. These steps would reduce consumption directly and promote investment in more efficient combustion technology. More efficient equipment could make a huge difference. On average, China's major industries consume some 30 to 90 percent more energy than like industries in the developed world. Its biggest wasters are its mostly coal-fired small and medium-sized industrial boilers and kilns,[71] which are far behind modern efficiency standards. Upgrading or replacing this equipment alone could save some 100 million tons of raw coal annually, nearly one-tenth the amount currently consumed.[72]

China could also promote substitutes for coal. Under one plausible model, for example, large-scale conversion to imported natural gas where feasible would cut CO_2 emissions by 25 percent.[73] Another proposal has been to expand China's installed base of hydroelectric power. The leading example would be the Three Gorges Dam—when finished next century, by far the largest dam in the world. Another proposal has been to substitute coal-mine methane gas for existing on-site power sources. This is doubly virtuous since it both substitutes a cleaner fuel and reduces methane releases into the atmosphere. Other proposals include "clean coal" technologies such as coal gasification and conversion to hydrogen for use in fuel cells, or large-scale biomass gasification of plantation-raised timber.[74]

Finally, other proposed solutions to China's undesirable contributions to global warming and climate change include virtually eliminating ozone-depleting substances via a large-scale industrial conversion.

Implementation of these various proposed solutions has been the trickier part, for a variety of political, economic, technological, and resource reasons. Rationalizing coal prices, for example, if done too quickly, would economically shock both the coal mining industry and energy-intensive industries that currently depend on cheap coal to stay afloat. Transition to a greater reliance on imported natural gas could occur, but probably not without a net cost compared with the costs of China's present energy path.[75] Hydroelectric power development could also be stepped up, but also not without serious environmental side effects. The Three Gorges Dam is only the leading example of this.[76] Methane use at coal sites is also feasible, but resistance from the coal bureaucracy has reportedly stymied its adoption.[77] There is good news, at least, on the ODS-front. A major international push for worldwide reduction or elimination of ODSs, organized under a series of meetings and agreement in the 1990s known as the Montreal Protocol, led to the formation of a Multilateral Fund for aiding developing countries in conversion away from ODSs. The total conversion cost in China has been roughly estimated at $1.4 billion, and some projects are already under way. Some of these projects hold much promise for foreign enterprises with the requisite technological abilities.[78]

DEPLETION OF NONRENEWABLE RESOURCES Technically, few resources are completely nonrenewable. But the time horizon for their replenishment—millions of years for oil and coal, hundreds of years for topsoil or groundwater—can be so extremely long that they are, practically speaking, nonrenewable. In some cases, substitutes may be found, such as rainfall for groundwater, or hydroelectric or solar power for coal. But these substitutes may be more theoretical than economically or technically feasible.

ARABLE AND OTHER LAND CONVERSION AND DEGRADATION Several of China's spatial natural resources are under threat, including forests, wetlands, wildlife habitat, and arable land. Natural forests are being steadily stripped away, as rural residents relentlessly seek fuel sources. Wetlands, both coastal and inland, are almost universally treated as little more than wastelands to be reclaimed. Wildlife habitats are under increasing pressure from encroaching human activities. And arable land is either being diverted to other uses (primarily urban development) or degraded. This degradation is occurring either through erosion, desertification, salinization, alkalization, or the ebbing away of the soil's long-term fertility.

The soil degradation problem is extremely serious. One aspect of this—the soil erosion problem—is among the worst in the world, with at least one-sixth of the nation's arable land affected. Soil losses are estimated at between 5,000 and 10,000 million metric tons per year, with fertility loss roughly equal to China's annual chemical fertilizer production of about 40 million tons.[79] Human-induced desertification is also worrisome, with nearly 2 percent of China's area now affected,[80] bringing the total deserts and desertified land of China to about 1.49 million square kilometers or 15.5 percent of the land area,[81] and affecting some 400 million people.[82] Salinization and alkalization—due largely to inefficient drainage and excessive irrigation—now affect roughly one-fifth of China's irrigated cropland, and the problem is growing.[83] Soil fertility losses are also very worrisome. To blame are double- and triple-cropping (that is, sowing and harvesting several times in a single growing season), a decline in crop rotation (which replenishes certain nutrients), failure on the small scale to prevent topsoil losses, and a neglect of investment in organic replenishment of soils—problems that are all especially pronounced in the post-1978 reform era. That neglect is due to increasingly tight rural demands for biomass as fuel[84] as well as the current property rights structures that give little incentive to the typical farmer to invest in the long-term fertility of any particular plot of farmland. As a result, the natural organic content of soils now averages a slim 1.5 percent.[85]

One potential long-term consequence of these trends would be China's incapacity to feed itself. Some have debated whether this is a problem;

after all, China could import food, particularly if its GDP per capita continues to grow. But China's massive population distinguishes it from other nations. It would take roughly 20 Frances, Great Britains, or Italys to equal China's population. And the impact on world agriculture would be great. Regardless, China has no shortage of other valuable uses for foreign exchange, so prudently managing its soils in order to preserve a domestic competitive advantage in satisfying most of its food demand would preserve that foreign exchange for other purposes, to say nothing of giving added security and flexibility to its leaders.

Noting the disturbing trends in the full group of land degradation problems is not to say that the central government is not trying. Ministry of Forestry officials estimate forest cover had climbed to 13.6 percent (131 million hectares) in 1992, up from 8.6 percent in 1949. Yet this is still far below the world average of 31 percent,[86] and most of the percentage gains have come from vast tree plantations whose post-planting tree survival rate—while improving since the 1980s—often has been quite low.[87] The government also has been working rapidly to create a system of nature reserves to protect species from overhunting, collecting, and other human pressures. The system has grown from 59 reserves in 1979 to 708 in mid-1993 encompassing over 40 million hectares.[88,89] Central government officials have also declared their intention to save wetlands, but local officials have usually foiled implementation and pressed ahead with reclaiming wetlands for other purposes. Efforts to control erosion or preserve soil fertility also have been made, though only the former have been implemented successfully on any large scale. Massive afforestation along with construction of some 30,000 erosion-control gully dams in the most badly eroded areas has helped, but the scale of the erosion problem is so great that net loss continues.[90]

FRESHWATER The United Nations predicts water will be the world's most critical natural resource issue by 2000. Shortages are already keenly felt in China, where over one-fifth of the world's people make do with 8 percent of its water,[91] and this is unevenly distributed in both time and place.[92] Officials estimate these shortages cost China $27 billion a year in lost industrial output,[93] and that does not begin to account for the human costs. In northern China, the groundwater table has been dropping 50 centimeters per year since about 1990, in Beijing about a full meter per year;[94] in some places it is now 70 meters lower than in the 1950s. Major cities like Shanghai and Tianjin—along with 45 other cities in the south—are literally sinking as they drain their underground reserves.

Most of the solutions proposed have been supply-side. In one scenario, three roughly 1000- to 1400-kilometer canals would carry water from the Changjiang River in the south to the northern region, making this one of the great engineering feats in history. Southerners have opposed this due to the likely impact on southern ports and harbors and the chance that salt water would enter city freshwater supplies.[95] Nevertheless, construction on the easternmost of these has already begun.

More recently, the government has begun to look at demand-side responses, which would conserve supplies through improved efficiency and pricing. By the early 1990s, China was already consuming about 460 billion cubic meters of water per year.[96] Eighty-seven percent of that was being used in agriculture, 7 percent in industry, and 6 percent for domestic purposes, with expectations of soaring demand ahead in the latter two categories. With World Bank staff help, China in the late 1980s saw the opportunity costs of the vast amounts of water being used for irrigation: one hectare of rice used as much water as 300 urban families would use in a year. The World Bank also showed how water pricing could make a difference. Beginning in Tianjin, officials designed a new cost structure for industrial water in which the price rose with consumption.[97] Improved metering of water, improved irrigation practices and water recycling have also been proposed.

Foreign enterprises interested in corporate citizenship could, at the most basic level, ensure that their own operations are water-efficient. Those that can bring technological solutions to industrial or agricultural water use could also make a great impact.

COAL Given all that has been said about China's huge coal reserves, it might seem a few hundred years premature to suggest that coal is a depleting, nonrenewable resource. But revised estimates of China's proved recoverable reserves of coal deserve mention. A survey reported in 1992 put these reserves at only 15 percent of the figure estimated only a few years before.[98] While in the short term this should make little difference, it may cause China's leadership to reexamine its long-term energy directions.

LOSS OF BIODIVERSITY China ranks among the top ten nations in biodiversity.[99] Over 700 species enjoy some official level of protection by the government, and many are endangered, including the giant panda, tiger, snow leopard, white-lip deer, golden monkey, green turtle, Yangzi dolphin, Korean pine, and dragon spruce. Human population pressures on China's plant and animal habitats are a large part of the problem. But hunting and collecting for taxidermy and medicine also have contributed to the decline.[100]

Beginning in earnest in 1979, Chinese authorities began creating nature reserves—some effectively managed—and some endangered species are recovering. But many reserves are ineffective, with both central bureaucracies and local management lacking funding and expertise even to monitor, let alone win, compliance with their mandates. Often overseers are preoccupied with short-term economic advantage or protect only isolated parts of the environment that relate to that particular bureaucracy's interests. Various international organizations, recognizing the difficulties and interested to work with China, have helped organize collaborative study and protection efforts; some of these are making important progress. But many environmentalists still judge that China is doing too little too late.

CAUSES, CONTEXTS, AND POSSIBLE SOLUTIONS

Now that conditions in China have been examined, it is worth revisiting, consolidating, and extending the causes and contexts of those conditions.

With regard to population, the vast majority of China's 1.2 billion people live in an area about the size of the part of the United States that is east of the Mississippi River. This population is also growing at about 15 million annually. Hence, creating the conditions in which nutrition, health, housing, and educational demands are met—and doing so in a way that keeps inequality of wealth distribution within socially tolerable limits presents a constant policy challenge. Furthermore, this huge population's environmental behaviors—personal, agricultural, industrial—even if individually much less environmentally offensive than in the developed world, will nevertheless have a correspondingly sizable impact. Chinese policy makers pondering the massive requisite behavioral changes face a daunting task.

With regard to the economic context: three aspects of China's economy and their implications merit notation. First is the low per capita income. Many of China's problems are related to its relatively low GDP per capita—by definition held low both by low aggregate income and by a huge population. Such low per capita income—300 million people live on less than $1 per day—helps account for China's stressed physical infrastructures such as water and sewage systems, as well as the stressed social services infrastructure—medical, educational, and so on. It also helps account for China's relatively low installed base of energy and pollution-control technologies and for the occasional lack of managerial and operating expertise that could lessen various adverse social and environmental outcomes. It also helps account for both social and environmental problems more directly. Poor people have less access to education and place a higher demand on the environment just to survive, yet the fact of their lower educations and overtaxed physical environments exacerbates their poverty.

Such low income per capita also helps account for China's furious drive for economic growth. The rate of that growth over the last 19 years has been breathtaking. Visit any major city today and you will see what looks like one giant construction zone. Visit the countryside—especially in the east and south—and you will see small- to medium-scale enterprises thrown up everywhere.

This growth has lifted hundreds of millions out of absolute poverty. And it unquestionably must continue if funds to overcome undesirable social welfare and environmental conditions are to be available.[101] Yet, at China's still-low economic level, growth itself brings a host of threats: more pollution, more resource degradation, the worsened health that flows from these, and so on. Witness the impact of the township-and-village enterprises among the major polluters. Or consider the consequences of heavy dependence on China's particular mix of coal. To grow, China needs energy, and coal will be the main source of that energy for the foreseeable future, regardless of the domestic or international environmental impact.

China is not unique in all of this. Typically, a poor country that begins to grow rapidly hits a point where it becomes severely polluted for a couple of decades and then gains enough economic and institutional strength to spend the money and enforce the laws needed to clean up.[102] What distinguishes China is, again, its sheer population size and the corresponding environmental demands. What environmental cost will have been paid before the effective clean-up stage hits?

With regard to China's economic structure as a third category of conditions accounting for it's present situation: China remains in a period of reform—from an economy premised on state ownership and centralized planning to one that permits more ownership forms and relies more on market signals to direct enterprise-level decision making. Yet, those reforms are still only partial and gradual, proceeding in fits and starts.

As one result, unequal rules and unequal outcomes typify the system. As seen earlier, the interior has been less free and therefore has grown less under reform than has the coastal region. The same holds true for rural areas relative to the cities. Understandably, to a certain extent, the political priority assigned to human welfare and environmental improvements varies accordingly.

As another result of partial and gradual reform, only some prices have been decontrolled to reflect true relative scarcities and only some institutions and enterprises freed to buy, produce, and sell strictly according to market disciplines. Relatively underpriced goods such as water or coal are normally overused. But if other prices are kept wrong, subsequent steps to rationalize the price of one kind of goods may produce economically abnormal responses or undesirable outcomes, including anything from unchanged usage patterns at one extreme to dramatic usage changes and subsequent employment disruptions at the other.

As a third result, property rights assignments are often still either ambiguous, misplaced, or counterproductive. Underinvestment is a typical response. For example, plots of farm land in China are normally merely leased rotationally and for relatively short terms. The typical farmer therefore has no incentive to forego current income to promote any particular plot's long-term fertility, since someone else will reap those benefits. The disastrous aggregate result is that China's soil fertility is rapidly plunging. Such underinvestment is a common manifestation of the larger set of "collective action," "public goods," or "cooperation" problems[103]—problems often also manifested in air or water pollution.[104]

One fixed product of reform is the replacement of the commune by the household as the base unit of rural organization. While observers have noted many benefits of this shift, including dramatically increased individual effort in agriculture, one drawback is the lost economies of scale that had previously made feasible both integrated pest management and conversion of various agricultural byproducts into bio-gas.

Quite apart from reform, China's particular natural resource endowments will continue to influence human welfare and environmental policies and outcomes. As a result, no one is likely to talk China out of continuing its heavy dependence on coal for the foreseeable future.

As is true of the economic context, the political context for China's human welfare and environmental situation is extremely complex.

The Structure of Political Power

Political power in China is, at a formal level, highly structured and, at an informal level, sharply personalistic. The formal structure is both vertical (with sharply independent bureaucracies) and horizontal (with power assigned to finely differentiated bureaucratic levels, including geographic units such as provinces and cities). On the informal, personal side, one secures and exercises power via or by virtue of the recognized strength of one's networks of relationships.

Consider first the formal, bureaucratic side. Several outcomes flow from the fragmentation of authority in this domain. Horizontally, what one bureaucracy is mandated to do, another may ignore or thwart. What one bureaucracy approves, another may disallow—assuming it is informed. Responsibility over closely related tasks such as environmental protection in rural areas may be ambiguously shared or uncertainly divided, leading to weakened or failed implementation of mandated policies. Vertically, lower levels do not necessarily share the interests or, therefore, the aims of their superiors, thereby weakening or effectively thwarting implementation. This is particularly relevant environmentally, since local levels have effective authority and frequently undermine central policies. Notably, environmental protection bureaus at almost every level are weaker than, or do not even have proper jurisdiction over, those they are charged with monitoring and from whom they are supposed to win compliance.[105] Finally, particularly at the lower levels, corruption is widespread. Taken together, common outcomes are conflict, stalemate, and policy slowdowns.

The depth of the problem can be underscored by the Beijing government's reaction to a Western gathering to benefit Chinese orphans in 1996. The story, in part, illustrates the Chinese special sensitivity to Western responses to its human welfare problems. But it also emphasizes how the Chinese bureaucracy and its rules and penchant for permits can discourage even the best intentions. In this April 1996 episode, 450 expatriate guests—including America's new ambassador, top American corporations' representatives, and even some Chinese officials—were to attend a benefit dinner for Chinese orphans. Organized by the Philip Hayden Charitable Foundation, a Christian charity founded by English teachers in China in 1995, the dinner was to feature a speech by Chinese-American author Amy Tan. An hour before the dinner, about 40 Beijing police officers entered, tearing down banners reading, "Love Children" and "Cherish Orphans," dismissing a greeting committee of local children and announcing there would be no speech.

The ostensible problem? Organizers apparently lacked a permit for the "mass gathering." The likely real problem? A general view that China can care for its own, as well as lingering touchiness about alleged mistreatment of children in Chinese orphanages raised by Human Rights Watch/Asia in its January 1996 report. The dinner was allowed to proceed, but only after the banquet hall was segmented into three portions, with police wandering among tables to make sure no impromptu speeches were offered. Ms. Tan and guests reportedly took it in stride, though, as plainclothes police watched them leave, many guests admitted that China often makes it tough to feel charitable.[106]

Leadership at the Top

While the personal side of power operates at every level, it can be partly seen in the issues surrounding human welfare and environmental policy making at the top—a circle of 25 to 35 people who are themselves led by a handful at the very apex. For a policy to be formed and executed, leaders first must know and care about a problem. In the late 1980s and early 1990s, it appears the top leadership's recognition of the seriousness and pervasiveness of China's environmental dilemmas increased. That recognition appears to grow weaker, though, the nearer one comes to the local level, where economic development remains by far the overriding policy aim. Beyond knowing and caring, the top leaders must believe that longer-term benefits such as those that derive from environmental protection and promotion of human welfare are worth the more immediate sacrifices that will be needed to win them. Currently, it appears those sacrifices would have to come from current economic growth. That trade-off is difficult enough, but, as is true elsewhere, when leadership transitions are incomplete, as they are now, caution is still greater.

Leadership Dilemmas

Beyond the personal and succession issues, China's top leaders face a number of tough dilemmas and challenges when weighing how to proceed on policies affecting China's human welfare and environmental conditions. Take, for example, the issue of how quickly to reform (including rationalizing prices, ending subsidies to energy-intensive enterprises, and so on). Reform too slowly and the result may be broad, deep discontent with the persistent problems of a partially reformed economy. But reform too quickly and the disjointed change may yield angry bureaucratic players (for example, the coal bureaucracy) and a large group of particularly aggrieved individuals (for example, people losing jobs in affected enterprises). Another example: the benefits of welfare and environmental policies are often not assigned to those who bear the costs. Still another: assigning permanent property rights for plots of farmland, for example, would yield losers (those who now direct the flows of benefits from those lands) as well as winners.

Beyond even the dilemmas, there are also the cases of simply competing priorities for these leaders' time and energy—issues like advancing foreign policy interests, coping with growing urban/rural and coastal/interior cleavages, uprooting official corruption, keeping a lid on inflation, suppressing dissent, dealing with social decay (crime, drugs, prostitution, family break-ups, and so forth), balancing power bureaucratically, quelling ethnic rebellion, and so on.

International Issues

China frequently suffers direct or indirect rebuke from developed countries for its domestic and international policies. On the environmental side, though, China's leadership is understandably unreceptive to some of the criticism. A case in point involves calls from the West, especially the U.S., for China to limit its energy consumption. For though it is now the world's second-largest energy consumer, its per capita level is less than one-tenth that in the U.S. Some argue that unless compensated, China should not forego several percentage points of its GNP to cut its CO_2 emissions, when the average American discharges far more than the average Chinese.[107]

OPPORTUNITIES AND CONSTRAINTS FOR FOREIGN-FUNDED ENTERPRISES

Chinese officials are considerably more sensitive about prominent foreign-led efforts addressing China's human welfare issues than its environmental conditions. An exception to this general rule is found in the government's Agenda 21 project list, which includes a few population and health initiatives.[108] One human welfare area, though, where foreign firms might make a difference would be in the area of treatment of labor employed by foreign firms, not only in one's own operations but also, through the promotion of labor standards within local foreign business associations, in the operations of other firms as well. Disfiguring accidents, deadly plant fires, dismal living conditions, and cruel treatment in foreign firms have made news over the last few years[109] and would be among the problems most readily subject to direct action by foreign firms.

On the environmental side, the government is clamoring for foreign participation in everything from financing, supplying, and even managing. Many projects are staked out as Agenda 21 projects, a list formulated in the wake of the 1992 U.N. Conference on Environment and Development (UNCED) in Rio de Janeiro. Project foci include environmental education, standards, and facilities; sustainable agricultural policies; cleaner industrial production; clean energy and transportation; conservation of natural resources; water pollution, solid waste, and hazardous waste;

poverty alleviation and regional development; and global change and diversity.[110]

More positives: considering just environmental goods and services, an estimated $15 billion was spent in 1994, with projections of 30 percent annual growth thereafter. Of this spending, 60 percent came from provincial and municipal governments, 20 percent from industrial ministries (plus the military), 10 percent from foreign investors, and 10 percent from multilateral and bilateral lending sources. The last of these categories may be the most attractive for many companies, both because funding for most of these projects is untied and, unlike other infrastructure projects in China that can face finance difficulties, these are all backed by adequate hard currency.[111]

Projects are initially proposed by local or provincial governments and then must be successively screened by China's National Environmental Protection Agency (NEPA), Ministry of Finance (MOF), and State Planning Commission (SPC), followed by the lending institution. Generally this last review takes 12 to 18 months, culminating in an implementation stage, during which foreign firms express interest in particular projects. The big financing sources include the World Bank, Asian Development Bank, U.N. Development Programme, Japanese loans (especially the Fourth Yen Loan), the Global Environment Facility (GEF and GEF II) trust fund and the Montreal Protocol's Multilateral Fund.[112]

Some examples help flesh out these generalities. First, to remedy their decrepit water works, various Chinese cities are discussing 20- to 30-year build-operate-transfer (BOT) agreements with private firms. Sino-French Holdings, a partnership between Lyonnaise des Eaux and Hong Kong's New World Development, appears to be a leader, in 1995 claiming contracts to supply industrial water in four cities, plus more on the way, with combined investment of $225 million.[113]

A second example: to cope with the troubling by-products of coal combustion, China has held talks with various foreign firms about remedies at every step of the process. One key step is cleaning the coal before transport. Besides sulphur, impurities account for 35 to 40 percent of its total weight, yet China cleans only about 19 percent of its coal, compared with nearly 100 percent in the West. Various proposed cleaning techniques would remove this and up to 75 percent of the sulphur, thereby dramatically reducing SO_2 output, lowering railway demand, and leaving less ash when burned. A menu of options for coal cleaning, capture of coal-mine methane for fuel, and other coal-related environmental aids has been put before the Chinese by several Western firms or consortiums, including Australia's Custom Coals, Switzerland's ABB Power Generation, and Dallas-based Powerbridge, Inc. The Chinese reportedly embraced the technologies but balked at the price. Financing assistance may help. But some speculate a more stubborn obstacle is China's coal bureaucracy, which apparently perceives some of the proposed projects as threats.[114]

CONCLUSION

While human welfare measures have improved considerably since the mid-20th century, economic growth—particularly during the reform era—has led to great environmental harm in China. Yet such reform must proceed if China is to afford remedies to its environmental situation. Whether merely by behaving responsibly in their own China operations, by raising an existing set of standards among their peers, or by taking on more ambitious roles in developing, adapting, or marketing appropriate technologies, foreign firms with a vision for global citizenship can play an important, perhaps pivotal, role in China's moving—healthy and environmentally safe—into the 21st century.

ENDNOTES

1. For further reading, see, for example, works by Stephan Schmidheiny, including Schmidheiny with the Business Council for Sustainable Development, 1992, *Changing Course: A Global Perspective on Development and the Environment* (Cambridge, Mass.: MIT Press) or Schmidheiny with the World Business Council for Sustainable Development, 1996, *Financing Change: The Financial Community, Eco-efficiency, and Sustainable Development* (Cambridge, Mass.: MIT Press).

2. See World Bank, 1996, *Poverty in China: What Do the Numbers Say?*, cited in (author unnamed), 12 October 1996, "How Poor Is China?," *The Economist*, pp. 35, 36. The $1-a-day line is preferred for international comparisons. Using China's internal standard of about 60 cents per day, the figure would be below 100 million.

3. UNICEF, 1996, *The State of the World's Children 1996* (New York: Oxford), pp. 81, 98.

4. UNICEF, 1996, pp. 81ff.

5. UNICEF, 1996, pp. 89, 97.

6. Economist Intelligence Unit (EIU) 1996. "Health," *Country Profile—China, 1995–96* (London: Economist Intelligence Unit), p. 25.

7. See, for example, Giles Hewitt, 2 June 1994, "China's Minorities Fight Poverty Trap," *The Chicago Tribune*, News section, p. 10.

8. See, for example, Renee Schoof, 19 February 1995, "China's Rural Poor Face Widening Education Gap," *Los Angeles Times*, p. A12; and EIU, 1996, "Health," *Country Profile—China, 1995/96*.

9. On conditions in urban areas, see, for example, Sheila Tefft, 29 September 1993, "Shortage of Housing Cramps Urban China," *Christian Science Monitor*, p. 8.

10. EIU, 1996, "Education," *Country Profile—China, 1995/96*, p. 25.

11. Author's own research in China in 1985 through 1987 and 1996.

12. Cv. EIU, 1996, "Education," *Country Profile—China, 1995/96*, pp. 24, 25.

13. *China Statistical Yearbook* and/or [ambiguous] the *Economist Intelligence Unit*, cited in Dominic Ziegler, 8 March 1997, "Ready to Face the World?," A Survey of China in *The Economist*, p. S4. Uncertainty about the precise number stems from statistical reporting that is still below developed world standards. Moreover, while these figures are given using the standard exchange-rate basis, quite different figures obtain if one uses a purchasing-power-parity (PPP) basis. The most recent World Bank PPP estimate is $1,800. See World Bank, 1996, *Poverty in China: What Do the Numbers Say?* cited in [anonymous], 12 October 1996, "How Poor Is China?," *The Economist*, p. 35.

14. The national Gini coefficient—where "0" signifies absolute equality and "100" absolute inequality—moved down from 27.4 in 1978 to 21.5 in 1984 but up to 30.7 in 1993. See Yvonne Ying, July-August 1996, "Poverty and Inequality in China," *Transition: The Newsletter about Reforming Economies*, 7, no. 7–8, pp. 3–4. (*Transition* is published by the World Bank.)

15. See the discussion in Kenneth Lieberthal, 1995, *Governing China* (New York: W. W. Norton), p. 305–308.

16. 1995 estimate. *China Statistical Yearbook* and/or [ambiguous] the Economist Intelligence Unit, cited in Dominic Ziegler, 8 March 1997, "Ready to Face the World?," A Survey of China in *The Economist*, p. S4.

17. Note, though, that these are partly explained by higher urban-rural ratios in coastal provinces.

18. For a rigorous analysis, as well as an interesting longer-term historical review, see Tianlun Jian, Jeffrey D. Sachs, and Andrew M. Warner, 1996, *Trends in Regional Inequality in China*, NBER Working Paper 5412 (Cambridge, Mass.: National Bureau of Economic Research).

19. EIU, 26 February 1997, "Post-Deng China Faces Period of FDI Uncertainty," *Crossborder Monitor* (New York: EIU), p. 1.

20. See discussion and notes in Lieberthal 1995, p. 307.

21. For an interesting narrative view of the labor migration phenomenon and some of the forces driving it, see Ann and James Tyson, September 1996, "China's Human Avalanche," *Current History*, pp. 277–283.

22. See "Much Like Others," 13 May 1995, *The Economist*, p. 38.

23. See, for example, Yan Shanping, September 1995, "Export-Oriented Rural Enterprises," *China Newsletter* (published by the Japan External Trade Organization), no. 118, pp. 15–16.

24. See Joseph C. H. Chai, 1996, "Divergent Development and Regional Income Gap in China," *Journal of Contemporary Asia*, 26, no. 1, pp. 46–58.

25. See Scott Rozelle, 1994, "Rural Industrialization and Increasing Inequality: Emerging Patterns in China's Reforming Economy," *Journal of Comparative Economics*, 19, pp. 362–391.

26. Ten years into reform, for example, while tax and subsidy combinations cut rural dwellers' net income, urban dwellers saw an average income enhancement of 64 percent. See Lieberthal 1995, p. 307.

27. For an accounting of this contribution, see EIU, 24 June 1996, "Migrant Labour: A Nation on the Move," *Business China*, pp. 2–3.

28. Michael Bruno and Lyn Squire, September-October 1996, "The Less Equal the Asset Distribution, the Slower the Growth," *Transition: The Newsletter about Reforming Economies*, 7, no. 9–10, p. 6. Excerpted from Bruno and Squire's article previously published in the *International Herald Tribune*. Note that their research showed no certain correlation between greater asset equality and greater income equality.

29. Richard Louis Edmonds, 1994, "China's Environment," in William A. Joseph (ed.), *China Briefing, 1994*, Deborah Field Washburn, series ed. (Boulder, CO: Westview Press, in cooperation with The Asia Society), p. 162.

30. Edmonds, 1994, p. 162.

31. Yu Shuwen, *et al.*, 1986, "Acid Rain Destroying Pine Forests," *Huanjing kexue* (Environmental Science), 6, no. 5, pp. 63–66, cited in Vaclav Smil 1993, *China's Environmental Crisis: An Inquiry into the Limits of National Development* (Armonk, N.Y.: M. E. Sharpe), p. 120.

32. In Michael Westlake (ed.), December 1994, *Asia Yearbook 1995* (Hong Kong: Far Eastern Economic Review), p. 64.

33. Amsden, Liu, and Zhang, 1996, p. 282.

34. Cao Hongfa, 1989, "Air Pollution and Its Effects on Plants in China," *Journal of Applied Ecology*, 26, p. 763, cited in Edmonds, 1994, p. 161.

35. "Cold Times in Shanghai," *The Financial Times*, 7 February 1997, p. 4.

36. Robert Livernash, 1994, "China," in *World Resources 1994–95*, a report by the World Resources Institute in collaboration with the U.N. Environment Programme and the U.N. Development Programme (New York: Oxford University Press), pp. 76–77.

37. Keith H. Florig, 1993, "Benefits of Air Pollution Reduction in China," mimeo prepared by the OECD Environment Directorate, Resources for the Future (Washington, D.C.: RFF), cited in Amsden, Liu, and Zhang, 1996, p. 281.

38. Smil, 1993, p. 121.

39. Livernash, 1994, p. 74.

40. Simply washing and molding coal into briquettes would help surprisingly much, since briquettes burn up to 30 percent more efficiently and, in residential settings, give off 70 percent less CO_2, 60 percent less dust, and 50 percent less SO_2. Source: Gregory Mock's energy section in Livernash, 1994, p. 69.

41. For a detailed discussion of solutions that have been tried or proposed, see Livernash, 1994, pp. 74–75.

42. Amsden, Liu, and Zhang, 1996, pp. 281–282. Other encouraging signs they identify relate to topics treated here later, including large-scale reforestation efforts that are off-setting the ongoing deforestation in the countryside, and increasing rates of treating wastewater and solid wastes.

43. Kari Huus, 17 November 1994, "A Question of Economy," part of a special section titled "Focus: Environment in Asia," *Far Eastern Economic Review*, p. 52.

44. Except as noted, this section draws primarily from Edmonds, 1994, pp. 156–157 and Livernash, 1994, pp. 75–76.

45. [Author unnamed], June 1993, "1992 Report on the Environment in China," *China Environment News*, no. 47, p. 5, cited in Livernash, 1994, p. 75.

46. Amsden, Liu, and Zhang, 1996, p. 282.

47. See Edmonds, 1994, p. 157.

48. [Author unnamed], June 1992, "1991 Communiqué on the State of the Environment in China," *China Environment News*, no. 35, p. 7, cited in Livernash, 1994, p. 77.

49. See Edmonds, 1994, p. 157.

50. World Bank, 1992, unpublished data (Washington, D.C.: World Bank), cited in Livernash, 1994, p. 77.

51. Amsden, Liu, and Zhang, 1996, p. 281.

52. [Author unnamed], June 1992, "1991 Communique on the State of the Environment in China," *China Environment News*, no. 35, p. 7, cited in Livernash, 1994, p. 77.

53. Amsden, Liu, and Zhang, 1996, p. 281.

54. See Livernash, 1994, p. 76.

55. Except as noted, this section draws primarily from Edmonds, 1994, pp. 157–159 and Livernash, 1994, pp. 77–78.

56. For a quite pessimistic view see, for example, Lester Brown, 1995, *Who Will Feed China?*, New York: W. W. Norton & Co., Inc. For a similarly sober but contrasting view, see Vaclav Smil, September 1995, "Feeding China," *Current History*, pp. 280–284.

57. United Press International, cited in Jian-Min Li and De An Yin, 13 December 1996, "Another Year of Bumper Crop, Storage a Problem," *China News Digest* (an Internet-based newsletter).

58. Han Chunru, 1989, "Recent Changes in the Rural Environment in China,"

Journal of Applied Ecology, 26, p. 806, cited in Edmonds, 1994, p. 158. Note, too, that this problem is exacerbated by the fact that returns to nitrogenous fertilizers are declining, with a 50–70 percent drop in marginal yields per unit of fertilizer between the 1970s and early 1990s. See Smil, 1995, p. 281.

59. Edmonds, 1994, p. 159.
60. For an excellent extended and technical treatment of China's soil situation, see Smil, 1993, pp. 138–187. A more recent and slightly less technical summary overview is found in Smil, 1995, pp. 281–282.
61. This section draws heavily from Edmonds, 1994, pp. 159–161.
62. Amsden, Liu, and Zhang, 1996, p. 282. [Sources: *China Statistical Yearbook,* various years (Beijing, China), and/or China Environmental Science Press, 1992, *National Report of the People's Republic of China on Environment and Development* (Beijing, China: CESP).]
63. See William Chandler, Alexei Makarov, and Zhou Dadi, September 1990, "Energy for the Soviet Union, Eastern Europe, and China," *Scientific American,* p. 121, and Mark Levine, Feng Liu and Jonathan Sinton, 1992, "China's Energy System: Historical Evolution, Current Issues, and Prospects," *Annual Review of Energy and the Environment,* p. 419, cited in Livernash, 1994, p. 66.
64. Jayant Sathaye, Patty Monahan, and Alan Sanstad, June 1996, "Costs of Reducing Carbon Emissions from the Energy Sector: A Comparison of China, India, and Brazil," *Ambio,* 25, p. 262.
65. Smil, 1993, p. 130.
66. Geoffrey Carliner, September 1995, "The China Card: Global Warming?," *Challenge,* pp. 57–58.
67. Smil, 1993, cited in Lieberthal, 1995, p. 289.
68. Livernash, 1994, p. 78.
69. Jessica Poppele, July 1994, "The CFC Challenge," in a special report on China's environment, *China Business Review,* p. 35.
70. National Environmental Protection Agency (NEPA), March 1993, "China Country Program for the Phaseout of Ozone-Depleting Substances under the Montreal Protocol," report submitted to the Ninth Meeting of the Executive Committee of the Multilateral Fund of the Montreal Protocol, Montreal, cited in Livernash, 1994, p. 78.
71. Wu Zongxin and Wei Zhihong, 1991, "Policies to Promote Energy Conservation in China," *Energy Policy,* 19, no. 10, pp. 936, cited in Livernash, 1994, p. 67.
72. Huang Yicheng, 1992, "Strategic Alternatives for Coordinated Development of Energy and Environment in China," recommendations to the China Council for International Cooperation on Environment and Development, Paper No. 5, Agenda Item 4C, Beijing, p. 3, cited in Livernash, 1994, p. 67.

73. Jayant Sathaye, Patty Monahan, and Alan Sanstad, June 1996, "Costs of Reducing Carbon Emissions from the Energy Sector: A Comparison of China, India, and Brazil," *Ambio,* 25, p. 262.

74. See discussion and references in Livernash, 1994, p. 70.

75. Sathaye, Monahan, and Sanstad, 1996, p. 262.

76. Befitting the Three Gorges Dam's status as the world's largest construction project, there is a very large literature analyzing its probable economic, environmental, and human welfare effects. These problems were considered serious enough that in May 1996, the U.S. Export-Import Bank turned down aid applications from U.S. firms hoping to sell equipment for the project. In early December 1996, the same decision was taken toward applications from several large Japanese firms by Japan's Export and Import bank, and for the same reasons. The stakes for these firms are high: the project is officially expected to cost about $25 billion but expected by outside analysts to cost as much as twice that. Yet the environmental stakes are also high. For the official Chinese view of the dam's environmental impact, see Lu Youmei, 8 July 1996, "Three Gorges Project Benefits Ecological Environment," *Beijing Review,* pp. 9–13. In short, the benefits touted are a tremendous supply of clean energy, flood control on the Changjiang (Yangtze) River that could save millions of lives, and a boom in inland-coastal shipping that would help alleviate poverty in the interior. For a more circumspect view, see Lawrence R. Sullivan, September 1995, "The Three Gorges Project: Damned if They Do?," *Current History,* pp. 266–269.

77. In Michael Westlake (ed.), 1994, *Asia Yearbook 1995,* p. 64.

78. For a detailed discussion, see Poppele, 1994.

79. Edmonds, 1994, p. 153.

80. Edmonds, 1994, p. 154.

81. Michael A. Fullen, and David J. Mitchell, March 1994, "Desertification and Reclamation in North-Central China," *Ambio,* 23, no. 2, p. 131.

82. [Author unnamed], 17 October 1995, *Renmin Ribao [People's Daily],* overseas edition, reprinted in 4 December 1995, *Beijing Review,* p. 24.

83. Edmonds, 1994, p. 155.

84. Livernash, 1994, p. 67.

85. Edmonds, 1994, p. 155.

86. See "1992 Report on the Environment in China," 1993, p. 5, and China Environmental Science Press, 1992, p. 7, cited in Livernash, 1994, p. 79.

87. Smil, 1993, pp. 59–62.

88. Livernash, 1994, p. 79.

89. Edmonds, 1994, p. 164.

90. Edmonds, 1994, pp. 153–154.

91. Except as noted, this section draws most heavily on Edmonds, 1994, pp. 150–151 and Livernash, 1994, pp. 72–73.

92. The northern 60 percent of the landmass has only about 20 percent of the freshwater resources. Smil, 1993, p. 41. (See extended discussion in Smil, 1993, pp. 38–52.)

93. Jonathan Karp, 1 June 1995, "Water, Water, Everwhere," *Far Eastern Economic Review,* p. 55.

94. Thomas Homer-Dixon, 4 September 1995, "China's Challenge," *MacLeans,* p. 27.

95. See Bruce Stone, 1983, "The Chang Jiang Diversion Project: An Overview of Economic and Environmental Issues" and Shen Huanting, Mao Zhichang, and Gu Guochuan, *et al.,* "The Effect of South-to-North Water Transfer on Saltwater Intrusion in the Chang Jian Estuary," both in *Long Distance Water Transfer: A Chinese Case Study and International Experiences,* Asit K. Biswas, Zuo Dakang, James E. Nickum, *et al.,* (eds.). Dublin, Ireland: Tycooly, pp. 194–197 and 352–359, respectively. See also Dong Shi, 2 April 1990, "Water Crisis in Northern China and Counter-Measures," *Beijing Review,* p. 33. All were cited in Livernash, 1994, p. 73.

96. China Environmental Science Press, 1992, p. 56.

97. Karp, 1995, p. 58.

98. See World Energy Conference, 1989, *1989 Survey of Energy Resources* (London: World Energy Conference), p. 17 and World Energy Council, 1992, *1992 Survey of Energy Resources* (London: World Energy Council), p. 20, cited in Livernash, 1994, p. 66.

99. Except where noted, this section draws from Edmonds, 1994, pp. 164–168 and Livernash, 1994, p. 79.

100. See Andrea Sachs, 8 April 1991, "A Grisly and Illicit Trade," *Time,* pp. 67–68.

101. Amsden, Liu, and Zhang, 1996, p. 281.

102. See discussion in Jim Rohwer, 1995, *Asia Rising* (New York: Simon & Schuster), pp. 84–87.

103. I use the familiar—albeit limited, misleading, and often biased—terms here. For interested readers, one of the best-argued and novel taxonomies of institutional choice problems known to this author is found in A. Allan Schmid's (1987) difficult but rewarding *Property, Power, & Public Choice: An Inquiry into Law and Economics,* 2nd ed. (New York: Praeger).

104. The jargon gets dense here, but, by way of reminder for the previously initiated, such problems typically appear when individually rational behaviors together yield collectively suboptimal outcomes, or, more basically, when "internalizing the externalities" of one party's behaviors is costly.

105. For an excellent brief discussion, see Kenneth Lieberthal, 1995, pp. 285–290. See also Barbara J. Sinkule and Leonard Ortolano, 1995, *Implementing Environmental Policy in China* (Westport, Conn.: Praeger).

106. "Charity Ends at Home," *The Economist,* 6 April 1996, p. 39 and "Police Disrupts Fund-Raiser for Children," *Facts on File News Digest,* 11 April 1996, p. 252.

107. Carliner, 1995, p. 58.

108. [Author unnamed], July 1994, "Agenda for Change," *China Business Review,* p. 28. These and other Agenda 21 projects are managed by the Administrative Center for China's Agenda 21 in Beijing.

109. See, for example, Joyce Barnathan and Matt Forney, 1 August 1994, "Damping Labor's Fires: Can Beijing Calm Workers and Sustain Growth?," *Business Week,* pp. 40–41.

110. [Author unnamed], July 1994, "Agenda for Change," *China Business Review,* p. 28.

111. [Author unknown], 15 February 1996, "How to Get into China's Lucrative Environmental Market," *East Asian Executive Reports,* 18, no. 2, p. 8.

112. [Author unknown], 15 February 1996, "How to Get into China's Lucrative Environmental Market," *East Asian Executive Reports,* 18, no. 2, pp. 17, 18.

113. Karp, 1 June 1995, p. 58.

114. Westlake (ed.), December 1994, pp. 64–66.

15

RUSSIA, UKRAINE, AND KAZAKSTAN

Corporate Citizenship in Unstable Environments

Benjamin E. Goldsmith[1]

The collapse of the soviet union is being translated, in large part,
as a complete victory for the proponents of a market economy.
With the primacy of capitalism thus understood, large transna-
tional corporations can grow even larger. These megacorporations
must now assume responsibility for resolving global problems
commensurate with a vast proportion of the world's resources that
they command. When capitalism is the only game in town, its per-
formance, both economically and in terms of social responsibility,
will be held by the public to a different standard
(Harvard Business Review, *July-Aug., 1994, p. 143).*

—Delwin A. Roy, President and CEO, The Hitachi Foundation

BY VIRTUE OF THEIR SIZE and resources, Russia, Ukraine, and Kazakstan represent the most important investment opportunities in the former Soviet Union. But most global corporations have been slow to commit for business—even slower to rally their global citizenship bandwagons.

SLOW PACE OF INVESTMENT

The relatively sluggish economic performance of the former Soviet region is indicated in its low level of trade with the rest of the world and in low levels of foreign direct investment. For example, although the Russian economy has declined in recent years, it is still at least three-fourths the size of China's. But Russia's *volume* of trade is much less than one-quarter of China's.

The immediate reasons for this great difference are no secret. First, the historical legacy of the Soviet economic system, with its headlong drive for autarky, is still strongly felt. The surviving structural and psychological barriers to global integration have to be overcome gradually. Second, foreign companies perceive great risk involved with the newly independent states of the former Soviet Union. The political situation is unstable, or has been until recently. The legal guarantees and protection against organized criminal gangs are nebulous and notoriously unreliable.

Why attempt corporate citizenship in what seems to be such an anarchic and corrupt business environment? Such activities can be a strategic asset for foreign firms. First, if designed well, a citizenship program can be a serious hedge against political risk. Second, corporate citizenship can serve to domesticize a firm's image for its customers, ameliorating the effect of any antiforeign backlash in the future. Third, citizenship can be an excellent tool to build bridges between MNC (multinational corporation) employees and local populations. Expatriate employees, and even local employees to some extent, tend to live sheltered from the basic hardships and turmoil of post-Soviet societies in transition. Ignorance of local conditions and basic needs can lead to an attitude unresponsive to customer needs; it can also contribute to the creation of uninformed illusions about the overall health, stability, and beliefs of the society that forms the workforce and the market in these countries.

THE BACKDROP OF TRADE

Compare the trade statistics shown in Table 15.1 (in billions of U.S. dollars):

Relative to their size, level of development, and potential, all three former Soviet republics are underperforming in terms of trade. They are significantly disengaged from the global economy. For those MNCs active in these markets, the expectation of the countries' increasing integration into the global economy is often the ultimate justification for investing in the

Table 15.1.   Comparison of Imports and Exports
(in Billions of U.S. Dollars).

	Russia	Ukraine	Kazakstan	Poland	China³	India	Brazil
Imports	26.8	2.4	0.4	18.8	242.5	22.8	27.7
Exports	44.3	3.1	1.3	14.1	227.0	21.6	38.6
Total trade	**71.1**	**5.5**	**1.7**	**32.9**	**469.5**	**44.4**	**66.3**

Source: United Nations Statistical Yearbook, 1993.
Note: Figures for China include Hong Kong.

region, that is, to establish market share now because the potential for growth will be enormous later—and a foothold advantageous. Even if profits are being made today—and there is a short-term justification of the investment—the expectation of growth and development of these states is important.

Doing business and investing in production and distribution of products in the former Soviet Union is in itself a contribution to the economic health of the region. But there are great needs at all levels of society in all states of the former Soviet Union (FSU).

Although Russia, Ukraine, and Kazakstan were part of the same state until 1991, there are significant differences between them in all socioeconomic areas. Noting some key differences, as well as some continuing similarities, will help emphasize the need to tailor citizenship activities to local environments. Some basic economic and developmental data are included in Table 15.2. Kazakstan is clearly the poorest of the three states, although it is still considerably more developed than China or India on a per capita basis. Kazakstan is a Central Asian republic with a Turkic ethnic and linguistic background. However, today around 60 percent of the population is made up of Slavic or other non-Turkic ethnicities (Germans, Jews), and Russian is spoken more than Kazak. There are about 17 million citizens of Kazakstan, with Russian speakers concentrated in the north and ethnic Kazaks in the south. The world's major oil companies have been active in the country since the fall of the USSR, due to the considerable untapped reserves in the north. United Nations data give the under-five mortality rate, a key health indicator, as 48 per 100,000. In Russia the figure is 31, and in Ukraine it is 25. Russia and Ukraine are overwhelmingly ethnically Slav, although Ukraine has sharp ethnic and cultural divisions between Russians and Ukranians; Russia is diverse but

Table 15.2. Comparative Statistics.

Country	Russia	Ukraine	Poland	Kazakstan	U.S.	India	China
GDP[1]	329,432	109,079	85,853	24,728	6,259,901	250,966	425,611
GNP per cap.[2]	2,340	2,210	2,260	1,560	24,740	300	490
Change in GDP 1990–94 (%)[3]	–21.1	–24.6	–10.1	–27.3			
Private sector share of GDP[4]	55	35	60	25	—		
Institutional reform ranking[5]	intermediate reformer	slow reformer	leading reformer	intermediate reformer		—	—
Corruption ranking (10 = no corruption; 0 = extremely corrupt)	2.54		5.57		7.66	2.63	2.43
Press freedom rating[6] (100 = no freedom; 0 = completely free)	58	39	21	62		83	83
Credit risk ranking[7] (178 states)	86	135	55	129	3	62	40

[1]World Tables 1995, pp. 27–33. Data are in millions of U.S. dollars for 1993.
[2]World Tables 1995, pp. 3, 5. Data are in U.S. dollars for 1993.
[3]Transition, 6(9–10), 1995, p. 20. Data are power-consumption-based GDP measures, more accurate than standard measures of GDP in transition economies.
[4]Transition, 7(7–8), 1996, p. 9. Data are for 1995.
[5]Transition, 7(7–8), 1996, p. 9. World Bank classification.
[6]Freedom House surveys, 1996, as reported in Transitions, 7(5–6), 1996, p. 5.
[7]Euromoney, 1996.

overwhelmingly Russian. The population of Ukraine is 51 million, and that of the Russian Federation is 147 million.

All three states share the legacy of the Soviet economic system, which was arranged hierarchically with limited horizontal coordination. This means that enterprises attempted to incorporate many inefficient or inappropriate functions. They tried to provide housing and other social services for their workforce, and they tried to incorporate all aspects of production and supply within one organization. This led to worker dependence on the enterprise for much more than a paycheck, and enterprise inefficiency because supplies and distribution were not subject to market forces. There was great duplication of efforts, sheltered from competition, and much that was done off-the-books.[2] One fairly consistent feature of the present business climate in all three states that stems directly from the Soviet system is corruption. Governments, state enterprises, and private firms are all enmeshed in a system of protection, extortion, and tax evasion, which is pervasive. Any type of significant business activity in these states will result in a demand for a bribe or protection money at some point, and possibly at many points. One tool to lessen the magnitude or danger of these demands is to specify what type of donations your firm makes to which philanthropic groups. In the case of government-based corruption, such arguments have proven to carry some weight and to discourage demands for bribes.[3]

THE ENVIRONMENTAL LEGACY

Another powerful legacy of the Soviet system is environmental degradation on a truly unprecedented scale. Ukraine's Chornobyl, Russia's Ural mountains, and Kazakstan's nuclear test sites in Atyrau oblast (Feshbach, 1995, p. 33) are the best known of the manifold environmental disasters, past and present. Not all important environmental problems are so well known or dramatic, however. The Communist Party diverted a major proportion of its resources into military production and industrial infrastructure. Infrastructure to support basic social needs was fairly low on the list of Soviet priorities. Two legacies of this lack of investment are poor-quality drinking water and inadequate sewage treatment. To make things worse, poorly treated sewage often gets into the water supply for human consumption, even in major metropolitan areas such as St. Petersburg. In Kyiv, not only are water quality and sewage treatment a problem, but previous and continuing contamination from Chornobyl, about 90 miles to the north of the city, makes the normally polluted water especially unhealthy (Feshbach, 1995, p. 33). As specialists such as Murray

Feshbach and Aleksei Yablokov have noted, documenting the health effects of environmental degradation in the former Soviet Union is especially difficult. Even if scientific confirmation is tentative so far, most specialists argue that these environmental problems, individually and in the aggregate, certainly make Russians, Ukranians, Kazaks, and citizens of other former Soviet republics less healthy. Children are especially vulnerable.

THE POLITICAL SYSTEM

All three societies share at least one fundamental characteristic in their political and social values that distinguishes them from Western Europe, North America, and Japan. They all place less value on "democracy" and personal economic and political freedom. Of the three, Ukranians are probably the closest to Western values in that they have significant historical ties to the West and an identification with the rugged individualistic values of the Ukranian Cossacks. Russians, on the other hand, are somewhat more wary of, or perhaps schizophrenic about, individualism. Soviet values, as well as those of some of the authors who shaped Russian identity such as Dostoevskii and Tolstoi, are more concerned with the good of the many than with the rights of the one. Kazak society and politics are still firmly in the developing stage, and neither democracy nor complete economic freedom have taken root, even to the extent that Russia and Ukraine have witnessed.

Kazakstan enjoys considerable political stability, and one does not find great resistance to the centralized political control that President Nazarbayev has imposed. Many elites and citizens appreciate the stability and sense of continuity that the Nazarbayev regime represents. Establishing strong high-level government connections and allies is therefore a key factor. Citizenship activities should take government goals and preferences into consideration while also meeting MNC goals and local needs.

A team of executives from major international corporations that visited Kazakstan in 1993 noted that government officials were concerned about educational and environmental issues, but state funds were lacking to address these issues in a meaningful way (Kazakstan Telecom Report, 1993, p. 20). This clearly presents a citizenship opportunity for MNCs.

Appropriate educational programs for local communities, perhaps beginning with employer-provided day care services for workers' children, can also include donations to local schools or provide adult education for workers and their families. Another is strong environmental ethics and concern. MNCs should demonstrate by example that they value

Kazakstan's environment no less than that of their home country by observing local laws and international standards—and going beyond these when they are deemed insufficient. MNCs can also participate in local cleanup efforts by providing know-how, sharing their experiences in other parts of the world, donating funds, and encouraging executives and rank-and-file employees to volunteer. Financial incentives or perquisites for volunteering should be avoided, however, because all Kazak citizens, just like all citizens of the former Soviet Union, are skilled at beating the system.[4] One area of clear concern and need is that of water supply. Potable water, filter systems, bottled water, and general water-supply infrastructure investment are key areas of concern for the government and citizens alike.

WHAT'S THE POINT?

There is no shortage of negative examples of corporate irresponsibility, exploitation of human and natural resources, and arrogant and ignorant approaches to the societies of the FSU. One clear problem, however, is that most of this activity is either legal or goes unpunished. Historically, the worst abuser of people and environment in the Soviet Union was the state itself. Industry was state-run, and both the environment and the workforce were severely damaged. As a result, citizens do not readily distinguish between business and government, and they tend to maintain a cynical attitude toward the capacity of those in power for progress and positive action, whether they are corporate executives or government ministers.

Worse, some of the major business successes in the former Soviet Union are based on questionable citizenship practices. Korea's Hyundai Corporation and other MNCs are, according to most sources, recklessly and irreparably damaging the great taiga forests of Siberia with their aggressive clear-cutting logging practices. Some of the greatest profits and fortunes have been amassed through illegal or semilegal trade in raw materials. Natural resources such as oil or iron are bought at government-controlled domestic prices and quietly shipped across the border and sold at world market prices. Huge profits are made, but miners go unpaid, further destabilizing local and national politics, and no investment is made in sustainable extraction.

Are there risks attached to such behavior in the post-Soviet context? Almost certainly. In the final years of Soviet power, some of the most potent political movements, including those with a nationalist and xenophobic character, were organized around environmental issues. There is nothing more important to a Russian's, Ukranian's, or Kazak's feeling of identify than the land itself. There is no reason to believe that rising nationalist sentiments in these states will turn a blind eye to foreign firms that damage the environment. The same can be said of other basic components of national identity such as language, socioeconomic well-being, and the health of the population. Such needs offer citizenship opportunities to the MNC. But they must proceed with caution and vigilantly monitor how their efforts are being publicly perceived.

THE SNICKERS SCENARIO

For instance, when Mars International, the U.S.-based confectioner, decided to break into the Soviet market, it pioneered TV advertising there. In June 1991, Mars agreed to sponsor a foreign rock music program on the television station run by Boris Yeltsin's Russian republican government. At the time, a republic TV official stated that he regretted the "MacDonaldsisation" of the USSR, but finding a sponsor was the only way the TV station could afford the music programming (Reuters, 6/7/91). By 1995 the tables had turned. Opposition politicians and those opposed to economic reforms had coined a new Russian word, "Snickerization," for the spread of foreign goods and the supposed displacement of domestic firms and domestic jobs (Reuters, 10/20/95).

Snickers has since served as an identifiable symbol of foreign infiltration into the Russian economy and to a lesser extent the Ukranian and Kazak economies—easy prey for nationalist politicians on the rise. But the backlash has roots in the general public as well. The extent of the phenomenon is astounding. In 1994, an article in *Advertising Age* noted:

> Attacks on candy bars have centered on Mars Inc.'s Snickers, the candy bar so popular in Russia that its name crops up in everything from jokes to Parliament speeches. But recent references to the heavily advertised candy bar have been negative. . . . The popular daily newspaper *Moskovsky Komsomolets* recently printed a front-page item that linked high diabetes rates here last year to a glut of Snickers bars, and there have been rumors that the bar has high lead content. . . . A girl interviewed on TV recently told viewers she does not eat Snickers bars because they are "poisonous" (*Advertising Age*, 1/24/94).

In May, the *Moscow News* characterized a crowd listening to Prime Minister Victor Chernomyrdin's Victory Day address as feeling that "faith in the Motherland has been replaced with the advertisement of Snickers—this was the general opinion of all present" (5/13/94). In June, a foreign ministry official decried the poor funding the ministry received from the federal budget, noting a "very dangerous trend" in which, as reported in the newspaper *Segodnia,* "new-comers do not stay at the ministry for long: They prefer to seek employment with private businesses selling chewing-gum and Snickers, earning 10–15 times more" (6/10/94).

At one event, a well-known film director, Stanislav Govorukhin, declared that Russia's present leadership is "leading us into a narrow canyon, where we drink Pepsi-Cola and eat Snickers. . . . The Russian soul has become a colony where the dollar is the currency. . . . How do you destroy Russia? You tear it from its roots," he concluded (*Reuters,* 5/29/94).

During the 1995 parliamentary elections, radical nationalist and xeno-phobe Vladimir Zhirinovskii wound up his party's campaign effort with a speech railing at "the West," saying, "While you were chewing gum and eating Snickers bars, we were conquering space" (Reuters, 12/15/95). At a Communist rally in Moscow in 1996, Father Victor, a well-known "red clergyman" likened Mars and Snickers to a Western "Trojan horse" sent to destroy Russia (Reuters, 9/30/96). And finally, the newspaper *Soviet Russia* asked whether the new Russia was "a mighty power, a worthy suc-cessor to . . . Peter the Great . . . , or a dying Third World semi-colony exchanging oil for Snickers?" (10/12/96).

Why Snickers? And what could it have done through citizenship efforts to counteract such a torrent of negativity? First, recognize that many multinationals do business in the FSU. Many—such as Pepsi, Coke, McDonald's, Mercedes Benz, and Procter & Gamble—are arguably as recognizable as Snickers. Coca-Cola, for example, began a $500-million investment program in Russia in 1991 and now has ten plants throughout Russia and others in Kazakstan, Uzbekistan, and other former republics, but it is still widely perceived as a high-end "foreign" product, unlike Pepsi. Mars, on a somewhat more modest scale, began with a joint ven-ture in 1991, has invested about $200 million, and operates one plant near Moscow. Snickers and Mars bars and other Mars products are still perceived as foreign (*Moscow Times,* 4/30/96; Reuters, 10/20/95).

No company wants to be identified as a negative influence on the soci-ety in which it sells its products. Even more to the point, in one of the most politically risky markets in the world, it is not good business practice to have your brand name on the tip of every radical xenophobe's tongue—this in spite of the major investment Mars has made, creating at least 1,000 jobs in the Moscow suburb of Stupino, where its $150-million factory is located. The factory itself is supplied largely by domestic pro-ducers, and its construction provided 3,500 Russians with jobs and used

60 percent local components (Reuters, 5/31/96; *RusData DiaLine-BizEkon News*, 5/28/96).

MARS CITIZENSHIP

Examining Mars' limited citizenship activities will help identify what should not be done by MNCs in such circumstances.

More attention to corporate citizenship values and activities would have likely softened the perception of Snickers and Mars as foreign invaders in certain sectors of society. In fact, there is scant evidence of any serious citizenship activity by Mars. In conjunction with several other major Western firms, including Chevron and Chase Manhattan, Mars supported the Russian National Symphony Orchestra—an independent and highly acclaimed orchestra based in Moscow (*Moscow Times*, 8/8/95). Mars also provided funding for the Russian Soccer Union in conjunction with an Italian and a Russian firm (*Moscow Times*, 3/15/94). In 1992, Mars sponsored an evening at the theater for underprivileged children in Moscow; however, from the citizenship standpoint this was little more than a farce; the event was unblushingly broadcast by Russian news as an overt advertisement for M&Ms and other products, which were handed out during the performance of Tchaikovsky's "Nutcracker" (Reuters, 11/27/92). This combination of self-serving publicity masquerading as altruism and obvious duplicity between the state-owned TV news and high-powered foreign money is exactly what MNCs want to avoid if they are seriously concerned with projecting an image of genuine concern for and commitment to post-Soviet society.

If there is one legacy of the Soviet period that remains and is common to regular people throughout the region, it is a general disdain for the arrogance and abuse of power. Mars's contribution—of questionable legality—of 62 million rubles to the parliamentary campaign of the Democratic Party of Russia is in the same vein (*Moscow News*, 5/6/94).

These limited and apparently unsuccessful attempts at corporate citizenship in the post-Soviet context by Mars are nevertheless instructive. Note that there are two distinct audiences to whom the activities are directed. Sponsoring an evening of ballet and candy for disadvantaged children and then broadcasting it to millions of viewers is clearly an attempt to influence mass public perceptions. Call this audience the "people," or "narod" in Russian and Ukranian. In contrast, contributing hefty sums to political campaigns, even in support of democratic ideals, is unquestionably an activity aimed at the elite strata of society. In this case, the Democratic Party fared miserably at the polls, and no friends were made among the opposition politicians whose strong showing made them all the more threatening to Mars.

Although citizenship may be more often conceived as activities aimed at the narod, in the post-Soviet context some form of citizenship principles should be developed to deal with post-Soviet elites, or *verkhushka*—those at the top—which as a group have great educational needs, often lack basic skills, and often are uncertain about how to best contribute to the progress of post-Soviet society.

CITIZENSHIP FOR THE NAROD

Most Russian consumers are slowly getting used to foreign products, especially foreign consumer goods, which have collectively captured a 40 percent market share. This has mixed implications for MNCs. On one hand, the likelihood of an antiforeign political backlash may be diminishing as foreign products become an accepted part of economic life. On the other hand, the initial appeal of foreign goods because they are foreign is diminishing as well. Studies across the country have shown that Russian consumers increasingly judge brands on quality, not on nationality, concluding that the prestige of Western goods had diminished. Factors familiar to businesses in other parts of the world are now much more important to FSU consumers: quality, reliability, and value. In Moscow, the Russian Red October brand candy was named best chocolate brand—not Mars or Snickers—while Mercedes was the car of choice. In Samara, a major industrial Russian city of over 1 million people, the local Rossiya brand candy was brand leader—and Rossiya has a foreign owner, Nestle, the world's largest food company (*Moscow Times*, 12/15/94).

Meanwhile, post-Soviet consumers are maturing. And this is perhaps best reflected in the fact that Mars had to lower prices on Snickers bars in 1995, cutting more than 200 rubles off the 2,200-ruble price, which the market previously bore (*Moscow Times*, 4/20/95).

BEST PRACTICES IN ACTION: NESTLE, CTW, AND "ULITSA SEZAM"

Contrast the Mars experience with that of Nestle. It is desirable and possible to design citizenship activities that have a simultaneous positive impact at the mass and elite levels, which is preferable to being seen as courting either group to the detriment of the other. One outstanding example of such citizenship best practices in the former Soviet Union is Nestlé's sponsorship of the Russian version of the children's television program, "Sesame Street."

The Swiss food giant joined George Soros and the U.S. Agency for International Development to provide some of the $6 million toward the development of a version of "Ulitsa Sezam"—Russian for Sesame Street— which would be tailored to the needs of Russian children. The process took six years, but in October 1996 the first episodes aired. Nestlé's decision to support an exceptionally appropriate project and to undertake a long-term commitment before realizing any significant reputational benefits distinguished it in this new market.

In choosing Sesame Street, Nestlé demonstrated exceptional judgment about which citizenship "investment" might have the greatest societal impact, and it showed an ability to think in terms of making a long-term contribution to the health of a society in which it plans to become a permanent citizen.

The New York-based Children's Television Workshop (CTW) has wide experience designing versions of Sesame Street for young viewers around the world. The Russian version is the 17th such locally tailored edition of the educational children's show. Perhaps the best testament to how well the process works is the following statement of Russia's deputy minister of education, Viktor Bolotov. "Six years ago, when we went to New York and met the Children's Television Workshop people, I thought this was another attempt to introduce American stuff into Russia—you know, the idea that the United States is the greatest country in the world. But when I saw different versions of 'Sesame Street' made for Latin American countries and Scandinavia, I realized they were very sensitive to the cultures of those countries" (*Washington Post*, 10/23/96).

The show's executive producer, Natasha Lance Rogoff, adds, "What you feel from the show is very much Russian culture—parts that are shot, produced, written in Russia. That provides the nature of the show, and that's what's most important."

Clearly, CTW thought long and hard about what sort of impact it wanted Sesame Street to have in Russia, and about how best to achieve that impact. In fact, much of the actual work was given to Russians themselves, but without abandoning CTW's unique contribution in terms of focus and goals. "We worked with over 300 Russians and had to develop very close relationships for this to succeed," noted Lance Rogoff. "I think the cooperation you see between Russian and American writers was phenomenal" (*Washington Post*, 10/23/96).

The Russian version of Sesame Street was coproduced by Moscow-based VideoArt, an advertising agency. The extent to which the show was designed with the special characteristics, needs, and circumstances of Russian children in mind is remarkable. One million dollars was devoted to test marketing version after version on Russian children in schools and focus groups across the country. American and Russian writers struggled to develop characters and skits that would appeal to the Russian sense of humor—often cynical or pessimistic—but still convey both an optimistic, hopeful tone and educational substance. "Life is very different and very intense here," states Lance Rogoff. But, Ulitsa Sezam had to create an environment, in this case a friendly courtyard rather than a street, inhabited by a creature named Zeliboba instead of Big Bird, which would provide an authentically Russian feel for a message of fun, learning, and humor, which was different from anything Russian children, or their parents, had ever seen.

But, different does not mean inappropriate, as Russian children's filmmaker and Ulitsa Sezam director Vladimir Grammatikov notes, "Sesame Street has a long and successful track record of educating while entertaining; a show like this could fill a critical programming void in our country" (*Moscow News,* 2/15/96).

Virtually all aspects of this project are instructive for MNCs designing citizenship programs for the FSU. Many have appeal at both the mass and elite levels. The educational focus has great appeal for an elite interested in improving the efficiency and abilities of the population, but also for parents. Education is perhaps the single most valuable type of social investment.

The high-quality product itself is further evidence that CTW, and by association Nestle, take Russia and Russian children very seriously. The investment is long-term, and dubbed-over U.S. shows or other adapted, hand-me-down products aren't good enough. This is a strong message to send, and one that can make a contribution to instilling pride in a disheartened community. Until Ulitsa Sezam made its debut, the *Moscow News* testified that, "The channels [were] overwhelmed with cheap cartoon series poor in quality and rich in violence" (2/15/96). The fact that CTW respects Russia enough to adapt its product, but nevertheless did not abandon its core production beliefs in optimism, humor, and education, is also exemplary. MNCs have unique perspectives and knowledge that they bring to the FSU, and adapting citizenship "products" to the local environment should not mean abandoning core values or proven practices.

And Nestle's approach to doing business in the FSU also betrays a particular sensitivity to basic citizenship issues. Nestle tends to operate through joint ventures, and exhibits a willingness to adapt products to local needs. Mars, on the other hand, tended to attempt to adapt local tastes to its products through saturation advertising. Both methods have met with business success, but Nestle's operations have been much less politically controversial—a positive citizenship asset.

Managing director of Nestle for Russia, Andreas Schlaepfer, made the following comments regarding a new ice cream factory that Nestle opened with Zhukovsky Khladokombinat of Moscow: "Traditional Russian ice cream will always remain popular because Russians are accustomed to their particular taste. That's why we decided to produce them as well as our ... brands. Nestle aims at becoming a Russian food company" (*Moscow Times*, 6/7/96). With the Rossiya and Konditer confectionery factories in Samara, Zhukovsky Ice Cream in Moscow, a planned baby food plant in St. Petersburg, and $400 million in 1996 sales, Nestle is experiencing dramatic business success in Russia, without the negative publicity that Mars encountered. Furthermore, Nestle's Nescafé brand coffee is continuously capturing market share of Russia's most popular food product besides tea—instant coffee—without any detectable political fallout. Nescafé has captured similar market share in Ukraine recently (Reuters, 11/20/96).

THE UNITED WAY

Another example of good corporate citizenship activity comes from United Way International, which helps firms get involved in directly improving the lives of many of the region's most disadvantaged and forgotten people. The United Way has several programs that involve MNCs through modest donations and employee participation. Increasingly, domestic firms in the former Soviet Union are also being involved in the work of UWI. The "Life Skills Program" helps orphans prepare for life's professional and personal challenges (*Moscow Times*, 9/12/96). The "Day of Caring" matches volunteers with sick, handicapped, or orphaned children twice annually (*Moscow Times*, 11/3/94). A major part of United Way International's activities is giving advice and providing networking opportunities—and occasionally some funding—for grassroots charities in the former Soviet Union. There is also a deliberate, but low-key, attempt to expand the number of domestic firms and volunteers who participate in citizenship activities (*Moscow Times*, 3/30/94). The United

Way also holds fundraising events aimed at expatriate communities, with proceeds given to local charities such as soup kitchens or medical training scholarships (*Moscow Times,* 2/22/96).

Companies involved in UWI activities include many of the major MNCs active in the region today. Hewlett Packard, Coca-Cola, Arthur Andersen, Procter & Gamble, Chevron, American Express, Marathon Oil, KPMG, and many other firms have been involved in United Way activities since its Moscow office opened in 1990 (*Moscow Times,* 3/30/94). UWI programs are instructive in two ways. First, they demonstrate how citizenship activities can be successfully run in the former Soviet Union, and second, they provide an indication of the impact of citizenship programs on post-Soviet society and on the firms and employees involved.

UWI's director for the FSU region, Paul Murphy, characterizes the organization's goal as something more than the sum of its programs. "Our idea has always been to establish this as a model by involving Westerners in a way that sets an example for community volunteerism. I really believe that the old attitudes toward volunteerism are changing, particularly with the younger generation. I think it is part of the evolution into a different society—knowing that you have to take somebody's hand and walk with them" (*Moscow Times,* 11/3/94). And more Russians are indeed participating in events such as UWI's "Day of Caring." In 1994, for example, a group of university students in Moscow participated in the October Day of Caring by visiting Moscow's Number 12 Orphanage. "I think it'll grow," declared Lena Gusakova, a 22-year-old linguistics student. "Russians are kind-natured and they take to heart other people's problems. . . . I'm going to tell my girlfriends about this and I think they'll come in the future." (*Moscow Times,* 11/3/94).[5]

Another example of the way in which citizenship activities can be successful at the grassroots level is the participation of Marathon Oil's Moscow-based employees in UWI events. At Marathon, the participation of Moscow office head David Denton in UWI's steering committee and other activities has led to widespread participation by employees, both expatriate and local. Denton's interpreter, for example, translated American pamphlets on coping with cancer into Russian, pro bono, for the Moscow Children's Oncological Institute. Other employees are closely involved with helping raise funds for the institute. "His attitude has rubbed off within his company," writes the *Moscow Times* of Denton.

United Way's programs in the former Soviet Union focus on direct involvement of volunteers, are aimed at specific local groups or institutions that unquestionably need help, and involve very limited financial resources.

THE SOCIAL BENEFIT

There are many advantages to small-scale, loosely organized programs in the former Soviet Union. Former Soviet citizens are, with excellent historical justification, wary of large-scale, centralized programs purporting to be interested in the common good. After all, the Communist Party of the Soviet Union was just such an organization! There is also a cultural inclination to view emotional, spontaneous, and decentralized activity as "genuine" and worthwhile. This hands-on approach can contribute to reputation, if properly publicized, in a way that direct self-promotion through advertising or simple charitable giving simply cannot. It will be perceived by people as genuine and sincere, whereas direct self-promotion is culturally and morally alien to former Soviet citizens, and saturation advertising leaves some negative residue.

Another benefit is internal. Employees—expatriate as well as local—feel pride and satisfaction at making a one-on-one, personal contribution to improving the lives of those hit hardest by the great socioeconomic transformation under way in the FSU. Many firms are making incredible sums of money in the Russian, Ukranian, and Kazak markets, and for employees with a conscience, this can create an uneasy feeling about their role in society. Such uneasiness is often translated into cynical rationalization and even extreme condescension toward locals, often most intensely expressed by successful Russians, Ukranians, and Kazaks themselves. These attitudes are bad for company morale and can make unethical behavior more likely within the company. On the other hand, making a concrete, hands-on, highly personal contribution to improving individual lives in these societies brings some healthy perspective to employees and heightens their sense of purpose on the job.

In terms of resources involved and actual impact on society, it is helpful to keep three points about the region in mind. First, there is great skepticism about any good deed that is impersonal and/or involves large sums of money. This has strong roots in Soviet and pre-revolutionary history. Billionaire financier George Soros has given at least $400 million away to support education, science, and other very worthy causes in the region. Nevertheless he is viewed with great suspicion by the security services (staffed by former KGB officers) and by the general public.

Second, the region is rich in resources but has a history of dismal exploitation of its own wealth. These people, historically and in the aggregate, don't know how to make use of what they have. Both Russia and Kazakstan have vast oil reserves, for example. Ukraine has what is potentially the most productive farmland in Europe, or the world. The human resources in all three countries are also world-class in many respects. Teaching these societies how to help themselves is truly a relevant goal—of more value than any donation in the long run.

Finally, and more concretely, firms are reluctant to give large sums of money in the former Soviet Union because there are few or no tax breaks or other incentives for such giving. In fact, large sums of money dedicated to any purpose not under the direct control of the donor MNC will probably be susceptible to all sorts of unintended diversions and semi-ethical or simply criminal misuse. Almost everyone in these societies is adept at exploiting the system and diverting resources for personal use.

Small-scale use of resources does not imply low impact or limited scope, however. Donations of employee time can be quite meaningful in both a qualitative and quantitative way. United Way's activities provide excellent examples. Teaching life skills to orphans will enable these most disadvantaged children to learn computer skills, foreign languages, or inspire them to pursue a university education, for example. Donating used office computers, or $1,000 to buy a few printers, or pamphlets or books, are small-scale activities that nevertheless vastly increase the resource base available to the disadvantaged.

CONFIRMATION FROM OTHERS

Other relatively successful citizenship programs in the former Soviet Union seem to confirm these conclusions about the appropriateness of UWI's model. Entrepreneurs at the Manhattan Express nightclub founded "Moscow Cares," a charitable group that works with orphans, providing free food to orphanages daily and occasional entertainment such as trips to hockey games. It invites participation from other expatriates such as Michael Roberts of KPMG in Moscow. "The long-term goal," Roberts declares, "is to make it a Russian organization" (*Moscow Times,* 5/12/94).

Action for Russia's Children (ARC) is an organization of over 120 expatriate volunteers. It broke away from the International Women's Club in 1996 and now includes men as well as women volunteers. The organization also focuses on Russian orphanages, providing food, clothing, medical care, and other services (*Moscow Times,* 4/3/96).

British American Tobacco (BAT) is a majority partner in the Yava tobacco factories in Moscow and Saratov. BAT has focused on improving working conditions and employee skills, as well as on updating the old factories it uses to ensure they are as environmentally safe as possible—screening out 99.5 percent of toxins by updating filter technology. There is much on-the-job training, and some fortunate workers attend training courses in Western Europe. A foreign trip is something of which the vast majority of citizens of the region can only dream, and the fact that BAT provides this opportunity as part of training conveys a message of valuing employees and common, long-term interests unimagined in the Soviet era. The impact is certainly great. BAT also attempts to play a constructive role in the municipal community, sponsoring events that bring citizens together, such as an air show and Moscow's high-profile City Day (*RusData DiaLine-BixEkon News*, 9/18/96).

The negative stigma attached to cigarettes in the United States is virtually nonexistent in the FSU, and no contradiction is perceived between the product's negative health effects and the company's positive effects on workforce and community. BAT has captured 70 percent of all domestic cigarette sales in Moscow but has suffered none of the negative consequences of such high visibility that Mars has. BAT is perceived as a domestic product, and the fact of foreign control has been made politically irrelevant, at least in part because of BAT's exemplary show of concern for its employees, the civic community, and Russia's environment. Its citizenship activities are locally focused, and its social role is perceived as constructive.

Note, however, that BAT has not attempted to involve its employees in volunteering to serve others in society. In the examples of volunteerism above, most of the volunteers are expatriate employees of MNCs, or executives of local origin, not the rank-and-file local workforce. Indeed, volunteerism has achieved a bad name in the former Soviet Union. This presents a formidable problem for MNCs with predominantly local employees if they hope to design citizenship programs to meaningfully affect society beyond those directly connected to the firm. Improving working conditions, providing training and travel, and operating in an ecologically ethical manner are exemplary, and rare, practices in former Soviet markets. But the ultimate goal of instilling a positive sense of responsibility for citizenship activity among employees is difficult to achieve and should be approached as a long-term, gradual project.

Several fundamental conclusions can be made about the cases of citizenship for the narod examined earlier. First, personal, small-scale programs are more appropriate than impersonal, large-scale ones. Second, expatriate employees are likely to be more receptive to these activities at first than Russian, Ukranian, or Kazak nationals. This is only natural, given the differing historical experiences, and local employees should not be pressured into some mandatory citizenship experience but rather should be welcome if they decide to participate on their own. Third, an MNC should not neglect its own rank-and-file employees as targets of citizenship activity. Improving working conditions, providing on-the-job training and travel, and letting employees know that local environmental and community concerns are important to the firm are excellent ways to instill pride and encourage loyalty and productivity among the workforce. BAT's activities in this area are exemplary.

CITIZENSHIP AT THE "VERKHUSHKA"

Because the Soviet state strove for autarky in the international arena and enforced rigid but superficial stability in domestic ethnic and political relations, those in positions of power and influence in Russia, Ukraine, and Kazakstan today have limited first-hand knowledge of nonauthoritarian methods for dealing with foreign influences, ethnic tensions, public disaffection, and a host of other challenges related to the transition from communism. Where can these political, business, and cultural leaders turn to discover reliable alternatives to the old methods? This is important because if elites cannot learn to use new methods of rule successfully, there is a good chance that the transition will fail, and authoritarian rule could return or chaos could become the norm.

Since the fall of the USSR, a plethora of Western "consultants" and other professional advice-givers have descended on these societies. The International Monetary Fund, World Bank, and the U.S. Agency for International Development have been especially active. Nongovernmental organizations such as Greenpeace and the Soros Foundations have also participated. The results of all of this good advice have been mixed. Beginning around 1993, there was a noticeable backlash among former Soviet elites, especially in Russia, due to the abundance of general advice and the scarcity of offers of resources or tailoring of prescriptions to really help untie the Gordian knots that decision makers in the FSU face daily.

This situation presents foreign business leaders operating in these markets with a unique opportunity. Unlike foreign consultants from governments or international organizations, foreign business people share many of the risks facing domestic elites. There is mutual interest in lessening social strife and political volatility, as well as in making positive strides on the economic front. Furthermore, international business leaders are among the best educated and most widely experienced people in the world. It is also their job to find innovative, practical, and efficient solutions to new and constantly changing problems. And, they are results-oriented, placing relatively little emphasis on ideology or dogma.

In addition, businesses in these countries need good relations with elites if they are to succeed. Elites can cut through red tape, ward off bribe takers and "protection" providers, and ensure the stability of laws and regulations. On the face of it, at least, there is considerable room for mutually beneficial cooperation. Elites can greatly smooth market entry and ensure that the rules of the game do not change drastically to the detriment of MNCs. For their part, MNCs can engage in activities that contribute to solving some key social, political, and cultural problems of societies in transition. They can cooperate with elites by providing direct financial support or in other ways to facilitate activities that the local, regional, or federal governments could not accomplish alone. And the business people can share their expertise and wide range of knowledge to help identify practical solutions to vexing problems.

THE BUSINESS-ELITE DATA

Is there evidence that such a synergy can work in practice? Several cases are instructive and encouraging, especially the growing phenomenon of City Days. One of BAT's activities was to help sponsor Moscow's City Day in 1996.[6] This annual celebration of municipal heritage and community was originated by Boris Yeltsin in 1987, when he was Moscow's Communist Party boss (*Moscow Times,* 8/31/94). Sponsoring a City Day can be considered part of a citizenship program aimed at the narod, but the major emphasis should be placed on its value to municipal elites, the local verkhushka. One strong indication that such events serve elite interests is in the fact that Yeltsin himself initiated the practice. The benefits for city elites are not hard to identify. The event gives citizens, otherwise known as voters, a chance to take pride in their city and to relax and enjoy themselves. There is no work requirement, no mandatory "volunteerism," just a day of celebration. And at the center of events is the incumbent political leadership of the city. They take much of the credit, express their love of the city, and are able to claim, "The entire event did not cost the city a single ruble since it was sponsored by. . . . " (*ITAR-TASS,* 9/4/94).

Yeltsin, of course, did not have the opportunity to find private sponsors for the first Moscow City Day, but the practice has spread throughout the former Soviet Union since the opening of the region's economies. And new national holidays have been created, which have special significance for the new elites of Russia, Ukraine, and Kazakstan. In Moscow, mayor Yuri

Luzhkov is especially active in promoting City Day. But the practice is widespread. Even in Lenin's home town, Ulianovsk, City Day is now celebrated, and local officials talk about new values in spite of the region's strong communist sentiments (*Moscow Times,* 6/15/96). At the national level, the central government encourages the celebration of Russian Independence Day (June 12) throughout the country, with the grandest celebrations taking place in the capital. There are also International Family Day, International Youth Day, and International Women's Day. These are promoted by elites to help inspire a sense of civility and community. Women's Day deserves special attention in Russia because it is the one holiday universally celebrated under the Soviet system that remains genuinely popular, relatively noncontroversial, and nondivisive.

In Kazakstan and Ukraine, however, the issue of corporate sponsorship of local and national holidays can be more complex. Awareness of the political and social context is absolutely necessary if MNCs hope to play positive and constructive roles in this way and avoid political debacles. In Kazakstan, Women's Day is still celebrated as an official state holiday on March 8 and is not considered controversial. However, Kazak Republic Day (October 25),[7] commemorating independence from the USSR, is potentially as divisive in some parts of the country—the largely Russian-speaking north, in particular—as it is unifying in other parts. Many ethnic Russians and other Russian speakers continue to regret the dissolution of the USSR and their diminished status in Kazak society, which followed.

Clearly, at least as much caution is urged when considering sponsoring celebrations of Muslim holidays such as Nauryz Meyramy (March 22, the Persian calendar New Year) or Ramadan (ending in early March), as well as traditionally "Soviet" holidays such as May Day, all of which, save for the month of Ramadan, are official state holidays in Kazakstan today (*Pravda,* 2/5/92). However, in avoiding controversy and emphasizing equal rights and national civic unity, MNCs will have strong allies in the Kazak central government. For example, President Nazarbayev expressed his view of the role of Islam in Kazak society. "If the Moslems, with their pure hearts, secure the unity of the country, social accord, and help the poor, it will help all of us to get through this difficult period" (BBC Monitoring Service, 3/7/95). Clearly, there is room for MNCs to contribute to such sentiments and join the central government in promoting civil accord. Allies among the elites, essential to doing business in authoritarian Kazakstan even more than in Russia or Ukraine, will be won, and genuine civil accord and political stability will be promoted.

In Ukraine there is at least as much reason to use caution in joining in elite-sponsored local and national celebrations. Ukranian society is divided by religion, ethnic identity, and language just as Kazakstan is. Also as in Kazakstan, these divisions are geographically as well as demographically based. Eastern Ukraine is largely Russian-speaking, Russian Orthodox, ethnically Russian, and one finds strong nostalgia for the USSR there as well. Western Ukraine is Ukranian Orthodox (of which there are several variations) or Catholic, ethnic Ukranian, Ukranian-speaking, and often strongly anti-Russian, with only negative memories of the former Soviet order. While perhaps less distinct to outsiders than the Islamic/Christian divide in Kazakstan, the sociopolitical divide in Ukraine is strongly felt and ignored at one's peril.[8]

In Ukraine, for example, even International Women's Day is controversial in western regions such as L'viv because it is identified with the Soviet approach to women's rights. Eastern Catholics and other traditionalist groups prefer to celebrate Mother's Day, May 12, and have recently taken to the streets to protest this and other Soviet-holdover holidays such as May Day and Victory Day, which is celebrated on May 9, as it was in the USSR, not on May 8 (*ITAR-TASS*, 4/30/96). In fact, local authorities in western Ukraine have established Mother's Day as an official holiday, with special emphasis on women's professional and political roles as well as on traditional child-care and homemaking roles (*ITAR-TASS*, 5/14/95). The central government in Kyiv continues to mark International Women's Day, in spite of the protest of top western Ukranian nationalist leaders (Reuters, 3/8/95). May 1, International Worker's Day, is also still an official holiday but is more often an occasion for conflict between national-democratic and leftist political movements, with demonstrations and counterdemonstrations throughout the country. Ukranian Independence Day is marked on August 24, but again, it is not widely celebrated in some eastern Ukranian cities.

How can MNCs participate constructively and safely in such holidays? The answer is to act locally. Many cities do have City Days as in Russia, and participating in these is perhaps the least controversial alternative if a firm is looking to build a reputation and solidify its good will with elites in local markets. Another option is to tailor participation in potentially controversial events to the local audience.

The potential synergy between a populace longing for some new communal activity, the elite verkhushka hoping to overcome the present plague of cynicism toward power and position, and business hoping to cement its reputation at both levels while contributing to social and political stability, makes local and national holidays an excellent target for citizenship activities.

LOCAL PARTICIPATION IN CITY DAYS

One good sign that this is an appropriate focus of citizenship activity is the high proportion of local firms participating in such events. They know the importance of recapturing the lost sense of community and of maintaining firm and cooperative relations with key political elites. For example, one of the region's largest banks, Moscow-based Stolichny Bank, claimed the general sponsorship of Moscow City Day in 1993. Every district of the city held its own events, and there was an air show, a fireworks display, and a carillon bell music festival (*Moscow News,* 9/3/93). Muscovites love these sorts of fun, relaxing, and traditionally Russian forms of celebration, and they really do contribute to some sort of communal identity and civic accord. In 1994, Khoper-Invest and Stipler were among the Russian companies sponsoring a concert on Moscow City Day (*Moscow Times,* 9/4/94). Most Bank was another major sponsor, gratefully acknowledged by Moscow's highest-ranking official for cultural affairs, Igor Bugaev, who stated, "We would like there to be more such holidays. . . . we still need to instill Muscovites with a sense of pride for their city" (*Moscow Times,* 8/31/94).

And the sums of money involved are often not exorbitant. "Millions of rubles" is really a bargain, given exchange rates, and $15,000 spent for a new city seal is quite reasonable if it gets Mayor Luzhkov's attention and praise. He is one of the most powerful and influential figures in all of Russian politics. He has been closely involved in City Day celebrations, as well as in the 1996 Navy Day celebrations, marking the tricentennial of the Russian Fleet.

Outside Moscow, two locally based Siberian banks have also set an example for citizenship activities related to national holidays. In Longepas, Siberia, the banks have sponsored a battered women's shelter. Siberian life can be especially brutal, and alcoholism can turn Russian men into abusers, so these relatively small local banks are making a real contribution to this community of 200,000, and they did it in the context of Women's Day celebrations in 1996 (*Moscow Times,* 3/8/96).

UNSUCCESSFUL SPONSORSHIPS

There are, of course, many other possible venues for citizenship activities aimed at post-Soviet elites. Perhaps the best known, and perhaps the least successful in many ways, is sponsorship of the rebuilding of Moscow's Christ the Savior Cathedral. Clearly, there are positive aspects to this, which have attracted many foreign and local sponsors. It is an extremely high-profile project, restoring one of Moscow's great landmarks after it was dynamited and bulldozed on Stalin's orders in 1934. The restoration of the beauty of the city, of Russian national pride, and of a central monument of the Russian Orthodox Church all have their appeal from a citizenship standpoint. The country's key politicians are all "for" this project, and the government and Orthodox Church are in great need of funds to meet the $500 million costs of construction. Firms that have contributed to the project include major local and international players: Credit Suisse Bank, Coca-Cola, McDonald's, Philips Electronics, and the Russian arms-export monopoly Rosvooruzhnie!

There are at least two negative aspects MNCs should consider before getting involved in such projects. First, the scale of the project and the consequent large sums of money involved may negate the positive aspects, because Russians tend to make automatic associations between big money and large-scale corruption, even when the Russian Orthodox Church is involved. Indeed, the reported construction of a major luxury apartment and shopping complex directly below the cathedral as part of the project only serves to confirm Russians' justifiable cynicism. This is a big-money project for those with big money, and at least has the potential for a serious backlash.[9] Second, the involvement of the Russian Orthodox Church itself is controversial because religion is still a controversial issue and deeply connected to all sorts of nationalist beliefs and senses of foreign infiltration. Foreign money going to rebuild such a central religious landmark may spark great suspicion. And, in addition to these concerns about the sensitivity of religion, there is also the fact that the Russian Orthodox Church has attracted wide publicity for its semilegal and wholly-for-profit business activities. The church, it seems, is involved in a big way in everything from diamonds to oil to cigarettes, and is taking full advantage of its tax-free, nonprofit status to rake in billions ($2 billion in oil revenues alone in 1996, by one account).

RESULTS OF SOME EFFORTS

Among other citizenship activities aimed at the post-Soviet verkhushka, several deserve mention here. Reebok has gained a very high-profile reputation as a sponsor of sporting events attended by Russia's political and economic elite. Reebok has been one of the consistent sponsors of the Kremlin Cup, and in recent years domestic firms such as Inkombank have jumped on the bandwagon. This can be considered a citizenship event, and not simply smart advertising, if it is remembered that all countries in the region are still attempting to overcome 70 years of political and cultural isolation. Supporting Russia's only regular world-class sporting event, which is shown on television throughout Russia, Ukraine, and Kazakstan, certainly contributes to reducing the feeling of cultural isolation. Besides, tennis is Yeltsin's favorite sport, and he is likely to smile on whoever helps keep the event solvent and successful. Reebok also sponsored the 1994 and 1996 Russian Olympic teams.

American Express has taken an approach uniquely tailored to its long-term business interests. In 1994, it donated $750,000 to promote "culture, education, and tourism" to Russia, Ukraine, Kazakstan, and other FSU states. It has a similar program in Central and Eastern Europe (and one in Hungary is fully described in Chapter Five). This commitment, although limited, nevertheless demonstrates to elites that American Express is serious about developing the tourism industry in the FSU and not simply cashing in on short-term profits. The company has made a commitment to involve other foreign sponsors in financing specific projects in conjunction with the American Express Foundation, including Delta and British Airlines and hotel operators working in Russia. Besides educating tourism professionals and improving tourism infrastructure, there are projects that allow students from high schools in the FSU to travel abroad (*ITAR-TASS*, 9/15/94). Such programs can be seen as very appropriate because of their dual focus on (1) improving a specific and potentially important domestic industry and (2) providing educational and cultural connections with the rest of the world. Indeed, American Express has been involved in student and cultural exchanges since at least 1987, when it helped support the American Soviet Youth Orchestra. This project continued, and in 1993 the group of Russian and American young musicians toured five U.S. cities and four Russian cities (*New York Times*, 6/23/93).

CITIZENS DEMOCRACY CORPS

One final citizenship-type program is the Citizens Democracy Corps (CDC). Like most of the United Way programs in the FSU, CDC is a volunteer-based operation. Unlike UWI, however, CDC takes only full-time volunteers who are willing to devote a considerable period of time to the programs. CDC, therefore, is not an option for direct MNC participation. Rather, it is presented here as a model from which to draw general principles about appropriate activities in the FSU aimed at local elites.

CDC has since 1992 been in the business of pairing U.S. volunteers with considerable business or technical experience with the most outwardly oriented and reform-minded firms in the FSU. It is a hands-on educational program based on the idea that, "the transition to the market implies not only reforms at the macro level, but also day-to-day work at the level of enterprises, public organizations and municipal services," according to Maureen Kiser of CDC's Moscow headquarters (*Moscow News,* 3/4/94).

The focus on one-on-one sharing of experience with local officials and entrepreneurs who have taken the initiative to request such assistance is one important aspect of this program. Helping others to help themselves is an excellent principle, but it only works if MNC involvement is perceived as helpful and instructive by those receiving the "aid." As Robert Jacoby says of the Business Entrepreneur Program that he directs, "We select a mere 10 percent of the total number of applications, counting on promising enterprises which seriously desire to reach out to the world market" (*Moscow News,* 3/4/94).

Another exemplary practice of CDC is the attention it pays to major population centers outside the capital. CDC has sent volunteers to work with firms, regional and municipal governments, and nongovernmental organizations in such major cities as Samara, Nizhnii Novgorod, Obninsk, and Voronezh, as well as Moscow and Moscow Region. Finally, CDC's focus on educating the elite class of business and government leaders at perhaps the second and third tiers of leadership, rather than at the highest levels, is also admirable and effective. This has the potential to make a long-term impact, spreading competence and expertise in business and public administration that will serve as a solid counterforce to irrational, arbitrary, or xenophobic tendencies of the more politicized "commanding heights" of the verkhushka.

Although direct participation in CDC is not really an option for multinationals, unless they simply want to give financial support or grant employees long-term leave, there are similar options in the FSU that are more practicable. One opportunity is to support business, financial, and other market-oriented technical education in the region.

In Almaty, the capital of Kazakstan, the Institute of Management Economics and Strategic Research has been graduating local MBAs since 1994. But its financial situation is reportedly shaky. It first relied on funding and teaching by Baptist missionaries, but the focus was often on proselytizing. The European Union, British KnowHow Fund, and London School of Economics have contributed in various ways since. It is just such institutions that can make the difference in preparing a new elite capable of stabilizing and developing society and business in the region (*Daily Telegraph,* Reuters, 3/21/94).

WHAT ROLE CAN FOREIGN FIRMS REALLY PLAY?

Says Karl M. Topp, president and CEO of Die West Development Company, Inc.:

> As utopian as it may sound, companies can actually make money in the process of helping Russians. . . . Working with local people, staying in fourth-class hotels, and bringing my own food and water, I have witnessed firsthand the great potential for doing business in Russia. The needs of its huge population are enormous, and those considering investing in Russia have a chance of success if they make an emotional commitment and take the time to build a sound business foundation (*Harvard Business Review,* May-June, 1994, p. 35).

Violence—Russians, Kazaks, and Ukranians want to believe—is not the only answer to the communal/capitalist "dialectic." Revolution, the corporate citizen hopes to demonstrate, can come in many forms.

One international group of executives from the University of Michigan Global Leadership Program visited Russia, Ukraine, and Kazakstan in 1994 and observed that, "Many in the Russian population resent all those who have prospered and, in fact, perceive everyone with money as criminal" (Russia Telecom Report, 1994, p. 4). This observation has great significance for citizenship program design in the former Soviet Union. Self-interest is usually perceived negatively, especially when it is demonstrated by the wealthy and powerful. Suspicion and resentment are aroused when self-interested outcomes are presented as if they are for the good of all. In Russia, and to some extent in Ukraine and Kazakstan, apparently selfless altruism is greatly respected and often taken at face value. One clear and recent example was the spectacle of Yeltsin's 1996 presidential campaign tactics. He would promise cash, benefits, and direct presidential intervention to just about anyone who could get his ear. Certainly, many viewed this as a cynical and irresponsible move to gain votes through impossible promises. But most Russians are greatly affected by such behavior.

What Westerners might call "enlightened self-interest," on the other hand, can be perceived as more self-interested than enlightened.

Therefore, citizenship activities should be designed to make a clear statement about ideals and about problems facing Russian, or Ukranian, or Kazak society. The ulterior motives of the MNC will probably not be questioned if the need is perceived and the effect is real. Communal values and identities have broken down, and this contributes a great deal to the psychological insecurity of many former Soviet citizens, especially the older generations who grew up under Khrushchev or Brezhnev. The effect of MNCs helping to rekindle citywide, regionwide, or even nationwide communal activities will probably have a positive impact on the firm's reputation and lessen the uncertainty and fear felt by regular people about the "new" ways and the "new" Russia, Ukraine, or Kazakstan.

CONDITIONS FACING WORKERS

Many people still consider it "normal" for employers to provide housing, medical care, access to special stocks of food, even special prices on appliances or cars. These socialist perquisites are disappearing, but some sort of communal security can still be provided by MNCs with vision and understanding of local perceptions and needs. Workplace standards are one area in which an MNC can prove it has the good of its workforce in mind. Soviet enterprises of all kinds were notorious for their disregard of basic worker needs, and for their health and safety. Establishing basic standards of safety, cleanliness, and a healthy work environment will show commitment to the workforce. BAT provides a good example of this in the earlier cases.

One simple place to start is to ensure adequate lighting, heating, air-conditioning, and janitorial services. The effect on worker morale is immediate and significant. Enlisting workers' participation and responsibility for maintaining such standards is one way to inculcate responsibility and a sense of ownership. Overcoming the traditional attitude toward "common" property at the workplace, however, is no mean feat. Socialist property was everybody's, and nobody's. All felt entitled to steal from the workplace; none felt obliged to maintain it for the common good. This is an internal citizenship challenge of the first order for any firm operating in the CIS.

In the former Soviet business environment nothing is certain except personal relationships. Laws bend easily; they also come and go with political swings and presidential decrees. Business ethics in general are low, and many of the new rich have made a great deal of money very quickly—and very illegally. Contracts are breached regularly, and the legislation and police mechanisms to make them enforceable are woefully inadequate. There is not yet a sense of permanence for businesses. The only thing that can overcome all of the mistrust, risk, and fluidity is a strong personal bond, which creates common interests and loyalties.

CONCLUSION

The citizenship principles for addressing issues at the mass (narod) and elite (verkhushka) levels are solid guiding principles for contributing to evolutionary change and building a solid reputation in Russia, Ukraine, and Kazakstan. At the narod level, the following principles should guide corporate citizenship design:

- Small-scale, personal programs maximize impact.
- Truly voluntary, not mandatory, activities are necessary.
- Practice intrafirm citizenship, including employees as beneficiaries.

When attempting to address relations with the verkhushka, a somewhat different set of rules applies:

- Use the synergy involved in helping elites rebuild communal civic values.
- Avoid overly controversial or sensitive issues such as religion.
- Help and educate those who are receptive.

The Nestle/CTW case helps demonstrate how these principles can be combined to reach both essential audiences and have an important social impact. The elite level is especially important for market entry, given the highly bureaucratized and unpredictable environment. Affecting the mass level in a meaningful and positive way is important to avoid political backlash. Contributing to both levels of society is really an essential activity for MNCs in this volatile part of the world. Multinational firms have the knowledge and the resources to contribute in a substantial way to the evolution of a stable social and political environment in the newly independent states of the region. If the private sector abrogates this role, the viability of the supposed potential of these new markets may be a risky proposition at best.

REFERENCES

Feshbach, M. *Ecological Disaster: Cleaning Up the Hidden Legacy of the Soviet Regime.* New York: Twentieth Century Fund Press, 1995.

Kazakstan Telecom Report. University of Michigan Global Leadership Program. Ann Arbor, Michigan, 1993.

Russia Telecom Report. University of Michigan Global Leadership Program. Ann Arbor, Michigan, 1994.

ENDNOTES

1. I gratefully acknowledge the advice and comments of Jonathan Halperin in the preparation of this chapter.
2. Hewett's *Reforming the Soviet Economy* gives an excellent description of how the Soviet system functioned and why certain problems were endemic to it. See especially Chapter 4.
3. Private communication with Jonathan Halperin, Nov. 15, 1996.
4. Two brief examples of this will suffice. In the post-Soviet Baltic republics, a booming market in "language certifications" has emerged. One can pay 1–2 month's salary for an official document certifying competence in the local language. This opens up many job opportunities, even if the language skills are nonexistent. A similar market in "experience" thrives among Soviet emigres in the Brighton Beach area of Brooklyn, New York, in the United States. Immigrants from all over the former USSR are able to purchase 1–5 years of verifiable experience working for U.S. companies. When prospective employers call to confirm this experience, someone is there to answer the phone and vouch for the applicant. This presents an attractive alternative to education or apprenticeships for many emigres.
5. Note the importance of being aware of cultural differences when designing citizenship programs. As the next chapter details, in India people are generally accepting of the fact of poverty and are quite unenthusiastic about any altruistically motivated attempt to help the poor. That they are poor because they deserve to be is a common sentiment. In the former USSR, the exact opposite is true. Poverty is not perceived as the fault of the poor, but rather as the unjust suffering of good people, perhaps the best, most selfless and honest members of society. Altruistic kindness and giving are perceived as good and useful activities with spiritual and material benefits.
6. I thank Jonathan Halperin for initially pointing out the importance of City Day and similar celebrations for corporate citizenship in the FSU.
7. Republic Day is doubly controversial in that it was originally celebrated on December 16, but this date coincides with the anniversary of an incident of Soviet repression of Kazak political protest in 1986. The date October 25 commemorates the Declaration of State Sovereignty of Kazakstan in 1991; the holiday celebrated until 1994 commemorated the Law on the State Independence of Kazakstan of December 16, 1991.
8. One example will illustrate. In 1994 I was conducting interviews with political elites in Kyiv. When interviewing a leading official of a nationalist party, and not even one of the more extreme nationalist parties, I was required to

use an interpreter because my Ukranian wasn't good enough at the time. Even though my Russian is very good, and the person I was interviewing also spoke perfect Russian, she absolutely refused to say anything substantive in Russian. I assured her that I was not a Russian chauvinist and that I was studying Ukranian, but to no avail. As a result, I have taken the time to become more proficient in Ukranian! Such situations will become more, not less, prevalent as time goes by and fewer people even study Russian in Ukraine.

9. Distrust of the Russian Orthodox Church is growing. In 1993 a survey showed that 60 percent of Russians trusted the church above all other institutions; only 40 percent felt that way by 1996 (*Moscow Times,* 11/5/96). Keep in mind that Russians don't really trust any public institutions, so if only two out of five put the church on top, this can be seen as a widespread perception that the church, like everything else, is seriously compromised.

16

CORPORATE CITIZENSHIP IN INDIA

Multinational Corporate Experiences and Best Practices

Benjamin E. Goldsmith

*True, there is no shortage of social initiatives that lend themselves
to photo opportunities without effecting real change. But the new
corporate philanthropy encourages companies to play a leadership
role in social problem solving by funding initiatives that incorporate the best thinking of governments and nonprofit
institutions. . . . Already powerful in the United States, the new
model of strategic philanthropy promises to be most effective for
U.S. companies internationally, particularly in emerging markets,
where even small grant programs can have a large impact*
(Harvard Business Review, *May 1994, p. 105).*

—Craig Smith, President, Corporate Citizen

BUSINESS CONTRIBUTES TO SOCIETY in two basic ways. *First, and fundamentally, business creates wealth and forms the core of a healthy economy*—jobs, tax revenues, consumer and industrial goods, trade
efficiencies, and economic growth. However, even if firms fulfill this primary function successfully, the overall health of society is not guaranteed.

Just as no market can function perfectly in the real world, no real-world society will be healthy if business leaders believe that creation of wealth through short-term profit maximization is their sole function. In the final analysis, business cannot flourish in a seriously ailing society. Social ills have a tendency to spill over, eventually, into politics. And politicians driven by fear, shoring up illegitimate power, or riding on popularity gained from impossible promises, cannot help but turn to forays of intervention into the economy.

In other words, *the second function of business—large and small, domestic and multinational—is to contribute to the health of society in ways that, in the aggregate, help correct market failures. This is corporate citizenship.*

CORPORATE CITIZENSHIP IN THE INDIAN CONTEXT

In India, the visible political hand has only recently begun to recede from economic life. The moderately good growth has also resulted in social dislocations and dissatisfaction, driven partly by economics and partly by perceptions. Any multinational operating in the Indian market should not underestimate the importance of these social problems.

Since the introduction of economic liberalization in 1991, two U.S. firms—Enron and PepsiCo—have learned first-hand about the importance of corporate reputation in society and how it can interact negatively with rising national sentiment in India. For multinational corporations (MNCs) in India, reputation is a key business asset, but understanding how to build a positive reputation is not a simple task. Western and other non-Indian values do not necessarily translate directly to Indian society. Building the valuable business asset, which a positive reputation is in India, means understanding a lot about Indian culture, history, business, bureaucracy, and politics. If these basics are ignored, results of corporate citizenship activities will likely be different than the MNC expected—different in the negative.

INDIA: RISING NATION, MNC CITIZENSHIP CHALLENGE

Neither its great size nor its location in the relatively successful Asian region make India immune to global pressures. World Bank economists estimate that a 6 to 6.5 percent annual gross domestic product (GDP) growth rate is necessary just to provide enough jobs for the increasing

Indian population to prevent increased unemployment. But in 1994, growth was only 5.9 percent. In 1995, the IMF (International Monetary Fund) measured real GDP growth at 6.2 percent, perhaps avoiding additions to the ranks of the unemployed; but a drop to 6.0 percent was predicted for 1996. In addition, consumer prices rose 10.0 percent in 1994, 10.2 percent in 1995, and a rise of 7.9 percent was predicted for 1996 (*IMF*, 5/96), further squeezing the vast majority of Indians who are poor or destitute. Although the 1980s and mid-1990s have witnessed some growth in the Indian GDP, the long-term record of under 2 percent annual growth since 1960 pales in comparison to the fast-growing economies of East Asia, which registered average long-term growth rates of 5 to 6 percent in the same period.

Since 1991, when Indian GDP growth was a miserable 1 percent, there has been significant success in shaking off the legacy of what came to be known as the "Hindu growth rate" among development experts (*IMF*, 12/95). However, history advises caution in predicting that Indian growth will someday match that of regional powerhouses such as China or many of the Association of Southeast Asian Nations (ASEAN) member states. Even at recent historically high rates, real GDP growth in India has consistently lagged 2 to 3 percentage points behind that of the average for all of Asia (*IMF*, 5/96, pp. 24, 121). And slower growth in India will probably mean greater social turmoil.

In both developed and developing societies, many conservatives feel that the core values of traditional societies are being eroded. The exodus of the young from rural to urban areas has caused massive changes in the social fabric. Traditional social structures such as cross-generational family and village ties are being eroded in a single generation. While conservative political leaders in the developed world point to free trade and immigration as global phenomena easily blamed for economic pains, politicians in the developing world achieve popular appeal by blaming the invasion of American television, Western evangelicals, consumerism and the growing presence of foreign products, foreign technology, foreign practices, and foreign-owned businesses for such changes.

In India, these phenomena have grown in frequency and force since 1991, and the major nationalist party, the Bharatiya Janata Party (BJP), has accumulated power and influence. A BJP slogan, "microchips, not potato chips," reflects a general opposition to foreign consumer goods, or at least a somewhat greater degree of tolerance for foreigners who bring valuable technology with them. Even though it was not able to maintain a governing coalition after the national elections in early 1996, its rural strength still made the BJP India's dominant political party, but it is uncertain for how long. Already the first governing United Front coalition put together under Prime Minister H. D. Deve Gowda lost power in early 1997, although it appeared that successors would likely pursue a strategy of moving to the right in order to take the nationalist wind out of BJP sails.

A wide range of foreign companies have encountered difficulties in India due to this backlash. Fast-food chains have experienced protests and threats of violence; demonstrations have been called for the purpose of smashing bottles of Pepsi and Coke; DuPont has had difficulty finding a site for a plant due to state governments' concern over public health risk, AES Transpower has also encountered state-level resistance in Orissa.

A poll conducted among urban residents—presumably the most open to foreign influence—indicated that over half of Indian city dwellers oppose foreign investment that does not bring high technology with it (*BusinessWeek*, 10/23/96).

Today it is hard to find an emerging market (or a developed market, for that matter) in which these forces do not exist and reinforce each other. No amount of spin will convince a Hindu farmer that DuPont, Coke, Enron, or KFC (Kentucky Fried Chicken) is "good" for India; genuine consideration for local sentiments and sensitivities, better health care, education, or job training in the community as a result of corporate activity might. Hence, true action through global citizenship by MNCs can have a real impact.

HIGH-PROFILE LESSONS: ENRON

The best-known recent cases in which foreign firms have run afoul of Indian pride are the experiences of PepsiCo's KFC in Bangalore and Enron Corporation's power plant project in Dabhol. Both of these high-profile cases flared in the summer of 1995, but their legacy remains. And MNCs and Indians have drawn largely different lessons from them.

In early August 1995, the Indian government—with no warning—effectively canceled the $2.8 billion deal it had made with Enron to build a 2,015 megawatt power plant in Dabhol, in Maharashtra state in west central India. The state government undertook a complete reassessment of the deal. The details of this case illustrate the risks of pioneering in emerging markets, but they also illustrate how ignoring basic citizenship issues can greatly increase those risks and raise costs considerably. One direct consequence of the cancellation, for example, was that Enron's stock, considered undervalued before the deal fell through, plummeted 10 percent in just two months (*BusinessWeek*, 9/4/95).

What did Enron do wrong in India? The bottom line is that Enron behaved with classic developed-world arrogance toward its host society. Rebecca Mark, head of the Houston-based company's international-power unit, drove the deal through with no concern for Indian political trends or public sentiment. Enron signed an initial agreement for the project in the summer of 1992. By 1994, the details had largely been worked out, and the Maharashtra State Electricity Board contracted to buy 90 percent of the power when the plant was completed. The government and Enron agreed that the specifics of the arrangement were to be kept secret. There was no bidding process involved in granting the contract, and the Indian government guaranteed loans to Enron. This reflects the advantage—at least as Mark must have perceived it—that Enron gained by pioneering the Indian energy market immediately after liberalizing reforms were introduced. Enron could squeeze the deal for all it was worth because the Indian government was desperate for foreign investment.

Hindsight provides clear and powerful lessons from this case. First, politics matter. Enron ignored the rising nationalist BJP, even after it called specifically for a reevaluation of the deal during the February 1995 state election campaign. The BJP had teamed up with a local movement, the Shiv Sena, to bring the issue into the political mainstream (*Business Week*, 10/23/95). Not only did Enron push its deal through before the election results were known, but, according to a U.S. diplomat, once the BJP had taken power in Maharashtra state, Enron "pushed like hell" and convinced the U.S. Department of Energy to issue a warning in June that canceling the deal would adversely affect other U.S. projects in India. This was perceived by the BJP as a belligerent U.S. threat (*Business Week*, 9/4/95).

The U.S. position left the BJP with no choice, politically. It had to make good on its campaign promise or be perceived as caving in to the exploiting MNC. This had the effect of moving the BJP farther to the right—exactly the outcome Enron should have, and probably could have, avoided. Enron, which had relied on what it felt was a solid relationship and a legal contract with the central government in New Delhi, was rudely awakened to the fact that India is a democracy. With national elections in the offing, then-Prime Minister Rao simply did not have the power to force the Dabhol plant on an unwilling public.

The second critical mistake Enron made was to keep the terms of its deal secret. Nothing ignites suspicion and resentment like secrecy, especially in an industry such as power generation, which touches the entire population directly. Secrecy breeds mistrust. A Mumbai consumer group sued to make the details public and learned that the rate of return granted

Enron was estimated at 23 percent, well above the 16 percent the government granted other investors. When Enron—desperately trying to save the deal—offered to lower its price from 7.4 cents per kilowatt-hour, opponents immediately took this as evidence that the original deal had been overly advantageous to Enron and unjustly exploitative of the Indian consumer (*BusinessWeek, 9/4/95*).

A third mistake was certainly that Enron suffered from overconfidence in its ability to understand local business conditions. It would have stood a greater chance of success, even given BJP opposition and public suspicion, if Enron had a local ally who understood how to surmount obstacles in India and how to anticipate political, legal, and other pitfalls. Enron, in spite of its size and power internationally and in the U.S., was clearly outmatched and outmaneuvered by opponents with a home-field advantage.[1]

Still, Enron seemed to ignore local developments right up until those developments overwhelmed the deal. One U.S. diplomat familiar with the case put it bluntly, "Enron just blasted on. . . . Public perception just didn't concern them" (*BusinessWeek, 9/4/96*). Indeed, the company seems to remain contentious after a year of contemplation. In October 1996, CEO Kenneth Lay claimed that, "Dabhol was one of the most politically approved power projects in the world. We had 50 different legal permits . . . and we would prefer never to go through what we went through in India again" (*Financial Times, 10/17/96*).

This suggests that even in retrospect Lay is making a naive mistake—confusing formal, legal approval with informal, political support. And this interpretation is borne out in the five "lessons" he claims that Enron learned from the experience: "First, the sanctity of contracts must be honored; two, legal recourse must be available . . .; three, there must be security of power purchases; four, electricity markets must be reformed . . .; and five, governments must assume foreign exchange rates" (*Financial Times, 10/17/96*). Although it eventually got approval for the Dabhol project from the Maharashtra government, the entire experience was costly for Enron in real terms, and the intangible damage in terms of Enron's reputation in India and globally is certainly great.

HIGH-PROFILE LESSONS: KFC

Another U.S. company that had to undergo a painful public lesson in India is PepsiCo's Kentucky Fried Chicken (KFC). KFC's first Indian franchise, in Bangalore, was confronted with protests and bureaucratic roadblocks that came to a head in August 1995, only three months after it opened. The major antagonist was the radical Karnataka Farmers

Association, which threatened to take "direct action" against the restaurant. The group was purportedly protesting KFC's preference for contracting with large farms for supplies, as well as the poor quality of the food (*The Guardian*, 10/26/96, p. 18). Another major actor was the radical nationalist party Swadeshi Jagran Manch (National Awareness Forum), which is ideologically opposed to MNCs operating in the consumer goods markets of India (*Agence France Presse*, 10/14/96). The KFC outlet was physically entered and ransacked at least twice during this tumultuous period.

These political movements found an ally in the Bangalore city government. This is especially indicative of the extent of anti-MNC sentiment, since Bangalore is well known as the center of foreign high-tech manufacturing with extensive operations by the likes of Digital Equipment, Hewlett-Packard, IBM, Texas Instruments, and Compaq (*International Herald Tribune*, 8/29/95). If there is any city government in India expected to show support for foreign investment, it is Bangalore's. The city did supply a police guard to protect the KFC outlet. However, it also declared the food "unfit for human consumption" due to the amount of monosodium glutamate and threatened to revoke the franchise's restaurant license (*United Press International*, 9/2/95).

Contrast KFC's response to that of Enron. Enron's leadership tried to muscle its way into the Indian market, responding to political resistance by mobilizing its connections in high places and making thinly veiled threats. This only served to unify and radicalize Enron's opponents and reduce the chance that a compromise could be found. KFC, on the other hand, exhibited patience and a commitment to making it in India by accommodating local needs as much as possible. From the time KFC had opened in June, it offered special vegetarian dishes developed specifically for the Indian market. Vegetarian food alone may not have stopped the radical groups from protesting, but it did indicate KFC's willingness to adapt and respect local preferences and tastes. One important fact is that these dishes were so successful, bringing in about 40 percent of total revenues, that the company decided to begin offering them in other outlets worldwide. In particular, KFC restaurants in Arab states, which cater to millions of resident alien Indians, were a logical target (*United Press International*, 9/7/95).

KFC also persevered with its plans to open two more outlets by the end of 1995, one each in Mumbai and New Delhi. In New Delhi an outlet did open its doors before year's end only to experience a replay of the incident in Bangalore—the city government closed it down for "health reasons." However, KFC challenged the ruling, and the Delhi High Court agreed, allowing the doors to reopen two weeks after the city's action (*Agence France Presse*, 10/27/96). KFC has not opened any more restaurants, apparently canceling or postponing the one planned for Mumbai. However, its initial steps can be seen as instructive. In fact, another PepsiCo fast-food subsidiary, Pizza Hut, has apparently taken KFC's experience to heart and enjoyed greater success.

In June 1996, the first Pizza Hut outlet made a low-key debut in Bangalore. The second opened just as quietly in New Delhi four months later. Thirty more are planned by 2003. There has been one incident in Bangalore, in which 50 farmers attacked the Pizza Hut, protesting that it was ruining "millions of farmers" and subverting Indian culture. But the farmers were quickly arrested. The trend seems to be toward less resistance.

THE MARKET ROAD TO CITIZENSHIP

Winning a place in the market is the first step to citizenship success. The key in the case of PepsiCo's franchises has been to respond in a firm but accommodating and respectful manner. Enough customers were won to keep the business operational, and management persevered, proving its staying power sufficient to subdue the vocal extremist groups who presented a threat. The next stage that high-profile companies must enter is that of winning customers and improving the company's reputation among the vast majority of Indians. This means showing genuine good intentions and long-term commitment to the host society—putting the lessons learned to work in more substantial corporate citizenship activities.

For PepsiCo's fast-food franchises, perseverance, keeping a low profile, and adapting products to suit local tastes proved important. Another fast-food franchise, McDonald's, seems to have learned from observation and is enjoying a relatively uneventful period of entry into the Indian marketplace. As journalist Suzanne Goldenberg observes, "McDonald's has learnt from example. It cajoled Indian journalists to stop in for a Maharaja burger at its opening [in Bangalore in October 1996], and was careful to incorporate replicas of traditional embroidery into its advertising. If that wasn't clear enough, promotional material promised: 'McDonald's India respects its local culture'" (*The Guardian*, 10/26/96). Bad publicity is minimized by projecting an image—and reality—of openness with the public and demonstrating a willingness to adapt in order to be accepted in the local society.

Of all fast-food franchises, McDonald's and other burger outlets would be expected to encounter the most resistance in India because of Hindu reverence for cows. However, by learning from other franchises's best practices with clear citizenship content, McDonald's has managed to make the smoothest entry yet of any fast-food franchise into the Indian market.

McDonald's took an obvious, important step by avoiding selling beef burgers in India, introducing mutton and vegetarian products instead. It also made a point of adopting and projecting an attitude of openness and commitment. Vikram Bakshi, McDonald's managing director in India, states that countering nationalist protests "is a question of information. We are a joint venture employing Indian people, everything we buy is from Indian suppliers and we are serving Indian customers. Our ingredients are those which would appear in any Indian family home. Once people know the facts, they will have a better opinion" (*Agence France Presse,* 10/18/96).

Actually, Bakshi spent three years getting domestic suppliers prepared for the franchise's standards. This had a significant positive impact—allowing these suppliers to not only serve the local Indian market but also begin to export; for example, they send iceberg lettuce to the Middle East and dairy products to the U.S. And, as a final strategic element, initial price of the "Maharajah Mac" and other food will be low, designed to "be competitive to reach as large a section of the population as possible" (*Agence France Presse,* 10/18/96).

UNDERSTANDING THE INDIAN PERSPECTIVE

At least part of the explanation for the current nationalist sentiment in India can be found in historical patterns and historically rooted sentiments. Arguably, the first Indian experience with an MNC began on December 31, 1600, when the British East India Company was established by a charter of Queen Elizabeth I. The British began to displace the Portuguese as the dominant colonizing power on the subcontinent—and enthusiastically, arrogantly, and brutally exploited India's resources and cheap labor, eventually bringing down the Mughal Empire and establishing their political and military control under the Crown Raj. This colonial legacy contributes even today—consciously, and especially unconsciously in the Indian psyche—to suspicion of any foreign business activity. "It is there. You cannot ignore it," says BJP economic adviser Jay Dubashi (*BusinessWeek,* 10/23/96).

Foreign activities have brought suspicion ever since. In the years leading up to independence, Mahatma Gandhi himself often fought against unfair foreign exploitation, for example by defying the British monopoly on sea salt in 1930.[2] Gandhi believed in the future of an independent Indian nation, but he had liberal and tolerant values, which allowed him to conceive of the nation as inclusive. But Gandhi was killed by a radical Hindu nationalist.

India itself is divided by often fierce national and ethnic rivalries, most notably between Hindu and Muslim. Each case must be judged on its own merits; each protest should be taken seriously, rather than dismissed out of hand. And, most importantly, understanding of the roots of discontent should be sought out—perhaps by asking adversaries of MNC activity directly what it would take to win them over.

To underscore the importance of establishing a positive corporate reputation as soon as possible, consider that on December 3, 1994, all of India joined the city of Bhopal in commemorating the passing of a decade since the worst industrial accident in history. The official list of those killed by the lethal gas leak from the Union Carbide plant in Bhopal contains 6,954 names (*New York Times,* 12/2/94). Unofficial estimates run as high as 16,000 (*Japan Economic Newswire,* 12/11/94).

Even after ten years, popular sentiment against Union Carbide is strong, even virulent, in Bhopal. This sentiment is transferred to other foreign firms, as well. One great irony of this incident is that Union Carbide, at least by most accounts, performed admirably and responsibly before and after the tragedy. The evidence is convincing that it was the local partner and its employees who were at fault for disregarding standard safety rules that Union Carbide had instituted. The Indian managers (the plant was staffed completely by Indians) were on a tea break when an employee, Union Carbide alleges, attempted to sabotage a chemical tank, not realizing the extent of the consequences. The Bhopal plant was apparently as safe as any other Union Carbide insecticide plant, and a large proportion of the people who were killed or injured were squatters who had illegally set up camps around the factory walls (Newton and Dillingham, 1994, pp. 30–38).

Two weeks after the deadly gas was released, 2,500 people were already dead and more were dying daily (*Los Angeles Times,* 12/4/94). Warren Anderson, Union Carbide CEO, had immediately flown to India with authorization to spend up to $5 million on the spot to aid the victims. And the company had "announced that [it] accepted full moral responsibility for the disaster and that the victims would be compensated." But, as victims were dying and local officials were overwhelmed, Anderson was detained in a company guest house; no Indian national or local officials would see him, and he was not allowed to distribute aid or investigate the incident in any way (Newton and Dillingham, 1994, pp.

37–39). In fact, he had been arrested upon his arrival and released only after posting bail (*Japan Economic Newswire*, 12/11/94). Union Carbide settled out of court in 1989 and paid $470 million in compensation, but in 1992 an arrest warrant was issued for Anderson in Bhopal on charges of "culpable homicide" made five years earlier (*Los Angeles Times*, 12/4/94).[3]

There are many facets of this case that are interesting, troubling, and instructive. What is of particular interest in the present context is the absolute futility of all of Union Carbide's apparently well-intentioned efforts. In this extreme case, we see clearly how essential a positive reputation is to doing business in India. Once the MNC's reputation had become completely negative, it was impossible to restore. The company eventually found a buyer for its 50.9 percent of the plant and donated all of the proceeds, $40 million, to build a hospital in Bhopal (*New York Times*, 12/2/1994). Nevertheless, protesters in 1994 shouted "Death to Union Carbide!" on the factory grounds, and children threw rocks at a 12-foot high "demon" effigy of Union Carbide.

In 1995, in the midst of controversy over a proposal by DuPont to build Asia's largest nylon factory near Bhopal, a group of local legislators protested, with clear reference to the Union Carbide incident a decade before: "We must not forget corporate ability to evade responsibility for harms inflicted as well as to defraud victims of corporate misconduct." One man was killed by the Indian police during a demonstration against the project, and environmental and nationalist groups treated it as a focal point around which to rally supporters to gain publicity. But DuPont had given the groups a rallying cry—a secret contract clause that absolved the parent multinational from all legal responsibility for any damages caused by the local joint venture (Inter Press Service, 2/6/95).[4]

To be sure, reputation is a key asset. No amount of citizenship activity may have been sufficient to shield Union Carbide from the outrage that forced it out of India. But a better reputation in-country might have served to counteract some of the most damaging effects of the disaster.

As it happened, however, Union Carbide was unable to participate in any way in the relief effort, leaving corrupt and inefficient bureaucracies to distribute the money it finally gave. As a result, less than one-third of the funds have been distributed 12 years after the disaster, and the suffering continues. Indeed, the entire process of reaching a settlement might well have been substantially different if the government had not cynically played on public outrage by asking for an impossible amount, over $3 billion, and tying the procedure up for five years.

No Union Carbide officials were allowed to inspect the scene of the accident. Union Carbide was denied the ability to defend its own interests and to fulfill what Anderson and other officials probably believed was their moral as well as corporate responsibility. The company has not only had to abandon its operations in India, it also has little chance of returning to the second largest country in the world for the foreseeable future. And Union Carbide's reputation globally has certainly been damaged.

BEST PRACTICES IN INDIA

To get a glimpse of what corporate efforts work best with the citizens of India, it is useful to examine citizenship practices in those firms that understand India best—wholly owned and operated Indian firms. For example, in Pune, four companies visited by a University of Michigan Global Leadership Program team in 1995 were running exemplary citizenship programs. Bajaj Auto, Bharat Forge Ltd., Kirloskar Cummins, and Telco Ltd. have programs that focus on maintaining the "health, safety, skills, and family life" of employees. These concerns are manifested in such practical, relatively inexpensive programs as legal aid, tax planning, professional counseling, classes in cooking, arts and crafts, family planning and family education, and physical fitness.

These programs share several features. First, they all have a narrow scope of activity—they all are aimed at improving the lives of employees and their families. This is not coincidental or trivial; Indians, perhaps for cultural and historical reasons, tend to be deeply suspicious of pure philanthropy. Unadulterated altruism does not pay in India, at least for those less saintly than Mahatma Gandhi or Mother Teresa. The typical Indian understands corporate good deeds done to improve the morale of the workforce or its health, and will form a positive image of a company that takes care of its own. They might not be so receptive to a program focused on improving conditions for the indigent rural poor—who are poor, it is widely believed, because they are lazy and like to be poor. Such attitudes are commonly referred to as Indian "resignation," or belief in one's fate.

This does not mean that extending help to the poor is impossible in India, but it does indicate that care must be taken to incorporate Indian norms in such citizenship design. Bajaj Auto and Telco Ltd. are both involved in local, but extensive, rural development projects, for example. These serve the immediate communities of the companies and their workforce, and therefore are perceived as appropriate, even though there are benefits for a wider circle of people. One key to their success is a focus on helping people to help themselves in very practical ways. Villagers are consulted in village meetings, and they help define what some key problems are and how they might be addressed. The result can be seen in small-scale effective programs for improving education for village youth, drinking water purification, women's empowerment clubs, bio-gas plants, and cattle cross-breeding programs. Larger Indian companies have been known to invest in housing, sanitation, and health care for employees (India Auto Report, 1995).

Another source for guidance on designing citizenship programs is the Confederation of Indian Industry (CII). This is the most important business organization in the country. CII has taken the initiative in outlining areas in which the business community could be constructively involved. These areas include education, basic transportation infrastructure, clean water, proper sewage treatment, improved health care facilities, housing for employees, child care for female workers, and local community involvement. CII's Corporate Citizenship Committee promotes rural development, facilitates links between business and Non-Governmental Organizations (NGOs), promotes health programs, AIDS awareness, population control, and education literacy programs.

In spite of these cases of citizenship activity and advocacy, it is nevertheless true that most Indian businesses are indifferent or even actively resistant to corporate citizenship activities. Philanthropic activities in India have traditionally been the product of individual, not corporate, giving. There is a largely religious orientation and motivation as well. It is common for donations to be made to hospitals and schools attached to certain religious communities. Rural development projects are often infused with Hindu or other beliefs and seek donations from individuals in the immediate community rather than from large Indian or foreign corporations. NRIs (Non-Resident Aliens) are also a source of philanthropic funding. Indian business culture differentiates between the role of companies and that of government, NGOs, and individuals in contributing to the good of society. Corporations' responsibilities are usually not considered to extend beyond the realm of generating shareholder profits and creating jobs.

As one University of Michigan Global Leadership Program team of executives concluded:

> The acceptance of. . . . an individual's position in society is a feature of the Indian psyche, which may lead to less action on many corporate citizenship issues than would be perceived as the norm by many MNCs. There is a risk that to do anything outside that which can be perceived as enlightened self-interest would create suspicion. . . . Adopting a positive stance on global citizenship issues is in the MNC's

long-term . . . interest. Taking care of the local workforce creates a better, more loyal, more productive workforce. Looking after the community wider than just employees helps to create a positive corporate image in the community and should assist in overcoming some of the anti-foreign feeling of which a manifestation is the Swadeshi movement.

More general charitable giving that cannot be directly related back to the corporation's own self-interest can be viewed with suspicion. The Indian may feel compromised, whether in integrity or in independence, by taking charitable money. For this reason local activity that can be seen in the corporation's long-term best interest is recommended. Public health and housing activities, which can benefit both employees and potentially the wider community, are a good starting point.

It will be helpful to find a local Indian to guide the corporation's efforts in the right direction (India Telecom Report, "Country Business Opportunity Assessment," 1995, pp. 18–19).

C-DOT: BEST PRACTICES IN ACTION

If Enron and portions of other examples suggest a disregard for corporate citizenship in India, then the story of Sam Pitroda and C-DOT is its polar opposite.[5] This is not, strictly speaking, a case of a foreign MNC building a positive citizenship reputation. However, it is perhaps the best example of effective citizenship practices in India, and it demonstrates a number of central principles in action. It is exceptional in its combination of U.S. and Indian perspectives and in the scale of its success. In short, C-DOT is a model from which MNCs can learn a great deal about how to design and run successful citizenship programs in India.

The Centre for Development of Telematics (C-DOT) was registered as a nonprofit Indian organization in August 1984. It was the brainchild of Sam Pitroda, a U.S. citizen and former vice president of U.S.-based Rockwell Corporation. Pitroda was born in 1942 in Titilagarh, an Indian village without phones or electric power in Orissa state. By the time he was 21, he had a master's degree in physics from an Indian university, but he had never used a telephone. By the time he was 30 he was a leading developer of digital switching technology for the U.S. giant GTE in Chicago. In 1974 he founded Wescom Switching Inc. with two partners, and in 1980 they sold out to Rockwell.

Pitroda agreed to work for Rockwell for three years as part of the deal, but his thoughts were pulling him in another direction. In 1981, he managed to convince an Indian government telecom committee to give him two hours of its attention. He presented them a message that had clearly been taking shape in his mind for some time: India should pull out all the stops to develop a state-of-the art telecom infrastructure throughout the country. In particular, Pitroda believed that India should abandon plans to install cheaper, but inefficient and outdated electromechanical switches and move directly to digital switching for large urban centers and especially for all rural areas, including the smallest Indian villages.

This strategy was surprising and unorthodox. India at the time had one telephone for every 280 Indians, and these were located almost exclusively in the major cities like New Delhi, Mumbai, and Calcutta. The common approach to telecom development was that it should take a back seat to what were considered more fundamental issues: water purification, sanitation, or population control. Putting telephones in impoverished villages was not considered the best approach to overall development. But Pitroda had a different idea about the role of communication technology. He believed it could be a powerful engine for economic and political development. Pitroda believed:

> To survive, India had to bring telecommunications to its towns and villages; to thrive, it had to do it with Indian talent and Indian technology.... I began to see that information technology played an indispensable role in promoting openness, accessibility, accountability, connectivity, democracy, decentralization—all the "soft" qualities so essential to effective social, economic, and political development.... Telecommunications was as critical and fundamental to nation building as water, agriculture, health, and without it, India's democracy could founder.

In other words, telecommunications technology is a key engine of growth and development, creating efficiencies and opening opportunities that accelerate economic activity and productivity, and help people accumulate the resources to improve their own lives and communities.

Pitroda's approach emphasizes two important points. First, it encourages self-reliance—helping people to help themselves by providing them with the tools they need. Second, it has a local, community-based focus. Even given the massive, nationwide scale of Pitroda's plan, the focus was on allowing individuals and small entrepreneurs to improve their lives.

Pitroda was convincing enough to gain a one-hour meeting with the prime minister, Indira Gandhi. An indication of how strongly he felt is that after he had first been offered a ten-minute audience with the prime minister, he turned it down saying there was no way he could explain his proposal in such a short time. Instead, he persevered and pushed until five months later, he had Mrs. Gandhi's commitment to listen for a full hour. The key, he explained to her in November 1981, was to develop a digital switch uniquely suited to Indian conditions. In particular, an efficient switch built to accommodate no more than 200 telephones was all that the vast majority of villages would need, and all they could afford. In the developed world, even the smallest towns installed switches built for 4,000 to 10,000 lines, because the cost was negligible. But, multiplied by hundreds of thousands of villages in India, this level of excess capacity was prohibitively expensive. In addition, domestic manufacturing of these small-capacity switches would create high-skilled jobs in India, further fueling development, and the switches could even be exported to other developing countries.

Mrs. Gandhi saw merit in the plan. Her son, a powerful political figure in his own right, became Pitroda's ally. There was resistance, of course—from skeptics, entrenched interests, and foreign telecom equipment suppliers. One European CEO took it upon himself to personally write a letter of protest to the prime minister. By August 1984, however, C-DOT had received permission to open up shop.

Recalling the experiences of Enron, PepsiCo, and McDonald's, we can note that Pitroda was politically cognizant from the start. Especially in the decade before India's real economic opening, he knew he needed the attention and support of the prime minister and those immediately around her. But, he also based his proposal on the concept that it was good for Indian development and the Indian people. It would improve village life and create high-tech jobs. Today, such jobs are a great source of national pride and political strength in India.

And C-DOT achieved significant results. Pitroda writes,

> By 1987, within our three-year limit, we had delivered a 128-line rural exchange, a 128-line private automatic branch exchange for businesses, a small central exchange with a capacity of 512 lines, and we were ready with field trials of a 10,000-line exchange.... [A]nd all of this was being manufactured in India to the international standard.... We had licensed some 40 public and private companies to manufacture and market C-DOT products, and more than 100 businesses had sprung up to manufacture ancillary parts and components.... Moreover, these rural exchanges were masterpieces of "appropriate" design.

Pitroda's team of young India engineers had designed switches that were self-cooling to avoid reliance on the poor Indian electrical grid, and they were protected against India's especially dusty conditions—all delivered for about $8,000 per switch.

In one test case in a village of 5,000 in Karnataka state, the installation of a 100-line digital exchange spurred local business and increased economic activity substantially, according to Pitroda. A small trucking company was enabled to more efficiently dispatch its drivers and find goods to transport. This, in turn, moved products more quickly and provided more jobs for drivers and others. Local farmers could call city markets and follow prices for their produce. Artisans could speak to customers, machine operators could arrange for services and repairs, shopkeepers could order goods—all by phone and in real time. In the six months after the introduction of service, total bank deposits in the town rose impressively. And nationwide, there are now 93.5 Indians for every telephone (compared with 280 when Pitroda got started) in the country (*AsiaWeek*, 3/15/96)—still well below developed-world standards, but a vast improvement from a decade earlier.

As a result, community functions can be organized, medical help can be summoned immediately, and schools can search for better or cheaper supplies. And this communication creates an openness and an attitude about information that is a democratizing force.

SOCIAL NEEDS FOR SUSTAINABLE DEVELOPMENT

Against that backdrop, what specific social needs might an MNC want to address in India?

India's economic liberalization program has achieved some stunning successes. Foreign reserves were only $1.1 billion in June 1991 but by October 1995 had reached $19 billion. From a virtual standstill pre-1991, GDP growth has consistently risen and is projected at around 6 percent for 1996. Nevertheless, India's socioeconomic ills are not being eradicated as quickly.

India's population is diverse—83 percent Hindu, 11 percent Muslim, and 2 percent Sikh; there are 24 languages spoken by a million or more people, with 30 percent of the population speaking Hindi. This leaves open the possibility of continued interethnic conflict, especially between Hindus and Muslims. Continuing impoverishment and heightened uncertainty about the future make this mixture possibly more volatile than in recent memory.

India's labor force of 340 million includes 15–50 million children. Sixty-seven percent of the workforce is employed in agriculture, while only 10 percent is in manufacturing. Agriculture supplies only 30 percent of GDP, however, while manufacturing accounts for 22 percent. Unemployment is 22 percent.

To continue the growth spurred by reform, Prime Minister H. D. Dewe Gowda's Common Minimum Program (CMP) announced on June 6, 1996, recognizes the need for $10 billion annually in foreign direct investment in India. Infrastructure and high-tech investment are encouraged. Only foreign investment can ensure India's economic success—and beyond that, corporations doing business in India have a stake in citizenship activities aimed at making growth politically and socially sustainable.

Individual corporations can take on relatively limited, localized parts of these larger problems. In the aggregate, a large number of dedicated corporate citizens in the form of multinationals operating in India will have a significant, nationwide, positive impact. One business directory lists 1,500 collaborations between Indian and U.S. firms alone (Purohit and Dalvi, 1995). The collective impact of 1,500 serious citizenship programs in India would be significant.

Helping to build and develop India's social infrastructure is a key area in which MNCs can have a significant impact. Specifically, community- or workforce-based housing, health, and educational programs are particularly promising. Projects in these areas can be limited and local—and focused on benefiting a company's workforce and the immediate community.

In 1973, 20.7 percent of Indians lived in cities. By 1983, this figure had risen to 23.8 percent. By 1993, urbanization in India was at 26.3 percent of the population (*IMF,* 5/96, pp. 354–55). If this trend continues, by 2000, when there will be 1 billion Indians, there may be as many as 300 million inhabitants of India's already overcrowded cities. Clearly, this begs two fundamental questions. First, how can these people be housed today? Second, how can further migration to urban centers by the poor and destitute be prevented or discouraged? Providing quality living conditions—or any living conditions—is the only real answer. In urban and rural settings, Indian communities need more housing.

A key concern of health specialists in India is access to safe drinking water and proper sanitation. Thirty percent of Indians do not have access to drinking water that meets even minimal international standards. A full 80 percent are without proper sanitation.

According to the International Monetary Fund, no progress was made on fighting malnutrition among Indian children from 1979 through 1990 (the last year for which data are available). Sixty-three percent of India's children suffered from malnutrition during this period (*IMF,* 5/96, pp. 354–55). By 1994, the U.N. reported that 53 percent suffered from malnutrition—a marked improvement but certainly a far cry from "good." Many poorer Asian countries manage to feed their children better than India; included among those with lower malnutrition rates are Cambodia

(40 percent), Myanmar (31 percent), Vietnam (45 percent), and Nepal (49 percent) (UNICEF, "The Progress of Nations," 1995, p. 52). There is little anecdotal evidence that would indicate that things have improved since 1994 in India. Care and concern for children is one of the truly universal values. The situation in India presents an opportunity to accomplish much good. A corporation could provide free lunches for children, for example, which meet basic nutritional needs. Educational programs, day care, or information on nutrition could also be provided.

DOING BUSINESS IN INDIA INTO THE 21ST CENTURY

India is the world's largest democracy. One legacy of British imperialism is an Indian parliamentary system not unlike Britain's. The prime minister is the key figure in Indian politics; he or she heads the executive branch and leads the governing party or coalition. Of the two houses of parliament, the lower house, Lok Sabha, is the most powerful. Indians take some pride in their judicial system, which can generally be relied on for fair, impartial, and nonpoliticized rulings. The system works, although it is slow and heavily bureaucratized. Overall, a functioning, reliable, and fair legal system is one of the positive aspects of doing business in India. It is only since 1991 that Indians have gained a measure of economic freedom, in the western, capitalist sense, to match their substantial political freedom.

The 1996 elections made Indian politics much more representative. In one sense, this is the fruition and maturation of Indian democracy; at the same time, the risk of popular reaction to MNC activity flaming onto the political scene is heightened. An important difference between Western and Indian democracy is that politically, the wealthy are not as influential in India because of their low numbers. The poor vote in huge numbers, while the rich and educated tend not to vote because there is little chance for influence. This makes political awareness extremely important.

One fundamental political factor often overlooked by foreigners intent on doing business in India is that of caste. The caste system was opposed by Mahatma Gandhi, and discrimination on the basis of caste is technically illegal in India. However, 3,000 years of practice and Hindu belief in the inherent value of different groups based on birth has not disappeared. Indeed, caste has now become "a principle of political mobilization rather than a matter of ritual distance," according to Ashis Nandy at the Center for the Study of Developing Societies in Delhi. The upper castes make up only 10–15 percent of India's 940 million people, and fear among them is growing—especially in the countryside, where tension between landless untouchables and upper-caste landlords is growing (*New York Times*, 10/20/96).

In business, managers are typically Brahmins (upper-caste), and the manual jobs and lowest-paying jobs go to members of the lower castes. Children of lower-caste parents often work instead of attending school. Human Rights Watch has released a study estimating that 115 million school-age Indian children are working as bonded laborers—virtual slaves. On the other hand, the lower castes have made marked progress in government and educational jobs, due to a system of "reservations," or quotas. There has also been progress in the political sphere as groups organize and fight for economic and social advancement (*New York Times*, 10/20/96).

But the caste system should be seen as a fundamentally Indian problem—or characteristic—by foreign firms. Rather than attempting to correct the perceived injustices of this ancient social and religious system, foreign business should be cognizant of the process of change, and open to it, while avoiding the appearance of manipulating this politically charged issue. Remember, altruism is not readily appreciated in India. Rather, Indians of all castes are likely to take a cynical view toward any firm's overt interference in this most Indian of Indian social issues. In addition, MNCs need to be aware of the undercurrents and implicit assumptions about such issues as poverty and illiteracy. Caste may not be explicitly mentioned, but it is probably an important factor in the perception of corporate citizenship activity among one's own employees—managers and rank and file—and the Indian public in general. This is yet another strong argument for maintaining a local, community-based, and employee-oriented focus to citizenship activities in India, while avoiding issues that are culturally divisive or have religious or political undertones.

CONCLUSION

India faces a plethora of challenges today that (1) are widely recognized by Indians, (2) are amenable to small-scale, locally based solutions, and (3) rely on empowering people to help themselves. Corporate citizenship activities in India should demonstrate that knowledge and underscore:

- Cultural awareness and respect.
- Practicality and frugality.
- Sustainability by self-reliance.

Cultural awareness and respect mean that MNCs should seek out issues on which broad cultural consensus exists. Respect also implies avoiding secrecy. Self-reliance is a fundamental principle that allows Indians to maintain their dignity and avoid the reality or appearance of dependence on foreigners.

It also appears from the cases examined that citizenship should be an integral part of any market-entry strategy. India has had some distasteful experiences with foreign businesses, which should be recognized and understood. The historical legacy of the British East India Company is more salient than foreigners might imagine, especially in its perhaps unconscious contribution to general suspicion of ulterior motives and exploitative tendencies of MNCs. India also suffered the consequences of the worst industrial accident in history. The Bhopal disaster, while not often mentioned, is certainly never forgotten.

The cases examined here point to three principles of citizenship which, when observed, seem to lead to some degree of acceptance upon which a reputation can be built. If, conversely, these principles are ignored, the consequences can be very costly, as they were for Enron.

- Politics matter in the Indian democratic system.

- Secrecy leads to suspicion and is usually futile; openness is appreciated.

- Find local allies who can help overcome obstacles.

The opportunities for citizenship activities in the vast Indian marketplace are as diverse as the needs are great.

REFERENCES

India Auto Report. University of Michigan Global Leadership Program. Ann Arbor, Michigan, 1995.

India Telecom Report. University of Michigan Global Leadership Program. Ann Arbor, Michigan, 1995.

ENDNOTES

1. Louis T. Wells and Eric S. Gleason explore themes relevant to Enron's experience and to infrastructure projects in emerging markets in general in their useful article, "Is Foreign Infrastructure Investment Still Risky?," *Harvard Business Review,* Sept.-Nov. 1995.

2. Wolpert gives an excellent and concise introduction to Indian history, culture, and politics in his 1991 book, *India*.
3. This charge was not dropped until September 1996 (*European Chemical News*, 9/23/96, p. 4, as reported by Reuters).
4. Note that such a clause is not necessarily a bad idea from the local perspective. It could create a sense of responsibility and culpability for the local JV partner. Lack of such responsibility seems to have been a major cause of the Bhopal disaster—the local managers did not follow safety rules and left the chemical tank unguarded. In the context of Bhopal in 1995, however, the objectionable nature of such a secret clause, left completely unjustified and unexplained to the public, should have been crystal clear to any firm aware of citizenship issues.
5. The details of this case are taken primarily from Mr. Pitroda's own account of it, "Development, Democracy, and the Village Telephone," *Harvard Business Review*, Nov.-Dec. 1993.

17

A GLOBAL MODEL FOR THE BUSINESS OF CORPORATE CITIZENSHIP

The Success Story of Focus: HOPE

Lynda St. Clair

THE CASES IN THIS BOOK have focused on companies that are first and foremost competitive businesses. Society has benefited because these companies have accepted the responsibility of serving as good corporate citizens. These citizenship activities, however, are clearly a supplement to their core business activities. Having organizations that are willing to serve the global community while pursuing a competitive business agenda is critical to maintaining a strong and healthy global society. Our economy depends upon businesses pursuing their corporate self-interest to sustain economic growth. This chapter, however, focuses on another type of organization—one that was initially founded as an act of citizenship but over time has evolved into a competitive business organization. In that, it serves as a model for developing self-reliance and economic and social success—a model that can be adopted and recreated anywhere in the world.

BACKGROUND

The Focus: HOPE mission statement is as follows:

> Recognizing the dignity and beauty of every person, we pledge intelligent and practical action to overcome racism, poverty, and injustice and to build a metropolitan community where all people may live in freedom, harmony, trust and affection—black and white, yellow, brown, and red—from Detroit and its suburbs, in every economic status, national origin, religious persuasion, we join in this covenant.

Focus: HOPE is a self-sufficient, not-for-profit organization in Detroit, Michigan, that trains inner-city young people to be highly sophisticated, state-of-the-art machinists. It was started on a shoestring as a food program by two enormously determined and energized people and has succeeded because of their fortitude and powerful ability to create and harness the energy of others. Father William Cunningham was a young priest teaching English at the Sacred Heart Seminary in Detroit when that city's destructive race riots broke out in 1967. During the riots, Father Cunningham looked around at the poverty, rage, and despair in the city's black neighborhoods and decided, "I can't keep teaching Beowulf and Shakespeare and English composition[1] . . . with the choppers coming and the half-tracks and the 50-caliber machine guns turned on the side of buildings and the encampment of Central High School. In the terrible days of watching people be shot in front of our eyes on the street, (we felt) we had to do something."[2] With the aid of Eleanor Josaitis, a suburban housewife at whose parish he had been a weekend pastor, Focus: HOPE was founded. Josaitis and her family moved back to the city of Detroit in 1968 and she, like Father Cunningham, has lived in the city ever since.

Beginning with literally nothing but the energy and initiative of two people, Focus: HOPE's operations now include over 1 million square feet of floor space spread through 12 buildings on 30 acres in the Detroit area. The story of Focus: HOPE exemplifies the fusion of soft-hearted compassion for individuals, hard-headed economic business thinking, and pragmatic concern for restoring the fragile social fabric that binds a community together.

1971: NOURISH

The overwhelming needs of the inner city might have caused lesser people to throw up their hands and declare that the problem was too big to even begin to attack. Cunningham and Josaitis, however, never considered the impossibility of the task that they were undertaking. Rather, they focused their attention on the most immediate need of the community and went to work. They commissioned studies that found that babies, if not given proper food and nutrition during their first three years, would lose a significant portion of their brain capacity.[3] Prompted by these results, they started a food program for babies and their mothers in 1971. In its early days the modest program fed fewer than 800 children and mothers. Today it feeds more than 24,000 low-income mothers and children each month.[4] Families collect their food from supermarket-like facilities where they push shopping carts and check out at a cash register much like traditional grocery stores. It might be more efficient to simply provide handouts in a box, but this is not the way of Cunningham and Josaitis. They feel families should have the dignity of choice in their food selections and, more importantly, they feel the children need the psychological imprint of a role model more like mainstream families than collectors of charity.

In addition to serving the needs of its original target population, Focus: HOPE has expanded the population it serves to reach the elderly poor. Eleanor Josaitis describes the event that sparked the expansion of Focus: HOPE's food program:

> This woman called and she said, "Mrs. Josaitis, I understand that you have food." And I went rattling on about this fabulous program for nursing mothers, and pregnant women, and babies. And then came a long, long pause. She said, "I am 72 years old. Do I have to get pregnant before I can get some help?" And she told me off, like only your grandmother can tell you off. But I had it coming to me. I heard every single word the woman said to me. What I did not hear was the fear in her voice.

Determined to respond to this latest challenge, Cunningham and Josaitis hired two researchers, gathered enough information to fill an entire room, and marched themselves to Washington, where they stood in front of Congress and asked if they could please give food to seniors. Five years and 32 hearings later, the determined pair got their wish and were granted national law to provide food to the elderly. Today, by way of intelligent and practical action, the Food for Seniors program reaches 27,000 low-income older adults in 45 metropolitan Detroit communities.

Although Focus: HOPE had successfully established programs to feed the hungry, it was clear to Cunningham and Josaitis that their efforts were only attending to symptoms, not to the insidious infection that was at the root of the problem. In the words of Eleanor Josaitis, "The realization began to dawn on us all that feeding the hungry is more than just giving them food. If we really believe in human dignity, it is providing them with something more—the wherewithal to provide for themselves."[5] Their next mission was to address the underlying problem: children were going hungry because their parents didn't have jobs. Providing food, although an enormously valuable service, did little to address that problem and thus would have little long-term impact. To stem the flood of poverty, Focus: HOPE needed to help the parents break with the failures and frustrations of their pasts and transition into becoming responsible, self-sufficient individuals.

To achieve that goal, jobs were needed—stable, well-paying jobs. In the Detroit area, it was virtually impossible to think about jobs and not think about the automobile industry. In evaluating the alternatives, Cunningham and Josaitis discovered that some of the best-paying and most stable jobs were as machinists, so they decided to take on the challenge of training inner-city workers to become machinists—"not just adequate machinists, not even above-average machinists, but the best machinists in the world." Their vision was that Focus: HOPE graduates would get and keep jobs not because socially conscious employers pitied them but because Focus: HOPE graduates would be solid, reliable workers with skills that the employers needed. As Cunningham described it before his death in the spring of 1997, "We [have] got to knock down the last vestige of racist conclusion that black men and women are not suited, not fitted for, not capable of, the highest positions of contribution to our society."[6]

1981: TRAIN

For Cunningham and Josaitis, the only way to break down those kinds of racist assumptions was to prove that they were untenable. But that left them with a very large problem. Because, regardless of their potential, the simple fact was that much of the population of the inner city did not currently have the skills necessary to succeed in the workplace.

Undaunted by that reality, Cunningham and Josaitis were determined to accomplish their goal. Just as they had been resolute in their goal to provide nourishment to those who could not afford it, so, too, were they determined to provide skills to those who they knew had the ability but lacked the training. Thus in 1981, Focus: HOPE's Machinist Training Institute (MTI) began preparing students for jobs in precision machining and metal working. The program is today accredited and has placed over 1,200 graduates in jobs since its inception, with approximately 250 individuals enrolled in the program at any given time.

Along with technical training, Focus: HOPE provides students with an opportunity to build their self-esteem. While setting stretch goals for its candidates, Focus: HOPE simultaneously offers the hope and support that those goals can be met. That, along with the obvious respect that the program leaders have for their students, serves to build the students' sense of self-worth and confidence in their ability to meet whatever challenges may come their way.

1987: SUPPORT

To get inner-city dwellers to achieve higher levels of skill and confidence, of course, meant that they had to participate in the program. But what about people who were unable to obtain training because of their child care responsibilities? Eliminating barriers is central to the identity of Focus: HOPE, so it seemed only natural in 1987 that a child care facility should become part of the operations.

Twenty-four-year-old Denecia Harvey, a single mother of three, says that Focus: HOPE's fully certified, well-staffed, up-to-date day care facility took away her best excuse for not completing her education or acquiring a trade. "I was always saying what I couldn't do. 'Oh, I can't do this because of my children.' Or, 'I don't have this for my children, I can't do this.' 'I don't have a baby-sitter.' I made an excuse for everything." Now she is studying to be a machinist, while her children are enrolled at Focus: HOPE's Center for Children. The 26,000-square-foot center provides infant care, toddler care, a Montessori school program, and a before/after-school program for the families of its students.[7]

1989: TEACH

Focus: HOPE's goal of creating opportunity for individuals who might otherwise have been left behind has led the organization to find ways of offering whatever tools might be necessary to make that mission a reality. One result of that mission was the development of FAST TRACK, a program that offers tutoring and remedial courses in math and language to fill educational gaps. When Cunningham and Josaitis tested 187 men and women with high school diplomas, they found that a mere 27 could pass the equivalent of a tenth-grade math test. Recognizing the need for corrective, intelligent action, the two created a fast-track education program designed to either improve students' short-term job skills or to prepare them for a longer course of study. Begun in 1989, FAST TRACK focuses on academic and communication skills, computer applications, and industry standards of discipline and personal conduct. Although the program now feeds many of its students into the Machinist Training Institute, it was actually MTI that led to the creation of FAST TRACK, as Focus: HOPE began having difficulty obtaining students who were qualified to enter directly into the MTI program. Once again, rather than concluding that they had done all they could, Father Cunningham and Eleanor Josaitis decided to create their own supply of MTI participants.

The desire to help people is never confused, however, with a willingness to let them slack off. Focus: HOPE maintains extremely high expectations for all its students. For example, students at FAST TRACK must be in class, logged onto their computers by 8:00 A.M., and not a second later. This policy is strictly enforced by Thomas Murphy, the ex-military sergeant at the helm, whose goal is to emulate real-world circumstances. "Companies don't tolerate tardy employees, and we don't either."[8]

1990: TRANSFORM

The Center for Advanced Technologies (CAT) is the most breathtaking undertaking at Focus: HOPE to date. The $100-million CAT program involves a coalition of six universities (University of Detroit Mercy, Wayne State University, Lawrence Technological University, Ohio's Central State University, Lehigh University, and the University of Michigan), six manufacturers (Ford, General Motors, Chrysler, Detroit Diesel, EDS, and Cincinnati Milacron), and the Society of Manufacturing Engineers. Its goal is fittingly ambitious: to reinvent how America teaches its engineers. Students split their time between "real-world" manufacturing and academic pursuits at the CAT facility. The curriculum includes not only sophisticated design and engineering courses but also business administration and language training. Graduates of the six-year master's degree program will be fluent in German and Japanese.

To help Focus: HOPE reach these lofty goals, Cunningham and Josaitis have developed an incredible network of support. The CAT project has pledges of support from the U.S. Departments of Defense, Labor, Education, and Commerce. The former president of General Motors, Lloyd Reuss, was drafted to play the crucial role of executive dean for the CAT. He in turn immediately recruited four more retired auto executives to join Focus: HOPE's ranks.[9] He continues to draft Big Three retirees today. "For 38 years I worked at shaping steel; now I'm shaping lives," a proud Reuss states.

Josaitis and Cunningham energized corporations to provide funding. Cunningham and Josaitis inspired Carl Levin, the Michigan senator who sits on the Armed Services Committee, to help arrange a $60-million Defense Department special industrial grant to build the CAT. "To witness what is going on here is simply breathtaking," Levin told the crowd at the center's dedication. And, they motivated the University of Michigan Engineering School, Lehigh University of Pennsylvania, and four other engineering institutions[10] to agree on a curriculum so that they would grant CAT graduates degrees from their institutions.

Equally critical to the success of the program has been the support that it has garnered from the inner-city residents who are its participants. Influenced by Cunningham and Josaitis's own exceedingly high expectations, candidates at the Center for Advanced Technologies have found that they, too, are constantly raising the high bar for themselves. George Smith, a typical CAT candidate, is one such example who has learned to settle for nothing less than the best. His end goal today is to complete a master's in engineering and to own his own business.

"Nobody owes you anything. You want something, you have to work for it," Cunningham says. In the spring of 1996, he explained his philosophy of bold action to a group of visiting Ford executives. "As leaders we do not set the goals high enough for our people," he said. "The exact synonym for consensus is mediocrity. You think of the lowest possible denominator. . . . Leadership is salesmanship—getting people to say, c'mon we can do this."[11]

The new high-tech center is designed as a total learning experience. It is important that the architecture symbolize and practically operate as "work of the future." Cunningham will not have hand-me-down computers or manufacturing equipment in the CAT, because he wants to energize and stretch his students and teachers to prepare for the 21st century. He has even set up an executive-style dining room for the students to learn how to interact socially in business settings. There is a world-class cook who prepares meals of different ethnic origin. The students have to learn how to set the tables, learn appropriate manners for different cultures, and learn how to carry on an appropriate business conversation. Against such a backdrop, beginning a culinary institute seemed only natural, so Focus: HOPE did that, too.

With all this attention to detail and their hard work, Cunningham, Josaitis, and the rest of the staff show their confidence in the students, and the students develop confidence in themselves. Andre Reynolds, a CAT student who graduated from the Machinist Training Program and now works at the organization's machine shop, plans to be a globe-trotting engineering troubleshooter. "So if they have a problem, let's just say, in Germany or in Japan," he explains, "they would say, 'Who can we get to solve this problem?' 'Well, call Andre Reynolds.' 'Where is he?' 'Last I heard, he was in Washington.' Well, they call me up and I fly down to Japan, and I won't need a translator because I already know the language myself."

The goal of the CAT program, and indeed all of Focus: HOPE, is truly the transformation of the individual. After describing the profile of a CAT student, Cunningham once asked an audience, "Where do they come from, these gems. Do we import them from Germany? Do we bring them in from Japan? Or do we even bring them in from MIT? They come from the streets of Detroit. They labored through the FAST TRACK program, they pushed their way through the Machinist Training Institute, they held a job, and now they're starting at the CAT and there's nothing like them in the world."[12]

THE BUSINESS OF CHARITY

Although it began as a charity, supplying food for mothers and infants, Focus: HOPE has grown into a business. So powerful is the Focus: HOPE model that in 1994, when U.S. President Bill Clinton hosted economic ministers of the G-7 leading countries in Detroit, the one side trip they made was to visit and see first-hand the world-class example in Detroit's inner city.

Today, Focus: HOPE continues with its food distribution program but now also prepares individuals to provide for themselves. Make no mistake, the CAT is a business. Sales volumes as of July 1995 were running around $10 million per year. And Focus: HOPE was a praised supplier to its automotive customers. Never content, Focus: HOPE's 1995 five-year sales projections called for sales of $60 million a year.

The work that the participants do is real work, supplying parts to companies such as Ford, GM, and Detroit Diesel. These companies purchase parts from Focus: HOPE, not out of any sense of social responsibility but because the parts produced meet the highest levels of quality. For example, Detroit Diesel president Ludwig Koci says he buys from Focus: HOPE because, "Although they [machined parts] look like a simple little piece of metal, they are a highly machined and highly accurate piece of metal. And Focus: HOPE is doing a terrific job for us there." In fact, Focus: HOPE has been able to manufacture parts at the CAT at such high quality levels and exacting tolerances that they are the sole provider for some Detroit Diesel parts.

To date, three for-profit companies have sprung from the not-for-profit roots of Focus: HOPE. High Quality Manufacturing, Inc. supplies engine hoses and assembles emission control harnesses. F&H Manufacturing, Inc. is a machine shop that serves as a supplier to Ford. Tec Express started in 1992 and serves General Motors as an exclusive national redistribution site for transmissions that are covered under dealer warranties.

CONCLUSION

In the 1990s, as Americans—indeed, people the world over—struggle with getting people off the welfare rolls and into the productive workforce, Focus: HOPE is a model of success. Not only has it placed more than 1,200 graduates in private sector jobs, it also operates a for-profit machine shop where its own graduates and volunteer retired machinists train others.

Cunningham and Josaitis are very clear about their own personal commitment and the fact that they are working with their clients in the struggle. As the students work to prepare themselves for self-sufficiency, Cunningham and Josaitis work alongside them, energetically raising funds, seeking new business opportunities, spreading the Focus: HOPE message, and creating a space where the students can thrive. They take meticulous care in all aspects of the environment—from the striking gardens and trees to the clean, graffiti-free retrofitted buildings making up the Focus: HOPE complex in inner-city Detroit. Once bombed out and abandoned buildings are now totally modernized.

The Child Development Center is high-tech, with computers for the kids as well as clean, modern interior design, all supportive of the tasks to be accomplished. Even the layout of its food distribution center is carefully thought out to look as much like a regular grocery store as possible. There are regular check-out lines, and the food is bagged, just like at the local supermarket. Such attention to detail serves multiple purposes: it helps to maintain the dignity of the clients; provides a model to the children of what it means to go to a store; and reflects the fundamental truth that Focus: HOPE sees itself and those it serves not as a charity for indigents but as a successful business serving equally successful clients.

The evolution of Focus: HOPE is a textbook example of leaders recognizing the complexity of social problems and proactively pursuing systemic solutions. These leaders have neither chosen to approach the problem with an eye toward public relations, nor have they thrown up their hands and declared the situation a lost cause. For tax purposes, Focus: HOPE may qualify as charity, but it is run according to serious, no-nonsense business principles. Like winning corporations, Focus: HOPE provides its clients/workers with a clear strategy—in this case, attaining economic self-sufficiency. It provides them with the necessary skills, both the job-specific ones needed to be a good machinist and the personal ones related to attendance, attire, and the demeanor needed to be a good employee. And it creates the energy to reach its lofty goals by supporting and encouraging those who have the determination to succeed.

The readers of this book can find no better example of an organization that has refined the art of corporate citizenship to the level of science and business than Focus: HOPE. It combines the best of local initiative with global thinking to ensure that the local students who graduate from its advanced programs are not only proficient in technology but also in a minimum of two languages other than English.

The energy and drive behind Focus: HOPE reflects a personal commitment far beyond what most organizations would be willing to commit to social activities, but the impact of their programs should give even the most hardened critics of social responsibility pause. For Focus: HOPE is not just about helping people, it is about excelling in business and creating enormous value for the organization and society as a whole. In that, it serves as a model to the world.

ENDNOTES

1. Taken from the MacNeil-Lehrer Report segment on Focus: HOPE. Public Broadcasting System, August 5, 1992.
2. Taken from the University of Michigan Business School's Business Leadership Awards acceptance speech by Father Cunningham, March 2, 1993.
3. See Business Leadership Awards.
4. *PR Newswire,* June 12, 1995.
5. *New York Times*, April 21, 1996, C1.
6. See Business Leadership Awards.
7. See *Corporate Detroit Magazine,* "Tech Trek," 7/95.
8. *Dallas Morning News,* 12/5/95, 13A.
9. See *Corporate Detroit Magazine,* "Engineering Change," 7/95.
10. University of Detroit Mercy, Wayne State University, Lawrence Technological University, and Central State in Ohio.
11. Taken from Ford Capstone Leadership Program speech at Focus: HOPE, April 22, 1996.
12. See Business Leadership Awards transcript.

18

AN AGENDA FOR CORPORATE GLOBAL CITIZENSHIP

Noel M. Tichy, Andrew R. McGill, and Lynda St. Clair

CORPORATE GLOBAL CITIZENSHIP'S time has come. It is no longer charity, no longer guilt money, no longer corporate do-goodism, no longer payoffs to satisfy a constituent, no longer the "chump-change" of the rich—more like a ticket-punch for the Social Register than the heartfelt energy that comes from getting down in the dirt with a less fortunate human being.

Those days of leading with the checkbook are over. To be sure, corporate global citizenship still requires money—lots of money. But much more, it requires heart and soul—human commitment, time, hours, energy. It requires leaders at every level of a corporation giving of their time to talk and listen, model and mentor, work hand-in-hand, counsel and cajole—leaders providing tough lessons and tough love.

A picture helps. Imagine Robert Knowling, a towering 290-pound former football All-American in the streets of Cleveland as part of an Ameritech team working to clean up the government-subsidized house of a family that is fresh from a homeless shelter. The mother and three children were very proud of their new home. But a skeptical eight-year-old—the man of the house—wanted to know everything Knowling and his team planned: weeding and cleaning, planting, painting, fence repair. "This flower should go here," the eight-year-old said, pointing. "This over there." He had a vision for what his house would become. "And the little kids need to help," their big brother added. "They need to own something that lives so they can care for it and help it grow." For six hours in the yard, Knowling worked side-by-side with the eight-year-old, talking and sharing as they worked. The home improvement was remarkable. Near the end of the day, Knowling asked the precocious youngster about his role models and whom he admired. "I never had anyone before today," the youngster replied, leaning against a teary-eyed Knowling. Money can't buy that caring imprint and what it did to the growth potential of one young man.

Multiply Knowling by 67,000 other employees at Ameritech. Multiply Ameritech by 999 other corporations in the *Fortune* 1000. Add the millions of smaller corporations—the dominant employers in the United States—that never make any lists. Do the same across the Americas. Add Europe and Asia. Suddenly, the seemingly impossible becomes reality. The scale is huge and significant—the time asked of any single individual minuscule when compared with the gain, coming together in a whole panorama of better lives the world over. This is what corporate global citizenship can become.

Recall the miraculous achievements of Focus: HOPE, which began as an inner-city program to nourish babies so their brains wouldn't deteriorate and rose to move some of those babies through its Advanced Engineering Center, the most high-tech, hands-on engineering graduate school in the world. Here, the visionary Father William Cunningham saw in the aftermath of a devastating riot the potential to build black-white relations and provide equity through real skills and ability, not handouts. The sequence is elegant in its simplicity: provide food to nourish people, teach skills to make them fully employable in well-paying jobs, offer quality day care so they needn't worry about their children, provide advanced education to enhance their skills, operate profitable manufacturing businesses to keep the wheels turning and advancing, share your model with the world. What began in the blood-drenched streets of Detroit beckons to be transplanted and adapted the world over, as corporations strive to improve the communities in which they do business. This is corporate global citizenship.

Corporate global citizenship is the price of admission to the 21st century—the century of the global corporation, the century of interdependence, the century of committed corporate citizenship—not itinerant corporate exploitation—the century of doing for others what governments can't or won't do, the century of making every place your corporate logo hangs a little bit better off for your presence.

BUSINESS AND CORPORATE GLOBAL CITIZENSHIP

Successful admission to the 21st century rests on the five cornerstones of corporate global citizenship that we introduced at the beginning of this book: understanding, values, commitment, actions, and cooperation (See Figure 18.1).

Understanding is the most basic requirement of any global business decision. What skills are required? What skills do local people possess? How can these be upgraded through training? What are the most significant social-cultural issues? How can they be supported and advanced? What must be done to enhance, not damage, the local environment?

Values represent an organization's core. Some choose hell-bent profit-making for shareholders at the expense of all else. Others see the world in a longer time frame and look for profits now and in the future. Hence, they want to optimize the potential of people—their employees (as workers) and their neighbors (as potential consumers and future employees.) They seek to replenish the environment, not deplete it, so it can contribute to their success in the short and long term.

Commitment comes from the courage to stick to these values in good times and bad. It requires a religious-like faith that doing the right things will pay off in the long run, not only in good feelings but in good busi-

Figure 18.1.   The Corporate Global Citizenship Approach.

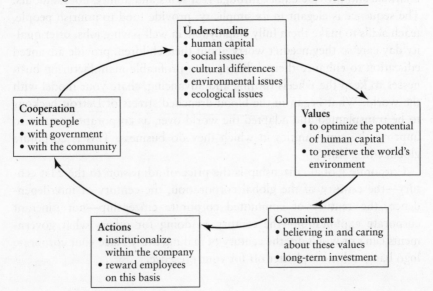

ness. And it requires having the courage to share these commitments with stockholders and help them understand and share in the value of following such a course.

Actions are the way these values and commitments become institutionalized in an organization. Do they receive action or lip-service from leaders? Are employees rewarded or promoted based on the importance they place on these beliefs? Does the corporation see a growth in its own human potential through these activities?

Cooperation represents the thread binding the entire citizenship process, for it acknowledges that only when people, government, and their communities work together can the full potential—the synergy—be achieved.

These elements form the core of most successful business leaders' vision. They also are at the root of corporate global citizenship. Business and its communities become intertwined, the people of the corporation and their citizen neighbors. They are interdependent. And just as business is finding in relationships throughout the chain from supplier to customer, one can no longer succeed—not for long, anyway—at the expense of those around them. But they can thrive by working together.

Against this backdrop, corporate global citizenship cannot be an afterthought. It must be core—part of everyday life in every organization. The brilliant social philosopher Amitai Etzioni, business strategist Charles Fombrun, and public policy researcher Mary Beth Tschirhart agree on this essential conclusion, despite their disparate starting points. Only through working together can government, nonprofit organizations, business, and individuals—each doing what they know best—conquer the health, nourishment, educational, housing, employment, environmental, and economic challenges facing a fast-developing world.

MIRACLES CAN HAPPEN

We have detailed some powerful first efforts. In education, recall the work of American Express and General Electric. American Express has combined with Hungarian governmental and nonprofit agencies to teach developing-country nationals the essentials of the travel business so that they, not foreign workers, can be employed as the industry unfolds in their homeland. This is progressive for the local community. And it also benefits American Express by having an employee population skilled at selling and delivering travel services, with at least a predisposition toward American Express. GE's efforts at affiliating with high schools in cities where its businesses are located provides a strong enhancement of science and math skills—areas where Americans have been deficient on a global scale traditionally—in communities from which GE will hire its next generation of workers. GE's Elfun Society volunteers serve as mentors to help the students learn and apply the skills they are taught. Again not merely altruistic, these same students become the population from which GE will hire its next generation of workers—people who need to have science and math skills to be successful. This is corporate global citizenship.

In the environmental arena, consider Compaq Computer and Procter & Gamble. Compaq's commitment to the energy-efficient, totally recyclable computer, first released in 1995, includes choosing design and components that lend themselves to easy service, upgradability and, eventually, dismantling and recycling. That commitment doesn't stop with the product. Compaq strives to eliminate emissions in the manufacturing process and even chooses its suppliers with the same goals in mind. Similarly, P&G voices a strong belief that "it is possible for humankind to progress without damaging the earth." Hence, P&G has maximized its efforts at producing "green" products that are environmentally friendly, while conserving energy and reducing the strain on the environment and recycling whatever is left over through composting and other techniques. P&G extends its practices to other stakeholders and shares best practices in environmental care with other corporations. While their environmental efforts help protect Compaq and P&G from potentially new restrictive regulations, ensuring their continued financial leadership in their respective industries, their efforts are not altogether self-serving. The efforts of both Compaq and P&G represent important gains on the road to sustainable development, a road to which there is, as described by our colleague, Professor Stuart Hart, no sensible alternative. As the world population increases, and rising demand for resources of every type produces growing environmental strain, the importance of sustainability cannot be overemphasized. It presents the only viable alternative to downright depletion. Getting this right is corporate global citizenship.

In health care, few have gone so far as Merck. Initially, the pharmaceutical maker had hoped to find commercial value in the human application of a drug that prevents a disease called river blindness, a disease rampant along the polluted waterways of Africa and South America. The drug had been medically and financially successful in Merck's veterinary business but became ensnared in the bureaucratic logjams of governments and nonprofit organizations when it came to its application to human beings—an example, perhaps, of how *not* to accomplish partnerships among business, government, and nonprofits. Merck persevered for more than a decade, but in the end its executives became so frustrated that they gave up on the product's commercial potential and agreed to provide it free to whomever needed it for as long as they needed it. Merck, the world's most admired corporation at the time according to *Fortune* magazine, has since saved tens of thousands of impoverished people from going blind. This underscores its commitment to people all over the world and to their health, with apparently little or no direct gains financially and the added costs of producing the drugs. Such a commitment to help humanity is corporate global citizenship.

In finance, J.P. Morgan has provided what often proves to be the most difficult obstacle for minorities and those less fortunate financially in starting up a business: money. Working through nonprofit and government agencies, Morgan has provided seed money, underwritten real estate, and invested direct capital in a variety of situations in New York City—most notably investing in a Ben & Jerry's ice cream store start-up in Harlem. But Morgan's efforts really begin in the city's high schools, where bankers work directly with teachers to improve their skills and teaching ability. As such, they are better able to produce educated youngsters with a better chance of being employable. In helping its community, Morgan certainly helps itself by producing future potential depositors, borrowers, and employees. But it also gives the less fortunate in its community an advantage. That is corporate global citizenship.

In serving their communities, it would be difficult to find better models than Ameritech or Sara Lee. Ameritech has shown itself to be more than just another telephone company by rallying employees like former executive Robert Knowling to paint and upgrade inner-city housing, deliver food to poor people or the infirm, help children learn to read, and a host of similar hands-on activities. Along the way, the Ameritech employees learn from interacting with their "clients" and sometimes even find business opportunities in learning how to serve them better. Likewise, Sara Lee employees work in a variety of ventures determined by its myriad of local subsidiaries and plants. They look to provide what would most benefit their local communities. While certainly a brand-equity enhancer for Ameritech and Sara Lee, their efforts also serve to bring them closer to their customers, to learn their needs and dreams, and sometimes to provide initial steps in those directions. That is corporate global citizenship.

Talk to anyone involved in any of the companies at the forefront of corporate global citizenship efforts, and one common takeaway will be the rich feeling they get from just being involved. For executives who spend most of their time inside hallowed corporate walls, it is an eye-opening opportunity to move outside. For those frustrated at their ability to exert much influence, it presents an opportunity to teach and lead eager followers. For those swamped by everyday corporate demands, it provides perspective. And for those sincerely wanting to make a difference, it provides a place to start.

A TIME FOR PROLIFERATION

This is only a beginning. Corporate global citizenship activities need to proliferate and show more and deeper commitment. They need to be more deeply connected to the corporate soul, not as a social obligation but as a cornerstone of good global business. Toward that end, three beliefs are essential—as outlined by our eminent sociologist colleague, Charles Kadushin: the belief (1) that citizenship activities are not only morally good but also contribute to the internal welfare of the organization and are economically beneficial, (2) that "everybody is doing it" and that corporations seeking cutting-edge visibility should be participating also, and (3) there must be a social construct—language and code words—inside the corporation that helps streamline, validate, and reinforce participation, much as with the rest of daily business.

From this starting point, corporate leaders can begin to develop a vision of how they see themselves and their firm in a world of corporate global citizens. What type of organizations would they most like to affiliate with? How does corporate global citizenship mesh with their overall corporate strategy? How might corporate global citizenship provide a competitive advantage? How would they like to see things different in ten years, and what does the new picture look like? With those questions answered, a rough sketch begins to emerge of the corporation as corporate global citizen—through deliberateness, not happenstance. This provides a vision for the future, especially on a global scale.

Consider, for example, a manufacturing corporation looking to begin operations in a developing country in Southeast Asia (although it could be anywhere in the world). As in the past, the company starts with a plant that will employ local residents. But the good corporate global citizen won't stop there. That corporation will see the benefit—social and corporate—of providing more than jobs and income to the local citizens. Consider the opportunities to install: training and education facilities to enhance employee skills even before they begin work; medical care facilities for workers and their families; housing for plant workers and their families; a dining facility and commissary to provide quality food; libraries; computers; recreational facilities; preschool and day care for children; a public school. While adding significantly to the cost structure of the venture, these added investments can raise the skill and productivity capacity of the workers and enhance the employability of their children. Equally or more importantly, they help the local government resolve a plethora of social challenges and, in the process, may give the new corporate investor a preferred position in the eyes of the government. The company could invest in on-going education, where its best workers assist in high school and trade school development programs to train the next generation of workers. This helps the local citizens and the corporation with a long-term focus. This is corporate global citizenship.

Such opportunities will afford themselves thousands of times over in the 21st century. As the chapters on China and India—the world's two most populous countries with more than 2.1 billion people between them—point out, the opportunities are immense. So, too, for business challenges in a former Soviet Union with former Eastern Bloc allies anxious to get better at free-market business. Those chapters (Fourteen, Fifteen, and Sixteen) portray dichotomies between corporations that did well at entering these developing countries with good corporate global citizenship in mind and those that came in as traditional heavy-handed exploiters. In the main, the days of entering developing countries with a boomlet of media attention, big money investments in causes near and dear to political leaders, and hard pushes to ramrod approval processes—assuming social acceptance thereafter—may not be the best long-term strategies. Enron and Mars found that out in India and Russia, respectively. In contrast, an entry strategy focused on providing what local citizens need in conjunction with what the entering corporation desires—in short, corporate global citizenship—offers a far more optimistic course, as was found by McDonald's and Sam Pitroda in India, Nestle in Russia, Owens-Corning in China, and the Children's Television Workshop in Russia.

UNIQUE CHALLENGES OF CORPORATE GLOBAL CITIZENSHIP

According to philosopher J. R. Danley (1994):

> In the global arena, there is no longer necessarily a congruence of interests between the major core corporations and the interests of the nation. There is no longer, if there ever was, much managerial flexibility. There is little room for sentimental attachments to regions or nations, for emotional ties to traditional labor resources or capital, or for cultural scruples against the penetration of new markets with products which are of dubious appropriateness there [p. 283].

In this book, we have emphasized the benefits of corporate global citizenship activities for society and for the companies that engage in those activities. We believe that such a positive emphasis is appropriate because the benefits of well-conceived and executed corporate global citizenship programs are indeed extraordinary. No discussion of corporate global citizenship would be complete, however, without recognizing that corporate global citizenship activities are not always successful, nor are they uniformly lauded.

As mentioned in the Introduction, some people believe strongly that when corporations engage in citizenship activities, they are going beyond their designated role. Not everyone agrees that businesses have some responsibility to the communities in which they operate. Some individuals believe that by engaging in corporate global citizenship, organizations are usurping the authority of the company's owners to decide where and how to contribute the profits of the corporation. Thus, organizations that believe corporate global citizenship is an imperative must first overcome the resistance of shareholders who regard these activities as inappropriate.

Even when there is agreement that corporations do have responsibilities to the communities in which they operate, there is often disagreement about how those responsibilities should be met. As demonstrated in many cases in this book, notably in the cases of J.P. Morgan and Merck, companies can be very effective if they take advantage of their core business competencies when developing their corporate global citizenship agendas. Unfortunately, it is often the case that there are unintended and unexpected consequences with any type of intervention. For example, economic development is often at odds with environmental protection. Similarly, providing antibiotics for disease control will only be effective if the drugs are taken correctly. Failure by patients to complete their course of treatment may lead to the emergence of new strains of diseases that are more resistant to treatment. Thus it may be considered insufficient to provide the medication without providing sufficient support services to ensure that the antibiotics are used appropriately. Such expanded responsibility is very costly and is also likely to take a company beyond its area of expertise.

Other examples of unintended consequences can cause companies to appear as villains, even when their original intentions were benevolent. In some cases, as Ackerman and Bauer (1975, p. 19) point out, attitudes change. What was once socially acceptable and even desirable later becomes anathema (for example, disposable plastic containers). In other cases, it is a question of focusing on short-term versus long-term needs.

For example, providing food distribution programs in underdeveloped regions may undermine efforts to improve agricultural production in those areas. As a consequence, those regions may become more and more dependent on imported foodstuffs to feed their populations. Similarly, providing education and training without creating opportunities for people to use that education may reduce satisfaction and encourage violence. Although some organizations such as Focus: HOPE have been exceedingly careful to develop their programs with an eye toward eliminating these types of unintended consequences, companies that are ultimately responsible to anxious shareholders may choose to forego engaging in corporate global citizenship activities rather than risk their reputations on an intervention that might, in retrospect, appear to have been ill-conceived at best or, at worst, an intentional plot to increase a community's dependence on the products or services of the organization.

For a multinational company, the question of how to behave in a socially responsible manner is greatly complicated. Like any organization, a multinational must address whether the interests of internal company shareholders should take precedence over "socially responsible" actions. Multinationals, however, have even more complicated agendas because the interests and values of different countries in which they operate may lead to different conclusions about the appropriate course of action. For example, from a local community perspective, closing a plant in the United States and relocating the work to a Third World country where labor is far less expensive seems like an example of poor social responsibility. If, however, the level of analysis is raised to the global community, it may turn out that the overall benefits to society are enhanced by providing opportunities to work and produce income in an area that otherwise would be destitute, with no opportunities to rise out of the depths of poverty. This is not to endorse one argument over the other, only to illustrate the conflicting aspects of some decisions in a global environment.

Finally, one of the biggest challenges to corporate global citizenship programs is motivational. The sheer magnitude of the undertaking at times is likely to overwhelm even the most dedicated reformer. Social problems tend to travel in packs. As the founders of Focus: HOPE recognized, poverty, poor health, and nutrition, and a lack of skills and opportunities for success, go hand in hand. Given limited resources, companies must make choices about where they will concentrate their energies. We must all overcome our tendencies to throw up our hands and declare the problem too big to be solved. Rather, we must each roll up our sleeves and ask, What can we do now?

GETTING STARTED

Skeptics should not feel that this discourse has provided them a rationale for doing nothing. Rather, they should take a chance—experiment for the good of mankind. In so doing, here's a suggested path to corporate global citizenship:

1. Take the corporate global citizenship Mirror Test as follows. When you evaluate business results, ask not only how they served your needs through profits and served your customers' needs through products or services but how they served your communities socially and environmentally. Future business success means doing equally well on all three dimensions.

2. If you're still skeptical that corporate global citizenship is little more than corporate do-goodism, try it once or twice, and give it the same consideration you would a new movie: a willing suspension of disbelief. When you're done ask, Are the people of the community better off? Is the business better off? Is our image enhanced? Do our corporate employees feel energized and better about themselves? And, finally, do I feel better about myself, and have I done something I'd be proud to go home and tell my children about?

3. Resist the temptation to rely on a corporate bureaucracy to oversee or coordinate your efforts at corporate global citizenship. Instead, make active commitment—in time, energy, and creativity, as well as money—a criterion upon which future leaders are evaluated for success and promotion. This may seem a heavy-handed way of forcing participation. Perhaps it is. But more importantly, it is a quite appropriate means of identifying future leaders with values important to the corporation in a 21st-century world. Those who hold differing values and attitudes may simply be selfselecting themselves out of consideration for future top jobs because they aren't right for the times.

4. Proliferate the process. Involving your suppliers and customers can make for a very rich interaction outside of normal work activity. In the process, teamwork improves and people form strong human relationships and bonds of trust and interdependence—qualities that also improve their ability to work together professionally and partner and depend upon one another.

CONCLUSION

In spite of the challenges, we remain resolutely convinced that corporations *can, should, and must* contribute to the global community. We can imagine no other scenario in which the pressing problems of population growth, inequities in the distribution of wealth and the depletion of environmental resources can begin to be addressed. The migration of power into the hands of global corporations requires a similar migration of responsibility and accountability. Expertise provides a further argument for the assumption of responsibility for global society by corporate entities. We are firmly convinced that corporate global citizenship is necessary and beneficial. We are not, however, blind to the difficulties and complexities that face companies as they engage in corporate global citizenship activities under the watchful view of multiple constituents. We are merely convinced that only those companies that manage to contribute to and sustain the communities in which they operate will be able to remain acceptable organizations in the public's eye in the 21st century and beyond.

REFERENCES

Ackerman, R. and Bauer, R. *Corporate Social Responsiveness: The Modern Dilemma*, Reston, Va.: Reston Publishing Company, Inc., 1976.

Danley, J. R. *The Role of the Modern Corporation in a Free Society.* Notre Dame: University of Notre Dame Press, 1994.

APPENDIX: COMPANY PROFILES AND CITIZENSHIP PROGRAMS

Charles Kadushin and Laurie Richardson

THE INFORMATION TO BE PRESENTED in this section was obtained by researchers under a grant from the Commonwealth Fund (Grant #92–41) at the University of Michigan Business School. The researchers who gathered the information were attempting to understand the underlying causal issues for a new era of corporate involvement with pressing community problems. *Their findings became the core base of knowledge from which the chapters and cases in this book were developed.*

The researchers conducted a comprehensive, analytical review of the nature and extent of corporate community programs. A survey team compiled an inventory of citizenship projects being undertaken by 12 companies that were members of the University of Michigan Business School's Global Leadership Consortium. The purpose of the survey was to provide a sense of the rationales for corporate citizenship as seen by the corporations themselves, the level of effort companies are making to improve the health and well-being of their communities, and the types of projects under way and how they are organized and managed by the companies.

This Appendix includes a summary of the information gathered in the course of that survey, which was conducted from March through September, 1992. Included is information about the rationales that companies used for explaining their participation in citizenship activities, descriptions of the structures that companies used to manage their citizenship activities, and a listing of the specific citizenship programs that companies had in place at the time of the survey.

THE RATIONALES FOR CITIZENSHIP ACTIVITIES

Every firm that engages in citizenship programs also offers a rationale for its community involvement, which is contained in the firm's annual report, in reports or brochures about the firm's foundation or corporate giving unit, or in written descriptions of citizenship programs. We examined company positions that have been institutionalized by being written down in publicly available literature. That the firms are impelled to offer a reason for engaging in citizenship is in itself worthy of note. While every firm has a "mission statement," firms do not necessarily have to state publicly why they exist or what their right to exist is. But citizenship is something that every profit-driven firm seems to have to justify in some way. Three kinds of rationales or reasons for involvement were offered in the corporate literature we surveyed: *practical, relational or contractual,* and/ or *moral.*

Among the practical rationales offered are those that insist that citizenship activities directly benefit the firm. These direct benefits can be internal to the firm, affecting its employees and the way they do business. Other kinds of direct benefits affect the firm's external environment, making it more favorable to the firm's profit-making activities. One such external benefit is making the firm generally more competitive. Another direct, external benefit lies in making the firm more attractive to future employees, thus ensuring a more capable workforce. There are also practical advantages of a citizenship program that indirectly benefits the firm. Most typical is the feeling that by educating people who are not members of the firm, the company eventually acquires a better-trained workforce. The final practical reason sees the firm as embedded in the community so that anything that benefits the community benefits the firm.

The practical advantages of citizenship are obvious. A more complex relational or contractual rationale explains that the firm has either a contractual relationship with the community that requires it to give something back to the community, or that the firm has relationships and obligations to groups other than its stockholders.

The most fundamental reason for corporate citizenship is an absolute moral one: because it is the right thing to do. Finally, there is a moral reason involved in explicitly making amends for past wrong-doings.

More than half of the firms (7 out of 12) find citizenship programs directly good for the firm because they positively affect the firm's environment. Seven firms find the practical value of a citizenship program in the embeddedness of the firm in the community; whatever benefits the community benefits the firm, and the reverse. About half of the firms pose a social contract argument, thus directly attacking the notion that only shareholders are stakeholders. Most talk about giving things back to the community. All of the companies in the survey saw citizenship as the morally right thing to do.

It is important to bear in mind that the reasons each firm gives for its citizenship program are very much driven by its own distinct history, its product line, and the particular interests of its CEO. The reasons are not ephemeral rationalizations; they are an integral part of the way the corporation does business. To the extent that each corporation is unique, so are its sets of reasons for engaging in citizenship activities.

THE ORGANIZATIONAL STRUCTURES OF CITIZENSHIP ACTIVITIES

By analyzing the organizational and structural attributes of corporate citizenship in the sampled companies, we hoped to develop a better understanding of how corporate citizenship fits within the overall structure of corporations. This should help in understanding why and to what extent some companies are involved in their communities, and why they do so with particular programs.

We collected information on nine characteristics of corporate citizenship structure. First, we noted the general place that citizenship programs have in the company and their relation to the overall operations of the company. We also noted the size and degree of professionalization of related staff people. How the corporation controls giving also concerned us. Most of the corporations have giving and/or policy committees that report directly or indirectly to the board, suggesting that senior management attempts to keep some control over corporate giving and other citizenship activities.

In most of the companies, citizenship activities are carried out by a corporate foundation, a corporate giving program, and direct corporate contributions. Citizenship programs—both corporate giving and employee volunteering programs—may be dominated by the corporate foundation or other structure, implying direct corporate control. The foundation may be controlled by the corporation or a corporate department, usually public or community affairs staffs. The staff handling citizenship activities often falls under a corporate department, while still having access to foundation funds. In these cases, the foundation may have no staff working directly for it, suggesting that the foundation serves as a holding tank for citizenship funds rather than an actor in the giving program.

We differentiated between companies whose citizenship efforts were proactive and those that were reactive. The difference emanated from the existence of multilevel decision-making authority and the size of the staff responsible for citizenship programs. In a sense, all programs are proactive, since each decides how and where it should contribute. For our purposes, "proactive" referred to those corporations that seemed to make efforts to operate as change agents, actively seeking to influence the areas in which they are involved.

In the proactive group, all of the companies have a large staff and a complex structure. For the most part, the reverse holds for the reactive group, with mostly small staffs and simple structures. We could also interpret the lack of readily available and accessible information as an indication of the level of citizenship commitment of these firms.

The data suggest that the corporate board and/or top-level committees are instrumental in creating proactive citizenship programs. When the time they can devote to citizenship activities is filled with reviewing and deciding on proposals, senior management—or those in charge of citizenship—may have little time left to develop the strategic posture necessary for a proactive program. By spreading the decision-making authority to lower levels, a corporation frees its senior management from these responsibilities, which otherwise prevent it from implementing proactive citizenship.

The existence of volunteer programs was at the core of our interests. Volunteer programs may be run through a public relations or community affairs office, through the foundation, or through some other arrangement. Those corporations categorized as proactive have more predominant volunteer programs. While most of the reactive companies have such programs as well, theirs do not exist on the same scale. Thus, an extensive volunteer program may require a large staff and multilevel decision-making authority. Significant volunteerism and general proactivity go hand in hand.

THE CITIZENSHIP PROGRAMS, SOCIAL PROBLEMS ADDRESSED, BENEFICIARIES, AND FOCUS

One part of the institutional character of corporate social policy is that it consists of a number of discrete programs, each with a definite social problem focus, a (generally fixed) term, and a localized target population. By evaluating the types of programs and assistance provided to communities, we attempt to understand how (and whether) these programs can add up to a coherent and effective corporate social policy.

Based on information on approximately 200 programs from 12 companies, we compiled an inventory and typology of programs, which is not intended to be exhaustive but representative of what the companies are most proud of. Areas addressed in corporate citizenship programs included employment, neighborhood deterioration, racial inequality, women's issues, hunger, substance abuse, homelessness, health, the disabled, the elderly, education, and the environment. These programs can be grouped into three areas: problems related to poverty, social inequality, and the "underclass"; problems related to "natural" handicaps; and societywide problems.

Education, the environment, and health are areas of activity for almost all of the companies surveyed. These problems are the ones most easily identified as having to do with public goods and are easily justified in terms of payoffs to the company. The social problems area and the handicaps area are distinguished by the relative safety and political uncomplicatedness of the latter and the fact that, for the most part, corporate activity cannot be seen as a cause of the latter.

How a company conceptualizes its relationship to the community seems to influence the areas in which it is active as a corporate citizen. Companies that articulate an awareness of their obligation to the community or society in which they operate tend to have programs that try to ameliorate basic social problems.

Corporate community programs are often seen as models of how a particular social problem can be dealt with, but in exploiting the luxury of being able to choose the areas it gets involved in, the corporate citizen chooses a version of the social contract that differs from the public sector. It can avoid dealing with the gigantic scale and scope of most social problems. Another important difference between private sector social contract and public sector social contract is that the former can be involved without any mechanisms of accountability to the people who are, or are not, helped by their actions.

Companies vary in the number of different areas addressed by their best-practice programs. Companies that state that a well-focused giving program is more effective than one that tries to be involved in too many areas do not necessarily demonstrate a high degree of focus in their best-practice programs. The inherent complexity of real-world social problems can involve companies in all sorts of things, despite the corporate policy emphasis on focus.

TYPES OF ASSISTANCE PROVIDED BY CORPORATE CITIZENSHIP PROGRAMS

The citizenship programs highlighted by the surveyed companies involved different forms of assistance to nonprofits and community organizations. Financial assistance includes grants, scholarships, matching funds, awards, and internships or jobs. Materials provided include equipment and facilities, either donated or loaned. Employee volunteers include top executives and rank and file. Most donations of equipment and facilities were in conjunction with volunteer programs.

EMPLOYEE VOLUNTEER PROGRAMS

Programs involving volunteering in one form or another were highlighted by almost all of the companies surveyed. Volunteer programs are generally outnumbered by cash programs, but for several companies, volunteer activities seem to form a large part of what they are proud of.

Volunteer citizenship activity varies according to content (problems addressed and beneficiaries), the level/kind of organizational involvement on the part of the company, and the general type of the program. The salient questions for our study included: What does the company have to offer? What sort of problem is being addressed? In what way is the company involved in organizing and supporting the program? What use is being made of company personnel?

The content of volunteer programs varies widely; work in schools is common, but volunteers also work in nonprofits and community organizations. Most companies do not keep track of the numbers of employees involved in volunteer activities. It is not possible to determine the degree to which program content derives from what employees are inclined to do, what the company thinks they ought to do, and what the needs of the community might be.

A distinction can be made between volunteer programs that make use of indigenous company skills and those that do not. Many programs do not emphasize work skills at all, suggesting that the company sees itself as being able to organize and channel significant numbers of willing and able persons, as opposed to being a repository of specific skills.

There are four identifiable kinds of organizational support for or involvement in volunteerism: encouragement, facilitation, supplementary support, and underwriting. Encouragement involves various forms of telling employees that volunteering is a good idea. Facilitation includes variations on having a volunteer coordination office. Under supplementary support, we include grants to schools and nonprofits where employees volunteer and internships funded by the company. Underwritten volunteer activity involves employees working in the community on company time.

At first glance, these different kinds of organizational support for volunteer programs suggest a scale of levels of involvement. Despite the different levels of organizational support, in many cases employees could just as easily volunteer with the same organizations on their own. What, beyond the provision of resources, is the real value added of the companies' involvement?

In the best-practice volunteer programs of the companies in the survey, volunteer activities fit into four broad categories: (1) placement in existing community organizations, including staff positions, consulting and advising, and sitting on boards; (2) teaching, tutoring, and so forth, in schools; (3) company-based initiatives; and (4) involvement in extracorporate drives and projects.

In the first two categories, corporate citizenship "happens" insofar as employees volunteer as individuals in their role as employee. Companies are sources of bodies to which skills, status, and resources are attached, by virtue of the bodies' membership in the company. The company plays the role of good citizen by supplying brokering information (to connect potential volunteers with schools and organizations) and incentives (material or ideological or both).

In both company-based initiatives and participation in extracorporate drives and projects, the company serves as more than a broker and a supplier of willing bodies. In these cases, the company provides a structure in which it is easy to organize people to do things, and what needs to be added to make corporate citizenship happen is the vision or idea (and a sponsor) and the authority and space for the ensuing activity. What the company has to offer—the value added it provides—derives in part from the fact that it is an organization, not just from material resources it can supply.

SUMMARY OF SURVEY FINDINGS

Volunteer activity is an important part of corporate citizenship in almost all of the 12 companies surveyed. The form and content of corporate citizenship in each company appears to be a reflection of the goals and values of the respective corporate leadership, though all agree that one reason to engage in corporate citizenship is simply that it is the right thing to do. But there is no standard pattern. Volunteerism is directed toward a wide variety of targets and fits into company organizations in quite diverse ways.

Two aspects of corporations as organizations are exploited through the organization of employee volunteerism. One builds on the corporation as an aggregate repository of socially useful skills, directable resources, and high social status; the other leverages the corporation as an organization that can direct groups of people toward goals that stem from a vision of corporate success, which goes beyond the production of goods and services for profit. Which type of approach is more socially valuable remains an issue for further research.

When corporate goals and rationales for citizenship focus on corporate volunteer activities, the paradoxical nature of corporate citizenship becomes more apparent. Not responsible either to community-based trustees as are nonprofit organizations nor to voters as are government organizations, corporations are free to pick and choose projects where they feel their resources can have the greatest impact. Freedom also means lack of accountability; this can be seen in the dearth of evaluations of the impact of citizenship programs on the community and on the corporation itself.

One message from this research is that taking citizenship seriously means holding citizenship programs to the same standards of accountability as other corporate programs—an aspect that was conspicuously absent from most of the citizenship undertakings analyzed in the survey.

COMPANY PROFILE: AMERICAN EXPRESS

Rationale for Citizenship Activities

A philanthropic program reflects the values of the company that sponsors it. At American Express, our programs are as diverse as the people they serve. As a global company, we support programs around the world. The communities and the countries where our philanthropic program operates are where our employees and our customers live and work. We take philanthropy seriously. That seriousness is evident both in the level of financial resources we commit and in the personal involvement of management and employees. We take an entrepreneurial, creative approach to philanthropy, just as we do to managing our business. . . . We have found that partnerships work, and that the public and private sectors—profit and nonprofit—working together can develop new solutions to tough problems. . . . Our philanthropic activities focus on three themes: community service; education and employment; and cultural diversity and national heritage.

We do this because: It's the right thing to do. The health of our business and the well-being of society are interdependent. Our record in the community helps attract and retain the best employees, clients, and business partners.

American Express is a company that understands it has other responsibilities, too. This is reflected in our initiatives in consumer affairs and volunteerism, and in our advocacy on behalf of issues affecting the communities where our employees live and in which we do business. It is reflected in the funds we commit each year to a broad range of cultural and philanthropic activities.

Our integrity as a corporate citizen was tested last year when we discovered that our own code of conduct had been violated in a matter involving a private banking competitor, Edmond Safra. We promptly acknowledged the problem, and made a sizeable charitable contribution as a gesture of conciliation and good will.

Organizational Structure of Citizenship Activities

At American Express, the audit and public responsibility committee of the board of directors has general responsibilities to oversee, among other things, the charitable contributions of the corporation. It consults with management's public responsibility committee. But the American Express Philanthropic Program actually coordinates both direct corporate and foundation giving. The foundation contributions total about twice the direct giving of the corporation. Both corporate and foundation giving go primarily to American Express operating locations and to national and international organizations.

Proposals originate from local and regional committees, which also make recommendations and participate in project development. These philanthropy committees exist in 16 states and are made up of senior managers from the area American Express subsidiaries. Managers of these local committees complete the initial review of proposals and forward them to the appropriate committee for a funding decision. The trustees of the Program make the decisions for proposals requesting more than $15,000, but before a proposal reaches the trustees it is screened by the staff of seven full-time professionals, seven full-time support personnel, and one part-time professional. If less than this amount, the decision falls to one of the state or regional committees.

Corporate departments also make contributions directly from their own funds.

American Express gives priority to projects over general support, to partnerships, to giving that involves more than grant support, and to high-profile grants demonstrating American Express's commitment to communities. The company attempts to provide a leadership role in the community through its citizenship activity and strongly encourages senior managers to participate in and promote good citizenship.

Specific Citizenship Programs

GENERAL PROGRAM AREA—EDUCATION AND EMPLOYMENT. The focus is on (1) preparing youth for employment, (2) promoting education reform from early childhood to secondary level, (3) work/family issues like child care, and (4) increasing literacy in geography.

We recognize that our future is tied to how well we educate the current generation. Grants in this area address education and workforce issues that are especially acute in the service sector.

GENERAL PROGRAM AREA—CULTURAL PROGRAMS. The focus is on (1) bringing projects to a larger audience, (2) increasing accessibility and developing new audiences, (3) educating youth in the arts, (4) preserving historic and cultural assets, and (5) encouraging innovative collaborations.

We believe that the arts and our cultural and national heritage make a vital contribution to the quality of life in our communities. As a global company we promote cultural diversity and cross-cultural communication.

GENERAL PROGRAM AREA—COMMUNITY SERVICE. The focus is on (1) critical human service needs: children at risk, drug abuse, AIDS, and homelessness; (2) promoting volunteerism to solve community problems with emphasis on projects with employee volunteer teams; and (3) strengthening the nonprofit sector.

We are committed to being good citizens in our communities. The company provides financial resources, while employees give their time and talents to address critical social issues.

Debt-For-Nature Swap: Project was completed in Costa Rica, Brazil, and Argentina in 1990. American Express Bank is a pioneer in a new technique for ecological and environmental project financing, which gets repaid from fees from subsequent tourist visits to the nature preserves.

National Academy Foundation: Established to encourage and support partnerships between business and education, to strengthen the preparedness of the American workforce; will enrich the resources and opportunities available to high schools and their students interested in emerging and expanding careers.

The Academy of Finance is supported by the foundation; bridges the gap between classroom and workplace; helps students develop career skills, evaluate their own potential for success, and establish personal goals; an elective two-year program in public high schools for juniors and seniors that includes specialized courses and activities, paid internships, college-level experience, and a chance to develop personal contacts. AmEx created and is the principal corporate sponsor; contributes $2 million per year, seed grants, two members on the board, 100 internships, mentorships, curriculum assistance, and speakers.

NAF academies enhance community economic and social well-being by focusing successfully on workforce preparation, dropout prevention, and motivating students to continue their education.

In addition to the Academies of Finance are academies of Travel and Tourism, Public Service, and Manufacturing Sciences (with Ford Motor Company).

Fund for Curricular Development in Ethics—Harvard University: Supports the Program in Ethics and the Professions to give ethics a more prominent place in undergraduate core curriculum at the Kennedy School; contributed $1.5 million over five years.

Geography Competition: Addresses geographic illiteracy of young by showing it can be fun, useful, and rewarding. Philanthropic Program has given $700,000 over three years; Travel Related Services has given $1,745,000 over three years.

Fund for Central/Eastern Europe: Goal: to foster development of tourism in Czechoslovakia, Hungary, and Poland. A three-year commitment was made to spend $500,000. See detailed case study on American Express and the development of the Academy of Travel and Tourism in Hungary in Chapter Five, this volume.

Historic Preservation/Environmental Issues: Philanthropic program theme: Grants promoting environmentally responsible or "green" tourism. American Express is one of the few corporate leaders in the preservation of the historical and cultural resources so essential to tourism; preservation of natural resources like parks, preserves, and wilderness areas is a logical fit.

COMPANY PROFILE: AT&T

Rationale for Citizenship Activities

As a high-tech competitor and a world employer, AT&T's long-term needs and interests coincide broadly with those of society: an educated, healthy workforce; improved social services; cultural enrichment through the arts; and the benefits of the full contribution of all citizens.

Our business touches on so many lives and is so widely deployed that it is plainly in our self-interest to be engaged in community issues. In fact, by serving people who need help, we enhance our corporate image as a company that cares, and that gives us a competitive edge.

America's nonprofit sector remains strong, bolstered by continued business support. AT&T is proud to be part of business community efforts that help shape the educational, social, and cultural agendas of the nation. As the international part of our business continues to grow, we will also seek to contribute to the communities we call home beyond our shores.

AT&T's commitment to public service is an important heritage, born of a unique corporate history. In a rapidly changing world filled with serious problems as well as splendid opportunities, it represents a lifeline that reaches out to touch millions of lives, year in and year out. It reaches inward as well. By participating actively in nonprofit institutions and causes, AT&T people benefit from the opportunity to learn, to develop leadership skills, to enlarge their vision, and to multiply their relationships.

For more than 100 years, AT&T has been steadfastly committed to public service and social responsibility. From the beginning, we've recognized that our business interests are entwined with the well-being of our society. As a result, AT&T has developed an ethic of not just doing well but doing good. At the heart of our corporate citizenship is a set of beliefs. We believe in innovation—in taking risks and trying new approaches. We believe in diversity—that we are richer when we embrace our differences, and learn from them. We believe in equality—that everyone should have an equal opportunity to achieve success and independence. We believe in investment—that investing in the talents and potential of people benefits everyone in the long run.

Our tradition of social responsibility extends beyond our commitment to employee welfare. When we act to protect the environment, improve education and health programs, celebrate diversity, and stimulate artistic expression, we invest in the future of our communities and tomorrow's workforce—in essence, the future of our business.

Organizational Structure of Citizenship Activities

AT&T citizenship rests on the cash giving of the company-sponsored foundation, part of the Public Relations Department. The foundation is the primary vehicle for the company's philanthropy, and as such controls most of the giving budget. The foundation defines and communicates AT&T's corporate social responsibility philosophy and develops the context for a corporate perspective on citizenship activities. A board of trustees, made up of 18 people from various corporate units, heads the foundation, meeting quarterly to review grants, set up the strategic direction of the foundation, and discuss grant proposals requesting more than $25,000. Trustees are appointed for life and rotate positions. Grants under $25,000 but over $10,000 only need executive committee approval; grants under $10,000 can be made directly by the foundation.

The foundation concentrates on check writing on a national scale, although it does fund locally administered programs that involve hands-on activity. Local-level AT&T councils made up of local managers decide which of these requests to fund. Twelve professionals and six support personnel staff the foundation, which is still trying to find its place within the post-break-up corporation. Funding occurs primarily in four areas—education, health and social action, arts and culture, and public policy—each guided by a separate section of the foundation and each with a program officer, a staff manager, and a secretary. Funding for education represents about 50 percent of company giving.

Direct corporate donations concentrate on in-kind gift giving in communities in which AT&T has a significant presence. Proactive programs are considered the company's best practices. The foundation creates them with the help of internal and external consulting and technical committees. Although the core of citizenship activity reflects a unique corporate expertise, competence, and culture, the periphery might be influenced by the involvement of other corporations.

Specific Citizenship Programs

GENERAL PROGRAM AREA—EDUCATION. The aim is to keep America's workforce competitive and restore excellence to education, foster collaboration among parents and educators to reform our public schools, and improve teacher preparation.

The connection among all of AT&T's education grants is a stress on individual achievement. Whether dollars and resources are destined for junior faculty at a top research university or for students and teachers in an urban middle school, the emphasis of AT&T's gifts is squarely on people, and enabling them to get things done.

Strategies include: (1) to advance excellence in teaching and research in engineering and the physical sciences at universities important to AT&T by supporting projects of selected departments or development of new curricula; (2) to support institutions and organizations that encourage and support minorities and women in the pursuit of higher education; (3) to support projects that strengthen the infrastructure of education; (4) to support programs that ensure the strength of independent higher education at institutions and in communities important to AT&T; (5) to support collaborative school reform efforts in cities where AT&T has a significant presence; (6) to build the future human resource base for school professionals (teachers, principals).

Goals are (1) to assure quality in American education in engineering and science fields important to AT&T, to the communications industry, and to the competitiveness of the nation; (2) to provide educational opportunity for minorities and women and to increase the pool of minority talent for American industry; (3) to advance excellence in liberal arts education and maintain the unique balance of independent and public higher education in the U.S.; (4) to advance the national effort to improve K–12 education; (5) to enhance corporate visibility and brand identification.

GENERAL PROGRAM AREA—HEALTH AND SOCIAL ACTION. The focus centers on children and families, health, environment, and the United Way; represents 33 percent of the foundation's giving; focuses on projects that can serve as models.

Despite the diversity reflected in AT&T's support of health and social needs, all efforts incorporate widespread community involvement in order to find enduring support for the goals they address. As a result, changes brought about by AT&T Foundation grants can represent, it is hoped, enduring improvements, not temporary stop-gaps.

Goals are (education): to improve community-based education for children and adolescents leading to productive participation and self-sufficiency in work and society; (health): to increase the availability of health care and social services for medically indigent populations; (environment): to support environmental programs that complement AT&T's environmental goals; (diversity): to promote diversity in America's workforce and in society; (AT&T brand): to enhance corporate visibility and brand identification for AT&T.

GENERAL PROGRAM AREA—ARTS AND CULTURE. The area represents about 15 percent of funding. Goals are: (1) to foster creativity and improve the quality of life in communities where AT&T employees live and work; (2) to contribute to the economic vitality of communities where AT&T does business; (3) to enhance corporate visibility and brand identification for AT&T.

GENERAL PROGRAM AREA—ENVIRONMENT. As a good corporate citizen and a global company, AT&T takes seriously its responsibility to protect the planet. AT&T believes that . . . environmental protection is not only a social issue but a business imperative . . . industry-related environmental problems are the result of operating defects that can be remedied through better-quality management and new technology . . . (AT&T) is developing a range of programs to get at the root causes of environmental problems.

GENERAL PROGRAM AREA—INTERNATIONAL. The AT&T Foundation supports U.S.-based nonprofit institutions that study the flow of information across national borders and broad public policy issues such as trade and taxation.

Goals are (1) to support AT&T's business interests outside the U.S.; (2) to have an impact on the global community in which we live and do business; (3) to broaden the knowledge and perspective of AT&T managers and officers through active participation with nonprofit institutions focused on international issues; (4) to enhance corporate visibility and brand identification for AT&T.

University Equipment Donation Program: Largest non-cash giving activity in 1988 and 1989; program donated computers to universities, which cannot be done by the foundation.

Family Care Development Fund: Fund available to improve the quality and quantity of child and elder care.

Voices that Count: Created by units in charge of communications services, project allows students to voice their views in national polls using free phone service.

Telephone Pioneers of America: World's largest voluntary association of industrial employees; 30 percent of 800,000 members are from AT&T, which provides about 30 percent of operating income—$900,000; annual total about $10 million.

Pioneering gives employees the opportunity to gain personal satisfaction from volunteer work, to attain new leadership and organizational skills, and, most critically, to demonstrate AT&T's long tradition of excellent service in a visible, community-based role.

GENERAL PROGRAM AREA—PUBLIC POLICY. Strategies are (1) to support think tanks focused on the domestic public policy agenda on issues AT&T cares about; (2) to support initiatives that make the nonprofit sector more effective.

Goals are: (1) to influence the public debate on public policy issues that AT&T cares about; (2) to broaden the knowledge and perspectives of AT&T managers and officers through active participation with nonprofit institutions focused on domestic issues; (3) to support the continued growth and prosperity of the nonprofit sector.

COMPANY PROFILE: AMOCO

Rationale for Citizenship Activities

We are aware of national public policy and social policy issues that affect Amoco and the rest of the business sector. . . . Our goal is to enhance the company's image by actively helping to meet the immediate and future needs of the communities where Amoco operates.

We respect the individual rights and dignity of all people. Our individual and collective actions and talents create our competitive advantage.

Amoco is committed to giving back to the communities where our employees live and work. Through the Community and Urban Affairs Department, we support Amoco educational and employee-volunteer initiatives, including programs focusing on elementary and pre-college education, school reform, and math and science careers.

Amoco is a worldwide integrated petroleum and chemical company. We find and develop petroleum resources and provide quality products and services for our customers. We conduct our business responsibly to achieve a superior financial return, balanced with our long-term growth, benefitting shareholders, and fulfilling our commitment to the community and the environment.

Organizational Structure of Citizenship Activities

Most of Amoco's citizenship activities appear to be organized by the company-sponsored foundation. The contributions committee of the corporate board of directors oversees these activities, which are further supported by the Community and Urban Affairs Department. This department concentrates on Amoco educational and employee-volunteer initiatives.

The corporation emphasizes as one of its core values the protection of the environment and the health and safety of consumers of Amoco products and the communities in which they operate. The company cites "environmental remediation" as among its obligations to the community.

Specific Citizenship Programs

Tulsa Annuitant Educators Club: Amoco brought together 35 Tulsa area retirees in 1990 to tutor students at local public schools and offer teacher assistance; foundation grants a yearly maximum of $1,000 per annuitant on behalf of the volunteer's time. The grants are targeted for use in the areas of math, science, or computer technology.

Service Station Dealers Scholarship Program: During the past five years, foundation has provided several grants to Amoco service station dealers to start scholarship programs for college-bound minority students; program is ongoing in Chicago, New York, Connecticut, and southern Florida.

Power Hour Program—Power Hour of Teachers: A TV program to recognize skills and contributions of Chicago public school teachers (K–8); awards to nine teachers; essay contest for students.

Amoco Fund for Neighborhood Economies: Effort to seek new approaches and solutions to inner-city problems. $1.4 million yearly to encourage and support community economic development in Chicago, Denver, Atlanta, and Houston.

Amoco's Summer Jobs for Youth Program: Has enabled economically disadvantaged minority high school students to gain business-related skills by working for nonprofit organizations and Amoco Corporation, while earning money from Amoco's payroll. In 1990, nearly 300 high school students participated in Chicago, Denver, Atlanta, New Orleans, Tulsa, and Texas City.

Amoco Educators Club: In 1989 and 1991, Amoco strongly encouraged its employees to consider running for Chicago Local School Councils. The club supported their efforts.

Science Enrichment Program: Developed by employees at Tulsa Research Center, program is hands-on, self-discovery approach to teaching science; offers innovative lab equipment, student and teacher manuals, organization, and training; a product schools can buy into—in Aurora, Chicago, Denver, Houston, and Tulsa. Program has been very successful, primarily because of its reliance on trained volunteers who learn science enrichment teaching methods and, in turn, train parents and other school volunteers to conduct lab experiments at the schools.

The New Explorers: A 13-part TV series being used to educate and promote science education. Goal is to encourage and increase student interest in science and science-related careers; sponsored in part by Amoco.

Midtown Center for Boys and Metro Center for Girls: Promotes the educational and personal development of Chicago's inner-city boys and girls—supplementary education, classes in human values, character development, and public speaking. About 95 percent of participants graduate from high school; 65 percent go to college; involves over 2,500 students from more than 50 schools.

Business Roundtable Adopt a State for Education: Partnership with governors of all 50 states to improve their K–12 systems; to address educational issues faced by those states. Governors and CEOs meet to discuss the issues and possible solutions or additional support needed for standing programs. Amoco has adopted Iowa.

Hispanic Alliance for Career Enhancement—Chicago: HACE is a nonprofit organization committed to increasing professional employment opportunities for Hispanics with the help of companies like Amoco. Annual conferences for Hispanic professionals and a job bank with more than 1,000 resumes.

Youth Motivation—Chicago: Volunteer speakers (Amoco employees) are provided at 61 high schools in Chicago. Program intended to keep all youngsters in school and demonstrate the importance of continuing their education; in 1989–90, 33 spoke; in 1990–91, 52 spoke; and in 1991–92, 64 spoke.

Volunteer Involvement Program: Grants of up to $1,000 to nonprofits at which Amoco employees serve as volunteers. In 1991, grants made to 225 organizations where 452 employees volunteered.

Volunteer Educational Awards Program: $56,000 awarded to 26 schools in 6 states on behalf of 23 employee volunteers via this program.

Children's Miracle Network: Amoco sponsored a golf tournament that raised money for CMN. President Bill Lowrie described his company's excitement about sponsoring the golf tournament, believing it would be a unique addition to the Tour, and would be very popular with spectators and the television fans.

University of Chicago School Mathematics Project: Amoco is one of several corporate sponsors of this University of Chicago-based initiative to upgrade mathematics curricula for American schools. UCSMP began in 1983 with a six-year grant from Amoco, which has committed funding through 1994. Amoco sponsored three "Amoco Centennial Public Lectures" as the fourth plenary session at the third UCSMP International Conference in 1991. One thrust of the program is to borrow math materials and methods from other countries.

COMPANY PROFILE: ARTHUR ANDERSEN

Rationale for Citizenship Activities

The public interest, as we see it, requires independent, innovative organizations capable of serving multinational business enterprises worldwide. The restructuring should enable the member firms to compete more effectively in the evolving world markets.

Civic activities are equally varied. In offices throughout the country, there are countless examples of Arthur Andersen people reaching out . . . giving something back to their communities. Reasons people get involved are as varied as the thousands of worthwhile organizations they support with their time, talent, and money.

Our firm's founder, Arthur Andersen, was an educator and a leader. He believed he could build the finest professional services firm in the world through education of personnel and dedication to excellence in client service. Throughout its history, the Firm has relied on professional education as a key element in its strategy for success. It is only natural that Firm personnel should make the school the focus of their efforts to contribute to their communities and continue the tradition of quality education as a priority.

A defining characteristic of a professional is the ability to effect positive change by providing quality service. At the Arthur Andersen Worldwide Organization we are keenly aware that this includes not only the service we provide to meet the needs of our clients, but also the service we render in addressing the needs of the community—whether the many local communities in which our offices operate, or the global community in which we are an active citizen.

In a world that technology has made smaller than ever before, we all have a vested interest in one another's success and well-being. We also have the power to make a difference. At the Arthur Andersen Worldwide Organization we will continue to devote our energies to helping people make their own unique contributions to the world in which we live.

The firm's objectives related to sustaining this core value [leadership] include: Providing opportunities for the personal and leadership growth of our partners and employees. . . . [and] improving the community and thus creating a better place to live and for business to grow and develop. [Also included is] demonstrating the leadership, skills, and talents of our people.

We believe it is our responsibility to help foster a capable, well-educated, and entrepreneurial populace in the communities where we operate.

To provide truly high-quality service—to go beyond minimum contractual requirements and provide added value—we must be attuned not only to changing technological or marketplace conditions, but also to the community and the culture in which our clients operate.

Organizational Structure of Citizenship Activities

The Arthur Andersen Foundation, administered by eight trustees, is the formal philanthropic arm of Arthur Andersen and has traditionally focused on education. While foundation funding comes from the Worldwide Organization and from partners (the firm contributes a mandatory 2 percent of partners' incomes), the majority of citizenship activity takes place at the local level. Local offices administer programs addressing the specific needs of their communities, often joining clients and local organizations. Each office has a contributions budget in addition to individual contributions. These are often used jointly to leverage additional support. In fact, 65 percent of foundation giving in 1991, which totaled $6.6 million, went through the Matching Gifts Program; giving historically averages 3 to 4 percent of earnings.

Specific Citizenship Programs

School of the Future: Attempts to define the steps necessary to transform elementary and secondary education to meet the needs of the Information Age; Northern California team is working with Alameda Unified School District. Systems approach to education in four stages: strategy; simplification; process alignment, automation, and integration; and performance reporting and independent audits. Working with the St. Charles School District, Community Unit School District 303, to develop prototype; projects include Baseline Data Study, Cooperative Learning Implementation, Process Writing Evaluation, Technology Plan, and Strategic Planning Support.

Fellowships for Doctoral Candidates: For those in accounting, tax, the information sciences, or other areas directly related to our practice; fellowship provides $1,500 per month plus tuition for no more than 12 months for completion of research and writing of dissertation; 166 fellowships have been awarded, averaging annually $80,000 to $100,000 and totaling $1.7 million.

Faculty Residencies: Those with full-time faculty appointment work as regular member of Arthur Andersen while on vacation or leave from school; regular and short-term. Begin with staff training schools; last two or three months devoted to research project of choice. Many publish results, with approval; salary same as at university; 276 professors have completed program.

Matching Gifts Program: Matches individual contributions to universities up to $2,500 per school year; $25 minimum. Consolidated and group contributions allowed.

Research Facilities: Subject files made up of work in accounting, auditing, taxes, systems, and general business. Indexed and cross-indexed. Available to faculty members in conjunction with any of their research within the limits of client confidentiality.

Publications: Will supply copies of publications for use in connection with the classroom responsibilities of those involved.

Speakers and Educational Materials: To fullest extent possible, program provides speakers to student and faculty organizations. Also have film and video presentations.

New Faculty Consortium: Sponsors, funds, and co-hosts with the American Accounting Association training workshop to help new faculty members become better teachers; also a workshop for those more experienced.

Arthur Andersen Alumni Professors Outstanding Faculty: Sponsors endowed chairs at leading universities.

Accounting and Audit Symposium: Annual two-day seminar on the impact that changing business requirements have on curriculum design.

Accounting Wealth and Opportunities Program: Guest lectures by firm professionals in freshman classes of select universities; tries to attract students to the accounting profession. Similar program targets high school level.

Basic and Advanced Camp Training Interview Program: Students from leading universities invited to Center for Professional Education for annual interviewing skills session.

Arthur Andersen Leadership Conferences: Held at Center for Professional Education and designed for college upperclassmen and graduate students with leadership responsibilities and academic credentials. Offers courses to reinforce skills necessary for leadership and activities that reinforce teamwork in competitive environment.

Ethics Program: Spanned five years with over $5 million invested. Involved more than 280 institutions.

Institute for Learning Sciences at Northwestern University: Andersen Consulting sponsors and provides $2.5 million per year on ten programmers; attempts to model human learning processes and develop advanced computer software for education.

Atlanta: AA office created a videotape to inspire employees to become more involved in volunteering.

Chicago: One of Boys and Girls Club of Chicago's largest corporate sponsors; hosts annual Pier Power Benefit Extravaganza. Last year raised more than $70,000; office provided resources to many arts organizations; gives money and professional services for planning and computer installation and sometimes loaned staff.

Detroit: Detroit Compact partnership between business and public schools intended to improve student performance and help business find qualified employees. Firm hires students for the summer. Firm provides office space and administrative support to INROADS, organization that helps develop and place talented minority youth.

Paint the Town—Houston: With Houston Committee for Private Sector Initiatives. Volunteers help repair homes of the elderly and handicapped twice a year.

Minneapolis: Under the firm's Community Action Program, office formed AACAP, a foundation organized to implement the office's charitable program. Surveyed needs of community, raised money, and selected activities—Holiday Fund-Raising, Paint-A-Thon, FoodShare, and Minnesota Accounting Aid Society Taxpayer Assistance Program.

Northern California: For six years the office contributed pro bono services to Crocker Art Museum and led in contribution campaign to upgrade gallery. Services provided freed up $250,000 for museum to use elsewhere.

For six years, underwriting a program at the American Conservatory Theater and making it available to San Francisco youth by providing tickets (70) to seventh and eighth graders.

Los Angeles: Employees and community members volunteered to help computerize and tabulate offers of help in "Rebuild L.A." database after the riots.

Nashville: Encore program with Nashville Symphony encourages employees to attend; firm pays 50 percent of subscription cost for season tickets.

National African-American Heritage Museum: Involved in initial planning phases; provided grant to fund planning and act as auditors of the museum organization.

Local Office Arts Programs: Each local office has its own arts program. Each handles own collection supporting local artists; provides stim-

ulating environment for employees and clients and recognizes commitment to preservation of cultural resources.

Faculty Planning: Hosted annual faculty planning meeting for new
teacher recruiting organization, Teach for America, which is devoted to
inner-city and rural schools.

Dallas: Community Care Team in Dallas office formed committee that
helps identify volunteer activities.

Washington, D.C.: An Andersen partner in the D.C. office was loaned
to the United Way in the district to provide professional assistance under
the Executive Loan Program.

COMPANY PROFILE: CHASE MANHATTAN BANK

Rationale for Citizenship Activities

We aim to improve the well-being of the communities in which we operate,
recognizing our responsibility to our customers, stockholders, employees,
and the citizenry at large. We realize that the vitality of the communities
we serve is crucial to the long-term success of the corporation.

However, financial grants are not the only way we participate in the
larger community. We actively encourage all staff members to volunteer
their time and talents to organizations aiding the common good. Since we
reestablished our in-house volunteer program several years ago, we have
been heartened by the ever-growing numbers of Chase volunteers—and
by the wide range of organizations that call on our staff members for
assistance.

Organizational Structure of Citizenship Activities

Philanthropy at Chase is a unit of the Corporate Communications Group.
The corporate responsibility committee, chaired by the CEO Thomas
Labreque, guides the Corporate Responsibility Program, which sets the
budget for six subcommittees, each representing an area of Chase involvement—community development and human services, culture and the arts,
education, international, nationwide grants, and public issues and community responsibility. The committee and subcommittees are made up
almost entirely of senior executives. Members of the committee also serve
as trustees of the corporate foundation. While the foundation concentrates
on giving outside of the United States, most of the company's citizenship
activity falls under the Philanthropy Department included in Corporate
Communications. Philanthropy has its own budget within Communi-

cations, which is set by the board of directors. This budget had been set at 2.4 percent of after-tax profits, but in 1991 because of the fluctuating economy, this practice was found too unstable and was discontinued.

Prior to 1988, the committees reviewed all grant proposals individually. Since then, the philanthropy staff of five officers, four contributions professionals, two full-time support personnel, and four graduate interns has acquired more responsibility. This staff makes recommendations to the committee and subcommittees and makes some funding decisions itself. However, it still forwards proposals that fall on the margins to the appropriate subcommittee.

The Voluntary Action Program reinforces the current philanthropy program, supports employees in their own volunteer commitments, and improves community relations. Employees are actively recruited, and a large database helps match employees with opportunities and tracks those involved—about 3,000 past and present employees.

Corporate divisions fall under CRC guidelines but otherwise operate independently of headquarters. They do not have to report citizenship activity, and while some managers make recommendations to the corporate committees, most of the division-level contributions come from direct giving.

Another aspect of the post-1988 shift includes a much greater emphasis on proactive philanthropy, the idea being to focus more closely on certain proposed key areas with CHASE IMPACT Grants, with the particular direction they take formulated by the committee.

Specific Citizenship Programs

Voluntary Action Program: Reinforces current philanthropy program, supports employees in their own commitments, and improves community relations. Annual recruitment of employees via survey describing volunteer program, identifying employee interest, and documenting current involvement. Follows up with creation of volunteer database, regular mailings, and presentation to management trainees. Chase encourages board memberships and professional skills volunteers; has team projects and annual reception.

Matching Gift Program: Established to encourage employees to support cultural and educational institutions. Gifts must be at least $25; maximum combined gift is $750 under Culture plan and $5,000 under Education plan.

Community School/Saturday College at P.S. 287: Partnership between Chase, School District 13, and P.S. 287 administration provides elementary school students with reading and art program. Employees act as mentors, help develop school newspaper, conduct skills workshops, Community School/Saturday College at P.S. 287 team-building seminars, and financial management courses for parents and teachers; also serve as link to cultural institutions.

GENERAL PROGRAM AREA—COMMUNITY DEVELOPMENT AND HUMAN SERVICES. The program is intended to fund efforts that bridge physical, economic, and social revitalization of communities and is particularly interested in programs supporting the needs of the homeless. The program was established to allow Chase to better prioritize and focus the budget toward revitalization of low-and moderate-income communities and to improve the lives of residents. The focus is on the greater NYC area and upstate NY.

The subcommittee mission statement: "This Subcommittee will have as its primary interest the development of housing and jobs for low and moderate income people, support for solutions for the homeless; plus consider grants for related social services and the United Way."

GENERAL PROGRAM AREA—CULTURE AND THE ARTS. The program funds projects that have community outreach component, that present new work and assist developing artists, and that are specific in objectives.

The subcommittee mission statement: "Grants are made to organizations with programs in the following disciplines: Dance, Music, Natural Science, Performing Arts, Service, Theater and Visual Arts."

GENERAL PROGRAM AREA—EDUCATION. The program is changed from 1981, when goals were determined by the education profile of employees and by recruiting efforts. Goals are to support (1) pre-college organizations or projects likely to make a lasting difference to reasonably large numbers of disadvantaged New York City youth; (2) graduate schools from which Chase recruits large numbers of employees; (3) minority higher education; and (4) other programs serving New Yorkers' educational needs. Special emphasis is on core reform of the NYC public schools and support for other pre-college education programs.

Smart Start: Four full-year scholarships to Brooklyn high school students attending a Brooklyn college. Students receive paid part-time internships; a Chase employee serves as mentor and provides career information and insight into workings of large corporation.

Project Live: Local junior high students receive one-on-one tutoring/mentoring from Chase employees for two hours per week at a Chase facility. Volunteers receive release time for one of the two hours.

Model Office Classroom Project: Volunteers pair up to teach three hour-long classes every other week at Brooklyn high school, where classroom is set up as an office; focus is on office operations and culture. Chase supplies furniture and volunteers.

Business and Industry After School Program: Volunteers teach a work readiness curriculum two to three hours per week; reached more than 200 students over past several years.

Co-Op Programs: Program with high school and university in which students are paid to participate; four high school students and five university students involved in 1991.

Classroom Inc.: Employees serve as mentors and instructors for students in computer-simulated work program at two Brooklyn high schools.

Murry Bergtraum High School Intern Program: Provides paid internships.

INROADS/NYC: Program is a career development organization servicing NYC; recruits, places, and supports college students in summer internships. In 1991, Chase hired five interns.

Nehemia Project: Effort to improve East Brooklyn education by encouraging completion of high school. Graduates guaranteed placement at CUNY if meet basic requirements. Chase hires and trains many students and offers workshops for schools and students.

Junior Achievement: Volunteers teach applied economics one hour per week for 12 weeks at NYC schools; given release time for activities during the school day; generally volunteer for three semesters.

Educational Visits: Officers use expertise to educate non-Chase businesses and nonprofit managers. Provide consultation, training, and lectures; regular visits to universities and graduate schools.

Public Service Marketing: Programs include Mrs. Bush's Story Time, Police Athletic League's Public Awareness Campaign, The Chase Manhattan Bank Public Awareness Campaign.

Direct Response Marketing: Supports the Children's Literacy Initiative; half a cent from each credit card transaction donated to buy books and tapes for Head Start. Chase holds readings in NYC and Minneapolis branches for inner-city children.

Choices and Decisions: "Choices and Decisions: Taking Charge of Your Life" teaches financial management skills to NYC area high school students with interactive videodisc and PC-based curriculum.

Educational Minibanks: Thirty-five to forty branches in Long Island region support educational programs. Employees open Minibank in schools where students can open savings accounts; also contribute giveaways and promo items.

Chase Your Dream: Chase volunteers read to groups of children in Baltimore inner-city school. Chase trains volunteers and covers cost of books.

University of Baltimore: Chase provides to the University of Baltimore: financial advice, fundraising assistance, lectures at the business school, presentations on behalf of the university.

Training Center: Provided 13 days of free space to over 450 individuals in New York; provides use of AV equipment and refreshments.

New York Universities: Furniture and equipment donations to NYC universities, high schools, and elementary schools.

GENERAL PROGRAM AREA—INTERNATIONAL GRANTS. The essential mission of the International Grants category of The Chase Manhattan Corporation is to promote development in the countries where Chase has a significant presence, primarily through private sector, grassroots-oriented, direct service programs. A secondary mission is to enhance the American public's understanding of international affairs.

Projects should promote economic development, aid children and health care, provide disaster relief, educate, exchange youth, and show treasures abroad.

GENERAL PROGRAM AREA—NATIONWIDE GRANTS. The program expanded into 11 markets (Arizona, California, Delaware, Florida, Georgia, Illinois, Maryland, Massachusetts, New York, Ohio, Texas) from a mostly New York City area in 1981. Subcommittee restricts states' budgets so that no more than 25 percent can go to cultural organizations and so at least 25 percent goes to housing for the needy and homeless programs.

GENERAL PROGRAM AREA—NEIGHBORHOOD GRANTS PROGRAM. Program objectives are to distribute philanthropic resources appropriately among Chase's downstate service areas; to develop partnerships between Chase and recipient organizations to meet neighborhood stabilization and revitalization goals; to serve as a foundation for the Metropolitan Community Bank's community relations efforts by focusing on small, community-based, nonprofit organizations; to support the Metropolitan Community Bank's marketing objectives; to afford the Metropolitan Community Bank the opportunity to participate in philanthropic decisions that affect branch market areas; to enhance the perception of Chase in neighborhoods where the bank has business interests.

GENERAL PROGRAM AREA—PUBLIC POLICIES AND COMMUNITY INVOLVEMENT. The program stresses the need to advocate policies that stimulate economic growth and community development, especially in the NYC area, and stresses the important contribution of nonprofit and government agencies. The program was established to allow Chase to focus on non-direct service organizations.

The subcommittee mission statement: "This Subcommittee will consider grants which, generally, are focused on promoting public policies that will benefit the communities we serve and improve the management of government agencies and nonprofit organizations. The Subcommittee will also consider worthy initiatives that do not fall within other Chase program areas."

Volunteer Seminars: Three volunteer seminars for employees; nonprofit representatives discuss their missions and needs; ongoing and one-time events included. Information and refreshments are provided; held at three locations, one at headquarters.

P.A.C.T.: Sponsors public awareness campaign for the Police Athletic League. Chase raises money through pro bono, broad-based public appeal, and tie-in promotion—The Chase Challenge. Direct solicitations to branch and credit card customers; branches advertise and distribute materials; visits to Chase Operations and Systems Department and "Adopt-A-Center" program link volunteers to PAL centers.

Holiday Gift Drive: Collects new toys, gifts, and clothing for needy children and distributes to area shelters and health centers. Drop-off points at many Chase locations; gift wrapping and refreshments provided; other donations encouraged; sponsored by Philanthropy and Public Services Marketing.

Walk for the Cure: Supports Juvenile Diabetes Foundation. Chase had largest corporate team in 1991; refreshments and Chase t-shirts provided.

Chase Grows in Brooklyn: Works with community residents and Neighborhood Housing Services in East Flatbush to spruce up the area; refreshments, lunch, baseball hat, materials provided.

COMPANY PROFILE: EASTMAN KODAK

Rationale for Citizenship Activities

At Eastman Kodak Company, we make it a habit to imagine the best, and then work toward it. But there's another strength that's just as important: The power of "shared optimism." Companies and communities prosper together. Kodak is the world leader in imaging today because our roots grow deep in communities that enrich and enlarge our vision. In return, we "give something back" to these communities by contributing time, energy, and funding. Our Community Relations programs give these efforts shape and direction.

Since its founding days, Eastman Kodak has recognized that the success of business depends upon the vitality of the society in which the company lives. . . . In our view, doing well financially as a business and doing good in the social sense are not separate concerns. The one is dependent upon the other, and both are important to the health of the company and the well-being of the communities in which Kodak has made sizeable commitments. . . . Like any other business activity, these investments are managed and administered in a way that increases the probability of substantial returns . . . for the company, for the communities where it operates, and for the people who live and work in those communities.

What is good for our planet is also good for our business future. At Eastman Kodak Chemical Company, strong environmental capabilities have become a competitive advantage in attracting new business.

The commitments we make are generally long term. We believe such investments in the not-for-profit sector are an essential aspect of corporate citizenship. Our contributions also acknowledge the direct relationship between vibrant communities and a healthy business climate. When individuals, colleges and universities, community organizations, and businesses work together on common concerns, we not only solve problems, but also strengthen each other.

Organizational Structure of Citizenship Activities

Eastman Kodak maintains a formal, structured direct giving program—the Corporate Giving Program. This program, run by a staff including one professional, supports a corporate contributions committee, which in turn recommends grants for the approval of the corporate board of directors. The giving program falls under the Eastman Kodak Charitable Trust, founded in 1952.

The company also gives nonmonetary support. Between 1989 and 1990 the estimated value of this support jumped from $250,000 to $4.8 million.

Eastman Kodak gives mostly in areas in which there is high Kodak employment. It gives nationally mainly to higher education.

Much of Kodak's citizenship activity concentrates on the environment. While their motivation for citizenship in general includes moral and relational elements, the environmental emphasis appears in more practical terms. CEO Kay Whitmore headed the management committee on environmental responsibility, which also included most senior executives. This committee, monitored by the board of director's public policy committee, focused on corporate attempts to reduce emissions, minimize waste, conserve energy, and recycle and reuse resources.

Specific Citizenship Programs

GENERAL PROGRAM AREA—COMMUNITY RELATIONS. In the belief that the unique contributions of individuals are a tremendous source of social energy, Kodak Community Relations sponsors programs in education, health and human services, and community revitalization, including culture and the arts. Kodak celebrates diversity, enhances the potential of individuals, and attempts to refresh community spirit—the values of the Community Relations programs.

Kodak/Alan Page Challenge in the Great Cities: Essay contest to encourage writing on the importance of education; topic for fourth graders, "With an Education, the Future is Yours." Page visits inner-city schools with a stay-in-school message.

The Brainpower Hall of Fame: Successful city school graduates return to share perspectives on career, importance of education, and ways to overcome obstacles.

The Kodak 21st Century Learning Challenge: Funds go to improve science and math achievement; ten-year partnership with pre-college educational institutions. Program contributes facilities, training, professional core courses, personal development programs, communications support, volunteers, funding.

United Way: George Eastman, Kodak founder, started Community Chest, the forerunner of the United Way. Kodak is largest contributor to any single United Way anywhere in the U.S.

Dollars for Doers: Grants for nonprofit organizations at request of employees volunteering for them.

Community Revitalization: Concentrates on youth services, environmental education and conservation, public policy research and leadership development, economic development, job training.

The Kodak Scholars Program and The Kodak Fellows Program: The first provides full undergraduate support in computer science, physical science, engineering, marketing, and quantitative business; required internship at Kodak and mentoring. The second provides doctoral support and an unrestricted grant for fellow's department.

GENERAL PROGRAM AREA—HEALTH AND HUMAN SERVICES. Programs in the health and human services sector add measurably to the quality of life in Kodak communities.

Goals for Greater Rochester: Financial, volunteer, and in-kind support. Group develops action plans in areas of alcohol and drugs, community design/natural resources, cultural resources, downtown, economic development, education, entertainment/recreation, housing, and human services.

Kodak for Scientific Awareness (KSA): Brings groups of students to Kodak facility to see technology in action. Hands-on experiments.

The Summer Science Work-Study Institute: Teachers spend month taking college credit and shadowing a Kodak employee.

GENERAL PROGRAM AREA—ENVIRONMENT. Kodak's environmental efforts are substantial; the company plans to do more—in manufacturing processes, product design, energy conservation, emissions control, and packaging—to positively affect the environment. Kodak feels a responsibility to customers, employees, shareowners, and the community, and embraces a sense of stewardship for the environment.

Customer Imaging Environmental Support Services: Information source on safety guidelines, water and energy conservation, minimization of chemical usage, recovering and reusing chemicals and managing waste.

COMPANY PROFILE: EXXON

Rationale for Citizenship Activities

Exxon's management believes that an educated citizenry is important to the preservation of our democracy and is important to the long-term well-being of the nation's economy. Educational institutions provide the trained manpower needed to operate and manage the nation's economy. They also provide much of the research that helps America's industry develop and compete technologically.

The foundation's objective is to be philanthropic rather than commercial. We believe that being educated means more than mastery of a narrow technical discipline. Our world is too interdependent and too rapidly changing to limit our educational philanthropy strictly to programs of immediate interest to the corporation. To be supportive of education implies a concern for general education as well as for specialized education. . . . Exxon Corporation itself makes educational contributions more directly related to the company's business.

Organizational Structure of Citizenship Activities

In 1989, the corporate board of directors established a public issues committee to review policies, programs, and practices that relate to public issues. There is also a company-sponsored foundation.

Giving strategy has recently shifted to an extended concentration on a few issues. The corporation believes such a disciplined strategy will more likely influence the area they stress—education.

Outside of their work in education, much of the company's citizenship activity attempts to prevent accidents, and, if they occur, to respond effectively to them.

Specific Citizenship Programs

GENERAL PROGRAM AREA—ENVIRONMENT. In 1991, Exxon's environmental grants were used primarily in support of preserving natural sites, developing and promoting public policy, and assisting scientific research in environmental matters; 75 grants for U.S. projects, 11 for international. This includes divisions and affiliates but not contributions by the Exxon Education Foundation.

GENERAL PROGRAM AREA—GRANTS FOR PUBLIC INFORMATION AND POLICY RESEARCH. The aim is to assist responsible organizations that approach complex policy questions with objectivity and balance, thus contributing to enlightened public discussion of important domestic and foreign policy issues.

GENERAL PROGRAM AREA—EDUCATION GRANTS (SEPARATE FROM EXXON EDUCATION FOUNDATION). A primary focus of Exxon's contributions to education in 1991 was to promote engineering and science education at the high school and college levels.

Since these grants do not fall within the guidelines of the EEF, they were provided by the Exxon Corporation and its affiliates.

Higher Education Minority Programs: Scholarship money given to specific colleges and universities for engineering students.

MBA Fellowship Program: Money for MBA student fellowships given to specific schools.

Other Minority Scholarship/Support Programs: Grants to specific schools for support of minority education, particularly in math and science.

High School Partnership Programs in Individual Affiliates: Through participation in high school partnership programs by individual affiliates,

Exxon employees provided mentoring for minority students taking part in the company's summer job opportunities.

Education Involvement Fund: Exxon encourages its employees to be personally involved in the communities in which they live; provides an Educational Involvement Fund that offers funding of $500 to local schools where Exxon employees or their spouses serve as volunteers.

United Appeals and Federated Drives: A substantial portion of Exxon's support for health and human services agencies is allocated through United Way organizations. Financial support was only one facet of Exxon's involvement with United Way. Last year, Exxon employees and annuitants volunteered their services to local and national United Way offices, providing valuable expertise to help ensure successful campaigns.

GENERAL PROGRAM AREA—HEALTH GRANTS. Contributions to health-related organizations are in three categories: (1) medical and health education; (2) health care delivery; (3) environmental health. Focus in 1 was on substance abuse prevention.

GENERAL PROGRAM AREA—CIVIC AND COMMUNITY SERVICE ORGANIZATIONS. Donations go to civic and community organizations. Priorities are to support initiatives dealing with issues related to children, local collaborative efforts addressing homelessness and unemployment, ongoing funding of national and community-based programs in the literacy field, broad-based nonprofit sector financial assistance, and encouragement of employees and annuitants who provide volunteer services in their communities.

Community Summer Jobs Program: Assists nonprofit agencies in its operating cities by providing temporary employment for college interns. Qualifying organizations receive a grant to fund an internship for a student seeking work experience in the nonprofit field.

Volunteer Involvement Fund: Exxon employees and annuitants can apply for grants of up to $1,000 for the nonprofit agency to which they provide volunteer services; projects in 1991 included the Waco, Texas, Civic Theater, the Greenwich, Connecticut, Adult Day Care, the YMCA of Baton Rouge, Louisiana, and the Silver Ridge Park, New Jersey, First Aid Squad.

GENERAL PROGRAM AREA—MINORITY- AND WOMEN-ORIENTED SERVICE ORGANIZATIONS. Contributions go to projects that have a substantial impact on women and minority groups, supporting activities that deal with issues of family and child welfare, youth unemployment, parental involvement in education, and neighborhood revitalization. About 50 percent go to national organizations to support research, project development, and implementation of programs to help bring women and minorities closer to achieving economic and social parity.

GENERAL PROGRAM AREA—ARTS, MUSEUMS, AND HISTORICAL ASSO-CIATIONS. In 1991, efforts were directed toward building audiences for the arts and helping cultural institutions strengthen their financial bases. Nearly 25 percent of contributions in this area were part of company's Cultural Matching Gifts Program. Company matches up to $1,000 annually of donations made by employees and annuitants to eligible cultural institutions.

Elementary and Secondary School Improvement Program: Objectives: (1) to enhance educators' understanding of the changing demographic profile of the school-age population; (2) to restructure schools in ways that will give teachers and administrators the flexibility to pursue those educational strategies best suited to student needs; (3) to prepare pre-service and in-service teachers to work effectively within redesigned school structures.

Undergraduate Developmental and General Education Programs: A five-year program of research about most effective methods in remedial education and most effective general education programs; research is done; programs are now in the dissemination-of-results mode.

Research and Training Program: Provides money to underwrite university-based research activities in science and engineering; closed to applications; gives grants; foundation seeks advice of Exxon affiliates, divisions, departments that have expertise in the areas under study.

Organizational Support Program: Recognizes importance of certain organizations to the American education system by providing unrestricted grants for their operations.

Special Projects Fund: Program not open to application. Allows the foundation to be responsive to exceptional funding opportunities that are consonant with its general concerns but that do not fit into other categories. Grants developed by staff often in consultation with outside advisers.

Educational Matching Gift Program: Open to retirees, surviving spouses, directors, and employees. Matching ratio is 3 to 1 on gifts up to $5,000. In 1991, the foundation matched 11,430 gifts to 967 colleges and universities; second largest matching gift program in the country.

COMPANY PROFILE: GENERAL MOTORS

Rationale for Citizenship Activities

General Motors believes that corporate philanthropy is an integral part of corporate social responsibility. A sound philanthropic program is in the best interest of the Corporation, its stockholders, its employees, and the communities in which it operates.

Specific Citizenship Programs

GENERAL PROGRAM AREA—CORPORATE SPONSORSHIPS. The program funds educational and public interest programs.

GENERAL PROGRAM AREA—HIGHER EDUCATION. Mostly cash contributions are given to science and engineering activities—mostly to those 75 on GM Key Institutions List.

GENERAL PROGRAM AREA—NONEDUCATIONAL CONTRIBUTIONS. Program is designed to improve the quality of life in local communities and nationally, giving financial, material, and professional support to charitable organizations and community activities. The program has many GM volunteers.

GENERAL PROGRAM AREA—PRE-COLLEGE PROGRAM. Three objectives: to stimulate educational reform in plant cities, to coordinate local GM efforts with state and national ones, and to support math and science material for national use.

GENERAL PROGRAM AREA—MINORITY SUPPORT PROGRAM. The program works to increase the numbers of minorities motivated and prepared for education.

COMPANY PROFILE: HONEYWELL

Rationale for Citizenship Activities

Volunteerism is a Honeywell tradition, a way of life. From the executive suite to the factory floor, Honeywellers are taking part in community issues. They are involved, personally, in everything from major social issues to small acts of making a single life just a little bit better.

At Honeywell, volunteerism is encouraged and nurtured because it benefits not only communities but also employees and the company. It is also an act of self-interest. There is a direct relationship between the health of the company and the communities in which its workforce and assets reside. In a pragmatic sense, volunteerism is a learning and skill-building experience. It teaches people how to work together and instills them with new insights and skills they can bring back to their jobs.

Volunteerism is the quid pro quo for the "privilege" of running a business in America. Business has a responsibility to help make communities healthy; the interests of the community can't be separated from those of business. Healthy communities make for healthy companies.

The CEO of a major Fortune 500 company—a company like many others—has a stake in the future of the children of America.

We recognize the commitment and leadership that Honeywell employees bring to their communities. Honeywell's community relations program began in 1975, with volunteerism as a key strategy. We continue to nurture employee involvement because the margin of difference in successful community efforts often comes from the hands-on efforts of people. Moreover, the foundation's board of directors looks for employee involvement when considering requests for funding. With this report, we celebrate our employees worldwide and the Honeywell tradition of people-to-people giving.

Organizational Structure of Citizenship Activities

A 12-member board of directors guides the company-sponsored foundation that oversees about three-fourths of Honeywell's contributions. The board, made up of Honeywell executives with some expertise relevant to the operation and funding of the foundation, sets giving policies and procedures and approves funds. A foundation staff of three full-time professionals, and one full-time and six part-time support personnel, studies and evaluates community needs and issues and reviews proposals. The staff learns of local concerns and needs by meeting with local nonprofit organizations, community members, and employee volunteers. Honeywell often involves employee committees in the decision-making process.

Honeywell maintains three priority categories for its citizenship activity—education, human services, and art and culture. Giving concentrates on communities with major company facilities, with the headquarters area of Minneapolis receiving the largest share of funds. In fact, Minnesota organizations get about 50 percent of Honeywell contributions.

The foundation also allocates funds to Honeywell divisions for use in their respective communities. The divisions supplement these allocations from their own operating budgets, with the amount depending on the number of employees, employee involvement, and community relations plans.

After the Honeywell restructuring in 1986, the Corporate and Community Responsibility Department was deeply reduced. This department manages foundation contributions, the company response to social policy issues, and employee volunteer efforts. Nonetheless, Honeywell has maintained a four-level approach to community involvement stressing dollars, volunteers, partnerships, and then companywide internalization of the issues. Senior management, including general managers of operating divisions, has through its extensive volunteer commitment set the tone for community responsibility at Honeywell.

Specific Citizenship Programs

Honeywell Retirees Volunteer Program (HRVP): Organization of Honeywell retirees working in cooperation with company to serve the community through volunteer activities; 1,200 involved, including retirees volunteering at least one day a week in Minneapolis area. In 1989, more than 1,400 retirees companywide contributed at least four hours per week; 1989 volunteer hours totaled more than 250,000.

Success by 6: James Renier, CEO, was first chairman of this multisector initiative to have every child ready to learn by the time he/she begins school; United Way has adopted program as part of its national strategy.

Phillips Community Initiatives for Children: Neighborhood initiative around headquarters spawned by Success by 6. Attempts to reduce numbers of low-birth-weight babies through increased prenatal care for women in poverty; workers trained to recruit people for program.

New Vistas School: School for pregnant teenagers established on-site at headquarters. Honeywell proposed the school, provides space and cleaning, equipped most of it (IBM gave computers), and provides some paid and unpaid jobs. The Minneapolis Public Schools provide the education, and Hennepin County provides child care. Daily exposure to the business world includes unpaid internships at Honeywell credit union and paid summer internships at the company.

New American Schools Development Corporation: James Renier appointed to board of directors of this nonprofit organization that will award contracts to various groups to help communities create schools that will reach national education goals (America 2000 Education Strategy).

Education Task Force: Honeywell created an Education Task Force of employees from divisions across the country to develop guidelines for company action in education and to recommend specific programs.

Adopting Schools: Employees volunteer as library aides and mentors, conduct factory tours and field trips, and help with computer programming; donate audiovisual equipment and even open print shops for school use.

LINK: In Seattle, pairs high schools and businesses to develop education-enhancement programs on team basis. Includes student-teacher internships, classroom lectures, professional development for teachers, plant tours, and career counseling.

Minneapolis Education and Recycling Center (MERC): Neighborhood center linked to alternative education programs; helps at-risk youth earn high school degree while getting work experience and making money; students shadow employees at work to learn about their jobs.

Education Ventures Inc. or Teacher Mini-Grants: Holding company formed by Honeywell and six others to sponsor education incentive programs and broaden base of community investment in education. Long-range goal is to initiate programs that will be attractive investments to other companies and organizations and individuals that want to play a role in strengthening public education; 1990 funding for 54 projects.

Honeywell Academies in Minneapolis: Honeywell, with 11 area school districts, established summer academy to expose math and science teachers and professors to technologies, business practices, and careers at company; goal of enriching classroom experience.

Strategic Planning: Helped define district's mission and laid out tactics to achieve equity and quality in public education—principal and teacher development, educational technology, dropout strategies, and marketing.

Summatech: Grades 9 to 12 at North Community High in Minneapolis. Attempt to desegregate by attracting other district students to school as a quality option. Attempt to create magnet program in math and science.

Way to Grow: Recognizes value of family as social asset. Recruits workers and trains them to help families take advantage of available services; neighbor helping neighbor program.

Honeywell Partnership School in Clearwater: Division on-site school for 75 employee children entering kindergarten or first grade. Partnership with Pinellas Community Schools.

Parents as Teachers in Albuquerque: Combines family involvement with basic principles to help children develop from birth to age three. Includes home visits by public school officials and vision, hearing, and educational development screening.

Helping the Homeless: Saginaw, Michigan, branch donated all their empty soda cans from work; money put into a fund for good works; received matching gift of another $200 from Foundation HELP fund. (This is only mention of community involvement in 1990 Employee Annual Report.)

Corporate Tutor Program: One-on-one tutoring by employees at local schools.

Adopt-A-High-Rise: Effort to meet friendship and support needs of elderly and disabled. In 1989, 42 employees worked at two high-rise buildings in Minneapolis and made social calls, delivered meals, and contributed food and clothing.

A Friend for a Day—Minnesota Special Olympics: Honeywell volunteers and friends participate in friendship with athletes. Volunteers sponsor sports events, hold clinics, and stage activities.

Business Partners Program: Minneapolis Office of Employment and Training program to enhance summer youth employment. Business volunteers serve as mentors to unemployed low-income youth; meet once a week during summer employment project.

Executives in the Community: Honeywell executives program to make volunteer commitments in their communities like membership on committees, task forces, or nonprofit boards. Work with community members to address important needs and issues and serve as advocates for important public policy issues.

Honeywell Employee-Launched Projects (HELP): Program for teams of four or more who design and participate in community project with Honeywell support from $100 to $500. In 1989, 35 teams delivered services for total of $17,588.

Management Assistance Project (MAP): A nonprofit organization with 26 corporate partners that matches volunteer expertise with nonprofit needs. In 1989, 57 Honeywell employees were placed; since 1981, 444 have been placed.

Metropolitan Paint-A-Thon: Effort of businesses, congregations, and civic groups to paint homes of elderly, low-income, or disabled to contribute to home maintenance and neighborhood improvement. In 1989, 300 Honeywell employees in 12 teams participated; $1,128 in Honeywell grants helped pay for supplies.

Minnesota FoodShare: To stock emergency food shelves conducted by congregations, corporations, employee groups, and civic clubs. In 1989, Honeywell employees raised more than $270,000, including 10,000 pounds of food, making company and employees largest non-food producing corporate contributor. In last seven years, Honeywell employees contributed equivalent of $2 million.

United Way: Raises and distributes local funds to meet community needs; 300 company volunteers lead collection effort.

COMPANY PROFILE: IBM

Rationale for Citizenship Activities

IBM will be permitted to grow and prosper only where people in governments understand that we are, indeed, helping to solve society's problems.

Because these investments benefit the larger community in which we all live and work, our participation makes good business sense. More than that, we believe it is the right thing to do.

There is no profit unless society as a whole profits.

Organizational Structure of Citizenship Activities

Corporate Citizenship at IBM was reorganized in 1990. Four departments—Education and University Relations, Social Policy and Programs, Cultural and Human Services, and Corporate Support Plans and Controls—now fall under the Office of Corporate Support. This office reports to the Corporate Contributions Planning Board of senior executives, which meets a few times a year to set citizenship policy and the budget level and to evaluate programs. The head of the Department of Social Policy and Programs formulates overall IBM policy responses to social issues on a worldwide basis.

IBM still breaks its social service work into six categories: Education, Environment, Health, Persons with Disabilities, Human Services, and Arts and Culture; and it has begun to research citizenship internally.

More than one-third of IBM's 100,000 United States employees are engaged in some sort of nonprofit activity outside of passive memberships in clubs and the like.

Specific Citizenship Programs

Matching Grant Program: One of nation's oldest and largest ($14 million in 1989); gives two-for-one match (as do Exxon and P&G); will match up to $5,000 per organization; higher education employees have option of two-for-one cash match or five-for-one equipment match; K–12 schools eligible for equipment only.

Faculty Loan Program: Employees teach minority or handicapped students in colleges or universities.

Community Service Assignments: Scientists, engineers, managers devote themselves to social causes while receiving full pay, and without fear of losing professional status; mostly short-term (hundreds of employees work four to six weeks with nonprofits); some loans for one to three years. IBM Europe, Africa, and MidEast have similar loaned executive program (IBM Europe uses the British term "seconding"). IBM Brazil is putting program into place.

IBM Scientific Centers: Seventeen centers around the world, as well as special IBM units for researching solutions to problems of the disabled, the environment, and education. These centers not pressed to produce new products and services but to conduct long-term research in computer applications. Often, projects involve university scientists too in work on "societal problems": in Third World, several IBM scientific centers are involved in efforts to promote technology transfers that relate to problems of poverty.

Fund for Community Service (FCS): Volunteering employees and retirees or their spouses can get donated computer systems for their favorite nonprofits. In 1990, IBM made 2,400 FCS contributions with an average value of $2,400; usually approved by local fund administrators; larger donations approved at national headquarters. About one-third of donations in 1990 were to health and welfare organizations; rest divided evenly between cultural, civic nonprofits, and schools.

COMPANY PROFILE: 3M

Rationale for Citizenship Activities

It is advantageous for a corporation to invest in its communities, for by doing so, it is investing in its future growth; and the entire community benefits from the investment. 3M is committed to establishing a partnership with each of the communities in which it is located. Those partnerships include a sharing of time and talent, of supporting activities that enhance the quality of life, and becoming involved in the process of giving the greatest good of the world community.

We're winning by making life better in 3M communities around the world. We do this by helping to reduce pollution, supporting health and education, and meeting the needs of our employees. 3M has a long-standing commitment to our environment. In 1975, we launched an innovative program called Pollution Prevention Pays (3P). The aim is to prevent pollution at its source, such as by redesigning products and manufacturing processes.

Organizational Structure of Citizenship Activities

Direct corporate citizenship at 3M proceeds through the Corporate Contributions Program, which is guided by the Corporate Contributions Committee made up of the CEO, several executive vice presidents, and others. The program, staffed by seven full-time professionals and seven full-time support personnel, emphasizes projects addressing community needs and suggesting solutions. It prefers projects that provide communities with skills to achieve positive social goals and that seek self-support or broad-based community support.

The corporate foundation funds about two-thirds of the cash contributions. Both the company and the foundation provide nonmonetary support budgeted at $14 million in 1991.

Specific Citizenship Programs

Pollution Prevention Pays (3P): Aim to prevent pollution at its source by redesigning products and processes.

3M Tutorial Project: A release time, business/education partnership; employees released once a week for about two hours to work with students at various school districts. Topics range from computer language to helping handicapped students; choice of services includes tutoring, enrichment, Teaching English to Speakers of Other Languages, LOGO computer language, Adult Literacy Program, or Bridge View School for the handicapped.

3M Community Volunteer Award: Given to employee actively engaged in voluntary activities benefiting community on a continuing basis; recipients gets plaque and $500 to give to a nonprofit agency of choice. Awards coincide with National Volunteer Week.

Junior Achievement: Employees work in a classroom for one or so hours a week on Applied Economics, Project Business, Company Program, Urban Outreach Program, or Business Basics Program.

Meals on Wheels: Employees deliver meals to homebound people during lunch hour.

Management Assistance Project (MAP): Management experience shared with a nonprofit by a 3M executive who serves on the board of the nonprofit or donates consulting services.

Business Economics Education Foundation (BEEF): Employees speak to high school visitors at 3M or in a classroom.

Metro Paint-A-Thon: 3M teams paint houses of low-income, elderly, and handicapped people.

COMPANY PROFILE: WHIRLPOOL

Rationale for Citizenship Activities

Competition was especially difficult in some of our product areas, like refrigeration, where we're dealing aggressively with both cost-competitive and quality issues preparing for new, strict government requirements in the areas of energy and the environment.

The Twin Cities area of Southwest Michigan has been the home of Whirlpool Corporation for 78 years. It will continue to be. And we have a commitment to enhancing the quality of life in this and other plant communities.

The decisions we make, and the actions we take, need to make us more competitive. But they also must take into account the interconnectedness of our world today and the responsibilities we have to this world.

The environment and the community are two primary concerns at Whirlpool. The real issue is that everyone has a role to play, and for us that means stewardship, not just compliance.

1989 was a pivotal year for Whirlpool. It was a year that saw our company assume leadership of the global home appliance industry—literally becoming at home, and in the home, around the world. It was a year characterized by further globalization and expansion initiatives. By a vigorous emphasis on the need for integration in operations and innovation on the job. By a compelling sense of responsibility for the world we share. It was a year for making some difficult decisions, tempered by a desire to be fair and considerate.

Whirlpool Corporation has long been guided by the view that doing well in a business sense and doing good in a social sense are interdependent responsibilities. Our corporate commitments to civic involvement and social responsibility, both in philosophy and in practice, date back to the company's beginnings in 1911. Whirlpool founders, Lou and Fred Upton, were men of integrity and honor, and were sensitive to the needs of their employees, the community and society at large.

Founded in, and still headquartered near, the rural community of St. Joseph, Michigan, Whirlpool has chosen to locate most of its plants in relatively small towns and cities. Just as we believe that the esprit de corps and family orientation of these communities have helped to nurture our business, we also feel that our position as the largest employer in most of these locations brings with it a profound obligation to make a positive and measurable difference in the social and economic climate.

We will serve responsibly as members of all communities in which we live and work, respecting cultural distinctions throughout the world. We will preserve the environment, prudently utilize natural resources, and maintain all property we are privileged to use.

Organizational Structure of Citizenship Activities

Whirlpool has three levels of corporate giving. The main instrument of financial giving at both the corporate and division levels is the Whirlpool Foundation, established in 1951. The foundation is staffed by two part-time professionals, one of whom also works in public relations, and one full-time support person. The foundation receives funding through an annual contribution from the corporation. This amount varies from year to year. Each of the corporate divisions reports to the trustees of the foundation, who meet twice a year and have final approval on all grants. The trustees are apparently very line-item oriented. Prior to 1986, funding decisions were based on vague benefits, but since then the trustees have made more strategic choices concentrating on education, social, and medical issues. Each of these areas now has a trustee advisory committee.

Direct company giving occurs through the Community Relations Department but for the most part only to local charitable organizations in the form of employee volunteerism, complementary advertising, and use of facilities and equipment. This second level of corporate giving is also necessary when recipients and/or their activities fall too close to Whirlpool business activities, and for non-501(k) status recipients.

Local budgets make up the third level. Each division has a few part-time people responsible for citizenship activity, usually falling under the local Human Resource Department.

The foundation staff characterized corporate citizenship as extremely decentralized.

Specific Citizenship Programs

GENERAL PROGRAM AREA—EDUCATION. The focus is on marketing and engineering and supports key programs at graduate and undergraduate universities. Scholarships for employees began in 1952.

The Whirlpool Scholarship Program: Scholarships provided for children of employees to attend college.

School Appliance Program: Supplies home economics departments of public and private schools with appliances and provides instruction on their safe use.

GENERAL PROGRAM AREA—HEALTH. The program focuses on research, health education, cost containment, and community-based alternative health care services.

Integrated Health Affairs Management Project: Objectives: to create a curriculum to teach businesses how to improve the administration of health-related programs; to make health care programs more cost-effective and responsive to employee needs.

GENERAL PROGRAM AREA—HUMAN SERVICES. The United Way is major recipient. Others include YMCA, YWCA, child abuse prevention organizations, and senior citizens projects.

The Whirlpool Village at Camp Rota-Kiwan: An Indian Village in the woods of Michigan for year-long use by the Cub Scouts.

GENERAL PROGRAM AREA—CULTURE AND THE ARTS. Supports cultural institutions in local communities to enable them to reach out to as many residents as possible.

Whirlpool Sculpture Competition: Annual competition now covers 14 states.

GENERAL PROGRAM AREA—CIVIC AND COMMUNITY. Program supports organizations that enhance the vitality of local communities.

Whirlpool Community Leaders' Visitation Project: Community leaders visit to gain better understanding of Whirlpool philosophies, while company gains better understanding of community needs.

Whirlpool Corporation Employee Volunteer Appreciation Program: Select employees receive recognition for volunteerism, including financial support for organization of their choice.

Adopt-A-Family or Needy Family Program: Each department in Danville plant adopts at least one needy family and provides them with things from rent to shoes to Christmas gifts.

Project Home Safe: Started by the American Home Economics Association and Whirlpool Foundation; addresses the problem of children in self-care. Corporation provides material and promotional support; Resource Center for parents, child-care professionals, media, researchers, and public. Sponsors initiative to develop standards and staffing, curriculum, safety, parent involvement, and so forth. Four components: National School-Age Child Care Resource Center, Training and Community Involvement, Research on Self-Care, School-Age Child Care Standards Initiative.

Short- and long-range strategies include informing children in self-care and their parents about safety and productive use of time, creating support services for children on their own, developing supervised before- and after-school programs, and addressing public and private policies that affect families' child care responsibilities.

Volunteer Appreciation Program: Donated $1,000 to nonprofits chosen by Most Valuable Volunteers, $250 to those chosen by Honorable Mentions.

Business Roundtable Michigan Education Task Force: Plan to develop pilot programs at all locations as soon as program is worked out. Mission: business must accept the responsibility to act as catalyst for education reform; company expects world-class employees, customers, and citizens who are literate, informed, and socially responsible; will work with governor, state board of education, legislature, communities, educators, universities and colleges, business leaders, parents, and employees to achieve this end.

Community Economic Development Corporation: Whirlpool support helped start CEDC. Local communities match Whirlpool money; CEDC leverages additional grants—$5 million as of July 1992.

INDEX

A

ABB Power Generation, 286

Academic studies, and institutionalization of corporate global citizenship, 78

Academy of Travel and Tourism in Hungary, 106, 118–133; aims of, 120; as coalition of values-based action, 132–133; creation of, 118–120; draft content for, 122–124; economic and social benefits of, 131–133; and Fund for Central/Eastern Europe, 118–119, 125–125; newspaper reports on, 131, 132; partnerships for, 126–128; structure of, 120–125; support for, 128–131. *See also* American Express

Accountability, 3–6

Acid rain, 15, 251. *See also* Air pollution

Ackerman, R., 366, 369

Action for Russia's Children (ARC), 311

Actions, as element of corporate global citizenship, 5, 6, 360, 361

Advertising Age, 302

Advertising, in former Soviet Union, 310

AES Transpower, 329

Affinity Group, 204

Agence France Presse, 332, 333, 334

Agriculture sustainability, 255

Aiken High School partnership, 169, 170, 176–177, 180–181. *See also* General Electric (GE) Elfun Society

Air pollution, 14–15; in China, 269–272; solutions to, in China, 271–272. *See also* Acid rain

Akers, J., 34

Alberthal, L., 90

Allen, B., 93

Alliances: best practices in developing, 191–193; for community service, 62–74; social partnerships for, 87–89. *See also* Government; Nonprofit organizations

Allstate: corporate global citizenship best practices of, 96–97; Helping Hands program of, 96–97

Altruism: view of, in former Soviet Union, 321–322; view of, in India, 337–338, 345

American Airlines, 95–96

American Express: Academies of Travel and Tourism of, 115; academy programs of, 114–118, 380; Academy of Travel and Tourism in Hungary of, 106, 118–133, 361; American Express Foundation of, 107, 112, 113–114, 319; "Blue Box Values" of, 107–108; case study of, 102, 105–133; cause-related marketing of, 66; citizenship activities at, rationale for, 377–378; citizenship activities at, organizational structure of, 378; citizenship programs of, 379–380; community service programs of, 379–380; company profile of, 377–380; cultural programs of, 379;

H